Race and Place

Race
and Place

Equity Issues in Urban America

John W. Frazier

Florence M. Margai

Eugene Tettey-Fio

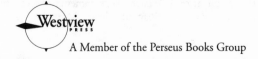

A Member of the Perseus Books Group

Copyright © 2003 by Westview Press, A Member of the Perseus Books Group

Westview Press books are available at special discounts for bulk purchases in the United States by corporations, institutions, and other organizations. For more information, please contact the Special Markets Department at the Perseus Books Group, 11 Cambridge Center, Cambridge MA 02142, or call (617) 252-5298 or (800) 255-1514 or email jmccrary@perseusbooks.com.

Published in 2003 in the United States of America by Westview Press, 5500 Central Avenue, Boulder, Colorado 80301-2877, and in the United Kingdom by Westview Press, 12 Hid's Copse Road, Cumnor Hill, Oxford OX2 9JJ

Find us on the World Wide Web at www.westviewpress.com

A Cataloging-in-Publication data record for this book is available from the Library of Congress.
ISBN 0-8133-4040-3 (HC)   ISBN 0-8133-4041-1 (pbk.)

Set in 10-pt Sabon by the Perseus Books Group

The paper used in this publication meets the requirements of the American National Standard for Permanence of Paper for Printed Library Materials Z39.48–1984.

10   9   8   7   6   5   4   3   2   1

We dedicate this book to our spouses,
Norah, William, and Joyce
And to our children,
Andrew, Jennifer, John, and Tonya
Luba and Konya
Ama, Afi, and Adjoa
And to their children.

Contents

Tables and Figures

Figures

Acronyms

AFDC	Aid to Families with Dependent Children
ALOHA	Areal Location of Hazardous Atmospheres
AOHC	Area of Hispanic Concentration
AOMC	Area of Minority Concentration
ARIP	Accidental Release Information Program
BHN	black-Hispanic neighborhood
BNL	Brookhaven National Laboratory
BRA	Boston Redevelopment Authority
CBD	central business district
CC	central city
CDBG	Community Development Block Grant
CDC	Centers for Disease Control
CO	central county
CPA	Center for Policy Alternatives
CPD	community property degradation/devaluation
CRA	Community Reinvestment Act
DOT	U.S. Department of Transportation
EJ	environmental justice
EPA	U.S. Environmental Protection Agency
ERNS	Emergency Response and Notification System
FHA	Federal Housing Act, the
FIRE	finance, insurance, and real estate
GMS	general merchandise store
HMDA	Home Mortgage Disclosure Act
HMIS	Hazardous Materials Information System
HUD	U.S. Department of Housing and Urban Development
IWG	Interagency Working Group
LULU	locally unwanted land use
NAACP	National Association for the Advancement of Colored People
NIMH	National Institute of Mental Health

NOAA	National Oceanic and Atmospheric Administration
NPL	(Superfund) National Priority List
NPTS	Nationwide Personal Transportation Survey
NSC	National Safety Council
NTC	National Toxics Campaign
OBD	office business district
PBS	Public Broadcasting Service
PIRG	Public Interest Research Group
PMSA	Primary Metropolitan Statistical Area
PUMS	Public Use Microdata Samples
SES	socioeconomic status
SMA	Standard Metropolitan Area
TIGER	Topologically Integrated Geographical Encoding and Referencing
TRI	Toxic Release Inventory
TSDF	toxic storage and disposal facility
UCC	United Church of Christ

Acknowledgments

We benefit from our discussions and interactions with others. The concepts and ideas in this book, though ours, have benefited greatly from our engagement with many people over a long period of time. We wish to acknowledge some of these.

John W. Frazier would like to thank the members of the national staff and regional directors and their staffs of the Fair Housing and Equal Opportunity Division of the U.S. Department of Housing and Urban Development (HUD) for sharing their insights about mapping and analyzing minority concentrations while he was a consultant in the mid-1990s.

Ibipo Johnston-Anumonwo and Blair Tinker deserve our special thanks. Ibipo is the author of Chapter 9, which provides insights on a topic—minority and gender issues related to travel behavior—that is crucial to understanding urban racial inequalities. Blair is the coauthor of Chapter 5, which provides an empirical analysis of various types of minority concentrations.

We also would like to thank a number of students whose participation in a number of applied urban geography seminars helped verify our concepts and crystallize our study approach. Also, we are grateful to Elbridge James, Juan Garcia Ellin, and Blair Tinker for their early testing of our minority concentration concept. We also thank Jennifer Frazier, Suzanna Klaf, and Karima Legette for commenting on specific chapters of the manuscript and Juan Garcia Ellin, Helena He, Joe LaCagnina, and Blair Tinker for their cartographic assistance. Florence Margai thanks McNair scholar Shannon Martin for her assistance in collection and integration of the environmental data used in Chapter 7.

We thank Debbie Standard and Lori Vandermark for typing early drafts of the manuscript.

Anonymous reviewers made very useful comments that led to revisions of some chapters, and we are very grateful for their advice.

Finally, we thank Westview senior editor Jill Rothenberg for her guidance and confidence. We gratefully acknowledge other members of the Westview editorial staff, especially Barbara Greer and Steven Baker, for their assistance in the production of this book.

Chapter 1

Race, Ethnicity, and Locational Inequalities

Introduction

The dawn of the twenty-first century in the United States is marked by a paradox in race relations and diversity. The nation has become more racially diverse (Armas, 2001), and racial discrimination has been legally prohibited. However, a series of events during the latter half of the twentieth century underscored the deep racial divide and underlying tensions that continue to threaten the nation's future peace and prosperity. One such event took place shortly after World War II when southern blacks demanded simple freedoms and equal treatment. The nonviolent marches, sit-ins, and bus boycotts signaled the beginning of African Americans' protests against racial injustices. By 1964 the Civil Rights Act outlawed discrimination in employment, and complementary legislation later "guaranteed" fair access to housing and public services. However, a year after this legislation, much of urban America was literally engulfed in the flames of race-based urban uprisings. Shortly after the 1965 "racial riots," two Americans who championed racial justice and equality, one black and one white, were assassinated. Violence and protests erupted again in subsequent years, notably 1980 in Miami and 1992 in Los Angeles.

The racial conflicts, struggles for civil and economic rights, and governmental responses in the latter half of the twentieth century also brought about some progress toward correcting socioeconomic imbalances among population subgroups. By the year 2000, a significant portion of the current African-American generation had achieved middle-class status, and for the first time in American history, an African-American man, Colin Powell, not only was considered a serious and desirable presidential candidate by white America in the 1990s but was appointed as the first black secretary of state in 2001. At the same time, however, racial polarization was clearly evident in the Rodney King and O. J. Simpson cases—reminders that racial division was deep in the United States. The racial tensions apparent from these cases received nearly the same media attention as the Gulf War, which revealed Colin Powell's strengths. Further, hate crimes, such as the death in Texas of a black who was dragged behind a pickup truck, reminded us of the racial hate that still raises its ugly head too often. As the black middle class emerged, by the close of the twentieth century, half of all black children were being born into urban poverty at a time when the United States was generating a federal budget surplus. These unmistakable, mixed signals call into doubt the progress of racial issues in America and suggest that W. E. B. Du Bois's "color line" extends into the twenty-first century as America's biggest social and moral issue (Du Bois, 1944, p. 23).

Not surprisingly, Americans differ greatly in their views of racial progress and racial equity. This is true for blacks and whites. The presence of Hispanics as the fastest growing American minority adds a new and significant dimension to the "browning of America" and promises among its consequences potential racial conflicts and moral controversy. Most Americans have very little understanding of emerging minority groups, such as the rapidly expanding U.S. Asian population. Many are also unaware of the diversity within this population or its distribution among all socioeconomic classes and employment groups. Racial and ethnic myths abound despite the nation's increasing diversity.

Amidst these demographic changes, there is a growing national concern that racial and ethnic minorities, particularly in urbanized communities, will face even greater inequalities with respect to housing, access to services and employment opportunities, and exposure to environmental pollution and related public health outcomes. Concerns over the increasing disparities between the population subgroups have received considerable attention in recent years from academics, local and national organizations, governmental agencies, the media, and social and environmental activists. As urban geographer Joe Darden (2002) stated, "It is not just segregation. It is the socioeconomic inequities associated with segregation that are important to address" (also see Darden, 1989). Based on the investigations taking place along these various fronts, it is now evident that there are several facets and dimensions of racial/ethnic inequities. In addition to studies of segregation and discrimination—particularly as they influence education, housing choice, and neighborhood condition—racial justice research now also embraces socioeconomic inequities in environmental quality, health care, housing, and other services. Due to the breadth of these maladies and the vagueness of the term *well-being*, we use the term *inequities* in much of our discussions.

Efforts to address these problems revolve around several questions: (1) What exactly constitutes inequalities or inequities among racial and ethnic groups? For example, are environmental inequities the result of deliberate, intentional siting of polluting facilities or merely a spatial coincidence resulting from the historical processes of urbanization and decisionmaking? (2) What causal mechanisms and sequence of events lead to the inequitable distribution of benefits (such as housing or services) and risks (such as environmental hazards)? (3) What actions are being taken at the state and federal levels to remedy the observed and/or perceived imbalances among social groups?

Along with the preceding questions are some basic issues and arguments surrounding racial and ethnic differences. Some question, for example, whether some individuals are truly disadvantaged due to racial discrimination or whether perhaps some fail to make socioeconomic progress simply because they are part of a racial subculture that suffers from certain social and structural weaknesses that are hard to overcome. Also, it has been argued that racism is on the decline and equity is on the rise, as evident from the significant growth of the black middle class in recent years. A corollary is that, given more time and additional education, minorities will continue to rise in status and equity. For example, the Asian American is frequently offered as a role model of success. The implications drawn by proponents of this myth are that Asian Americans form a ubiquitous culture that is more industrious and more willing to sacrifice and places a higher value on education than other cultures. Such arguments suggest superiority of one set of cultural virtues over those of another. There are also counterpoints to these views and to those regarding the growth of the minority middle class. Among them is the contention that minorities of education and experience equal to whites' receive less pay for the same work and are still ostracized and victimized in the job and housing markets. Consequently, there are inequalities in employment opportunities, socioeconomic status, and housing quality.

Another argument that is frequently provided as a justification for differential success and inequity among ethnic and racial groups is that progress takes time and hard work. Some would argue, for example, that recent Mexican immigrants residing in inner cities are not unlike their twentieth-century European counterparts, who labored long and hard to earn their place in America and opened the road to a better life for their children by their efforts. Such views are strongly countered by those who speak of oppression and exploitation of the poor and disadvantaged.

The primary objective of this book is to address these issues in an empirical fashion after examining different sociological and geographic perspectives in some detail. We hope to provide a basic understanding of the scope and multifaceted nature of racial inequalities in urban America, both in a broad context and in separate analyses of housing, services, and employment differences between groups, as well as in the degree of exposure to environmental problems.

This chapter proceeds by defining useful terms that serve as overriding concepts in the book. First, we clarify the differences between race and ethnicity as two of the most common elements of group identification in the United States. Next, we examine the linkages between race and place. The discussion of place allows us to introduce important concepts, such as *Areas of Minority Concentration,* and to illustrate race-place connections in urban America. A third concept discussed at length in this chapter is equity, which, as we reveal later, is one of the book's principal themes. We discuss the different aspects of equity and later, in the empirical chapters, provide concrete examples of locational inequities among the racial/ethnic groups. The chapter ends with a preview of the book's remaining chapters.

Race and Ethnicity

Social groups are distinguished by a host of characteristics, such as race, ethnicity, national origin, religious background, and sexual orientation. Within the United States, two of the most significant and historical bases for group identification are race and ethnicity. Given the relevance of these two elements in discussing majority-minority relationships and the plight of underrepresented groups in the nation, it is necessary to clarify the meaning of both concepts and describe the context in which they are used in subsequent chapters.

Racial groups are traditionally defined on the basis of the inherent physical and/or biological attributes of a group of people, such as their skin color, facial features, hair color and texture, and other visible physiological features. Although there is a wide range of physical attributes used in different parts of the world, the specific criterion that has been used historically to delineate between racial groups varies from one society to another. In the United States, for example, race has been defined primarily on the basis of three categories of skin color (black, yellow, and white). Up until the most recent U.S. Census, in 2000, when significant changes were made in racial group categorization, Hispanics were forced to declare themselves "black" or "white" on the survey form (Farley, 1977; Glazer, 1999), even though they are often popularly referred to as "Brown." In other countries, such as Brazil, several categories of skin color are used to differentiate between the racial groups. Some researchers have argued, correctly, that, given the mixed ancestry and interbreeding among population groups, there are no pure races within the genetic pool and therefore the biological distinction of groups is of little relevance today. Groups overlap so much that no single physical attribute remains a statistically exclusive characteristic of any one racial group (Schaefer, 1995; Gonzales, 1996).

Within the United States, one finds an evolving interpretation of race that is associated with American society's unique historical experiences as well as the changes in the nation's immigration history. This trend is perhaps best described by Stephen B. Thomas (2001):

The color line is not fixed but ripples through time, finding expression at distinct stages of our development as a nation. As the meaning of race has changed over time, its burdens and privileges have shifted among population groups. At one time in our history, for instance, the Irish and Italians were considered "non-white," along with other immigrants who were not descendants of the early Anglo-Saxon Protestant settlers [p. 10].

The concept of race in the United States has taken on a socially constructed meaning that transcends the biological distinctions of groups, with implications for how those groups are perceived and treated by others within the larger society. As Schaefer (1995) indicates:

In a modern, complex industrial society, we find little adaptive utility in the presence or absence of prominent chins, epicanthic folds of eyelids or the comparative amount of melanin in the skin. What is important is not that people are genetically different but that they approach each other with dissimilar perspectives. It is in this social setting that race is decisive. Race is significant because people have given it significance [p. 12].

This sociological interpretation of race now takes precedence over the biological meaning and has become firmly entrenched in the American mindset.

Others have argued that, even with the biological and social relevance attributed to race, the concept does not adequately describe or reflect the current diversity of the U.S. population (Oppenheimer, 2001). For example, Asians are typically differentiated from other racial groups because of their regional origin but more so because they share certain physical attributes that are tied to their genetic pool. Yet within the Asian-American community, there are many subgroups with different customs, nationalities, languages, and religious backgrounds. Japanese, Chinese, Koreans, Filipinos, Vietnamese, Hindus, Sikhs, Pakistanis, and many more subgroups comprise the Asian-American community. As such, the use of race as a common denominator for group identification is inadequate. Instead, a group taxonomy of ethnicity provides a more exhaustive categorization of people based on cultural, behavioral, environmental, physical, as well as some biological characteristics that are linked to their heritage. The term *ethnicity* is thus used to refer to a group of people who share one or more attributes such as language, religion, nationality or regional characteristics, unique customs and practices, and race. Ethnic groups are best identified by a set of internal and homogenous attributes that contribute to group affinity and cohesiveness and reflect how they see themselves ("we-ness"). These commonalities may also contribute to external attributes that make the groups distinct and influence how they are seen by others ("they-ness") within the larger society (Ringer and Lawless, 1989).

There is an ongoing debate over the appropriateness of using the terms *race* and *ethnicity* in the discourse on social inequality in the United States. Some contend that race must be separated from ethnicity, because, as we indicated earlier, race focuses on the biological characteristics of humanity whereas ethnicity addresses the social and cultural aspects. Others have argued even further that the concept of race must be eliminated from the discourse, particularly when dealing with group disparities, and that instead the focus must be on ethnicity as a more appropriate means of group affiliation (Cooper, 1994; Fullilove, 1998). For instance, David Kaplan and Steven Holloway (1998), noting the mixed ancestry and multiple definitions of race, opted to use ethnicity rather than race in their study. They suggested a more inclusive interpretation of ethnicity that made race and ethnicity synonymous, thus redefining groups such as African Americans as ethnic groups:

> We thus define ethnicity to include all groups that feel themselves different from others, or are felt to be different by the others, where the difference is based on culture, physical appearance, or ancestry, depending on the context [p. 5].

Throughout this book, however, we will use both concepts in the combined term *race/ethnicity* to address issues relating to group disparities in the United States. Our decision is based on a number of factors. First, as Gerald Oppenheimer (2001) argues, the substitution of ethnicity for race may have serious social implications since most studies of race bring attention to issues of poverty, segregation, accessibility to health care, distribution of environmental pollutants, and other matters relating to discrimination and prejudice (p. 1057). This view is also supported by Michael Omi (2000), who contends that the elimination of racial categories from data collection efforts, in particular, would hinder all attempts to monitor specific forms of discrimination, such as home mortgage and other financial loan practices, health-care delivery patterns, prison sentencing, and more recently, racial profiling incidences. A second reason for adopting the term *race/ethnicity* is that it already exists; it is widely used by social scientists, both for descriptive and analytical purposes; and it is now accepted by various academic and professional organizations (Oppenheimer, 2001; G. E. Thomas, 1995; Ringer and Lawless, 1989).

Given this book's stated objectives, the synonymous use of these concepts is warranted. We, like most in this line of research, support the basic premise that both race and ethnicity are socially created concepts that draw attention to population subgroups within the larger society, affect how those groups are perceived and treated by others, and, more important, serve as objective dimensions for collecting and analyzing data relating racial prejudice and discrimination. Below we discuss the historical and present-day linkages between these concepts and racism in America.

Race, Racism, and Racialism

Race, as indicated earlier, has previously been defined on a biological basis. However, in the United States, race has been linked to racism and specifically has had the connotation until very recently of white versus black. This sociological context of race has been clear since the first slave touched American soil. Race in this context is rooted in racialism, the belief that racial differences result from black inferiority and white superiority. Unfortunately, although many Americans, regardless of their color, were outraged by the racialism of South African whites, racialism is alive and well in much of the United States. Gunnar Myrdal's observation of more than fifty years ago—that the American race dilemma created a paradox because a nation committed to global equality and justice could not solve its "Negro problem"—unfortunately still rings true as the nation begins the twenty-first century. This observation was also confirmed by Andrew Hacker (1992).

Racism—the practice of segregation, discrimination, and dominance of one race by another at any given time—is unfortunately present and continues to take on new forms as the nation becomes increasingly diverse. Racism has become complicated as it has taken on multiple meanings. Included in this complexity is the issue of racial categories noted above—the issue of who belongs to which racial category and who is being affected by what forms of racism (Hartman, 1997). Furthermore, the implications of racism have become less clear with the use of a changing racial/ethnic vocabulary. They also become less apparent when socioeconomic status and nationality combine to blur racially motivated behaviors.

Until recently, racial division and racial tension in the United States were largely a black-white issue. The psychological divisions have been constant in some form since the colonial era. Even during the Civil Rights Movement, Kenneth Clark (1965) agonized over the state of urban black America and quoted a National Institute of Mental Health (NIMH) staff paper that commented on the "new" black-white relationship:

> Another fundamental that must be grasped is the magnitude of the present psychological gulf between Whites and non-Whites . . . the growing anger . . . fanned and fed by a growing impatience . . . when such Whites do come face to face with the Negro world they discover in themselves an entirely new response: fear. They sense the Negro's envy of the "privileged caste," they sense some of his bitterness. . . . And in this alien world they discover a complement to the White man's rejection: the Negro's distrust . . . the gulf that exists is wide and deep. Bridging it will not be easy [p. 224–225].

The persistence of black-white tensions has led to issues debated by both groups. One of the concerns shared by many blacks today is that racism is a permanent condition (Hartman, 1997). However, some black conservatives are tired of what they see as black whining and reverse racism. They stress the undeniable gains by black America and claim that programs such as affirmative action have run their course and are now crutches (Hamblin, 1999). They are critical of blacks who are unwilling to admit progress and of white liberals who "feel compelled to bleed" (p. 135). There is no denial that discrimination abounds, but black conservatives maintain that hard work and well-timed life challenges lead to acceptable results. Blacks are urged not only to recognize their gains as part of America but to "move ahead" in their thinking about history and the future. Despite these reassurances some, such as Benjamin DeMott (1997), claim that these revisionists' accounts in the media overlook important "truths":

> People forget the theoretically unforgettable—the caste history of American Blacks, the connection between no schools for longer than a century and bad school performance now, between hateful social attitudes and zero employment opportunities, between minority anguish and majority fear. . . . Where there is work, it is miserably paid and ugly. Space allotments at home and at work cramp body and mind. Positive expectation withers in infancy. . . .
>
> . . . revisionism loses touch with two fundamental truths of race in America: namely, that because of what happened in the past, Blacks and Whites cannot yet be the same; . . . the past was not just a matter of ill will or insult, but the outcome of an established caste structure . . . [DeMott, 1997, pp. 42–44].

Thus, there is a lingering concern among black social scientists about the permanence of racism. Many have expressed impatience over the continuing negative impacts of racism and draw examples from various experiences to illustrate their point. The literature is replete with examples involving politics, poverty, and the economic well-being of blacks. Beyond black-white issues, which because of American history dominate the literature, other segregation and isolation trends among other racial/ethnic groups have raised a new set of equity questions. These issues involve the consequences of racism for American minorities, including those who have played by white rules but experienced employment and wage discrimination, segregation, and isolation.

Our purpose in this chapter, however, is not to provide an exhaustive detail of these issues. Some of these will be raised during our sociological and geographic narratives and in empirical chapters later. We do want to note that segregation and isolation inevitably result in questions about places and geographic space. People spend most of their lives in selected few places, either by choice or by restrictions imposed by society. Place involves social and physical environments to which meanings are attached by the individual residing there and by societal groups. Places also are located relative to other places, which results in differential access to the resources and amenities necessary to live and enjoy life. Some places are more valued and more valuable than others. Perceptions and treatment of places and their inhabitants also vary. These are parts of the race-place connections that are a major focus of this book.

Race and Place

One of the continuing outcomes of racism is the segregation of African Americans, and more recently, poor Hispanics and Asian Americans, into inner-city ghettoes and barrios with little hope of escape. However, racial and ethnic outcomes are spatially concentrated everywhere, not just in the well-publicized ghetto but in the schools, on the job, and in several other places. Minorities have been and continue to be clustered in high concentrations in the United States. It is therefore necessary to examine race in conjunction with places of minority concentration. We will attempt to do so in this section by first defining place, as a general and empirical concept, and then proceeding to our own definitions of "areas of minority concentration."

Place as a General Concept. Place is a concept generally applied by most of us in everyday life. We give little thought to the different scales to which we apply the concept. This is because *place* has long been used to characterize any type of location that carries a special connotation or meaning. Typically we use a word to characterize the place we have in mind because it elicits a visualization of some sort for us and for the person for whom the description of a place is made. We often use locational or environmental descriptors in naming a place. This is because they immediately offer an image to the listener. *Antarctica* is one example. Almost anyone upon hearing the term has a vision of a white, ice-covered landscape that is bitterly cold and even deadly to inhabitants. Similarly, *the Amazon* conjures up for most of us an image of a place of other weather extremes, uncomfortably hot and humid temperatures, and a jungle-like landscape with potentially harmful creatures hidden in the vegetation or in the swampy waters. Place names are numerous and create mental images of the physical landscape and often its inhabitants (for example, *Appalachia, the Sahara, Siberia,* and *Southern California*).

At a different scale, however, we refer to urban places that are smaller in territory than those identified above but provide the same useful function: the visualization of specific locations that hold special meaning. The meanings can vary based on one's knowledge, beliefs, and experience but provide the basis for one's visualization of that particular place. Examples in urban America abound. Consider the specific places and the images provided by reference to *Central Park, Chinatown, Little Italy, Market Square, The Flats, Fanueil Hall,* and *the Wharf.* Some of these create clear images, even rough boundaries, for the individual perception. Others are vague recollections of tourist places visited once on a family vacation. Frequently we also use place descriptors to conjure up images of places in urban America. Some are more functional and sometimes emotional, including place images that result in anger, fear, pity, or some other perception of the city. Among these are *inner city, downtown,* and *ghetto.* One can imagine declining conditions—economically, architecturally, socially, and otherwise declining. However, these images can be vague and without borders (J. W. Frazier, 1999). They can be useful for imagining a place where we have been, places that others talk about, and places that appear to be in need of some type of social planning. However, because they are subjective and lack any concrete boundaries, they offer no empirical basis for analysis and social action.

Place as an Empirical Concept.   Place as an empirical concept moves from the general purpose of creating an image of a location and its inhabitants to one of bounded space with attributes that are measurable and imply internal homogeneity. In this sense a place is a region. Some criterion is applied to draw boundaries, and the area encompassed by the place is the subject for analysis over time. We have many examples of empirically defined places. Perhaps the most frequently used, however, are those designed for administrative purposes by the U.S. Bureau of the Census. The Bureau developed census geography to provide for census tabulation and reporting. Its geographic definitions have become the mainstay of longitudinal analysis, as well as the basis for government and private-sector planning. Numerous examples exist, but among the most frequently used administrative and spatial units in the United States is the county. Counties have been the basis of regional planning at both the multicounty agency level and at the federal level; for example, the county is used as the definition and operation of the Appalachian Regional Commission.

Perhaps even more frequently used is the empirically designated census tract. Originally, tracts were defined as places containing between 4,000 and 8,000 persons, with relatively fixed or stable boundaries (major streets/highways, bodies of water, or railroad tracks). They also were initially designed to represent places of relative homogeneity. Although this last objective is somewhat questionable, tracts continue to be the best spatial basis for conducting urban research, because population and race data are collected and forecasted regularly for this spatial unit. Census tracts have had wide application in social science, including empirical work and deductions about the relationships between race and poverty on a spatial basis. Reynolds Farley and others created indices of dissimilarity using census-tract race data to examine trends in racial segregation in the 1970s and 1980s and other aspects of race in relation to social and economic conditions (Farley, 1977; Farley and Allen, 1987; Farley and Frey, 1994). Others have analyzed the geographic concentration of poverty in U.S. cities and concluded that the most important factor in explaining poverty concentration is segregation (e.g., Massey and Denton, 1987; Denton and Massey, 1988; Massey, Gross, and Shibuya, 1994). In all of these cases, the census tract is used as an empirical building block to represent ethnic/racial "neighborhoods," or places that have boundaries and measurable attributes. There are other examples in which census tracts provide the spatial data basis for the creation and monitoring of places, either as they exist or are created for government-monitoring purposes. Examples include Historic Districts, Economic Development Zones, and Empowerment Zones. The census tract is also the building block for our definition of minority concentrations.

Areas of Minority Concentration

We propose that places containing high proportions of minorities, independent of economic class, are disproportionately impacted by inequities as compared to places that have less concentration or no concentration of minority populations. This is in keeping with the argument of A. Hacker (1992) and others (Fainstein, 1993; G. Miller, 2001) that race, not class, determines inequalities. We believe that this is especially true where minorities are highly concentrated and that examination of equity issues in housing, services, and environmental hazards will reveal a series of inequalities for minorities residing in Areas of Minority Concentration.

Definitions of a range of urban terms designed to capture the plight of urban minorities have been discussed elsewhere (J. W. Frazier, 1999). For concepts of minority concentration, it is important to note that both theoretical and practical concerns have led to definitions of minority concentrations. Harold Rose (1971) theorized about urban geography three decades ago when he constructed an empirically based vocabulary that included a ghetto center and ghetto neighborhood. A quarter century later, the Fair Housing Division of the U.S. Department of Housing and Urban Development (HUD) introduced the concept *Area of Minority Concentration* (AOMC). J. W. Frazier noted the similarity and differences between the Rose and HUD vocabularies. Rose's concern was only to empirically define and analyze black centers and neighborhoods, while Fair Housing had a broader minority audience, all nonwhites, in mind when it directed local fair housing planners to scrutinize

[p]ublic policies that restrict the provision of housing and community development resources to areas of minority concentration, . . . [and] . . . that restrict interdepartmental coordination between other local agencies in providing housing and community development resources to areas of minority concentration. . . . [U.S. Department of Housing and Urban Development, Fair Housing and Equal Opportunity, 1996, pp. 4–6]

The HUD definition included not only all nonwhite racial categories but also all Hispanics. The vocabularies were similar, however, in terms of the spatial unit and numerical threshold applied. Both used the census tract and established a threshold for inclusion at greater than 50 percent of the tract population. In other words, any census tract containing more than 50 percent minorities (blacks in Rose's case) was designated as an Area of Minority Concentration (a ghetto neighborhood in Rose's case). The HUD definition of AOMC was used in preliminary analyses (J. W. Frazier, 1997; J. W. Frazier and James, 1998). However, these studies led to the modification of HUD's nomenclature in important ways.

Given the rapid increase in the urban Hispanic population, it is necessary to separate Hispanics from other minorities. When this is done, the AOMC becomes predominately black in American urban counties; few Asians, Native Americans, or other minorities are concentrated at the urban census tract level (a few notable exceptions exist). Thus, the AOMCs used in this book follow the HUD definition, except for the removal of Hispanics, which results in black dominance. The *Area of Hispanic Concentration* (AOHC) is defined as any census tract containing 30 percent or more Hispanics of any racial category. This is an arbitrary proportion, but it is more than three times the overall proportion of Hispanics in the United States, so we believe that it adequately reflects places of Hispanic concentration. A sample map of Cook County, Illinois, is provided (Figure 1.1) to illustrate the distribution of AOMCs and AOHCs in a large urban county. The figure also shows another type of concentration: places where both black and Hispanic populations live in large proportions. Specifically, any census tract containing at least 50 percent non-Hispanic minorities (largely black) and containing at least 30 percent Hispanics is designated as a *black-Hispanic neighborhood* (BHN). We believe that these places are also affected by disparities in services, well-being, and environmental inequity.

The empirical analyses presented in this book are based on urban counties in the United States. We use census geography to spatially differentiate urban subareas within the counties. Areas of Minority Concentration are delineated by census tract using the definitions presented above. We also use the empirical concepts of central city and urban county. Every urban county has a central city, typically with a population of 50,000 or more. In some of these analyses, we compare Areas of Minority Concentration (AOMCs, AOHCs, and BHNs) with population attributes, housing, services, and polluting facilities in the urban county and the central city. To accomplish this, we always subtract (extract) all of the minority areas and their attributes from the central city before making comparative analyses. We do the same for the urban county, which typically contains other municipalities outside of the central city. In short, our empirically-defined places do not overlap geographically.

A visualization of the various minority concentrations within the continental United States clarifies their regional and local patterns in 1998. Figure 1.2(a) is a 3-D map of census tracts within the continental United States with greater than 50 percent of the tract's total population being African American. Figure 1.2(b) represents the same for Hispanics except with 30 percent as the threshold. Figures 1.3(a) and (b) illustrate the census tracts that contain Asian-

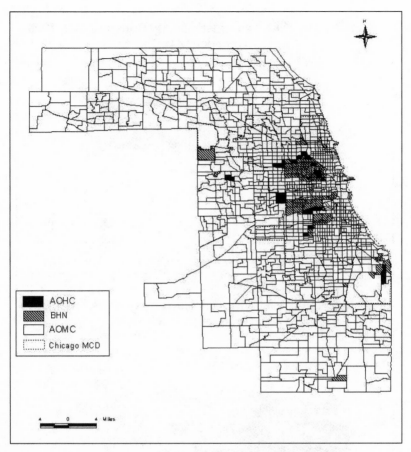

FIGURE 1.1   Cook County, Illinois, 1990: Areas of Minority Concentration
(AOMCs), Areas of Hispanic Concentration (AOHCs), and black-Hispanic
neighborhoods (BHNs)

American populations that exceed 20 percent of the total population of the
tract on a regional basis (Southwest and Northeast United States). The patterns
are obvious. African Americans are highly concentrated in the eastern United
States and are highly segregated on a local basis; Hispanics are highly concentrated in U.S.-Mexico border states but have emerged virtually in all other regions on an urban basis and are highly concentrated locally as well. Asian
Americans are highly concentrated on both coasts but particularly in California.
Despite these concentrations, Asian Americans are also dispersing and are appearing in other U.S. regions within particular urban centers. Chapter 2 will detail the settlement and dispersion process for each of these major groups. How
these groups are segregated and how they come together to share space and a
quality of life that is less than that of whites is one of this book's key themes.

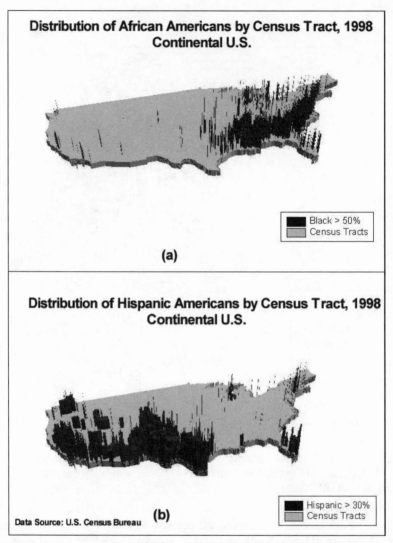

FIGURE 1.2   (a) Distribution of African Americans by census tract, 1998.
(b) Distribution of Hispanic Americans by census tract, 1998. Source: U.S. Census
Bureau, www.census.gov/population/socdemo/race

Equity and Racial Disparities

Another step toward understanding the complex dimensions of racial/ethnic
inequalities involves an operational definition of equity. This is necessary
for empirical analyses since the literature is replete with terms that are occa-
sionally subject to misunderstandings. In fact, some of the inconsistencies in

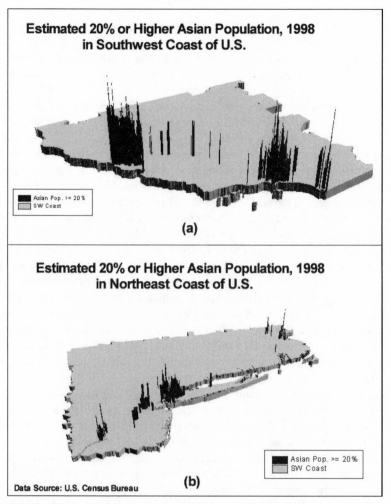

FIGURE 1.3 (a) Estimated 20 percent or higher Asian population, 1998, in the Southwest Coast of the United States. (b) Estimated 20 percent or higher Asian population, 1998, in the Northeast Coast of the United States. Source: U.S. Census Bureau, www.census.gov/population/socdemo/race

research findings from previous investigations are partly due to incomplete or ambiguous definitions. To avoid such problems, we need to clarify the term *equity* and identify its basic components. In addition, one of the stated objectives of this book is not only to document the historical and present-day outcomes of racism but also to provide meaningful ways of resolving these inequities. A thorough understanding of this concept is therefore critical to the development of policy initiatives aimed at eliminating the disparities between racial and ethnic groups.

At a broad conceptual level, *equity* refers to the fair distribution of risks, costs, services, and benefits across demographic groups, neighborhoods, counties, states, countries, and even generations. In a socioeconomic and geographic context for urban America, this concept has been used to examine the disparities in the distribution of income, housing, and basic services (banks, real estate sales, public services) between the "inner cities" and their suburbs and between black "ghettos" and white neighborhoods in American metropolitan areas (W. J. Wilson, 1987; Jencks, 1992; J. W. Frazier and James, 1998). The application of this concept to environmental issues is centered on the notion that environmental hazards are disproportionately distributed among demographic groups in urbanized and industrialized communities. Notable attempts at clarifying this concept from an environmental perspective and documenting the outcomes include the articles by Bowen, Salling, Kingsley, and Cyran (1995), Cutter (1995), Kraft and Scheberle (1995), and Margai (2001).

There are four attributes of equity. The first, and perhaps the most relevant to empirical analyses, is the *spatial scale, pattern, and distribution* of risks, costs, services, and benefits. Delineating the spatial scale or unit of analysis is vital for the validation of equity. Some studies are conducted at national, regional, or county level, and others are performed at less aggregate scales, such as the census tract, zip code, or block group level. But as some studies have shown, changes in the spatial unit of analysis are often likely to result in different and sometimes conflicting research findings about inequities. The areal distribution of the services, costs, or hazards is also useful for specifying proximity, evaluating accessibility to services, identifying host communities of hazards, and demarcating risk zones and potential health consequences. For example, using spatial distribution patterns and proximity-based measures, some communities of color have been found to host a disproportionate number of noxious facilities such as hazardous waste sites, large industrial plants, sewage treatment plants, landfills, and incinerators. Depending on the distance to these neighboring facilities, residents are likely to suffer from excessive exposure to air pollutants as well as other dangerous chemicals that could result in chronic health problems. In another study, the areal distribution of travel cost between resident locations and schools was evaluated to determine whether accessibility to schools was greater for children from high-income neighborhoods and lower for those from low-income areas (Talen, 2001). The results confirmed the existence of spatial inequities in access to schools, with significant implications for student achievement.

Equity incorporates three other components: *social, generational,* and *procedural.* The social component represents the socioeconomic factors that assist in the creation of economic, service, or environmental inequalities among population groups, based on class structure, race, ethnicity, income, or age. For example, some have argued that the social geography of places coupled with urbanization and industrial locational attributes such as property values, transportation access, and agglomeration effects account for the emergence of the observed disparities (Cutter, 1995). The procedural component of equity refers to the observed or perceived differences in governmental policies, enforcement of regulations, and remedies that address disproportionate distribution of benefits, services, and risks. Finally, the generational aspect of equity involves an attempt to evaluate the long-term impact of these disparities on the young and future generations. For example, what are the social or economic consequences and ramifications of segregation, urban environmental pollution, and other disparities on minority children, or all children for that matter? As Cutter (1995) argued, the goal is to ensure that "society does not mortgage its future for a short-term gain" (p. 112). Unfortunately, in most investigations of racial inequities, emphasis is placed on the spatial, social, and procedural dimensions with only a cursory examination of the fate of future generations. In this book, we hope to examine these different facets of the problem in a more comprehensive approach.

Outline of the Book

The discussion in this introductory chapter makes clear that this book examines the complex issues surrounding the increasing racial/ethnic diversity in the United States and the ongoing problems and locational outcomes of racism and group inequalities particularly in urban areas. We believe that the most useful concepts for addressing these concerns include race/ethnicity, place, and equity, all of which have been carefully defined in the preceding sections. These concepts will enable us to examine, both theoretically and empirically, the different forms of inequalities (socioeconomic, housing, service, and environmental) in urban America on a spatial basis. For example, using equity as one of the central themes of this book, we will investigate the extent of fairness or lack thereof in the distribution of benefits and risks across space, ethnic or racial categories, demographic groups, or merely in the enforcement of governmental regulations. The other two concepts, race and place, are intricately linked in several ways, particularly in urban environments, and to some extent are subsumed under the broad rubric of spatial inequities or, more appropriately, spatially patterned landscapes of inequalities.

There are eight premises that guide this book and its organization. We wish to make them explicit.

1. The U.S. white majority has maintained a sociological context of race that is deeply rooted in the racialism of the nation's history.
2. The twin consequences of American racism are racial segregation and isolation. These were made possible by legal and institutional mechanisms that have geographically restricted minority living space.

3. As a result of the historical and contemporary actions of the U.S. white majority, U.S. racial/ethnic minorities have unique histories in the United States that are too rarely mentioned and need to be told.
4. Immigration processes have and continue to play a vital role in the shaping of the American urban landscape. They will be no less influential in the next century than they were in previous centuries.
5. Widely ranging beliefs about American racism exist in the United States. These divergent perspectives and their implications require careful consideration as we debate America's urban future.
6. Geographic space—its structure and the forces that organize it—is too infrequently considered by students of racism. Space contains attributes, such as location, relative location, and places of varying content and subjective value for those who consciously design its use. As with sociological theories of racism, geography contains differing perspectives on the nature of spatial relations in urban America, including the nature of race-place connections. These perspectives too will be part of the debate of America's urban future.
7. One of the most important race-place connections in urban America involves race-place inequalities.
8. The nature and extent of race-place inequalities in urban America are sobering. These require immediate attention if the United States is to continue its self-appointed global role as defender of moral justice and equity and is to avoid the racial conflict that has been a significant element of American history.

The remainder of this book is organized around these premises. Chapter 2 examines the settlement, dispersion, concentration, and potential growth of minorities in the United States. In Chapter 3 we explore the similarities and differences between the major sociological perspectives on ethnic/racial pluralism and equality in the United States. Chapter 4 examines the theories of urban relationships, the expansion and restructuring of urban space, and the processes that have helped shape current geographic distributions of the different population subgroups. In Chapter 5, we examine the issues of segregation and the impacts on socioeconomic, housing, service, and environmental inequities on a race-and-place basis. These issues are addressed at a national level using a sample of urban counties. After reviewing the findings of other equity analyses, we provide our own analysis and add new dimensions. Chapters 3 and 4, then, not only provide key sociological narratives of racism but explain how these play out in geographic space on a theoretical basis. Chapter 5 also addresses one of the common criticisms of census-based analyses, that of data unreliability due to a time lapse between censuses. Although the 1990 data have merit of their own, at least from a historical point of view, it is useful to raise the issue of continuity of minority concentrations as an empirical concept and to challenge the continuity of inequalities discovered in those data. To this end, Chapter 5 explores two other issues. First, we examine the stability of AOMCs from 1990 to 1998, using race data estimates for 1998. Second, we test for the persistence of inequalities, using some 2000 socioeconomic data estimates.

In Chapter 6, we explore Asian-American concentrations on a micro basis, using Alameda County, California, an urban area of multiracial and multiethnic concentrations. This complex mosaic may be an indication of what other multiracial communities will look like over the next quarter century as racial mix changes and racial dispersion continues. Chapter 7 moves the equity discussion to the environmental arena. We review the urban processes and institutional forces that have led to the inequitable distribution of environmental hazards. We also explore the role of governmental policies and grassroots activism in addressing these problems. In Chapter 8 we investigate the changing distributions of economic activities in the American city and the implications for racial equity in access to particular services, including the cost of access and price differentials for particular goods. Chapter 9 addresses racial equity issues regarding employment status and race and gender differentials in not only access to employment but also commuting to work. Finally, we conclude in Chapter 10 with a summary of our findings and a discussion of U.S. policy and the future. We offer some ideas for creating new policies and attitudes and a healthier, more equitable landscape for the new multiracial America that will emerge this century.

Chapter 2

U.S. Minority Population

Settlement Patterns, Dispersion, and Growth Trends

A new America, one with a different complexion, is emerging in the twenty-first century. Demographers expect that the United States, previously dominated by its European white population during the twentieth century, will experience "browning" over the next half century, resulting in a slim white majority (52 percent) by 2050. However, the United States' changing racial composition will involve more than just browning. All races will grow at a rate faster than white America, and this will be complicated by further spatial concentrations of racial/ethnic subgroups, their differential access to benefits and services, and the resulting landscapes of inequalities.

Policy decisions (or lack of them) during the next few decades will likely shape the nation's future well-being. Given the potential ramifications, it is important to review the demographic patterns that emerged in the twentieth century and to predict those that are likely to evolve in this century. To do so, we must first examine the processes that resulted in the present-day distribution of minority populations. We can also better understand future scenarios and their implications by classifying and mapping the existing distributions. This chapter reviews the history of minority population settlements. In addition, the migration patterns of minority populations, both at the national and local levels, are considered, as are the likely changes in their growth and distribution. The chapter is organized into three sections. The first is devoted to a chronology of the settlement and dispersion patterns of blacks, Hispanics, and Asians in the United States. In the second section, future growth patterns and trends are discussed, based on a cartographical analysis of projected estimates. The chapter concludes with a few implications that arise from the expanding ethnic mosaics nationally, regionally, and locally in metropolitan areas.

Minority Population Settlement and Dispersion

African-American Settlement Patterns

The story of black America is one of fluctuating growth due to a variety of factors. Black settlement patterns can be traced to colonial times, but generally their early settlement in the United States was tied to slavery and, thus, was largely rural prior to World War II. The formation of urban black ghetto centers, though beginning well before 1920, occurred throughout the United States largely after World War II, intensifying after 1950 with mass black migrations northward and westward.

Historically, the creation and expansion of a tobacco-growing economy in the southern colonies in the 1600s and 1700s resulted in the need for a large, cheap manual-labor force. White colonists viewed blacks as inferior, and the slave trade was accepted as an economic panacea; blacks became white property, a commodity to be bought and sold. Although blacks lived in the American colonies at least as early as 1619 (Farley and Allen, 1987) and were initially brought to Jamestown, Virginia, as indentured servants, their plight quickly changed. Indentured servitude was not a long-term labor solution for the colonies' tobacco industry, which required a stable workforce. The need for hand labor intensified with the rise of the cotton economy. By 1790 the black population of the United States had grown to 757,000 persons; the annual growth rate was 3 to 4 percent during the eighteenth century (Farley and Allen, 1987). By 1800, approximately 90 percent of blacks resided in the southern states.

After 1790 and until the Civil War, black population growth rates were modest. The reasons for the rate decline are not definite, but Reynolds Farley and Walter Allen (1987) attributed them to disease and lack of medical care. Similarly, improved accessibility to health care services and medicines probably contributed to the higher growth rates that occurred after World War II.

During the period 1940–1990, the black population more than doubled in the United States. However, as shown in Table 2.1, the black proportion of the total population in the nation changed little during that half century. By 1940 slightly less than 13 million African Americans accounted for nearly one-tenth (or 9.8 percent) of the total population. However, by 1990 there were nearly 30 million blacks, constituting only 12 percent of the national population. Little change occurred by 2000. The biggest problem for whites was not the size of the black population. Rather, their rapid relocation, especially of large numbers to the North and, later, to selected cities in the West, led to several issues. First, early black migrations overwhelmed northern blacks and led to problems unique to the North (Du Bois, 1901). Second, the Great Migration led to the eventual development of a national ghetto system (Farley and Allen, 1987; Rose, 1971).

TABLE 2.1   Populations of Selected Racial Groups, 1940–1990 (thousands)

	1940	%	1950	%	1960	%	1970	%	1980	%	1990	%
White not-hisp.	116,353	88.5	134,478*	89.5	158,838*	88.5	169,653	83.4	180,603	79.7	169,653	68.2
Black	12,866	9.8	15,045	10.0	18,849	10.5	22,539	11.1	26,482	11.7	29,931	12.0
Hispanic	1,861	1.4	N/A	–	N/A	–	9,073	4.5	14,604	6.4	22,608	8.8
Asian/ Pacific Is.	255	<1.0	320	<1.0	891	1.0	1,526	<1.0	3,726	1.6	7,227	2.9
Total	131,669	100	150,216	100	179,362	100	203,210	100	226,546	100	248,710	100

+ Rounded to nearest Thousand; *Hispanics were not separated from whites, which inflates white total.
SOURCE: U.S. Census Bureau, 1999.

Changes in Black Settlement Patterns in the 1800s.   Black settlement patterns underwent fundamental changes during the twentieth century. Prior to 1920, black settlement remained relatively fixed, except for a few large northern urban centers at the end of the nineteenth century (Du Bois, 1901). Black rights achieved under Reconstruction were largely lost to the southern Jim Crow laws, which created push factors that might have led to a black exodus northward before the turn of the twentieth century. However, forces in both the North and South discouraged black relocation (Farley and Allen, 1987). In the North, white industrialists and workers withheld potential job opportunities because of their fear of blacks and social-Darwinist beliefs. Fears were exacerbated by cases of industrial firms hiring blacks as "union busters" or as cheaper labor replacements for whites (W. J. Wilson, 1987, pp. 67–68). Such efforts led to disorder in Chicago, East St. Louis, and Detroit during the first two decades of the twentieth century.

Other factors combined to discourage black out-migration from the South prior to World War I. Efforts by southern interests to retain blacks as cheap labor, initially in anticipation of the renaissance of the cotton economy and later for other agricultural pursuits, kept them from migrating in substantial numbers. Additionally, little effort by the print media to reach southern African Americans, combined with their high illiteracy rates and rural location, served to retard black migration (Farley and Allen, 1987). In fact, rather than positive information, southern blacks received no information or anecdotal reports of "disappointment and failure" from the North (p. 112). Despite these influences, three northern cities did experience a significant in-migration of southern blacks. Their impacts were noted by a black sociologist, W. E. B. Du Bois, who published a series of articles in the *New York Times* describing the "peculiar problems" that arose when southern black attitudes and behaviors differed from those of northern blacks. He also detailed the settlement locations and conditions of African Americans (Du Bois, 1901; all four articles are included in Shenton and Brown, 1978).

According to Du Bois, before southern migrants arrived, approximately 750,000 blacks resided "north of the Mason Dixon line" by 1900, with nearly 400,000 living in New England and the Middle Atlantic Regions (Du Bois, 1901). He made several points about the black problems existing in the North prior to the mass arrival of southern blacks. These problems originated during the early colonial period and varied over time. They included a range of issues such as education, riots, restricted rights, poverty, crime, and prejudice. Du Bois included New York City, Philadelphia, and Boston in his case studies. For example, he argued that New York City had had a "Negro problem" since its inception. Its black population increased steadily between 1700 and 1900. In 1700 roughly 1,500 blacks resided in the city, but by 1800 the total had reached 9,000; by 1880 it was 20,000, and in 1900, 36,000. Not only were the numbers of blacks increasing geometrically in specific older areas of the city during most of the nineteenth century, but their mass was even greater after annexed areas were included. This raised the total number of blacks residing in New York City to about 60,000 in 1900 (Du Bois, 1901).

The spatial concentration of blacks within specific neighborhoods was as striking as their increasing numbers. Du Bois reported that these "negro districts" emerged early in the city's history and included the "Tenderloin," "Brooklyn," and later, parts of "Coney Island" (Du Bois, 1901). The social attributes of the black North included a disproportionate number of very young males who, without families and despite their full employment and efficiency, could not afford to marry because they earned "a third less per week than the other nationalities" (p. 168). Although blacks shared in some of the same prejudices experienced by white immigrants, such as Irish or Italians, racial discrimination in the form of voting rights, exclusion from employment, violence, and poor housing conditions were unique to the African-American communities. Du Bois described the housing conditions facing blacks:

> In no better way can one see the effects of color prejudice on the mass of Negroes than by studying their homes . . . 19 percent living in one and two room tenements, 37 percent in three rooms, and 44 percent in four or more rooms. Had the rooms been of good size and the rents fair this would be a good showing; but 400 of the rooms had no access to the outer air and 655 had but one window. Moreover, for these accommodations the negroes pay from $1.00 to $2.00 a month more than the whites pay for similar tenement . . . [p. 169].

Du Bois made similar observations regarding housing, crowding conditions, and enforced segregation in Philadelphia and Boston.

Du Bois suggested that a class structure emerged early among northern blacks in all three of the large urban centers studied. The bulk of the African-American workers were kept out of the growing industries by labor unions through exclusion tactics, forcing them to become low-wage laborers and domestic workers. A small proportion of blacks became professionals; thus the northern black elite. Generally, however, the African-American masses suffered in the North just as they had in the South, but an urban class structure had taken form before southern black migrants arrived.

This led to another of the interesting "peculiarities" Du Bois found between northern and southern blacks. He observed that the northern black population evolved into a class structure based on regional origin. Those born in the North were urbanites, who had established certain attitudes and customs that included assimilation with whites. Northern black urbanites were routinely "overrun" by rural southern blacks, who had developed traits distinctive to their own subculture due to their southern upbringing and experiences. The two groups, one urban and entrenched in the North and the other migrant and rural, intermingled, but their variations in education and attainment led to a class distinction. Further, and to the dismay of northern blacks who fought hard to assimilate, southern blacks voluntarily segregated, creating a harmful "color line" for northern whites to exploit. He maintained that this exacerbated the prejudices of northern whites toward African Americans.

The fearful and prejudiced white masses hardly needed this as a motivating factor to enforce the racial segregation desired by some blacks. Their minds were already made up even before this convenience appeared. They manipulated African Americans, as they had other immigrant groups, by threats of violence and, when that did not work, real violence. Whites also controlled the housing market and manipulated it to restrict blacks to "acceptable places" in the inner cities. As a result, the racial tone was set in the North, and the development of a national ghetto system described by Harold Rose evolved in the twentieth century.

Development of the National Ghetto System. Changes that occurred in the United States between the world wars led to mass migration of southern blacks northward and westward into existing urban centers. This process evolved over an entire generation, accelerating to a peak in the 1960s and resulting in a new urban form, the "black ghetto" (Rose, 1971).

After World War I, agricultural changes became push factors for a southern African-American population eager to leave Jim Crow behind and find opportunity elsewhere. The push factors included the further decline of the cotton industry and lower prices for key agricultural crops. The result, of course, was less labor needed in the South, which was furthered by gains in mechanization. Simultaneously, pull factors attracted southern blacks to other U.S. regions. These included increased labor demand related to World War I and the labor shortages created by the quota system of the 1920 U.S. immigration law. These led the northern press and recruiters to encourage blacks northward and westward, suggesting that new social and economic promised lands awaited (Davis and Donaldson, 1975; Farley and Allen, 1987).

Rose (1969a, 1969b) documented the redistribution of black Americans into urban centers and described the development of the national ghetto system as a process that "accelerated" during and after World War II. He identified three stages of ghetto formation, including the first by 1920, the next between 1920 and 1950, and the third post-1950. In the first period, black migration streams from southern regions flowed to particular northern and western areas. Rose noted that the South lost more than a half million blacks during the 1910–1920 decade, most moving to the Midwest. He categorized cities as "ghetto centers" after their black populations reached 25,000 persons. By this definition, first-generation ghetto centers included a small group of "northern" cities (Chicago, Cincinnati, Pittsburgh, and St. Louis) that joined seven southern and Atlantic seaboard communities to constitute the early "national ghetto system." He noted that only the largest northern and midwestern cities had experienced sufficient black in-migration before the end of World War I to create ghetto centers.

The second-generation centers, or "new ghetto centers," emerged between 1920 and 1950, when, except for the Depression years, blacks migrated en masse out of the South, seeking industrial employment opportunities in northern and midwestern cities. During this period the mass migration of white Europeans slowed substantially due to both the quota system and World War II. The result was an expansion of existing southern and northern ghettos and the creation of new ghettos. Among the centers were Dallas and Houston in the South; Los Angeles, San Francisco, and Oakland in the West; Cleveland and Detroit in the Midwest; and Newark on the Atlantic Coast.

Rose (1969b) identified a group of third-generation ghetto centers resulting from post-1950 black migration northward, which grew and expanded due to "white flight" in northern cities. These centers were numerous and widespread geographically, including Boston, Buffalo, Rochester, Milwaukee, Denver, San Diego, and Seattle. By 1970, fifteen of the twenty-eight ghetto centers were outside the South. By the 1990s, scores of American cities had black ghettos and the twenty largest black ghetto centers were located almost equally between the South and other regions of the United States.

As noted above, nationwide, white Americans' real concerns were not necessarily the numbers or proportion of black Americans; rather, they involved their locations in great numbers. Not only did the African-American population dramatically relocate regionally between 1940 and 1970, it also became highly concentrated in certain cities. This rural-urban shift created problems for the white society, who restricted the housing choices of blacks through mechanisms of the housing market. Farley and Allen (1987) noted the proportional disparities between blacks and whites in urbanized areas:

At the turn of [the twentieth] century the proportion [of blacks] living in urban places was about half as much for Blacks as for whites: 23 percent compared to

43 percent. During World War II, for the first time a majority of Blacks lived in cities rather than in the rural South, and by 1960, Blacks were more urbanized than whites. This urbanization has been so complete that the concentration of Blacks in large metropolitan areas has become a major issue in our society [pp. 103–104].

These authors referred to both the spatial concentration within the nation and the formation of black ghettos, particularly in northern and midwestern cities. The fact that the nation's economy was undergoing major stress due to economic restructuring, shifting most employment away from manufacturing to services, made a difficult situation worse. Between 1960 and 1990, in response to foreign competition, many U.S. manufacturers cut jobs and relocated either outside the North or out of the country. As a result, blacks, in addition to job discrimination, found fewer factory jobs available. This resulted in unemployment or low-paying employment for many. Coupled with housing discrimination, this led to the formation of more ghettos and what was later termed the "ghetto underclass" of millions of black Americans.

By 1990 the concentration of African Americans spatially and in large metropolitan areas was clear. The twenty metropolitan areas in the United States with the largest African-American populations in 1990 are listed in Table 2.2. Of the largest six (rankings are also in Table 2.2), five are in the Midwest or on the East Coast. The total black population in these areas (Northeast/East Coast and Midwest) is approximately 5.5 million. This is nearly twice the number of African Americans residing in the South's largest black centers (about 3.1 million) and more than six times the number of blacks in Los Angeles and Oakland, the West's only two metropolitan areas with very large black populations. In fact, New York and Washington, D.C., combined have nearly as many African Americans as the eight southern cities listed in Table 2.2 and contain approximately 2 million more blacks than Los Angeles and Oakland. In summary, these statistics underscore Du Bois's earlier point that northern blacks were literally "overrun" by waves of southern black migrants over a short period of time. This has become the settlement legacy of the postslavery era.

Hispanic Population and Settlement Patterns

In 1940, when African Americans were 10 percent of the U.S. population and were being restricted to urban ghettos, Hispanics accounted for slightly more than 1 percent of Americans. Hispanic Americans (1.8 million in 1940) almost exclusively were associated with the American West and Southwest, particularly Texas and California. By 1970 more than 9 million Hispanics resided in the United States, and that number more than doubled, to nearly 22 million, by 1990. Today Hispanics are the fastest-growing minority group in the nation (see Table 2.1). Reynolds Farley and William Frey (1993) reported a 53 percent

TABLE 2.2   Twenty U.S. Metropolitan Areas with the Largest African-American Populations, 1990

	1990 Black Population	Rank
Northeast/East Coast		
Baltimore	616,065	8
Boston	233,819	20
Newark	422,802	12
New York	2,250,026	1
Philadelphia	929,907	6
Washington D.C.	1,041,934	3
Midwest		
Chicago	1,332,919	2
Cleveland	355,619	16
Detroit	943,479	5
St Louis	423,182	11
South		
Atlanta	736,153	7
Birmingham	245,726	19
Dallas	410,766	13
Houston	611,243	9
Memphis	399,011	14
Miami	397,993	15
New Orleans	430,470	10
Richmond	252,340	18
West		
Los Angeles	992,974	4
Oakland	303,826	17

SOURCE: U.S. Census Bureau, 1990.

growth in the Hispanic population in the 1980s, with more dramatic increases in the 1990s. Hispanic growth basically dwarfed white, black, and Asian-American population growth rates. As with other minorities, Hispanic settlement and dispersion patterns are likely to greatly influence societal issues of the twenty-first century.

Early Settlement Patterns.   Hispanics are a significant part of American history for two major reasons. One has to do with the fact that Spain was the first European nation to settle in what is now the United States. The other reason is tied to the history and "legacy of linkages" between the United States and Mexico (Haverluk, 1997). In investigating the historical geography of Hispanic settlement in the United States, Terrence Haverluk provided an excellent chronology that began with four *entradas* (settlement periods). These occurred between 1598, when the first Spanish *entrada* brought settlers to the Rio Grande Valley, and 1769, when the last *entrada* created a northernmost buffer between the Spanish territory and "Russian settlements in the

Pacific Northwest" (Haverluk, 1997, p. 199). The Spanish settlement strategy, designed to halt the spatial advance of French and Russian settlements, established a lasting geographic pattern of cultural landscapes in the southwestern United States.

Spain's hold on parts of North America weakened as Mexico evolved during the nineteenth century, gaining its independence by 1821. Thirty-five years later, Mexico lost a war to the United States and yielded its lands through the Mexican Cession and Gadsden Purchase. This history, as noted by Haverluk, resulted in a legacy of migration between Mexico and the United States (Haverluk, 1997).

Haverluk (1997) identifies two subsequent periods of Hispanic settlement in the American West, one between the 1850s and 1920s and the other between the 1920s and 1940s. In the first period, whites migrated westward in great numbers. However, at the same time, Mexicans continued to move into the region, as well. This Hispanic population, despite its minority status, was still increasing, particularly in southwestern states. By the beginning of this period, "Hispanic homelands" (land grants awarded to Hispanics by the Spanish crown or Mexican government in what is now Texas, New Mexico, and Arizona) had reached their maximum size, and the practice of using cheap Hispanic manual labor in U.S. agriculture had begun. Initially, Hispanics were used to clear land and dig irrigation canals; later, they were used to plant and harvest crops. In the second period, the 1920s to 1940s, the agricultural economy of the Western states expanded rapidly, and labor was in great demand. The lack of a border patrol, the demand for labor, and the Mexican legacy resulted in the in-migration of 700,000 Mexicans during just a five-year period, 1920–1925. By 1930 the U.S. Census Bureau reported 1.4 million ethnic Mexicans among the U.S. population (Haverluk, 1997). Just as African-American migration was a response to northern labor markets hurt by the quota system, Mexicans became the chief source of cheap manual labor for the West. It is important to note also that the U.S. State Department permitted Mexicans to immigrate despite the stipulations of U.S. immigration law. This was due, at least in part, to their proximity and to the belief that Mexicans could easily be returned to Mexico when their labor was not needed. In fact, during the Depression, thousands of Mexicans were sent home forcibly and the immigration tide turned until World War II, when pre-Depression figures were quickly resumed (Haverluk, 1997). During World War II, the "bracero program" allowed guest workers entry to the United States, but its rigorous requirements led many agriculturalists to ignore it and opt for illegals (Haverluk, 1997). Nonetheless, this program and illegals brought hundreds of thousands of Mexicans into the American West during the 1940s and 1950s. Although repatriation strategies such as the 1954 "Operation Wetback" operated periodically, immigration continued and resulted in a doubling of the Mexican population in the United States between 1930 and 1960 (Haverluk, 1997).

Recent Hispanic Settlement Trends.   The 1920 National Origins Act established the quota system, which greatly favored western and northern Europe over other global regions. We have illustrated that, despite this restrictive system, the labor needs of American business opened the doors to Mexican migration, though the intent was to admit guest workers rather than permanent immigrants.

The entry status of Mexicans, and more generally Hispanics, changed dramatically. By 1960 the bracero program had established migration streams from Mexico for illegals. In 1965 the Hart-Celler Act provided access on a legal basis. By marriage and other means provided in the act, many illegals became legals and, since the act allowed for admission of immediate family members, brought family to the United States.

The entry of Mexican illegals continued to be a problem. Congressional efforts to deal with the problem include the 1986 Immigration Reform and Control Act, which provided general amnesty for post-1982 illegals who resided in the United States continuously, as well as provisions for "guest agricultural workers" and penalties for those employing illegals. This effort to control illegal entries resulted in the acceptance of approximately 2 million Mexicans who had entered the United States illegally. Despite these efforts and others, such as border patrol efforts, illegals remain a problem in the twenty-first century.

Perhaps the most dramatic and important trend since 1965 is the immigration of non-Mexican Hispanics into the United States. Politics, policy, and economics have resulted in massive increases in the numbers of Cubans and other Latin Americans, such as Haitians and Dominicans. Some have come legally; others as illegal refugees fleeing U.S.-supported, right-wing governments. Such was the case of Salvadoran immigrants (Lopez, Popkin and Telles, 1996). Puerto Ricans, who are U.S. citizens, also were attracted to the U.S. mainland by relatively inexpensive airfares and the perception of economic self-improvement. Their numbers in the United States have increased by a factor of sixteen in recent decades (Haverluk, 1997).

These changes in immigration trends are important because each Hispanic racial/ethnic group has brought its own unique culture to particular regions of the United States. Each has had a tendency to concentrate due to a geographic preference for a specific region, state, or city. The result has been dispersion away from the highly concentrated pattern of Hispanic settlement in the Southwest. Extreme concentration has been replaced by a more balanced set of regional patterns. However, within these major regions, Hispanic cultures have concentrated in the urban areas of only a few states, including those of the Mexican West, Cuban Florida, and Puerto Rican and Dominican New York, among others. Farley and Frey (1993) elaborated on this pattern, noting that approximately two-thirds of all Mexican Americans reside in the West and Southwest, including 58 percent in the state of California; 70 percent of all Cubans live in Florida; and the same proportion of Puerto Ricans reside in northeastern communities, especially in the broader New York City region.

Although six states contained the majority of Hispanic Americans in 1990, certain urban centers of those states had a disproportionate share of the Hispanic population. Figure 2.1(a) illustrates the distribution of urban counties in the southern-western crescent of the United States, sometimes referred to as the Sunbelt, containing 50,000 or more Hispanic residents in 1997 (U.S. Census Bureau, 1997). Twenty-four counties in California fall into this category and account for slightly more than 9.5 million Hispanics, or nearly 30 percent of the U.S. total. Another thirteen counties in Texas account for 4.1 million, or 13 percent. Thus, these two states combined account for approximately 13.7 million Hispanics living in thirty-seven urban counties. When urban counties in Arizona, Florida, and New Mexico are added, the total is approximately 16.5 million (more than one-half the national total) residing in forty-nine urban counties.

Figure 2.1(b) shows northern urban counties that contained 50,000 or more Hispanics in 1997. This map illustrates the concentration of urban Hispanics in the megalopolis, extending from metropolitan Washington, D.C., to the north of Boston and along the Atlantic seaboard. It also shows the concentration of Hispanics in three midwestern metropolitan areas. The first begins in Chicago and stretches through five contiguous urban counties, including Lake County, Indiana, the location of Gary. The second is Milwaukee, Wisconsin. The third is Wayne County, Michigan, which contains the city of Detroit. These thirty counties located in eighteen states contain 5 million Hispanics. Not shown are other significant distributions of Hispanic Americans in non-Sunbelt states in the West such as Washington, Utah, and Colorado. Together, forty-nine counties of all three regions contain more than 22 million Hispanics, more than two-thirds of the total Hispanic population in the United States.

Hispanic labor was imported initially to work in agriculture. However, by the end of the twentieth century, Hispanic Americans had become attracted to urban centers. In some cases they became significant proportions of local communities. Among the twenty counties in which at least 200,000 Hispanics resided in 1990, the Hispanic proportion of the local population ranged from approximately 23 percent to 65 percent. Also, even in instances where Hispanics were less than 23 percent, they sometimes constituted a large local concentration. Examples include Chicago/Cook County (with 867,250 Hispanics), San Diego (696,718), Phoenix/Maricopa County (526,540), and Dallas (415,700). Overall, twelve urban counties in California and Texas have more than a quarter million Hispanics among their populations. Another twenty-seven urban counties located there and in Florida, Arizona, New Mexico, and Nevada contain Hispanic populations in excess of 100,000 each.

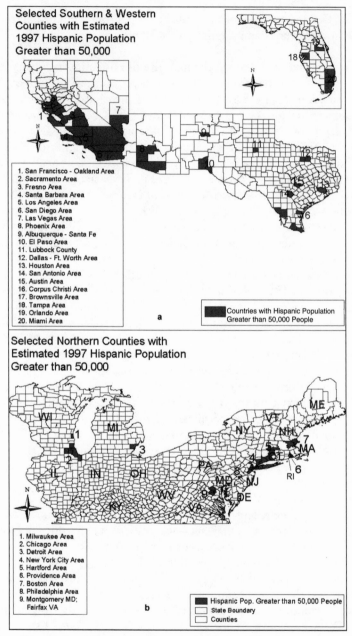

Selected Southern & Western Counties with Estimated 1997 Hispanic Population Greater than 50,000

1. San Francisco - Oakland Area
2. Sacramento Area
3. Fresno Area
4. Santa Barbara Area
5. Los Angeles Area
6. San Diego Area
7. Las Vegas Area
8. Phoenix Area
9. Albuquerque - Santa Fe
10. El Paso Area
11. Lubbock County
12. Dallas - Ft. Worth Area
13. Houston Area
14. San Antonio Area
15. Austin Area
16. Corpus Christi Area
17. Brownsville Area
18. Tampa Area
19. Orlando Area
20. Miami Area

Countries with Hispanic Population Greater than 50,000 People

a

Selected Northern Counties with Estimated 1997 Hispanic Population Greater than 50,000

1. Milwaukee Area
2. Chicago Area
3. Detroit Area
4. New York City Area
5. Hartford Area
6. Providence Area
7. Boston Area
8. Philadelphia Area
9. Montgomery MD; Fairfax VA

Hispanic Pop. Greater than 50,000 People
State Boundary
Counties

b

FIGURE 2.1   (a) Selected southern and western counties with estimated 1997 Hispanic population greater than 50,000. (b) Selected northern counties with estimated 1997 Hispanic population greater than 50,000. Source: U.S. Census Bureau (1997 estimate), www.census.gov/raceandHispanicorigin/estimates/counties, 1998.

In the north-central region of the United States, three urban counties have an excess of one-half million Hispanics, two others have more than 400,000, one has more than 200,000, and five other counties have more than 100,000 Hispanics within their borders. The U.S. Hispanic population not only has grown dramatically and spread eastward but also has become very urbanized.

As Farley and Frey (1993) have noted, minority populations have increased such that many cities now can be classified as multiracial, containing various combinations of African Americans, Hispanics, and Asians. On a municipal basis, three, or even two, races can account for widely varying proportions of the total population. Blacks and Hispanics are an example. In some counties, such as those of southeastern Pennsylvania, these two minorities account for only a small fraction of the total population. However, because they are highly concentrated in a few neighborhoods, they are readily observable as two subcommunities. In Lehigh County, for example, Puerto Ricans from New York and Philadelphia have settled in inner-city Allentown, a former steel town of the industrial era. By the 2000 census, they constituted 25 percent of that city's total population. Combined with the locally concentrated African-American community, they account for one-third of the Allentown population. In many larger urban counties, the same situation occurs; minorities are a low proportion of the population (less than 10 percent) but are highly segregated.

In many cases where African Americans and Hispanics coexist, one minority population is numerically dominant. For example, in Bernalillo County (Albuquerque), New Mexico, the Mexican population accounts for approximately one-third of the county's population, while African Americans constitute only 2.7 percent. The opposite scenario occurs in urban counties like Cuyahoga County (Cleveland), Ohio, where nearly one-quarter of the population is black and Hispanics are only 2.1 percent of the population. Yet in other urban counties their respective populations are more balanced. Examples include counties such as Tarrant and Harris Counties in Texas; Hartford, Connecticut; and Clark County, Nevada. When these two populations exist in urban counties, regardless of their proportions, they tend to be spatially concentrated and segregated from white populations. They also are overrepresented in the counties' central cities. Finally, there are instances in which a third minority group, Asian American, coexists with African Americans and Hispanics to form a racial mosaic of local minorities. We will examine such situations following our review of Asian-American settlement patterns.

Asian-American Settlements
Like their European, African, and Hispanic counterparts, Asians provided the inexpensive labor that helped build the American agricultural and industrial economies. They also experienced the same forms of racial prejudice and discrimination, including violence, deportation, and second-class citizenship.

Asians, like their counterparts of other races, had reached the Americas as early as the 1600s, when Chinese and Filipinos landed in Mexico. Filipinos also settled in Louisiana as early as the 1700s, when a few men jumped ship in New Orleans (Chan, 1982). The Chinese were in Philadelphia as early as the 1700s (Cheng, 1948). By the 1800s, Chinese "peddlers" were common in New York City and "sugar masters" worked in Hawaii. However, it was the discovery of gold in California in 1848 that first brought significant numbers of Asians to the United States, when Chinese miners came to San Francisco. Due to a host of push factors (a rebellion, a war lost to Britain, crop failures, and famine) and the pull of potential wealth, Chinese entered the United States in record numbers during the last half of the nineteenth century. In a single year alone, 1852, 20,000 Chinese miners entered California (Chan, 1982). The discovery of gold in the Pacific Northwest, notably in the state of Washington, provided additional impetus to the "Chinese forty-niner" rush to the United States. Te-Chao Cheng provided U.S. Census data to illustrate that Chinese immigration reached nearly 35,000 by 1850 as a result of the gold rush, peaking at 107,488 in 1890, before three decades of precipitous decline due to U.S. government restrictions (Cheng, 1948).

In the 1860s, Chinese were recruited by the Central Pacific Railroad Company to build the transcontinental railroad, which was completed by 1870. Chinese workers were also recruited in logging camps and fish canneries in the Pacific Northwest (Dowdell and Dowdell, 1972; Daniels, 1988). Hawaii became very dependent on the contract labor of these migrant workers. Hawaii's sugar plantations had been destinations for Chinese labor since the 1840s.

Japanese migrant workers also were attracted to Hawaiian plantations. This was due in part to the opening of Japanese ports by the 1850s and the subsequent economic upheaval that led to the loss of lands by Japanese farmers. With the annexation of Hawaii in 1898 and passage of the 1890 Organic Act, which applied U.S. laws to Hawaii, contract labor ceased in the islands, and Japanese migrant workers began traveling to the U.S. mainland, especially to California and the Pacific Northwest (Chan, 1982). Direct migration streams also provided the United States with Japanese migrants for inexpensive agricultural labor, especially in the production of agricultural produce for urban markets. The Japanese also worked in the extraction and processing industries, such as fish canneries and sawmills, and for the railroads.

Filipino migrants joined the Asian migrations to the U.S. West Coast. Their numbers increased dramatically after the 1882 Chinese Exclusion Act, which sharply reduced the numbers of Chinese that were permitted to enter the United States (Cheng, 1948). At the close of the Spanish-American War in 1898, the United States acquired the Philippines and held it as a colony until the conclusion of World War II. As a result of this acquisition, the status of U.S. nationals was applied to Filipinos, allowing them the freedom to migrate anywhere within U.S. borders (Bautista, 1998). Just as Chinese and

Japanese migrants were attracted by economic opportunities and the proximity of the American West Coast to Asia, thousands of Filipinos migrated to the United States, especially to the states of California and Washington after 1898. Like their fellow Asians, Filipinos provided an inexpensive labor pool that helped drive the development of the agricultural, fish-processing, and lumber industries.

While the Chinese, Japanese, and Filipinos were the three largest Asian ethnic groups to enter the United States early, other Asians also came and provided cheap manual labor. The most notable by their numbers were the Koreans and Asian Indians. These Asians contributed to the development of the U.S. economy in much the same way white European immigrants did, in the factories of eastern and midwestern cities. It was when Asian migrants were perceived as "outsiders" competing for employment in urban economies of the West that cultures clashed. Conflict was rooted in economic issues, especially in times of economic hardship. Just as blacks and Mexicans were "outsiders" and "different," Asians, though received initially as acceptable hard workers, later were rebuffed, first in California and the West, then in the East. The changing location of Asian settlement did not stop white fear, resentment, and discrimination.

Early Asian Dispersion, 1880–1920. Te-Chao Cheng (1948) explained why the Chinese population moved eastward after the Gold Rush:

> . . . Chinese "coolie" labor power was readily sought for and welcomed with open arms. . . . [However,] [a]s soon as the speculative bubble burst and whites were thrown out of employment the cry arose "The Chinese must go," for the once industrious cheap "coolie" labor had now become a competitive economic pinch to the American labor [p. 53].

The Chinese were victimized by white violence and massacres and had little choice but to change occupations and disperse themselves from California. As a result, Chinese men (very few Chinese women came to the United States in this early period) changed from predominately being miners and laborers before 1870 to being domestic and personal service workers (Cheng, 1948). They also became involved, though in smaller numbers, in trade and retailing.

> They quit mining and picked up the work usually done by women in China, such as cooking, washing, gardening, and so forth. But they soon found that this work was very much in demand as there was at that time a very great shortage of women in the frontier West [Cheng, 1948, p. 56].

Cheng used U.S. Census data for the years 1880 through 1920 to illustrate changes in Chinese occupations and the population's dispersal from the West

Coast. He noted that of all Chinese in the United States in 1880, 83 percent lived on the West coast. By 1920, only 55 percent resided there. Some of their experiences will be chronicled in Chapter 6.

Among the other regions of the country in 1920, three stand out for their proportion of the total U.S. Chinese populations: the Middle Atlantic (14.2 percent), east-north central (8.2 percent), and mountain (7 percent) regions. Together, these three regions contained nearly 30 percent of all Chinese residents in the nation. The remaining four U.S. regions all had less than 3 percent each (Cheng, 1948). Clearly, the Chinese had dispersed themselves away from California and the Pacific Coast but were disproportionately settled in other U.S. regions.

Before the mass migration from the Pacific Coast to the eastern United States, some Chinese settlers had arrived in Philadelphia, New York, and Boston. However, it was the eastward migration from California that brought large numbers of Chinese men, who would continue to dominate the Chinese population in the absence of women immigrants, to work as laundrymen and domestics, first in New Jersey and then in Philadelphia (Cheng, 1948). Chinese men then spread to other occupations, most notably in retailing and other service positions. As in the West, their occupations shifted from primary industries and heavy labor to urban service industries. In Philadelphia they became highly concentrated in the Race Street "Chinatown" area and in "satellite communities" in New Jersey and Delaware (Cheng, 1948). Chinese settlements also developed in New York City and Boston.

The increases in Chinese population in the eastern communities were in large part due to interregional migration within the United States, since their immigration to the country had decreased after the Chinese Exclusion Act. These increases, of course, slowed during the lean years of the Depression. Asian populations did not grow significantly in the United States again until the 1960s, when U.S. immigration policy changed in favor of the Eastern Hemisphere. Although not by design, the Hart-Celler Act of 1965 influenced Asian immigration to the United States. The Act's stipulation for skills-based entry resulted in a wave of highly skilled Chinese, Taiwanese, Korean, and Asian Indians into the country in unprecedented numbers. In addition to this first Asian wave came a second, consisting of immigrants from Vietnam, Thailand, Cambodia, and Laos, among others, in large numbers after 1965. Some came to seek security and economic opportunity. Many of this second wave, however, sought refugee status. The immigrants of this wave differed significantly from those highly skilled Asians who entered during the first wave. These were more similar to the existing segments of the black and Hispanic low-skilled, undereducated communities.

These dramatic increases in U.S. minorities, which are supported by the 2000 U.S. Census reports, are likely to cause major changes in American diversity and attitudes during this century.

Projected Growth of American Minorities

A review of projected estimates of the American population reveals dramatic changes in racial composition beginning as early as the first quarter of the twenty-first century. The African-American population is expected to increase modestly during the first half of this century. However, significant increases are projected for the Hispanic-American and Asian-American subgroups. The number of Hispanic Americans will increase most dramatically due to their large population base in the year 2000. The projected numerical and percent changes for all races for the period 2000–2025 are presented in Table 2.3. These data suggest that the total U.S. population is expected to increase by approximately 63.4 million, to 340.8 million, by the year 2025. The result is an annual rate of growth of less than 1 percent (0.9 percent) for the first quarter of this century, based on a twenty-five-year growth rate of 22.8 percent.

Table 2.3 also reveals significant differences in growth rates among racial groups. The U.S. white non-Hispanic population is expected to approach zero population growth, 0.2 percent per year, for the twenty-five-year period. However, all three minority groups will grow at annual rates of more than 1 percent. Over the period 2000–2025, the white population will increase by only 6.1 percent, while minority groups grow at dramatically higher rates: African Americans, 34.1 percent, American Indians, 38.1 percent, Hispanic Americans, nearly 88 percent, and Asian Americans, 95.4 percent.

The increasing rates translate into approximately 50 million new minority persons between 2000 and 2025, while the white population increases by only 12 million for the same period. As Table 2.3 reports, the Asian-American population is projected to increase by about 10 million for the period. Asians will almost double their year-2000 population base in a quarter century. In fact, the Asian-American population more than doubles from 1990, when it was 2.9 percent of the total U.S. population, to 2025, when it will constitute 6.5 percent, with nearly 22 million people. The Hispanic-American population, which experienced the highest rate of growth during the 1990s, anticipates the second highest growth rate (88 percent) for the period 2000–2025. The Hispanic-American population increases from approximately 31 million in 2000 to nearly 59 million in 2025 and becomes the largest single minority in the United States. Hispanics accounted for only 9 percent of the total population in 1990. By 2025 they will represent one in every four Americans (26 percent). Black Americans will represent only 13 percent of the U.S. population in 2025. Thus, not only is this "browning" of America likely to lessen the white majority by 2025, but minority relationships will also be changing. In 1990, for every Asian American, there were four black Americans and three Hispanic Americans. By 2025 that relationship will be substantially altered. Although the 3:1 ratio of Hispanics to Asians roughly remains the same, there

TABLE 2.3   Projected U.S. Population by Race and Hispanic Origin, 2000–2025
(thousands)

	2000		2005		2000–2005%	Average annual
		%		%	change	rate%
American Indian	2,401	0.9	3,317	1.0	38.1	1.5
Black	35,441	12.8	47,539	13.9	34.1	1.36
Hispanic	31,360	11.3	58,925	17.3	87.9	3.5
Asian/Pacific Is.	11,245	4.0	21,971	6.5	95.4	3.8
White non-Hisp	197,062	71.0	209,113	61.3	6.1	0.2
TOTALS	**277,509**	**100.0**	**340,865**	**100.0**	**22.8**	**0.91**
Nonwhite Majority						
Totals	80,447	29.0	131,752	38.7		

SOURCE: U.S. Census Bureau, 1994, (see PPL #47).

will be only slightly more than two blacks per Asian. More significantly, black-Hispanic ratios will reverse during the same period, from 1.36 blacks for every Hispanic in 1990 to 1.24 Hispanics for every black American in 2025.

The white population of the United States, after a long period of supermajority status last century (80 percent of the total), is very likely to lessen its hold on minorities. By 2025 the white majority will barely exceed 60 percent. For the first time in U.S. history, minorities will exceed 131 million people. By 2050 white Americans are likely to hold a slim 52 percent majority. Given the radical change in minority position, proportionately and numerically, it is necessary to analyze the projected minority populations on a spatial basis. The geographic locations of minorities and the subsequent distribution of risks and benefits are likely to greatly influence economics, politics, health, and cultural landscapes for future American generations.

Estimated African-American Population Growth, 2000–2025
Although the African-American population's rate of growth is modest compared to other minorities, its growth over the next quarter century will be unevenly felt geographically (see Figure 2.2[a] and [b]). Figure 2.2(b) illustrates the increase in numbers of African Americans between 2000 and 2025. Four states will gain at least 1 million additional African Americans during this twenty-five-year period: Texas, Florida, Georgia, and California (in rank order). Four additional states will add between a half million and one million African Americans within the same period: New York, Maryland, North Carolina, and Virginia. Thus, the majority of states that will add large numbers of additional African Americans during this generation will be on the East Coast, stretching from New York to Florida. Together these six states will add slightly more than 6 million additional African Americans to their year-2000 totals.

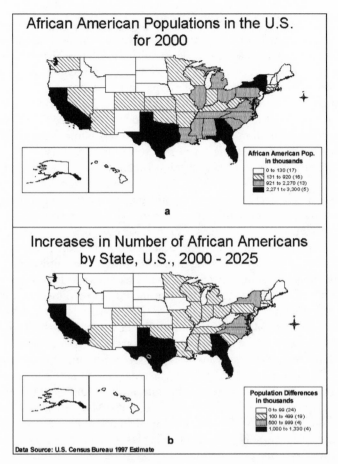

FIGURE 2.2   (a) African-American populations in the United States for 2000.
(b) Increases in number of African Americans by U.S. state, 2000–2025. Source: U.S.
Census Bureau (1997 estimate), www.census.gov/population/projections/state/
stpjrace.txt, 1998.

The occurrence of growth will be predominately urban unless some great
change in locational preference and housing market restrictions occurs during
this twenty-five-year period. These trends were reported earlier in Table 2.2
for metropolitan areas with the largest numbers of African Americans. These
urban regions and others with significant black populations are the most
likely to see major increases in the first quarter of the twenty-first century.

Changing Landscapes: Hispanic Growth and Dispersion by 2025
The distribution of the Hispanic population changed dramatically in the last
quarter of the twentieth century due to new immigrant locational preferences,

the increasing number of Hispanic ethnic groups entering the United States, and the perceived economic opportunities in various states and metropolitan areas across the nation. Generally, we have shown that a historic geographic shift in Hispanic-American populations occurred by the end of the last century, coupled with the migration of Hispanic Americans from West to East and major increases in immigration by non-Mexican Hispanics into eastern states. A general rural-to-urban mass migration also occurred in the twentieth century and included all races. The dispersion of Hispanic Americans is likely to continue during the first quarter of the twenty-first century.

Figure 2.3 illustrates the likely growth of the Hispanic-American population by U.S. state from 1990 to 2025. States with traditionally large Hispanic populations are expected to have big gains during the periods shown, including a doubling and then tripling of Hispanic-American populations among the fourteen states with the largest numbers of Hispanics. By 2025, an additional fourteen states will contain at least 200,000 Hispanic Americans. Figure 2.3(a) reveals that by 1990 the distribution of states with populations of 200,000 or more Hispanic Americans had already expanded to include eight states outside of the West, including one in the South (Florida), two in the Midwest (Illinois and Michigan), and five in the Northeast (New York, New Jersey, Pennsylvania, Massachusetts and Connecticut). However, the majority—more than 13 million Hispanic Americans—still resided in the Western states of California, Arizona, New Mexico, Colorado, and Washington.

By 2005, as Figure 2.3(b) shows, six other states with 200,000-plus Hispanics are to be scattered widely across the nation, including Georgia, Maryland, and Virginia on the Atlantic seaboard; Ohio in the Midwest; and Nevada and Oregon in the West. By 2025, eight additional states will have at least 200,000 Hispanic Americans (see Figure 2.3[c]). This last stage can be viewed as a "filling in" process within each of the major U.S. regions, including Utah and Idaho in the West, Kansas and Oklahoma in the central United States, North Carolina and Louisiana in the South, and Indiana and Wisconsin in the Midwest. In less than a generation, the number of states containing 200,000 or more Hispanic Americans is predicted to double, from fourteen to twenty-eight, resulting in the majority of U.S. states containing a relatively large number of Hispanic Americans.

The dangers of long-term forecasts are well-known. Still, it is useful to examine the potential future demographic and racial changes on a metropolitan basis. Private economic forecasts, such as those of Woods and Poole Economics (2000), provide a variety of insights as to what metropolitan America might look like in the year 2025. African-American and Hispanic-American population estimates as a percent of their total metropolitan populations were included. A Standard Metropolitan Area (SMA) is a U.S. Census term that refers to the metropolitan character of urban America. Typically, it has a

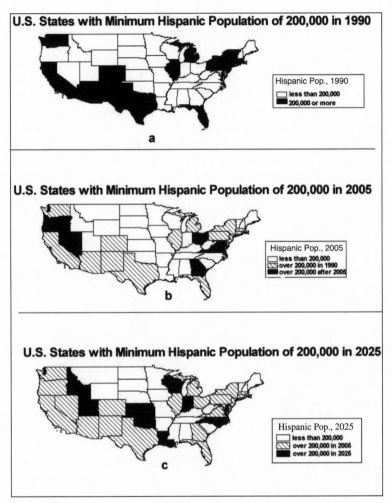

FIGURE 2.3   (a) States with minimum Hispanic population of 200,000 in 1990.
(b) States with minimum Hispanic population of 200,000 in 2005. (c) States with
minimum Hispanic population of 200,000 in 2025. Source: U.S. Census Bureau
(projections), www.census.gov/population/projections/state/stpjrace.txt, 1998.

central city of 50,000 or more people and meets the criteria of having a non-
agricultural labor force and spatial integration between or among counties
within the SMA. The spatial integration criterion is based on linkages between labor forces and employment centers of adjacent counties. For a particular county to be included within an SMA, a minimum exchange of labor
forces must occur between it and the central county of the SMA. In addition
to SMAs, these authors use Primary Metropolitan Statistical Areas (PMSAs),
which are SMAs of greater than 1 million people that have external links to

nearby counties as well. Thus, PMSAs refer to very large, integrated population centers.

Table 2.4 shows the percentages that Blacks and what Woods and Poole call "Hispanics" will represent in 2000 and 2025 in the thirty largest PMSAs. The percentage-point change in each group's share of the total population between 2000 and 2025 is also reported. Woods and Poole included people of all races in their Hispanic totals (i.e., they did not differentiate among Hispanic Asians, Hispanic blacks, etc.); therefore, some caution must be exercised in the interpretation and comparison of these numbers to other Hispanic-American statistics. Also, these forecasters did not provide projections for the Asian-American population.

Examination of these projected data reveals that generally the percent increases of African Americans in the thirty largest metropolitan regions will be smaller than those of Hispanic Americans. In fact, four metropolitan regions (Los Angeles–Long Beach, Dallas, Houston, and Miami) will likely see modest decreases in the proportion of African Americans. Another eight metropolitan areas, located in several regions of the United States, will have virtually no change in the proportion of black residents. Seven additional metropolitan areas will show a scant 1 percentage point increase, meaning that nearly two-thirds of these thirty largest centers will experience changes that range from a 1 percentage point gain to a 2 percentage point loss in their proportion of black populations. Of the remaining PMSAs, only two (Baltimore and Minneapolis–St. Paul) will experience a gain of 5 percentage points between 2000 and 2025. The remaining SMAs are scattered throughout the United States and will likely show increases of 2 to 4 percentage points in their African-American populations in this twenty-five-year period.

Hispanics, in contrast, will increase their percentages by substantially greater margins. Of the thirty PMSAs reported, twenty-five will increase their Hispanic proportion between 6 and 15 percent (Woods and Poole Economics, 2000). These can be divided into two groups, those that are forecasted to increase by 10 percent or more and those with estimated increases of 6 to 9 percent. In the first group, Miami will gain the largest (15 percent), followed by Phoenix, Los Angeles, Las Vegas, Dallas–Fort Worth, Sacramento, Tampa, Washington, D.C., Riverside–San Bernardino, New York, and Denver. Seven of these PMSAs are in three states, California (three PMSAs), Texas (two) and Florida (two). In each of the twelve cases, the African-American population increase is likely to be countered by a double-digit increase in the percent of Hispanics. In the second and largest group, fourteen SMAs/PMSAs scattered about the United States are expected to increase the Hispanic percent of the total population, in the range of 6 to 9 percent.

The final group of the thirty PMSAs includes Baltimore, Houston, Minneapolis–St. Paul, and Pittsburgh. These are likely to experience gains of

TABLE 2.4   Projected Changes in African American and Hispanic (all races) Percent of PMSA Populations, 2000 and 2025

PMSA Rank in 2005 (projected)	2000		2005		% Change, 2000–2025	
	Black	Hispanic	Black	Hispanic	Black	Hispanic
1. LA–Long Beach	11	44	9	56	–2	12
2. Chicago	19	15	19	24	0	9
3. New York	29	26	30	36	1	10
4. Boston	6	6	9	13	3	7
5. Washington D.C.	25	8	25	19	0	11
6. Houston	19	26	18	30	–1	4
7. Atlanta	26	4	28	10	2	6
8. Philadelphia	20	5	22	11	2	6
9. Phoenix	4	22	6	35	2	13
10. Detroit	23	3	24	9	1	6
11. Riverside–San B.	7	34	7	44	0	10
12. Dallas	16	18	15	30	–1	12
13. San Diego	6	26	6	32	0	6
14. Minneapolis–St. Paul	5	3	10	7	5	4
15. Orange County	2	29	2	35	0	6
16. Seattle	5	5	6	10	1	5
17. Baltimore	28	2	33	6	5	4
18. Oakland	15	17	15	20	0	5
19. Tampa	11	10	14	21	3	11
20. St. Louis	18	2	19	7	1	5
21. Nassau-Suffolk	9	8	12	15	3	7
22. Denver	6	16	8	26	2	10
23. Portland	3	6	4	14	1	8
24. Miami	20	58	19	73	–1	15
25. Orlando	14	12	18	21	4	9
26. Las Vegas	9	17	10	29	1	12
27. Ft. Worth	11	15	12	27	1	12
28. Pittsburgh	9	1	12	5	3	4
29. Sacramento	8	15	8	26	0	11
30. San Antonio	7	55	7	61	0	6

SOURCE: Woods and Poole Economics, 2000, pp. 323–885.

5 percent or less in their proportions of the population that are Hispanic. These four metropolitan regions are located in four different U.S. regions.

Four conclusions may be drawn from our earlier discussions and this brief analysis of expected growth trends in urbanized areas. First, Hispanic populations of all national origins will experience the largest numerical increases of any minority within their metropolitan areas through 2025. This is due to high Hispanic birth rates relative to all other groups and Hispanic Americans' relatively large population base. Second, black population increases will be relatively minimal between 2000 and 2025. This is reflected in small increases, no change, or reductions in their percent of the total population in most of the thirty largest PMSAs. Third, there is substantial geographical variation in the percent changes of blacks and Hispanics. There also is likely variation among the counties that are located within each of these large PMSAs. Fourth, we have every reason to believe that future urban landscapes will contain highly segregated black and Hispanic concentrations, as well as zones where blacks and Hispanics share space, if only on a temporary basis. These conclusions are important to the empirical analyses of future chapters, as we will point out later in the chapter.

Changing Landscapes:
Asian-American Population Growth by 2025

Although only 3 percent of the total U.S. population was Asian in 2000, this population will continue to grow significantly in future decades. The largest single Asian ethnic group in 2000 was Chinese. Although the Chinese have a long history in the United States, many were foreign born in 1990, reflecting recent Chinese immigration trends. Filipino Americans are the second largest Asian-American population; Asian-Indian Americans rank third. These three groups are followed by Japanese, Koreans, and Vietnamese. As a single race, the Asian population in the United States is projected to grow at an annual rate of 3.8 percent, reaching nearly 22 million persons by the year 2025. This addition of millions of Asians to the U.S. population is likely to dramatically change their settlement geography. According to the 2000 Census, New York City contained 873,000 Asians, while Los Angeles's Asian total reached 407,000. Despite these large concentrations, regional distributions occurred. In 2000 the U.S. West contained less than a majority (49 percent) of the total Asian population. Other regions continued to account for a larger proportion of the total.

Figure 2.4(a) illustrates the projected distributions of Asians across states with a minimum of 100,000 Asians in 1995. Although not shown on the map, some redistribution from the western to eastern United States had already occurred by 1995 into southern, midwestern, and northeastern states. Figure 2.4(b) illustrates the likely expansion of each of the existing subregions to include twenty-six states by the year 2025. A crescent of six western states stretching from Washington to Texas (with the exception of New Mexico) likely will contain 5.5 million Asians. In the Southeast, Florida and Georgia combined will account for nearly a half million Asians, while the eleven northeastern states will have a combined total of more than 3.3 million Asians.

The changes in Asian population between 2000 and 2025 are shown in Figure 2.4(c). This map reveals that the highest levels of change will occur in states with historic Asian populations (such as California, Washington, New Jersey, and Massachusetts) and states that more recently increased their Asian

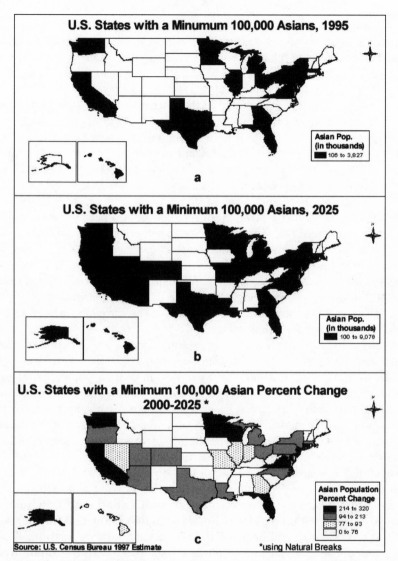

FIGURE 2.4 (a) States with a minimum of 100,000 Asians, 1995. (b) States with a minimum of 100,000 Asians, 2025. (c) States with a minimum of 100,000 Asians, percent change 2000–2025. Source: U.S. Census Bureau (1997 estimate), www.census.gov/population/projections/state/stpjrace.txt, 1998.

populations (including Florida, Connecticut, Minnesota, and Wisconsin). Thus, the exceptional growth rate of Asians in the United States will result in not only approximately 10 million additional Asians by 2025 but also a much more dispersed geographical pattern among the fifty states than ever before.

Since Asians are a highly urbanized group in the United States and many Asian immigrants tend to enter and, at least for a time, remain in gateway cities, it is important to examine the nature of their distributions. Our analysis is based on American SMAs. There are 318 SMAs of varying size. These contain more than 70 percent of the nation's total population. However, more than 90 percent of all Asian Americans live within these areas. In fact, a very high proportion of all Asian Americans (80 percent) reside in only seventy-four metropolitan regions. According to 1990 data tabulated by Susan Gall and Timothy Gall (1993), nearly 40 percent of all Asian Americans lived in only ten metro areas in 1990. These ten contained slightly more than 3.1 million Asian Americans. The ten regions are located in six states and the District of Columbia, but six are in California, indicating its dominant position in the nation.

In addition, ten other metropolitan regions contain nearly 1 million additional Asian Americans. The largest Asian-American metropolitan region among these ten is the Seattle, Washington, PMSA, with 128,656 Asians. The smallest population (ranked twentieth) is the Nassau-Suffolk, New York, PMSA, with 62,050 Asian Americans. All major U.S. regions, with the exception of the mountains and Plains, are represented in this list of metro areas with substantial numbers of Asian Americans. The list includes metropolitan areas located in eight different states.

Together, the twenty metropolitan regions contain about 4 million Asian Americans, or 56 percent of all Asian Americans. Clearly Asians are urbanites. In addition, though a significant proportion of their population remains in California and the West Coast, large numbers of migrants and new immigrants have resulted in a greater dispersion of Asian Americans into metropolitan regions across the United States. Asian Americans, however, are located unevenly within the national metropolitan system, with the majority located within a relatively small number of metropolitan areas.

There also is a substantial variation in the percentage of Asian Americans within their respective communities. Given the location and history of the Hawaiian Islands, it is not surprising that Asians are the majority (63 percent) population within the Honolulu SMA. In the continental United States, California is the cultural heart of the Asian American population. We already noted California's historic role in Asian settlement. In addition to the California Gold Rush, its proximity to Asia was and is one of the leading factors in Asian immigration to the area. As a result, California not only contains the largest Asian-American population but also has metropolitan areas that contain a relatively large proportion of Asian Americans. The San Francisco PMSA stands out as the metropolitan area with the greatest proportion of Asian Americans: one in five residents. Nearby, the San Jose PMSA is a close second, where only slightly less than one in five residents is Asian American. In three other California metropolitan areas—LA–Long Beach, Oakland, and Anaheim–Santa Ana—at least 10 percent of their respective populations is Asian American. Other California metropolitan areas also have similar Asian-American proportions of their populations. Examples include the Stockton SMA and the Vallejo-Fairfield-Napa PMSA. Of the twenty metropolitan regions containing the greatest numbers of Asian Americans, seven are located in California, totaling approximately 2.4 million people, or about 58 percent of all Asian Americans.

Asian-American representation in metropolitan areas falls precipitously as one leaves California. Three eastern metropolitan areas, New York and Washington, D.C., along the East Coast, and Chicago in the Midwest, together, contain nearly 1 million Asian Americans, with the New York City PMSA containing the majority (56 percent). Despite the relatively large number of Asian Americans in these large eastern metropolitan areas, the proportion of Asians is always low, especially when compared to California metropolitan communities. For instance, in 1990 in the New York City PMSA, Asian Americans constituted only 6.5 percent of the metropolitan population. In the Chicago PMSA, the third largest in 1990, Asian Americans constituted a rather meager 3.8 percent. The Washington, D.C., SMA's Asian-American population, by contrast, though somewhat smaller than Chicago's, makes up a greater share of the total population (5.2 percent).

In the second ten metropolitan areas, California is much less prominent than it is in the first ten. Eight metropolitan areas are outside California, and only Seattle is on the West Coast. However, in keeping with the West Coast pattern of relatively high proportions of Asian Americans within their metro populations, Sacramento and Seattle have the largest percent of Asian Americans in the ten SMAs—7.7 percent and 6.9 percent, respectively. Of the remaining metro areas, the Bergen-Passaic, New Jersey, PMSA has the largest percentage of Asian Americans, 5.2 percent. Of the other six metropolitan areas, only Houston and Boston have Asian-American percentages that exceed the percentage of Asian Americans in the national population, which is 2.9 percent.

Asian Ethnic Concentrations Within Metropolitan Areas

There is substantial variation in the representation of particular Asian ethnic groups within U.S. metropolitan areas. In some cases, both historically and since 2000, large numbers of a specific ethnic group came to a particular urban community and, for the most part, kept a presence there. In some cases, the group has become dominant in terms of its share of the local Asian population. In other cases, new Asian cultures have entered communities previously occupied by one or more Asian ethnic groups and created an ethnic-Asian mosaic. As a result, numerous Asian ethnic geographic patterns exist throughout urban America.

The percent of particular Asian ethnic groups (of the total Asian/Pacific Islander population) in selected metropolitan regions of the United States was reported by Gall and Gall for 1990 (Gall and Gall, 1993). The data were organized by U.S. region. On the West Coast, significant percentages of Chinese and Filipinos were present in all but one of the metropolitan regions, the Vallejo-Fairfield-Napa metropolitan area, which was dominated by Filipinos only. Another exception was San Francisco, where Chinese Americans were about one-half of all Asians and their proportion was nearly double that of Filipinos. In addition, three of these metropolitan areas contained a great diversity of ethnic Asian groups, especially Japanese, Koreans, and Vietnamese, as well as Chinese and Filipinos. These include the Seattle, LA–Long Beach, and Anaheim–Santa Ana regions. In the Anaheim–Santa Ana region, the Vietnamese were the largest single ethnic group.

The South and Southwest are strikingly different from the West due to the presence of a broader mix of Asian ethnic groups. Unlike the West Coast, where Chinese and Filipinos are the most common groups, five different Asian ethnic groups are broadly represented among the six large metropolitan areas reported (Gall and Gall, 1993). This is due in part to the historical pattern of immigration. Recent immigrants have had more diverse origins and have located outside the major western metropolitan areas. This diversity is reflected in Atlanta's Asian-American population. Three groups in Atlanta, Asian Indians, Chinese, and Koreans, have equal percentages of the total Asian-American population and together total 60 percent of that population. Other metro areas of the region illustrate Asian diversity, including New Orleans, Nashville, Houston, Dallas, and Ft. Worth.

The Northeast and Atlantic Coast have the most ethnically diverse Asian-American populations of any region. In 1990 the Norfolk–Virginia Beach–Newport News SMA, a Naval center, had a predominantly Filipino-Asian population. Eleven other metropolitan areas in these regions, however, had a minimum of three Asian ethnic groups that represented at least 10 percent of the total Asian population. The northern and midwestern regions also contain metropolitan regions of ethnically diverse Asian-American populations.

A Summary of Nonwhite Trends

There are common threads among the nonwhite population and settlement experiences in the United States. Historically, each minority group experienced some form of white hostility relating to skin color and cultural differences. Each was highly segregated and then experienced dispersal on a regional basis. Segregation persists among the nonwhite populations on a metropolitan basis.

There also are important differences. African Americans, who were originally brought to North America by force and whose position in the caste system has persisted, became segregated into a national ghetto system. The U.S. Hispanic population has a long Mexican legacy that resulted in Mexican Americans and Chicanos representing a large proportion of the Hispanic population. This changed after 1960, when other Hispanic populations—Cubans, Puerto Ricans, and other Latin Americans—entered the United States in growing numbers. Despite this ethnic diversity, Hispanics are increasingly segregated in American cities. Barrios are an important dimension of urban America, as are black-Hispanic neighborhoods (BHNs). Asian Americans also have a long American history. Once huddled in western Chinatowns, Asians dispersed early in their history in reaction to violence. Although still disproportionately located in the American West (49 percent), Asians are dispersing throughout the American urban system, which is where 90 percent of Asians live. The Asian-American population, once dominated by Japanese, Chinese, and Filipino ethnic groups, has greatly diversified since 1965. This is reflected on a regional basis in U.S. metropolitan regions. Although the Asian population of the United States is relatively small, it will continue to grow. Asians are an important part of the emerging American racial mosaic.

Each of these unique minority histories needs to be better incorporated into American history. Each racial/ethnic group discussed not only contributed to the development of the United States but is important to what the country will become in the twenty-first century and beyond.

Implications for Research and Policy

This chapter has focused on the demographic history and emerging growth patterns of minority groups in the United States. We have provided data and maps to illustrate the dispersion and resettlement patterns of these groups, their current distributions, and projected growth rates in the next few decades. Our findings suggest dramatic changes in the racial and ethnic composition of the population at national, regional, and local levels as the proportion of nonwhites increases faster than the white majority. These trends are perhaps most evident today in California, where the white majority is now a "minority" constituting merely 49 percent of the state's total population. Other states will likely reach the same status in future decades.

Besides the demographic shifts that are sweeping across the states and the nation as a whole, there are even more dramatic changes expected among the minority groups themselves, as some racial/ethnic groups begin to outnumber others. As we noted earlier, the Hispanic populations will experience the largest numerical increases compared to the other minorities. Blacks will be replaced by Hispanics as the largest minority group in the nation. The Asian-American population is also expected to grow substantially in selected parts of the country.

Another significant trend that we have documented in this chapter is the increasing concentration of the minorities in large metropolitan areas. African

Americans relocated and settled in large cities such as New York, Atlanta, Washington, D.C., Baltimore, and Detroit, where they now constitute more than 20 percent of the total population. We anticipate these race-place patterns to continue in the next few decades. We have also noted that Asians, who are currently the most highly urbanized minority group, will likely remain in large or highly specialized metropolitan areas. Our data also suggest the increasing concentration of Hispanics in urban counties in the Sunbelt states, the Boston-Washington megalopolis and the midwestern cities of Chicago, Milwaukee, and Detroit. Hispanic groups, such as Puerto Ricans, however, are also migrating to smaller cities, where they are having a substantial impact.

These emerging trends signal the need to confront a number of research and policy questions that will likely arise during the course of the next quarter century. Specifically, what are the current and foreseeable impacts of these demographic trends on the status of existing minority groups? These issues relate to the groups' size, composition, and ability to assimilate with the majority, to their aspirations to retain significant dimensions of their native cultures, as well as to their equity rights. Will racial segregation and isolation increase, decline, or desist? Are the existing power relationships and disparate patterns between majority and minority groups likely to remain? More precisely, are the socioeconomic, health, and other disparities likely to persist? Are we likely to see a realignment of groups and even greater competition as some groups vie for limited opportunities and resources? Will racial strife take on new locational and political dimensions? Omi (2000) has noted that, in cities such as Miami and Oakland, minority groups already control certain urban functions, such as the administration of social services and distribution of economic resources. This trend, however, has resulted in group conflicts, particularly between blacks and Hispanics, over educational programs, minority business opportunities, and political power (p. 253). Are we likely to see these conflicts extend into other cities, or should we expect the emergence of new alliances and coalitions that would improve race relations and possibly bring about racial equality?

Unfortunately, due to the history and endurance of institutionalized discriminatory practices in the United States, the increasing size and diversity of the population do not necessarily imply a more equitable society. The socioeconomic disparities between the population subgroups are likely to persist even with the projected increase in racial and ethnic groups. As Steinberg argued, one of the fatal flaws of the increasing diversity, pluralism, or multiculturalism in the United States is that its foundation seems to rest on systematic inequalities (Steinberg, 1989). The long-term systemic structure of racialism and prejudice makes it very difficult for the perceived and real differences between racial/ethnic groups to be erased overnight. As a result their geography persists, and new locational patterns of inequalities emerge. It is this set of problems that we explore in subsequent chapters as we take an in-depth look at housing, retail, employment, and environmental hazards.

Another issue addressed in the following chapters has to do with the restructuring of urban space and the further expansion of ghettos, barrios, and minority concentrations that will likely result in even greater segregation and isolation within metropolitan communities. Even the casual observer can see that most minorities, often in large numbers, are affiliated with American "inner cities," where they tend to be highly segregated. Many immigrants also are segregated in urban counties, especially those closest to the metropolitan area's old "central city." Even the often cited "emerging black middle class" is segregated within metropolitan America. One of the policy implications that arises from this is the direct linkage between these minority spaces and the spatially visible outcomes of racially motivated behaviors and practices. The residential locations of minority groups are directly impacted by access to educational and employment opportunities and retail, health care, and other services. Some of these areas also serve as host communities for noxious or locally unwanted land uses. As such, with inadequate awareness and a lack of any corrective measures by state and local governments to address these inequities, the expected growth of Areas of Minority Concentration will serve only to exacerbate the problems. In effect, some minority communities in urban America will continue to suffer from high levels of unemployment and limited access to jobs and retail, financial, and health care facilities. Further, residents in these communities will continue to face exposure to disproportionate amounts of environmental pollutants and consequently more disabilities, poor health, and other associated outcomes.

Future research and policy implications of projected growth patterns will include not only questions about racial/ethnic equity but also issues of empowerment in the Areas of Minority Concentration. Issues such as political redistricting that avoids gerrymandering and a wide range of other policy matters will arise. Minority living conditions and empowerment are likely to vary a great deal depending on where minorities reside and what power relationships they develop. Racial history teaches that, once a tension threshold is exceeded, racial violence occurs. Identifying and monitoring Areas of Minority Concentration and their levels of inequalities may well be an important and necessary challenge for policymakers and for minorities who wish to empower themselves. Although it is dangerous to forecast racial composition and location on a micro basis far into the future, one can examine race-based data by census tract to ascertain some of the likely patterns.

We hope to explore several of these issues in the following chapters. From an empirical perspective, we will be using several of the concepts introduced in Chapter 1.

The concepts of race, place, and Area of Minority Concentration will be particularly useful for understanding the spatial view of minority population distributions and the consequences of rapid in-migration, segregation, and discrimination. Specifically, the notion of Areas of Minority Concentration (AOMCs) illustrates that, when U.S. Census tracts of 50 percent or more minority populations are contiguous, they give rise to urban subregions that are distinctive by race and equity relationships. The continued growth of minority populations in the next quarter century is likely to change many aspects of American life. One aspect that is likely to remain in some form and magnitude, however, is the existence of cultural mosaics in urban America, including the continuing concentrations of each of the racial groups, highly segregated from one another in certain areas of the same city. However, in other communities, Areas of Minority Concentration will involve highly segregated spaces and neighborhoods of mixed races, even if only on a temporary basis, if the process of succession (one racial group replacing the other) is at work. These minority concentrations may involve spaces segregated by class, race, or some other criterion.

The concepts of segregation, isolation, and race-place patterns of equity will therefore be addressed in some detail. In the twentieth century, different racial groups experienced varying levels of segregation. Farley and Frey (1993) noted that blacks were the most highly segregated race in twentieth-century America but that their level of segregation dropped between 1980 and 1990. Hispanics were less segregated than blacks during the same period, but their level of segregation increased from the previous decade. Asians were the least segregated of these three minority groups, indicating that they were more easily assimilated into the white majority. Despite these general national trends, each of the three groups has been victimized by discrimination from time to time and place to place. As a result, in certain places each of the racial groups is highly segregated and has formed or become part of an AOMC. In other cases, new Hispanic and Asian immigrants may cluster in the old city center—as early twentieth-century immigrants did, alone or in coexistence with African Americans—whereas second- and third-generation Hispanics and Asians have either assimilated into suburbia or relocated to some other ethnic-based neighborhood outside the inner city. It is important to make general observations about AOMCs on a national basis. It is equally important to realize that every community has a unique history and elements that require its examination as an individual case. Although some or all of the generalizations about racism, discrimination, and Areas of Minority Concentration may hold in some communities, it is imperative to understand each individual case in its historical and contemporary contexts. Similarly, not all races or combinations of races in an area are the same. We need to clarify the racial nature of local AOMCs when examining data and conducting analyses. Our case studies presented in later chapters provide this perspective. They may also suggest future power relationships.

Before undertaking specific empirical analyses, however, it is necessary to establish broad theoretical understandings. The history of racial and spatial inequalities in the United States is linked to the sociology and geography of racism. In the next chapter, we provide a number of sociological narratives to explore the origins and persistence of U.S. racism. This is followed by a discussion of geographical perspectives on the organization and restructuring of urban space as they relate to minority patterns of well-being.

Chapter 3

Sociological Narratives of Racism in America

In the first two chapters of this book, we broadly discussed the concepts of race and place in the United States, as well as the growth trends among the nation's races and ethnic groups. We examined the early dispersal and recent relocations of racial and minority groups in response to both discrimination and the perception of improved economic opportunity in areas distant from their origins. We also emphasized that U.S. minorities had become more urbanized and, due to restricted housing choices and other forms of discrimination, highly segregated in urban centers. Economic discrimination, segregation, and isolation have led to the low socioeconomic status of most minorities. These geographic and economic patterns were reinforced by the creation of large African-American ghettoes and Mexican barrios in large American cities. As a result, race (black), place (ghetto), and poverty became linked in white consciousness, as did ethnicity (Mexican), place (barrio), and poverty.

During the last quarter of the twentieth century, some minorities escaped their lower socioeconomic class status and ghetto/barrio life in the United States when they joined the growing minority middle class. However, millions remain stranded in the stigmatized inner-city environments characterized by poverty, high unemployment and crime rates, drug infestations, poor housing, and other maladies associated with ghetto life. These minorities have little prospect of escape. Some analysts question whether those minorities fortunate enough to escape the curses of urban America's underbelly have really achieved full middle-class status. Free housing choice, equal access to services and employment, and equal pay for equal work seem still elusive to most minorities, including suburban, professional-class blacks. Questions related to why these situations are so persistent have led to sociological debates regarding racism. Race and racism are emotionally charged terms because explanations and potential remedies for racism vary widely. Americans interpret the causes, impacts, and permanence of racism differently. Permanence is widely and hotly debated today among minorities, social scientists, humanists, politicians, and the media.

In this chapter, we will examine some of the major narratives that place racism at the center of racial and ethnic inequalities. Ultimately these inequalities are distinguishable spatial patterns that are associated with the workplace, neighborhoods, recreational areas, and other places where people spend their lives. These narratives include:

1. Race and the underclass
2. Race and minority self-help
3. Racism and the economic system
4. Race, not class; professional-class racial inequalities; and minority rage

We examine these viewpoints because they are diverse and provide perspectives for the ongoing debates. For some Americans, for example, racism exists because of ignorance, a lack of education. What is needed, therefore, is a better brand of good capitalist enterprise that will bring more investment, more jobs, and, especially, education and training that lead to even better jobs. Such a process will lead to a decline in U.S. racism. For others, the minor shortcomings of the free market system result in a maldistribution of good jobs and the demand for new skills. American racism and discrimination make this bad but temporary situation even worse because they lead to minority disadvantage and white advantage. Proponents suggest patience and the need for government intervention in the form of social policy that will lead to fair treatment of minorities and all poor Americans, especially through the provision of employment and social benefits. When minorities gain resources and interact more fully with white society, racism will decline. For yet others, racism and capitalism are intertwined so tightly that only the removal of capitalism will lead to an end of racism. Finally, there is the view that racism exists beyond class, including beyond the class struggle of Marxism and the socioeconomic underpinnings of capitalism. Racism, from this vantage point, is an ugly reality imbedded in the American psyche. Racists differentiate human value not by socioeconomic class but by appearance, especially skin color. White racism punishes the minority doctor and lawyer as it does the minority street cleaner or the minority unemployed person. It hurts the child and the adult. It does so because they are different from whites and because white privilege and rules apply everywhere in the United States, with the government's sanctions.

To these well-established sociological narratives we add our own voice. We believe that it is impossible to understand the depth and persistence of U.S. racism without addressing the political and intellectual climate into which it was born and has persisted. Our thesis is that racial images have been shaped and fostered in large part by American political leaders and the media. We provide examples in this chapter. As American racial composition changes over the next quarter century, sociological and geographic perspectives will become increasingly important to the debates on dealing with racism. These perspectives are likely to drive policy and social action in one way or another. To be informed is to be able to participate intelligently in these debates. Accordingly, we summarize the important sociological narratives of our time and conclude the chapter with our own viewpoint as to how the threads of racial prejudice and discrimination have been spun in America. This chapter ends with some conclusions.

Diversity of Perspectives

Race and the Underclass: A Liberal Viewpoint

Not surprisingly, much of the race and class research has focused on the intersection of race and poverty. The leading advocate of the minority poor has been William Julius Wilson, who coined the term *underclass* to describe ghetto residents' sociocultural and economic existence. The terminology was promoted by the press, and a long, heated debate between Wilson and other researchers ensued. In three books, Wilson focused on the significance of race in the United States, the emergence of a ghetto culture, the consequences of the redistribution of employment in metropolitan America, and the nature of the "American belief system" (W. J. Wilson, 1980, 1987, 1996). In his response to critics of the "underclass" concept, Wilson presented empirical findings to substantiate the disappearance of work from the inner city and the growth of related problems. He argued that the increasing magnitude of an already severe economic and racial condition will continue until ghetto problems are solved. In making recommendations to address what he considered unique American problems, Wilson endorsed an approach that incorporates black ghetto problems and solutions into broader American social issues and policy (W. J. Wilson, 1996). This is necessary, Wilson argued, because it will lead to the broader realization that societal inequities, not racial deficiencies, contribute to the socioeconomic marginality of minorities.

In *When Work Disappears* (1996), Wilson systematically examined the decline of the inner-city ghetto environment beginning with the depopulation that led to the flight of business and decline in the inner city's employment base. Wilson explained that the increasing concentration of urban poor, especially African Americans, stems not only from segregation but from the "color line" that emerged and locked blacks out of certain occupations and reduced their social mobility. Wilson used the phrase "the new urban poverty" to refer to "poor, segregated neighborhoods in which a substantial majority of individual adults either are unemployed or have dropped out of the labor force altogether" (W. J. Wilson, 1996, p. 19). The result is a depressing environment of devalued and declining housing, limited access to basic services, and crowded living conditions that leads to a full range of negative emotions: low self-esteem, frustration, anger, and rage. The black underclass emerged as a subculture with a range of aberrant behaviors as compared to the white majority's norms. Fatherless households, drugs, and crime were part of the daily ghetto experience. Wilson emphasized that social organization in the ghetto declined as employment disappeared. He suggested three dimensions of social organization (social networks, collective supervision, and organizational participation) that contribute to a neighborhood's stability and health through collective teaching and supervision of children. Unfortunately, the high joblessness in inner-city ghettos that created "the new urban poverty" had simultaneously contributed to a decline in these important dimensions of social organization. Wilson believed that the societal changes that made these inner-city minority neighborhoods so vulnerable created "ghetto-related behavior" due to segregation and isolation. The ghetto became a place characterized by the negative attributes of the new urban underclass:

> . . . the segregated ghetto is the product of systematic racial practices such as restrictive covenants, redlining by banks and insurance companies, zoning, panic peddling by real estate agents, and the creation of massive public housing projects in low income areas. Segregation in ghettos exacerbates employment problems because it leads to weak informal employment networks and contributes to the social isolation of individuals and families . . . [W. J. Wilson, 1996, p. 24].

Wilson used data to demonstrate the decrease in real wages among minority men between 1970 and 1990 and noted that the majority of new jobs were located in the low-paying service sector. The staggering loss of manufacturing jobs, especially in northeastern and midwestern cities, had a very significant impact on minorities, especially males. Relocation of employment opportunities to the suburbs created a spatial mismatch between inner-city minorities and outer-city jobs. Beyond this, however, were the factors of racial bias and harassment, which, when coupled with the reality of ghetto dwellers' lack of skills and whites' negative cultural perception of the ghetto associated with underclass behaviors, translated into severely limited employment chances. The resulting stereotypes of young black males were that they are angry, unreliable, dishonest, and lazy. Stereotypes became linked to place. Wilson quoted one employer:

> I necessarily can't tell from looking at an address whether someone's from Cabrini Green or not, but if I could tell, I don't think I'd want to hire them because it reflects on your credibility. If you came in here with this survey [which Wilson made of Chicago employers], and you were from one of those neighbor-

hoods, I don't know if I'd want to answer your questions. I'd wonder about your credibility [W. J. Wilson, 1996, p. 116].

Employers' negative sense of ghetto neighborhoods that produce the unemployable is also acknowledged by ghetto job seekers, Wilson found:

Honestly, I believe they look at the address and—your attitudes, your address, your surround—you know, your environment has a lot to do with your employment status. The people with the best addresses have the best chances, I feel so, I feel so [Wilson, quoting a survey participant, 1996, p. 137].

For Wilson, this amounts to contemporary discrimination (or rational decisions by employers) in hiring that is a result of previous institutional racism that kept blacks from employment and educational opportunities. Beyond this, racial discrimination exists in a variety of contemporary forms in the workplace. It is difficult to recognize because it is often masked, such as the practice of selective recruitment efforts that systematically exclude minorities by avoiding some neighborhoods and schools while focusing efforts on targeted populations and places. The result is often the systematic exclusion of minorities.

Finally, Wilson (1996) analyzed the shortcomings of "the American belief system" regarding welfare policy (p. 149). He described U.S. policy efforts as "narrowly targeted and fragmented" antipoverty programs, as compared to the broader efforts of Europeans to enhance the "social rights" of the poor (p. 155). Wilson further explained the uniqueness of American beliefs and their impacts on the perception of societal problems. Perhaps not surprisingly, because white America's strong belief in "rugged individualism" has such a long history (Zelinsky, 1992), public sentiment in the United States favors individual initiative over social and economic structures as an explanation for poverty and welfare. Wilson cites national surveys administered during three separate decades that yield strikingly similar results as evidence that Americans accept "individual" explanations for success and improvement over structural causes. This finding applies to racism. Beliefs help shape behaviors and, in this case, have a negative impact on policy that affects the ghetto dweller.

More recent surveys illustrate that several groups of Americans hold negative attitudes toward welfare programs. Further, these groups believe that the cause of the welfare problem lies not in the socioeconomic inequalities of the American system but in the moral failure of individual Americans to want to work for a living. Wilson maintains that the U.S. Congress adopted the same ideology. The resulting two themes, which are shared by liberals and conservatives and shape federal legislation, are individual responsibility and workfare. The welfare recipient must accept certain responsibilities, including a code of behavior, in return for the government's obligation to provide welfare. Recipients must also understand that welfare now equals workfare. Wilson maintained that the overriding American belief is one of suspicion that people on welfare, due to morality problems, systematically avoid "obligations as citizens," preferring instead the life of public assistance. This removes government responsibility for any structural economic problems, placing the burden instead on the victim. The result has been a new "liberal-conservative consensus," beginning in the Reagan years and continuing into the first decade of this century. Examples of policy changes under this new leadership include tightening welfare payment conditions, limiting welfare payments to two years, terminating or denying Aid to Families with Dependent Children (AFDC) benefits under certain conditions, and using fixed-revenue-amount grants that are comparable to HUD's aid to local communities (W. J. Wilson, 1996). These actions reflect the emerging American belief system that previous social programs helped cause rather than fix culture-of-poverty problems in the American minority underclass.

Wilson's vision of new social policy initiatives places the needs of the underclass into the broader context of U.S. poverty. School performance standards and universal family policies, for example, are linked to educational improvements that will yield long-term gains for all disadvantaged Americans, including the underclass. In the meantime, on a more immediate basis, he suggested universal health coverage that would improve the lives of all low-income Americans. He urged consideration of car-pooling incentives and job centers that could reduce the spatial mismatch of central-city employees and suburban employers. Finally, Wilson affirmed the need for a broadly based political coalition of poor and working-class Americans "to change the current course and direction taken by policy makers. Perhaps the best way to accomplish this is through coalition politics that promote *race-neutral* programs such as job creation, further expansion of the earned income tax credit, public school reform, childcare programs, and universal health insurance" (p. 235). Wilson argued that such an effort is capable of profoundly changing U.S. ghettos while improving the larger society.

Wilson's views have been widely criticized. Among his most ardent critics is Stephen Steinberg, who accused Wilson of joining the "liberal backlash" against the Civil Rights Movement (Steinberg, 2001). He maintained that Wilson and other liberals joined conservatives in blaming blacks for their slow economic and social progress since the civil rights era. Steinberg faults the liberal leadership for this backlash, especially Senator Daniel Patrick Moynihan, because his voice was most influential in focusing on the "problem" of black social structure. Racial inequalities were no longer a result of structural problems in the economy or of white racism; rather, black culture factors, especially the dismal state of the black nuclear family, were the culprits to be confronted. Steinberg was disgusted by this victim-blaming mentality. He argued that Wilson's greatest sins included absolving racism and providing inaccurate depictions of the significance of race that helped undercut policy initiatives that could have helped minorities. Steinberg argued that Wilson's major concepts and conclusions, including the spatial mismatch hypothesis and the argument that blacks lacked adequate education and skills for new service jobs, had inadequate empirical foundations. He suggested, for example, that many service jobs needed no skills and were occupied by others with comparable education levels. Specifically, Steinberg noted that unskilled jobs were going to uneducated nonblacks and that Wilson's theories did not hold up under this empirical evidence. Most of all, however, Steinberg faulted Wilson's unrelenting support for the explanatory power of black cultural factors. He noted that, although Wilson had rediscovered racism's significance by 1997, he still clung to the belief that the "cultural factor also plays a very strong, strong role" (Steinberg, 2001, p. 153).

Waldinger (1996) stands out among other recent Wilson critics because he offers a theoretical and empirical alternative, not only to Wilson's mismatch theory but also to its alternative, the restructuring hypothesis. Waldinger assaulted Wilson's position on theoretical grounds as not fitting the facts. He disagreed with this model, including its skills and spatial mismatches arguments. He objected to the model's failure to explain immigrant success and black failure in securing low-end jobs during New York City's rebound. He used data for the last quarter century to illustrate that, although New York City was again becoming an American immigrant haven and low-skill, no-skill jobs were plentiful, African Americans made little progress in filling these openings. His explanation was that African Americans are different from new immigrants. First-generation newcomers are willing to accept practically any position and wage, whereas blacks, not surprisingly, have higher aspirations that are similar to those of other American natives. Waldinger disagreed with Wilson's argument for a skills mismatch, namely, that African Americans aspire to the same jobs as whites but lack the education and skills to adequately compete.

Waldinger also was critical of the restructuring hypothesis, which maintains that globalization and the new services economy, especially producer services, have created an "hourglass" labor market, dominated by growth in high-paying and low-end, but not mid-level, service jobs. Low-end job creation has resulted in high demand for immigrants to fill especially the low-end service positions. Waldinger suggests that the restructuring hypothesis collapses under the weight of facts and from its inability to deal with African Americans. In short, neither of these hypotheses adequately accounts, theoretically or empirically, for the employment patterns of blacks and immigrants.

Waldinger maintained that the best explanation for New York City lies in his model of "ethnic queues" and "ethnic niches." The job queue suggests that, as jobs become available, either because employees leave or new jobs are created, job seekers fill them in an orderly way based on ability or some measure of attractiveness. The term *ethnic niche* refers to the ability of ethnic ties to favorably sort work eligibility among the available jobs. It suggests that workers are directed into particular specializations because of ethnic ties and that these ethnic niches persist over time (Waldinger, 1996). For example, the job queue changed in the city when whites left at a rate faster than employment losses in the 1970s, and the resulting job openings were eventually filled by new immigrants. Although the queue explains opportunities, the ethnic ties operating within ethnic employment niches explain the allocation of those job opportunities. This, according to Waldinger, explains African-American failure and ethnic immigrant success in establishing long-term employment-sector niches that continue to serve particular ethnic groups while prohibiting any significant penetration by blacks. He maintained that ethnic employment niches are well established in the United States. Once a niche is formed, networks operate in a fashion that links and benefits employer and immigrant alike. Waldinger emphasizes ethnic networks and their importance over time for establishing and maintaining employment niches:

> . . . the continuing importance of ethnic networks shapes a group's employment distribution into the second, and later, generations . . . the second generation's search for advancement takes on a collective form. Starting out from an immigrant niche, the second generation is already imbedded in a cluster of interlocking organizations, networks, and activities. Not only do these commonalities shape aspirations, they also create the organizational framework. . . . Thus, the social organization of the second generation serves as a mechanism for channeling people into the labor market . . . [Waldinger, 1996, p. 23].

Competition is added to this equation. Once ethnic niches and networks are established, group dynamics operate such that niches are "politically" protected from outsiders. One result is that African Americans find it difficult to enter employment sectors that have long been or recently become the "property" of ethnic groups.

One of the problems with generalizing the findings of these two similar explanations is that they are developed for the United States' two largest and most unique global cities. The experiences of many African Americans across the nation's large and small cities probably fit this explanation less well. Blacks in a great variety of cities too often find themselves on the wrong side of opportunity's door, including places where fewer or no immigrants have entered. Further, Waldinger's explanation, even if successful in explaining employment niches in a large, unique "immigrant city," did not address the other overt forms of discrimination in housing, education, and other areas, which are all part of a larger process involving multiple forms of racism. For many social theorists and civil rights practitioners, other explanations are necessary. These range from extremely conservative viewpoints to Marxism.

Conservative Voices on Racism
and Arguments for Minority Self-Help

In opposition to the views of Wilson and other liberals are conservatives, who not only call for minority self-help but insist on an end to excessive federal spending and affirmative action policies. Such views have been linked to the Reagan and first Bush administrations and their followers, including conservative minority leaders. Prominent members of minorities have become associated with a new conservative-liberal coalition that favors moderation on the same issues. They include Colin Powell, Andrew Young, Coleman Young, and several black civil rights and religious leaders, including Ralph Abernathy and Hosea Williams. However, it has been the minority media who seem to be the most vocal in representing black conservative America to a daily audience. Ken Hamblin and Tony Brown, though differing in their actions related to achieving the conservative agenda, are two well-known writers and talk-show hosts. Hamblin, in *Plain Talk,* used a collection of his recently published articles to take a conservative stand on issues ranging from affirmative action and crime to capital punishment and immigration (Hamblin, 1999). He applied personal experiences to illustrate the prevalence of racial discrimination. However, his message was clear: Minorities must pick their battles and be firm when fighting discrimination. He was equally clear about the existence of black racism against whites. Further, Hamblin was troubled by white liberal judgments about black problems. For example, he questioned the motives of a Centers for Disease Control (CDC) report on increasing suicide rates among young blacks and blamed liberals and inner-city blacks for the problem.

In discussing racism and the consequences of 150 years of postslavery inequalities, Hamblin suggested that minorities should realize their gains and move to the pursuit of their goals and aspirations. Affirmative action is *not* the path to equality, he argued. In an open letter, Hamblin told Jesse Jackson that he and others were wrong for protesting California's anti-affirmative-action ballot initiative, Proposition 209. He stated that the burden for success today lies with the individual person, not the government. He chastised Jackson, the National Association for the Advancement of Colored People (NAACP), the Black Caucus, and others for dredging up history and urged them instead to lead black youth out of the ghetto and into America's mainstream.

Hamblin was joined in his criticism of the black establishment by Tony Brown, a former Public Broadcasting Service (PBS) commentator, author, and syndicated talk-show host. Brown's position included a moral viewpoint that challenged blacks, whites, and others. As a born-again Republican, Brown wrote his book with a political interest in mind. He espoused a Reaganite foundation for building a better America: federal tax cuts, a reduction in federal entitlement programs, and the individual's moral obligation to help others who are less fortunate. This polemic statement is of interest here because of the clear black conservative perspective it offers. Brown, who fears black genocide unless a black-white conservative coalition is built, warns that black anger in the United States could turn to rage, erupting in a race war. His warnings include a collapse of the U.S. economy that, when it lowers the white standard of living, will cause whites to blame minorities and lead to a race war.

Brown noted that whites, though many of them are racists, are not the only cause of black economic underdevelopment. According to Brown, in addition to the damage of white racism, socialism has infected young black minds against private enterprise while its black leaders earn fat salaries. Also, black leadership has failed. Among previous black leaders, it was only Martin Luther King who, though an assimilationist, pointed to the road of self-sufficiency. Socialism and assimilation are the wrong paths for blacks. Socialism is flawed, and assimilation fails because it cannot lead to equality. Assimilationist black leaders become trapped in the deadly web of seeking white approval, Brown asserted (Brown, 1995). White people will not solve black problems. In fact, blacks will be potential targets of genocide should a "triage" system be adopted by the white majority in response to financial crisis. Just as in medical triage victims are prioritized for treatment according to their likelihood of survival, so in a national financial crisis, in order to save valuable resources, blacks' well-being would be the lowest priority. Brown argued that most blacks have good cause to fear whites, given the historical and contemporary efforts by whites not only to terrorize and murder blacks but more recently, according to Brown, to place drugs in American inner cities and to tell lies, such as those related to the "AIDS epidemic" (Brown, 1995).

Given all the tension and the potential for rage on both sides, a race war is definitely possible, Brown claimed, and should blacks be drawn into it, the consequences for them would be dire. Brown sees white America "sleep walking on the edge of a volcano of ethnic and racial differences" (Sanford Cloud, Jr., quoted in Brown, 1995, p. 118). When awakened, it will respond under the tension of crisis to its image of the black "gangsta" with a force that is genocidal. He proposes "a cooling-off period" that includes "mutual respect and common decency" but racial separation rather than integration (p. 118).

Brown's answer to America's racial crisis and black inequalities is to end the "twin shackles of entitlement socialism and racism" through "sacrifice and change" that can lead to black economic development and self-reliance (Brown, 1995, p. 208). America will change in the first quarter of the twenty-first century, whether it wants to or not, as a matter of global economic survival. For Brown, the fact is that the American labor pool inevitably will be more female and more brown, black, and yellow. His politically charged suggestion, "Brown's Team America," calls for a racially integrated but not assimilated America. "Cultural diversity is good business" and is "performance-oriented" in Brown's "democratic capitalism" (p. 217). Education and technology, along with the eradication of America's "informal racial apartheid," are the centerpieces of the creation of future American wealth and a more level playing field. Education may mean sacrifice now, but the dividends pay handsomely in the future. For Brown, poverty results from low self-esteem and lack of capital, both human and social. Long-term racism and socialistic programs failed to empower black America, but it is not too late to overcome these problems. The answers involve instilling morals; educating the black masses, especially in the emerging computer-related technical fields; and being more entrepreneurial. Overall, Brown's viewpoint is rooted in the belief that racism, which continues as a "covert war against Black America" a century and a half after the abolition of slavery, can be overcome only by broadening affirmative action to include all people in need and by racial separation that requires blacks to sacrifice and change in order to create and control their own destiny (Brown, 1998, p. 165).

It should be clear that the conservative position of some blacks, especially those summarized in this section, mirrors to some extent the conservative free-market approach of American capitalism. The conservative position also differs from both earlier viewpoints in its emphasis on strategies for dealing with racism, specifically in proposing self-reliance and separatism. As we will see in the next section, other black leaders, especially academics, have quite different views regarding capitalism and its impacts on minority well-being.

Racism in a Capitalist Society

The common ground between people like Wilson and Brown lies in their mutual belief that, though racism exists and has severely negative consequences for American minorities, the American economic and political systems are still the best in the world. There are hope and means to counterbalance racism and its impacts. Their beliefs differ greatly from those who believe that capitalism is not only inherently flawed economically, politically, and socially but also has racism deeply imbedded in its core and results in geographic isolation of minorities.

In the 1980s, following a decade that included an oil embargo, the United States' international embarrassment by the Iranian hostage crisis, double-digit inflation, relatively high unemployment and recession, business failures, and continued failure of urban policy, a wave of conservatism swept the country and put Ronald Reagan in the White House. Conservatives began to dominate Congress, and early in the 1990s Newt Gingrich was elected speaker of the house. This conservative swing was briefly described in the previous section. Minority leaders who jumped on this wave, beginning with the 1980 San Francisco conference attended by former civil rights leaders and aspiring politicians, were considered turncoats and opportunists by hardcore liberals and by socialists who believed racism is imbedded in capitalism. This meeting of black conservatives, hosted by the Institute for Contemporary Studies, had the purpose of defining black conservative themes. One critic of this meeting and a leading Marxist authority, Manning Marable, has linked racism with capitalism.

Wishing to strike back at capitalism in general and the Reagan revolution in particular, Marable wrote *How Capitalism Underdeveloped Black America* (2000, originally published in 1983). Marable admits that his work is greatly influenced by two black socialists, Walter Rodney, author of *How Europe Underdeveloped Africa* (1982), and W. E. B. Du Bois, who argued that the "twin pillars of White capitalist oligarchy were domestic racism and colonialism" (Marable, 2000, p. 11). Du Bois scoffed at the notion of American democracy, contending that an inextricable link exists between capitalism and racism. He believed in the boom-and-bust cycles of capitalism and that only socialism would break them and lead to real democracy and racial equity.

Marable endorsed these Marxist principles in comparing the black-American dilemma to what he believes is capitalism's "iron fist of force," which extracts labor value from workers by coercion when necessary. Under capitalism's profit motive, labor is a commodity that permits capital accumulation by the elite. Competition in the free market allows capitalists to accumulate profits and protect their interests through reinvestments that secure even more profits. In this system, human needs are lost to market needs, and groups of people are reduced to "labor" and depersonalized on the way. Marginalization of the working class occurs for the benefit of production needs and the profit seeking of the ruling class. Blacks receive a disproportionate amount of coercion via intimidation and threatened and real violence from capitalist societies. Marable noted that, historically, northern and southern white capitalists and politicians found legal and other means to oppress black labor, ranging from midwestern voting restrictions to southern Jim Crow laws. Marable also reviewed the racism of the justice system under capitalism, noting the bias toward minorities in arrests, jury formation, and severity of punishments. It should be noted, however, that non-Marxists also have raised the issues of segregation's impact on criminal behavior and the differential incarceration rates of whites as compared to Hispanics and African Americans (Kennedy, 2000; Blumstein, 2000).

For Marable, racism is inherent in capitalist society, builds during economic downturns, passes from generation to generation, and finally explodes as racial violence. Racism is a deliberate outcome of a morally bankrupt system that seeks to maximize profits at all times, consciously at great human expense. The marginal and the weak are kept in their place by consensus and coercion. The white middle class is pinched during capitalist busts and is manipulated by the elite, who instill racism in working-class whites that leads to racial violence.

Marable places African Americans and their institutions within the context of a manipulative capitalist system and explains their roles and uses by capitalists. For example, he fears that black entrepreneurial capitalists end up on the side of conservatives, authoritarians, capitalists, and politicians. He maintained that the U.S. "black elite" evolved in a fashion similar to the colonial elite of West Africa, who turned on their own, enslaving other Africans for "crumbs of wealth and privilege" (Marable, 2000, p. 136). The four major occupations of the black elite ("politicians, clergymen, educators and entrepreneurs") amount to buffering positions between white capitalists and the oppressed black working class. Black entrepreneurs, in particular, are under the control of white capital through direct and government-sponsored investments. On top of this, white capitalists have pursued the emerging lucrative black middle-class market at the potential expense of the black entrepreneur. Given the daily pressures on business, especially small business, in the U.S. economy, Marable argued:

> The economic demands of day-to-day entrepreneurial struggle tend, in every capitalist society, to push the politics of small business persons to the right. . . . In short, the crisis of modern capitalism may push the advocates of Black Capitalism squarely into the political camp of the most racist and conservative forces of White America [p. 167].

Black politicians become part of a political system that offers "black Brahmin" status in exchange for accommodation, even from the most progressive black politician. Thus, blacks succumb to corporate interest and become black capitalists, seeking personal profit and ego fulfillment at the expense of the black working class. Power is purely symbolic. Black Brahmins, consisting of Reagan-like black conservatives and civil rights–oriented liberals, do not try to prevent the white establishment from oppressing the black masses, because that establishment is the source of their finances. Rather, these two similarly motivated groups, despite their distinction as Republicans and civil rights leaders, end up quarreling over a range of public policy matters that neither can control because the American political and economic systems are totally controlled by powerful whites. Marable explains that criminal justice and education are also manipulated to the advantage of the elite and the detriment of minorities.

In summary, Marable's analysis of black history and experiences in the United States concluded that the elimination of oppression and racism cannot occur under the system that breeds them. Only a radical separation from capitalism will break the long-term process of underdevelopment that a racist, capitalistic America has provided to African Americans since the early 1600s.

Marable noted that black separatism and street riots are not the answers. This would only lead to fascism. Rather, a long, protracted struggle by all workers and poor people will move the United States to a fairer system, socialism. Black Americans appear to have only two choices, socialism or genocide. The working class and poor should expect in the end to face "raw coercion" by the capitalist ruling class; they will do "whatever is necessary to stay in power" (p. 261). In his "critical reassessment" of this argument, published in 2000, Marable maintains his basic ideology:

> I remain convinced that Black people as a group will never achieve the historical objectives of their long struggle for freedom within the political economy of capitalism. Capitalism has shown the remarkable ability to mutate into various social formations and types of state rule, but its essentially oppressive character, grounded in the continuing dynamics of capital accumulation and the exploitation of labor power, remains the same [p. xxxviii].

It will be apparent in the next chapter that some of the same Marxist insights provided by Marable are also a part of Marxist and postmodern geography. However, Marable focuses on the racist flaw, its consequences for minority Americans, and actions necessary to change the system.

In the final section of this chapter we focus on another view, one different from Marable's because of its belief that racism transcends class in America. The argument is that "race matters," independent of other considerations, in all walks of life. It contends that racism permeates the daily lives of even successful minorities and results in less pay, exclusion, and sometimes acts of hatred. This view does not claim a philosophical basis and, therefore, does not fit neatly into a single ism. Therefore, we simply identify it as the "race, not class," perspective.

Race, Not Class

On the Permanence of Racism.   Racism in the United States is particularly troubling, not just because of the periodic violence it creates but because in the world's wealthiest nation, which preaches global human rights, the daily consequences of white privilege, minority poverty status, and middle-class black anguish are too visibly painful. Unfortunately, racial polarity seems to be increasing since the 1990s among the American populace. The national congressional elections of the 1990s and the presidential election of 2000 revealed different attitudes between American haves and have-nots. They also revealed a much deeper separation between races. Many middle-class and even lower-class whites seemed to abandon not only their long-term association with the Democratic party but their beliefs in justice for working-class labor, improved domestic welfare and services, and social justice through government leadership. This is not a statement in support of or against a particular political party. It is an observation that has been explained as resulting from economic stress due to high taxes and an unstable economy coupled with a "race-weary" attitude. Whatever the cause, the now moderately leaning public is more weary of federal programs that issue financial support to the poor and that also provide government employment disproportionately to middle-class minorities. One of the key issues of racism in America traditionally has been the intersection of race and poverty. However, recent developments, including the changing attitudes of average white and nonwhite people, suggest that racial/ethnic problems are much deeper than those typically associated with poverty and also cut across social and economic lines.

Although the U.S. economy's health at the close of the twentieth century was practically indisputable, what was debatable is its impact. Clearly, American poverty declined during the 1990s but not equally for all societal groups. Further, the long-term effects of the economic gains of minorities in the 1990s are being debated, as noted in Chapter 1. Specifically, it has been argued that those who are on the margins of the economy—poor whites and, disproportionately, minorities, especially blacks—will be the first to slip back into poverty during future recessions. The latter belief involves not just discussions of the racialization of poverty but more general debates on the permanence of racism in America (Kobayashi and Peake, 2000). This leads to the argument that American economic and service inequalities affect all minorities and are due to race, not class. This has led back to a debate on racism's "permanence." More and more, the assertion of many minority scholars is that racism is not a temporary evil but a permanent condition.

Near the close of the twentieth century, this debate became public and generated a number of publications, including *Double Exposure: Poverty and Race in America* (Hartman, 1997). On one side of this discussion are people like Paul Ong (1997), who object to the use of the term *permanent* because it is viewed as unnecessarily pessimistic. For Ong, racial injustice exists but has changed over time. One cannot ignore some improvements in race relations, yet we must continue to battle in a war that has not been lost. The challenge is to carefully revisit what we are struggling against, realizing that racism is an intergenerational battle against a target that continually mutates. We must persevere in our fight for progressive change.

José Padilla (1997), though sensitive to the evils of racism, has hope for its eradication. He reported local examples of racism within the context of his experiences as a Hispanic youth. He admits that failing to heed the early racial bias warnings of his mother were personally costly. Padilla cited his experiences as evidence of deep racial divisions in society, often masked by socialized patterns. He noted that these divisions often involve class differences, yet he suggested that, "were we to eliminate class difference, racism would not exist to separate economically but might exist to separate socially"

(p. 33). He maintained that "on the edges" of racial relations "raw hatred will continue to characterize American racism" (p. 33). He included examples of murder, reverse hatred, and the mistreatment of immigrants by any race. Not totally pessimistic, however, Padilla has hope for America's future:

> ... only where there exists a cultural leadership that learns to communicate across ethnic lines, that learns to mediate across the language obstacles and across the multicolored masses of people, will racism be defeated and left to the economics of our time [p. 35].

When addressing the issue of permanence, Leslye Orloff (1997) placed racism on a continuum, ranging from those who "react instinctively to racism against others" to the "devoutly racist." Of interest in her continuum are two categories that perhaps contain the largest proportion of Americans. One adamantly maintains that they are not racists and probably behave in a politically correct way. The other class is perhaps best described as indifferent. People of this ilk were raised in single-race communities and have planned their lives to avoid multiracial contact and any confrontation with racism. As such, their indifference contributes to ongoing racism and perpetuation of the status quo in race relations. For Orloff racism is not immutable; rather, it is a function of experience. Her answer is to create as much diversity as possible in our daily lives, forcing us to rethink racism, including our own, while pushing closer to a multicultural society of equal justice.

There are others, however, who echo the view of racial permanence. Derrick Bell (1992), for example, wrote that African Americans will never gain full equality in this country. He insisted that this fact must be accepted, "not as a sign of submission, but as an act of ultimate defiance." John Brittain (1997) agrees with Bell and is resigned to permanent white racism at all levels, as well as to the belief that white America will never willingly allow black equality. Whites may yield on occasion when it benefits them, but due to the permanence of racism, blacks and other minorities must always struggle to combat racism in all of its variant forms.

Other opinions on the permanence of racism include that of Benjamin DeMott (1997), who is particularly troubled by Hollywood's promotion of the "feel good" aspects of contemporary racial encounters and is even more frustrated by what he sees as efforts to whitewash historical facts related to black experiences in America. His objection is that such efforts move racial injustice and the future of racism to the individual American rather than to the broader society. They also ignore historical realities. Focus on individual actions wrongly suggests that racism is nonpermanent and will evaporate as soon as individual white fear of African Americans is eliminated. Such fantasy for DeMott blurs the atrocities of historical and contemporary racism:

The chance of striking through the mask of corporate-underwritten, feel-good, historical racism grows daily more remote. The trade-off—Whites promise friendship, Blacks accept the status quo—begins to seem like a good deal. Cosseted by Hollywood's magic lantern and soothed by press releases from Washington and the American Enterprise Institute, we should never forget what we see and hear for ourselves. . . . The history of Black America fully explains . . . how the disaster happened and why neither guilt, money nor lectures on personal responsibility can, in and of themselves, repair the damage. The vision of friendship and sympathy placing Blacks and Whites "all in the same boat," rendering them equally able to do each other favors, . . . is a smiling but monstrous lie [DeMott, 1997, p. 45].

Regardless of individual viewpoints of racism's permanence, all of the observers reviewed in this section see racism as a historical and contemporary American evil to be dealt with. Some see racism as tied to class struggles. Others see it as mutable. Still others are pessimistic and believe it to be part of the human psyche. Despite the variance in these views of permanence, most of these observers see racism as existing beyond the issue of socioeconomic class. Below we present two viewpoints that extend the race-not-class argument by providing insights into the treatment of the black professional class. One involves quantitative analysis; the other reports the results of qualitative approaches that address this issue.

Racism and the Black Professional Class: Quantitative Analysis of Inequalities. Although many views of racism link race and poverty, there are very important perspectives that place racism in a much broader context. Such viewpoints recognize the bifurcation of minority populations along social and economic dimensions (Grant, Oliver, and James, 1996; Ortiz, 1996; Cheng and Yang, 1996). The case presented here is by Fainstein, who maintains that class is not as important as race.

Fainstein has been troubled by the focus of social science research on the underclass because it "implicitly rejects the importance of race" by emphasizing ghetto poverty (Fainstein, 1993, p. 385). By doing so it ignores the

. . . highly politicized questions about wage structure, the condition of the millions of poor blacks and others who are fully employed at poverty wages, or about the ways in which public finance and services affect the life chances of low-income populations [pp. 385–386].

He also objects to the implication that successful blacks leaving the ghetto contribute to the problems of the underclass, the notion that black success causes black failure. Further, it frustrates Fainstein that the compulsion to monitor the underclass seems to eliminate the necessity for analyzing the plight of the "other" black classes, namely the minority professional and middle class. He is particularly critical of Wilson's work because he believes it minimizes the serious racial problems that plague all minorities, especially African Americans.

Fainstein tackled the issue of race and class empirically to illustrate the growing economic inequalities over two decades between middle-class blacks and whites. He also criticized conservative policies that abandoned domestic programs and contributed to fewer services being available to blacks of all classes. Further, Fainstein reported that income segregation between black groups is lower than for other minorities and, in fact, is modest by these standards. This debunks the underclass zealots' claim that successful blacks have a greater propensity for separation than others. In fact, he maintains that African Americans are not significantly different from other groups in this respect.

Fainstein analyzed racial disparities in socioeconomic status holding social class constant. He studied income, educational impact, assets, and services. According to his findings, the impact of education on earnings is negative. "There is little reason from this evidence to think that college education is closing the racial gap in earnings" (Fainstein, 1993, p. 393). Further, earnings within the middle class on a race basis, while showing mixed results, are also negative. Fainstein also concludes that high-income blacks are "asset poor" due to the depressed "racial value" of homes (p. 395). He provides evidence that racism cuts across economic classes. Regardless of the indicator applied, race appears to overwhelm class on all counts. He also argues that government policies have failed and, in some cases, have promoted segregation and isolation. The result is segregation across classes.

> Middle-class Blacks, working-class Blacks, and poor Blacks are equally segregated from their White class counterparts. Clearly, better class standing does little to buy African Americans a racially integrated environment. Nor does it allow Black households to distance themselves from lower-class cultural influences to the same extent as Whites . . . [p. 398].

There are other consequences of segregation, isolation, and discrimination that reach into the soul of the minority individual. Daily treatment of minority professionals shows that race more than class matters in the United States. Below are two summaries of qualitative assessments of the race-not-class viewpoint.

Racial Inequalities and the Black Professional Class: Frustration, Anger, and Rage.   Two major works clarify what it means to be an American middle-class/professional-class black. One, by Joe Feagin and Melvin Sikes (1994), provided an understanding of this black dilemma through analysis of 209 interviews with middle-class African Americans. Their study involved a broadly representative sample (although not random) of well-educated (80 percent had a college degree), middle-income (one-half had annual incomes in excess of $55,000 and only 30 percent earned less than $36,000 per year), white-collar workers from across the United States (although the cities of the South and Southwest were overrepresented). They sought experiential depth and, through the individual stories of ministers, lawyers, merchants, and other black professionals, provided informative and touching images of unfavorable black encounters in "white places" (restaurants, stores, parks, streets, etc.).

The four generalizations Feagin and Sikes distilled from the interviews clarified black experience with white racial hostility and explained African-American frustration, despair, and anger about the past and their concerns for the future. The first generalization is that racism must be understood as a "lived experience." African Americans do not learn about racism from textbooks and lectures; racism is routinely experienced from their daily lives. Second, racial hostility has "a cumulative impact on particular individuals" (p. 16) that becomes a part of family experience and shared pain, resulting in African Americans' often speaking of "we" not "I" when relating experiences. This creates a black group consciousness. Third, the constant repetition of racist experiences leads to a perspective that contributes to a behavioral pattern of coping and responsive behaviors. Fourth, racial hostility is learned behavior that has many dimensions but has evolved into a broadly based set of institutional discriminatory behaviors, which include both intentional and unconscious acts by whites. Both types of acts are hurtful and lead to black realizations that are disturbing:

> Individual Black Americans soon come to see that no amount of hard work or achieved status can protect them from racial oppression across numerous institutional arenas of this society. White discriminators typically only see the color of their skins and not their great efforts, sacrifices, and personal achievements. Moreover, through institutionalized discrimination whites not only restrict personal mobility but also social, economic and political mobility for Black Americans as a group [Feagin and Sikes, 1994, pp. 17–18].

For Feagin and Sikes the results are clear: "The discriminatory actions of many White Americans in many institutions—and not some vague agent called 'racial divisions'—are the major reason for continuing Black-White problems and persistent Black protest" (p. 18).

Fainstein's empirical results were published in the same year as a book by Ellis Cose entitled *The Rage of a Privileged Middle Class* (1993), which is the other qualitative study explaining the frustration and rage of black professionals. Cose's work offered numerous examples of the rage felt by many African Americans. The inability of many black professionals and middle-class workers to realize the same type of success experienced by whites, whether in the choice of a home, neighborhood, or workplace, leads to anger and potentially to rage. Cose, a well-known journalist and editor, reported that, despite the economic gains of the twentieth century, the depth of daily pain experienced by black Americans, who though they have played by white society's rules and believed their promises, is so severe that it is likely to spill over into rage. Cose, like Feagin and Sikes, paints a very vivid picture of racism and the emotions that it generates among bright, successful African Americans. He does not use statistics. Rather, he presents the cases of individual minorities hurt by white behaviors, including minority doctors, lawyers, teachers, executives, journalists and managers. Cose suggested not only that this group of African Americans appeared more alienated from American society before the 1992 LA riots than their "underclass" counterparts but also that their level of discomfort as a group soared after the riots to a point much greater than that of poorer blacks. Clearly, the belief that what happened to Rodney King amounted to racial injustice that could easily happen to them influenced their feelings. For minorities this is not a singular event. Cose related a personal story in which two white policemen stopped him because he appeared "suspicious" sitting on his car at a particular location. His professional dress apparently diffused the potential problem, but Cose concluded that "the only suspicious behavior I had exhibited was being Black on a block where few—if any—Blacks lived" (Cose, 1993, p. 104).

Cose explained that the current U.S. environment prohibits progress on race relations. Most whites believe that racial barriers blocking minority opportunities have been leveled. In fact, they believe that it is more likely that a white will be harmed by reverse discrimination than minorities will be at risk from racism. The white feeling that great progress in racial equality has been realized supports the attitude that "middle-class Blacks have nothing to complain about" (p. 35). Such a view typically includes whites' indifference or inability to fathom the pain and anger minorities feel when they experience rejection and discrimination. In Cose's words:

> . . . America is filled with attitudes, assumptions, stereo-types, and behaviors that make it virtually impossible for Blacks to believe that the nation is serious about its promise of equality—even (perhaps especially) for those who have been blessed with material success [p. 5].

Cose argued that engagement through dialogue is essential to changing society but that both blacks and whites, for different reasons, fear racial discussions. Race defines the existence of blacks. Black fear of potential white alienation is real and potentially affects most aspects of a black person's well-being. This reluctance to engage the issue of race perpetuates the myth that "everything racial is moving along nicely." As a result, black middle-class rage simmers just below the surface of white-black contact. This silence may also negatively influence white labeling of the frustrated average black who speaks up. He may be the "chronic complainer" or the "troublemaker." Ghetto rage is apparently understandable; middle-class black rage is whining, self-pity.

Added to this rage felt by the black professional and middle class is the white assignment of guilt or responsibility to the black middle class for betterment of the ghetto underclass. How, whites ask, can successful blacks turn their backs on their poor, less fortunate brethren? For Cose, this silly but sometimes effective practice ignores the fact that better-off African Americans are not only as pessimistic as whites about the future of African-American ghettos but continue to routinely suffer themselves from more discrimination than ghetto dwellers. Many black professionals perceive their own quality of life as declining. All of this contributes to the belief that their status is provisional, yet they are expected to solve the ghetto problem created by whites. The results are frustration, disbelief, anger, and sometimes rage.

The African-American middle class "faces demons" with which it must cope: not fitting in, being excluded from social clubs and assigned unreasonably low expectations, and facing derailed hopes, dim praise, presumptions of failure, limitations in job placement, fatigue, invisibility, expected quiet, mendacity, and stereotyping (Cose, 1993). African Americans grow tired of the view that they must "overcome," that they are suited for only certain jobs (community relations, public affairs, and student affairs), that they cannot afford to be seen as "black" in order to "fit in" and be successful, that they must not speak up when passed over and must continue lying that their corporations are color blind, that they should not be upset when mistaken for criminals, or that implicitly they should feel "guilty by association" about crime committed by other blacks.

All of these stressors, individually or collectively, lead to the anger and rage felt by middle-class African Americans. What often is attributed to historical mistreatment of blacks by whites (and the attitude "I don't want to be held responsible for something that happened a long time ago") is really anchored in today's experience. Speaking of daily racial wrongs, Cose noted:

> Taken separately, such episodes may not amount to much; everyone, regardless of race, experiences occasional slights and even outright rejection. But for many Black professionals, these are not so much isolated incidents as insistent and galling reminders. . . .
>
> In the workplace, the continuing relevance of race takes on a special force, partly because . . . even people who accept that they will not be treated fairly in the world often hold out hope that their work will be treated fairly—that even a society that keeps neighborhoods racially separate and often makes after-hours social relations awkward will properly reward hard labor and competence.

What most African Americans discover, however, is that the racial demons that have plagued them all their lives do not recognize business hours—that the stress of coping extends to a non-work world that is chronically unwilling (or simply unable) to acknowledge the status their professions ought to confer.

...the price of this continual coping is not insignificant [Cose, 1993, pp. 55–56].

Probably nowhere are minority stereotypes more pronounced than in white perceptions of black youths as criminals. The old story of teenage behavior clarifies the stereotype. Four white teenagers can be cruising with windows down and music blaring and they are perceived as "looking for a good time." Four minority youths (black, Hispanic, or Asian) involved in the same cruising "are out looking for trouble." The same simplistic deductions by American politicians reinforce the stereotype. Cose noted Senator Moynihan's reading of a James Q. Wilson quotation into the *Congressional Record*—"The best way to reduce racism . . . is to reduce the Black crime rate . . . "—and former mayor Ed Koch's contention "that 'even those who feel deeply about discrimination against Blacks . . . feel estranged from the Black community' as a consequence of Black violence" (p. 94). Cose found these to be absurd and unfair implications about black males. He reported that in 1991, contradicting the implication of statistics that "blacks account for 45% of those arrested for America's violent crimes" (p. 94), the actual number of African-American arrests translated into less than 1 percent of the black population. Blacks are not vicious criminals by nature, but statistics and media reporting lead to stereotyping. Further, as Cose noted, it is no more the black person's burden to account for and clean up black crime than it is the Italian's responsibility to crush the Mafia or the Irish person's burden to save society from Irish alcoholics. Cose also noted the absurdity of the stereotypical view that black criminals prey on innocent white victims. In fact, an African American is far more likely (thirteen times) than any white individual to be victimized by a racially motivated crime. Also, there is a certain irony in the white fear of blacks: Historically and today blacks have had good reason to fear whites, from North and South.

Racial hurt and racial prejudice are not limited to adults. Cose relates the experiences of black parents who face the choice of sheltering their kids from prejudice to protect them or preparing them to struggle against the beast, which can lead to its own prejudice. Cose concludes that racial harmony is *not* a natural state. Unfortunately, stereotypes are not created only at home and are not necessarily eliminated through higher education. Misinformation and confusion over results of affirmative action–like programs, the resentment felt by whites and minorities with regard to the other's privilege, and feelings of hatred perpetuated by parents of all races lead to racial disharmony. These lend support to Cose's contention that "the state of race relations is bad" (p. 145). Cose cites college events, like "Dress like a Nigger

Night," Oneonta College officials' release of the names of all African-American students to police, and other episodes, as supporting the "inescapable conclusion" that the "next generation, for all its idealism ... is not even close to mastering the art of how to get along" racially (p. 146). This evidence also demonstrates that institutions of higher learning are not exempt from racial turmoil and violence. Cose explains the uncertainty for black parents preparing their children for tomorrow:

> In the past, one knew White people didn't like Black folks. . . . One knew that the color line, at some points, could never be crossed, and that it was worse than useless to try. In short, one knew one's place. For the parents of today, such certainty does not exist. Yet they still must help their children find their place in a world in which no one, White or Black, knows precisely where that place will—or can—be [p. 151].

White people have focused recently on black (reverse) racism. Cose noted former mayor Koch's stance that the majority of African Americans are anti-Jewish. He countered that roughly the same proportion of blacks and whites, according to recent polls, are anti-Semitic. However, he also highlighted a major difference in the stereotyping by blacks and by whites. Racist blacks describe Jews as intelligent, strong, and ambitious—positive descriptors. White racists, however, "even those who harbor African Americans no ill-will, tend to see blacks as significantly less intelligent and less motivated than Whites" (p. 156). The unfortunate fact is that too many whites see blacks as genetically flawed or culturally inadequate, Cose asserts. This contributes heavily to black fatigue and generates the near-the-surface rage that characterizes much of the black professional and middle-class community.

Many African Americans have played by white rules. They have pursued education, obeyed the laws, set a strong moral code at home, worked hard, and "jumped through all the hoops" required for membership in a hostile workplace but still find themselves and their children hurt by racism. They try to engage with an environment that they can see and even long for. However, invisible walls separate them from "white privilege," locking them out of what they feel they have earned and into places they want to leave. Segregation and discrimination force them to live with inequalities inherent in certain places and to do without the level and quality of pay and services that most professional-class Americans take for granted. Cose is not a fatalist. It is not that all whites are racists or that racism is immutable. However, we are rapidly approaching the time when the rage will be expressed in overt ways. It is also likely that all minorities are or will become angry not just due to the dehumanizing stereotypes cast upon them but also because of the inequalities that those stereotypes perpetuate. Though not a fatalist, Cose posits a clear message: The black and the other minority middle-class communities have grown tired of the empty promises of "play by the rules and any American can succeed." There exists a range of emotions—hurt, frustration, disappointment, anger, and now even rage. Until true equality is realized by all Americans, there lurks in the darkest corners of urban America the threat of potential violence.

Taken together, these views of racial inequalities, one based in empirical evidence and the other on reflections of the shared experiences of middle- and upper-middle-income blacks, clarify the notion that, despite economic and educational achievement, race matters more than class in the United States. To this African-American situation we must now consider the addition of the plight and feelings of millions of Hispanic and Asian immigrants of the 1990s. Recent analyses support the idea that Hispanics and Asian groups are experiencing great frustration over American myths, such as that a willingness to work hard leads to economic success and equal pay for all Americans (Waldinger and Bozorgmehr, 1996).

Recent immigrants aspire to better treatment and a chance for equality in the United States. Some will likely fare better than others due to their educational attainment before migrating to the United States and to being received into a group that has established employment niches. Some also will find assimilation easier because they have the benefit of lighter skin. However, among the millions of other immigrant minorities, many have joined inner-city blacks, or live in their own ghettos, and are experiencing deplorable living conditions and an unbalanced playing field (see Chapter 6). Although these groups are willing to sacrifice for the short-term, accepting lower pay and low-quality housing, their children are likely to respond like the African-American professional class. They will want social and economic mobility in this land of opportunity. They will want to join the ranks of the professional classes. They also will expect equal pay for equal work. Playing by the rules will mean expectations of fairness. African Americans, by contrast, are not likely to stand by passively and watch immigrants achieve equity while black inequalities continue. Access to better living conditions and employment opportunities now associated with white privilege will become expectations for all minorities. Barriers to racial equity likely will pose real threats of interracial conflict and thus will challenge the nation's political leadership.

How did the United States ever evolve to a situation of white advantage, racialism, and concomitant racial inequalities? It is important for all Americans to address this question. We believe an honest look at the facts from the past two-plus centuries readily provides an answer. We spend the remainder of this chapter providing our perspective, which is formed through examination of the threads of prejudice and discrimination practiced continuously by our political and intellectual leaders. These provide some of the most important clues for understanding racial attitudes and behaviors that are practiced by rank-and-file Americans and that are exacerbated by the ignorance and isolation of racial groups in urban America.

A Historical Context for U.S. Racism

The Socioeconomic-Political Milieu

Human geography, sometimes referred to as the study of spatial patterns and cultural landscapes, informs us that our beliefs and values are transmitted to our living spaces and are visible reflections of us as people. As such, the American landscape is a confusing mix of beauty and neglect, of successes and failures. Any nation creates places of pride, respect, and hope. They also, wittingly or unwittingly, create landscapes of fear, despair, and shame. In the United States, more often than not, our minority concentrations create the latter. They reflect America's willingness to perpetuate two societies, one with too much and one with too little. The media's depictions of these places and the people that occupy them too often result in images of fear and defiance, where people become objects or appear as inanimate beings with rage but no other feelings. Our society has been successful in putting great distances, psychological and physical, between the two societies, resulting in indifference and often disdain for one another.

Despite Hollywood's efforts to bridge that distance with occasional feel-good movies about racial harmony, our geography, attitudes, policy, and well-being separate Americans in space and in mind. Largely, we share little space while working, playing, living. Separation, as the saying goes, breeds fondness, or it creates indifference. Unfortunately, the latter is generally true regarding white attitudes toward racial inequalities. Yet the American white culture is able to rationalize the me-first attitude, underlaid by a feeling of entitlement, with its self-perception of tolerance and caring. This is in part due to the fact that white privilege and feelings of white superiority have been present since American colonial times and have permeated our history of race relations. In earlier chapters, we have presented some examples of the key discriminatory behaviors of white America based on its prejudice toward nonwhites. Federal legislation restricting Asian immigration and local restrictive covenants were two such examples. Others included the South's Jim Crow laws and the North's institutional racism. We also provided instances of white violence against nonwhites that resulted in loss of property and lives. We tried to make it clear that discrimination may have varied by sort but not by U.S. region. In 1835 Alexis de Tocqueville made important observations about pre–Civil War racial prejudice in the North and the roots of inequalities between the races:

... the legal barrier which separated the two races is falling away, ... but the prejudice to which it has given birth is immovable. ... [I]n those parts of the Union in which the Negroes are no longer, ... the prejudice of race appears to be stronger in the states that have abolished slavery than in those where it still exists; and nowhere is it so intolerant as in those states where servitude has never been known. ... The electoral franchise has been conferred upon the Negroes, ... but if they come forward to vote, their lives are in danger. If oppressed, they may bring an action at law, but they will find none but Whites among their judges. ... The same schools do not receive the children of the Black and of the European. In the theaters gold cannot procure a seat for the servile races beside their former masters; in the hospitals they lie apart; and although they are allowed to invoke the same God, ... it must be ... in their own churches, with their own clergy. Thus the Negro ... can share neither the rights, nor the pleasures, nor the labor, nor the afflictions, nor the tomb of him whose equal he has been declared to be ... [Reeve, Bowen, and Bradley, 1945].

Of course, stereotypes of blacks by American leadership were already established before the Civil War. Thomas Jefferson stated: "In general their [blacks'] existence appears to participate more of sensation then reflection. ... It appears to me that in memory they are equal to the whites; in reason much the inferior ... and that in imagination they are dull, tasteless and anomalous." (Quoted by Davis and Donaldson, 1975, p. 156). Even President Abraham Lincoln, just before his assassination, admitted that integrating blacks into the broader society was more than a challenge. This is why he advised a black delegation that black colonization outside the United States was essential and that equality was possible under those circumstances rather than in the United States (Henry, 1999).

White behavior during Reconstruction proved Lincoln correct. In the South, the famous "black codes" cleared the way for discrimination against blacks, including the imposition of the death penalty for selected crimes committed by nonwhites. In 1866, following the 1863 New York City riots, a "political race riot" broke out in New Orleans and brought "widespread and unprovoked attacks upon innocent Negroes" (Henry, 1999, p. 185). What had been largely a white privilege, the right to vote, was now being offered by the federal government as a "right" of the black man. North and South alike were repulsed by this notion and, as Henry notes, northern states were rejecting Negro suffrage: "Northern states which could vote for themselves were voting it down wherever the question was presented. Connecticut, Wisconsin and Minnesota had rejected it in 1865" (Henry, 1999, p. 211).

Passage of the Thirteenth Amendment certainly did nothing to change the dominant white society's prevailing attitude of black inferiority. As we noted in Chapter 2, prejudice and discrimination were not reserved for blacks. Both

Mexicans and Asians were also deemed inferior, and even the "darker races" of Europe were suspect.

In the East, mob action was intensely directed at blacks. The combination of economic stress rooted in perceived job losses to and wage reductions because of freed blacks, Social Darwinian beliefs in black inferiority, and the fear that black men's sexuality made them both immoral and peculiarly attracted to white women resulted in white mob violence in both the North and South during and after the Civil War, and again in the early 1900s. We remind the reader of the racial tension that occurred between whites and Asians in California during the same period (Chapter 2; see also Chapter 6), a time when the ethnic Chinese dispersed from California to the eastern United States. During the 1870s and 1880s Chinese suffered white prejudice and mob violence, and by 1882 the Chinese Exclusion Act was law. In 1907 the American-Japanese Gentleman's Agreement was signed and anticoolie clubs harassed and attacked Asians' basic freedoms. There was pressure to destroy Oakland's Chinatown, and Chinese were forcibly separated from whites until World War II.

Between the two world wars various riots in all major U.S. regions continued to reflect deeply rooted racial hostilities. Joseph Boskin (1976) described the causes of two of these riots.

> . . . each of these riots had notably different characteristics. The riots in Los Angeles, for example, highlighted the racial prejudices of the Caucasian. Called the "Zoot-Suit Riots" because of the type of dress being worn by male Mexican-Americans (and by many other young males throughout the nation at that time) they took place in the Mexican-American area of Los Angeles and were racially oriented clashes.
>
> . . . the Detroit riot . . . stemmed from discrimination in a housing project and White attitudes toward equal employment rulings. . . . Roosevelt's significant Executive Order 8802, in which discrimination was prohibited, had angered Whites. In the months prior to the riot, several unauthorized walkouts had occurred in automobile plants, one of them numbering almost twenty thousand workers. Several of these "walks" had been prompted by the upgrading of Black workers. White supremacist advocates, such as Gerald L. K. Smith, Father Charles Coughlin, and others, further stirred prejudices among White southerners who had also migrated to Detroit . . . [pp. 55–56].

We have already characterized the subsequent riots of the 1960s as caused by continued black frustration with a system that preaches international freedom and tolerance but practices discrimination that perpetuates racial inequalities at home. The results were the racial clashes and other violence of the civil rights era.

These historical threads of racial prejudice, discrimination, and violence help clarify the continuous racial strife within the socioeconomic-political and racial history of the United States. We now turn to the intellectual context for racism. The history of ideas and beliefs provides a context for understanding, at least in part, the socioeconomic-political history of U.S. racism.

The Intellectual Framework for White Domination, Prejudice, and Discrimination

After emphasizing the prejudice and oppressive behavior of the dominant white culture in the twentieth-century United States, it is useful to provide a historical and social context for such attitudes and behaviors. Though choosing different discriminatory behaviors, the white leadership of the North, South, and West clearly portrayed Social Darwinian beliefs in their actions toward minorities, especially African Americans. To understand the context for these beliefs, we believe we must look to Victorian Europe and European and American scientific and popular literature during the late nineteenth and early twentieth centuries.

The Victorian era in England was a period of immense change and hardship related to urbanization and industrialization. The period seemed to substantiate Thomas Malthus's pessimistic conception of the future of human enterprise. Struggles were obvious in English life. Out of this environment rose Darwin, who, influenced by Malthus and others, fashioned his theory of evolution around the concepts of struggle, change, and survival leading to environmental improvement (Urbanowicz, 1996). This was a period of intellectual flowering and feverish interaction among the learned. Charles Urbanowicz noted that Darwin's work evolved through interactive criticism, which he incorporated into later editions of his work, and he accepted the language of others, such as "survival of the fittest," which he took from Herbert Spencer (Urbanowicz, 1996). In fact, it was Spencer who, because of his journalistic skill and wide acceptance by the readership of the day, brought Darwin's biological concepts to the social sciences and into everyday use. In fact, Robert Young (1998) claimed that Spencer not only was Britain's most "prolific thinker" but belonged in the company of Hegel:

> [Spencer] . . . can be said to be Britain's most prolific and bold thinker—the nearest the nation has had to a domestic Hegel. Lest this conception seem far-fetched, . . . He was the most influential single source for the main tradition in Anglo-Saxon thinking devoted to the naturalization of value systems in the physical, biological and human sciences [p. 4].

Spencer argued that humans were part of their environment and, so situated, were subject to the same "progressive adjustments" as the rest of nature. If the government minded its business (laissez-faire), then society would be improved due to the attributes it inherited based on those adjustments (Young, 1998). Spencer's insights and understandings of natural selection and adjustments were widely adopted. One area of impact was in the study of racial groups.

Pat Shipman (1994) provided insight into the evolution of racism, including in the early-twentieth-century United States, within the context of the abuse of science. A useful context for understanding the mindset of nineteenth-century leaders, which carried over to some early-twentieth-century Americans, was provided by Robert Wright (1994) when reviewing Shipman's book:

> . . . pronounced physical differences among the different racial groups . . . were being encountered with some regularity by European explorers. . . . These perceived physical differences were only heightened and reinforced by differences in dress, mores, manners, and beliefs. Those living among people of widely different cultural traditions were bewildered and sometimes defeated by the social and behavioral chasms that separated them. . . .
> . . . Like many others of his day and class, he [Darwin] simply did not believe that these savages . . . were human in the same sense that he himself was [p. 7].

This type of thinking became widespread and was given intellectual impetus by Spencer, who was "welcomed like royalty" in the United States in 1882, especially for his optimism and theories that favored capitalism (Young, 1998). In fact, his influence reached academia and the public sphere. There was both scientific and public interest in culture and cultural change; the concept of evolutionary change had wide appeal, and scientists routinely gave lectures and wrote books for public consumption. The result was substantial influence by Darwin and Social Darwinists on professors and popular writers.

It was the application of Darwinian biological concepts to the other sciences that led to abuses and racism. In geology and geography, for example, it is well established that Nathaniel Shaler and William Morris Davis, both well known in their disciplines at the turn of the century, adopted evolutionary doctrine and incorporated its language into their work (P. E. James, 1972). Preston James discovered that Davis adopted from Shaler the framework of the Darwinian concept of man as part of nature but endorsed Spencer's Social Darwinism (p. 358) and treated humans as organisms. As a result, explanations of human-environment interactions and relationships were thought to be "between some inorganic element of the earth on which we live, acting as a control, and some element of the existence or growth of behavior or distribution of the earth's organic inhabitants, serving as a response" (Davis, 1909, p. 8). This expression of Social Darwinism was termed *environmental determinism.*

Although short-lived, this type of determinism had a wide audience that helped shape the thinking of leaders and the public. One prolific writer of the period was Ellsworth Huntington, a student of Davis at Harvard and a writer of popular books and articles (James, 1972). Huntington developed a fascination with climatic influences on culture. Based on his own world travels and sweeping generalizations, Huntington offered explanations of historical events in terms of rapid pulsatile fluctuations in climate. More specifically, he believed human actions, including, for example, social crises, had been shaped by climate. Climates also were seen as affecting disease rates. More to our point, however, environment could alter human progress by controlling human productivity. Although he did point out that "climate is only one of the conditions" that shapes civilization, he often saw it as the primary causal factor (Huntington and Cushing, 1924, p. 259). Thus, when comparing the climates of the Bahamas and Canada, Huntington and Cushing wrote:

> The original White settlers in both places were of the same stock . . . English colonists. . . . Today the descendants of the Loyalists in Canada are one of the strongest elements in causing that country to be conspicuously well governed and progressive. In the Bahamas, the descendants of similar Loyalists probably show a larger proportion of inefficient, incompetent individuals than can be found in almost any other Anglo-Saxon community. Among the Canadians, practically everyone has a fairly good education. Among the Bahamans, a large number have never been to school, and many who learned to read and write in their childhood have forgotten these arts because they do not practice them. The main cause of these differences is the climate, although other factors such as the presence of negroes in the Bahamas play an important part . . . [pp. 257–258].

For Huntington race, like climate, was an important point that colored the "canvas" of civilization, its tints "sometimes good, sometimes bad . . . " (p 259). When climatic and race factors met, they predictably could lead to problems. Thus, some Mexicans, who were a mix of Indian and Spanish bloods, had a racial composition that reflected the good and the bad. On one hand, "Indians as a whole do not seem to be endowed with minds equal to the more advanced races of Europe." Spanish descendants, on the other hand, are "intelligent, bold and adventurous" (Huntington, 1921, p. 258). The Indians' dull ancestry is a function of climatic influences, whereas the Spanish have benefited greatly from a climate that produced superiority. These two blood types mixed to produce the Mexican civilization, which contains extremes in intelligence. However, Huntington concluded that Mexican social character reflected a lack of stimulation, leading to immorality, boastfulness, and a general disrespect for the law, or the dishonesty of Mexicans (Huntington, 1921, p. 259).

These Social Darwinian beliefs led to Huntington's participation in the American Eugenics Society, which he served as president and as lead author for its 1935 volume, *Tomorrow's Children: The Goal of Eugenics*. Both *environmental determinism* and *eugenics* later became ugly words. However, their advocates at the turn of the century were quite strong.

As we noted above, Spencer was well received in late-nineteenth-century America. During the same period, Darwin's cousin, Francis Galton, coined the word *eugenics*, which he intended to mean science directed at "improving human stock" by providing advantage to "the more suitable races or strains of blood" (Kevels, 1985). Galton argued for intelligence through heredity, rather than allowing for factors such as social advantage. Like Spencer, Galton wrote and spoke to the educated and general public alike. Although he found Africans to be among the "inferior races," his work only minimally dealt with these racial issues (Kevels, 1985). Rather, he leaped from Darwin's foundation of social progress and change to the suggestions that eugenics would hasten achievement of these important social goals.

Galton's torch for eugenics was elevated by Karl Pearson, the well-known British statistician. However, eugenics' entry into the United States came via highly regarded biologist Charles Davenport, who utilized the theories of inheritance credited to biologist Gregor Mendel (Kevels, 1985). Like Pearson, Davenport had unusual quantitative training and also had studied engineering. He quickly succeeded in establishing an experimental laboratory for evolution studies, funded by the Carnegie Institute (Kevels, 1985). What determinism's climatic causation was to an environmentalist like Huntington hereditary theory was for biologists. In short, social scientists were using environmental causation to explain racial behavior, while biologists sought explanations from studies based on theories of heredity. Daniel Kevels (1985) wrote of Davenport's work:

> Like many scientists of his time, Davenport held that physiological and anatomical mechanisms made some people alcoholics, others manic-depressives, still others "feebleminded." . . . Davenport similarly reduced pauperism to "relative inefficiency [which] in turn usually means mental inferiority." Of course, he conceded, human breeding was complicated, and human progeny were the products of both "conditions and blood." But attention to environment was not to obscure the crucial role of protoplasm in human fate. Heredity determined the characteristics both of Negroes—Davenport's views on Black Americans conformed for the most part to the standard racism of the day—and of the immigrants then flooding into the United States [p. 46].

In the early 1900s, eugenics reached popular status in Great Britain and the United States thanks to an aged Galton and Pearson's publications. Davenport worked with family records to establish his theories both in scientific and popular media. They were successful and strengthened the movement. Famous capitalists, among them the Rockefeller and Eastman families, contributed funds for the public teaching of eugenics and many middle- and upper-middle-class, literate Americans (largely WASPs) found eugenics a valuable concept. It was, however, the flood of European immigrants and the availability of immigration data that led urban industrial America to embrace eugenics and incorporate it into state and federal policymaking. As Kevels (1985) related, the "Anglo-American may have always known prostitution, crime, alcoholism, and disease, but neither society had ever before possessed the weight of statistical information, expanding yearly by volumes, that numerically detailed the magnitude of its problems . . . afflictions such as mental defectiveness and criminality were worsening every year" (p. 72). As we noted in Chapter 2, approximately three-quarters of a million blacks already resided in northern cities by 1900, and that population was steadily increasing. Du Bois's color line was already visible, not only in the existence of black ghettos but also in the treatment of blacks, who earned "a third less per week than the other nationalities, shared the same prejudices as Italians, but also suffered additional discrimination by white northerners in the numerous forms, including violence" (Du Bois, quoted in Shenton and Brown, 1978, p. 169). It is in the same time period that negative associations of race were directed to the "darker races" and eugenicists became concerned with understanding declining "Nordic fertility" and the growing numbers of "others" (Kevels, 1985).

It is true that the followers of eugenics were broadly concerned with all non-Nordic races. As such, the Irish, Italians, Jews, and Chinese, among other groups, were of concern as potential polluters of the WASP gene pool and, therefore, were unacceptable future immigrants. These beliefs led the Eugenics Society to lobby at the state and local levels for policies for race improvement. This amounted to a dominant role for the society in the passage of sterilization laws in numerous states and to lesser roles in other areas, such as coalitions to establish new marriage laws and to pass the immigration laws that resulted in the quota system.

Throughout the first part of this book we have focused on various forms of prejudice and violence tied to economic and political issues. Here we have attempted to illustrate the use of science to influence political and economic leadership and the general public. Negative eugenics was written into U.S. law at a time when the dominant white-dominated American society was being overwhelmed by immigrants and the black population was expanding in northern cities. Clearly, prejudice was in place in the northern and southern United States before eugenics entered the scene. But Social Darwinism in its many forms influenced racial perceptions and economic and political behaviors. Science was used to shape thought and action. Although white "minority races" (European ethnic groups) were subjected to the abuse of this science, blacks—already assumed to be inferior to all races—and mixed races received the brunt of eugenics philosophy. As Kevels pointed out,

Davenport and other Anglo-American eugenicists embraced the standard views of the day concerning the hereditary biological inferiority of non-Whites. . . . So Davenport believed . . . a 1929 study, *Race Crossing in Jamaica*, . . . of . . . the relative capacity of negroes, mulattoes, and whites to carry on a White man's civilization. The authors concluded not only that blacks were inferior in mental capacity to whites but that a larger portion of browns than of either pure group were "muddled and wuzzle-headed" [Kevels, 1985, p. 75].

Blacks were frequently lumped into the category of the "feeble-minded" and were subjected to culturally bound IQ tests, the results of which were used publicly to inform society of "black inferiority." Although Americans were horrified by Germany's use of eugenic principles in World War II, they had less trouble accepting their own use to discriminate and oppress "others" and to classify blacks and others as inferior. Like the environmental determinism before it, eugenics fell into disrepute. Unfortunately, however, its questions of race and intelligence (intelligence testing) continued after World War II and remain issues in segments of the scientific community today.

Taken together, then, the socioeconomic-political histories of prejudice, discrimination, and racial tensions, coupled with the extensions of Social Darwinian thought into the American mainstream of the twentieth century, shaped a belief system that not only disrupts racial harmony but helps explain the persistence of racism, racialism, and racial inequalities. One other issue that deserves clarification here is the role of the media in shaping our racial images.

Racial Constructions and the Visual Media

Opinion leaders, government officials, scientists, and others formulate racial images and promulgate them to the general public. Although the racial constructions of family and friends are important input into individual consciousness and the racial images of individuals, the media have become an increasingly crucial force in shaping opinion of all types. We have just reviewed the abuses of science that contributed to negative images of nonwhite races. In the twentieth century, the visual media have played key roles in producing racial images of all kinds. Earlier we mentioned the "Zoot-Suit riots." Carey McWilliams wrote of the role of the press in this 1943 event.

Immediate responsibility for the outbreak of the riots must be placed upon the Los Angeles press and the Los Angeles police. For more than a year now the press (and particularly the Hearst press) has been building up anti-Mexican sentiment in Los Angeles. Using the familiar Harlem "crime-wave" technique, the press has headlined every case in which a Mexican has been arrested, featured photographs of Mexicans dressed in "zoot-suits," checked back over the criminal records to "prove" that there has been an increase in Mexican "crime" and constantly needled the police to make more arrests. . . . The constant repetition of the phrase "zoot-suit," coupled with Mexican names and pictures of Mexicans, had the effect of convincing the public that all Mexicans were zoot-suiters and all zoot-suiters were criminals; ergo, all Mexicans were criminals . . . [quoted in Boskin, 1976, p. 62].

McWilliams noted that the crime rate of Mexican youth in this period had actually risen "less than that of other ethnic groups and less than the citywide average." He also saw as "nonsense" the official position taken by major news companies that racism was not an issue and identified racially charged newspaper stories such as "Zoot-Suit Gangsters Plan War on Navy," which appeared in the *LA Daily News* (McWilliams quoted in Boskin, 1976, p. 63).

Productions of black and white images also trouble critics. One is the effort of 1990s filmmakers to produce an image of racial harmony that is subject to generalization. DeMott (1997) is one who thinks that this perhaps well-intended effort is off the mark, because in romanticizing black-white relations it eliminates "the constraints of objective reality and [redistributes] resources, status, and capabilities" (p. 40). He identifies movies like *Pulp Fiction, Die Hard: With a Vengeance, Lethal Weapon,* and *White Men Can't Jump* as examples of this same excess. He also cites advertisers, talk shows, and other media as broadcasting "messages of comfort" that turn racism away from the political arena and into the hearts and good intentions of the individual white person. In DeMott's eyes, this continuous media assault provides the wrong message and excises the historical realities of black experience.

The good news at the movies obscures the bad news in the streets and confirms the Supreme Court's recent decisions on busing, affirmative action, and redistricting. Like the plot of *White Men Can't Jump,* the Court postulates the existence of a society no longer troubled by racism. Because Black-White friendship is now understood to be the rule, there is no need for integrated schools or a Congressional Black Caucus or affirmative action. The Congress and state governors can guiltlessly cut welfare, food assistance, fuel assistance, Head Start, housing money, fellowship money, vaccine money [DeMott, 1997, pp. 40–41].

For other critics, such as Patricia McKee (1999), it is the differential power available to the races that is of concern. She argued that racial identities become visual through "image production and change." McKee places the concerns of DeMott and others into a critical theoretical framework. In introducing her critical analysis of three popular authors, Henry James, William Faulkner, and Toni Morrison, McKee lays out her position as to why it is important to think critically about media images and imagery.

McKee's theoretical framework considers other critical analysts who see a necessary difference between "whiteness" and "blackness" and between

American "White Culture" and "Black Culture." She reviews Morrison's position that Black Culture involves a history of black responsiveness through the media of song and dance that helps preserve elements of their racial identity. These nonvisual elements of blacks' racial identity get assigned to their history and result in black-produced identities that differ greatly from the black identities produced by whites. Black self-identities are created with consistency through time through a social medium of group responsiveness (call-and-respond mode) that involves responsibility to the group. As such, Morrison sees a black identity created through character exchange that moves identity from individual to group. Black individuals must interact with and become a part their group. This produces a black collective identity with features that stand in stark contrast to the white characterization of "blackness," refuting the white depiction of blacks as mere objects rather than subjects (McKee, 1999).

Morrison also argued that "whiteness" in media productions depends on characterizations of African Americans. In short, the representation of "others" (those without whiteness) involves depictions of nonwhite characters as objects or bodies, whereas white characters are abstract subjects. McKee noted the importance of Morrison's view:

> . . . Morrison adds much to an understanding of White identity as an abstraction, because she identifies White representations of race in America with a kind of symbolic visual field. The White identity can be distinguished only against a ground of darkness and materiality. "Otherness" becomes a constituent of the abstract ideal rather than left out of it. African persons were put in place of otherness by White writers and thereby seen to materialize not only qualities White people did not want to be identified with but also the difference between White people and those undesirable qualities [p. 13].

McKee goes beyond this argument by claiming that whiteness is a visual culture that creates racial identities that privilege U.S. white culture. She maintains that visual culture, as portrayed in the James or Faulkner novels, appears as both image and as the views of particular characters. As such, the abstraction of "whiteness" occurs and permits "a theoretical consistency of individual and group" (p. 13). This permits a consciousness of openness as expressed through the "liberal white" identity constructed by James for individual characters. This provides whiteness a power and influence not available to other American races. Because whiteness can be portrayed in so many beneficial and varied ways in the public eye, even exclusive groups, such as white males, have been represented as "open to differences" (p. 14). McKee notes the contemporary scene is no different: "Similarly, in the more visual terms of twenty-first century public life, there is a wide range of images of whiteness. White persons, therefore, can experience their identity not merely as self-same but as diverse. They thus enter into exchanges of identity that seem open and inclusive of differences even as they are exclusive" (pp. 13–14).

There are, thus, very different modes of production of races in America, and McKee seeks to explain them within the context of the history of power relationships, particularly within the context of how capitalism serves and is served by racism. One need not adopt her ideological stance to see the distinctions in racial productions in America.

The media greatly influence racial identities in the United States. Often the daily resources available for us to help young people shape more accurate and tolerant racial identities of one another are overlooked. This is the message of Beverly Tatum's work (1999). She reminds us that friends, teachers, clerks, and many others are important to such identities. However, as important, she forcefully tells us we know little to nothing about the development of racial identities among our children. She points out that white prejudice in America amounts to an oppressive system of cultural messages and institutional policies and practices, reflecting the beliefs and actions of individuals. The results, of course, as noted by critics cited above, are white advantage and racial inequalities, including those discussed throughout this book. The concern about racial identity development is that it occurs in youngsters, usually adolescents, who self-define by what they hear, see, and cognize about themselves and their group, especially their racial group. Their decisions about who they are and how they will behave often follow them for a lifetime. Given the discussion of racial identity production by McKee, Morrison, and others, it is not surprising that Tatum tells us that the dominant white male culture rarely mentions its traits for self-identification while the "others" (women, Jews, the mentally disabled, gays, and racial minorities), or subordinate groups, frequently mention their group when self-identifying (Tatum, 1999). Also not surprising, these "other" groups internalize what is said about them by the dominant group and this makes self-confidence difficult. Dominants, who rarely if ever live the experiences of others nor come into close contact with them, learn and project what they see as the abnormalities or unattractive qualities of the "other" groups. Any parent, white or nonwhite, of a child with any type of disability recognizes the pattern. In fact, dominants, who have rationalized members of minorities as "other," do not really want to know them at all. This type of depersonalization leads at best to shunning these others and at worst to brutalizing them when they "don't stay in their place." Subordinates, in contrast, withdraw as a strategy and, as Tatum notes, this can mean avoidance of "learning by minorities, who see teachers as belonging to the dominant group" (p. 26).

Tatum implicitly poses the question why black children in particular think racially. It is so, she answers, because the world thinks of them that way, too. She explains a model of racial identity development that involves a transition through five stages. She argues that, in the first stage, African-American children largely absorb the values of whites in a preencounter stage before adolescence because racial grouping attachment is not yet relevant. However, as the black child develops, sooner or later he or she must encounter "the personal impact of racism" through some meaningful event that calls attention to the fact that being black matters (Tatum, 1999, p. 55).

At this second stage, Tatum explains, both becoming angry and turning to one's own age and race group are normal in trying to address one's identity. It is also common for "an oppositional identity" to develop that distances the dominant group and creates a shell of defense from further attacks on the existing identity. This often is expressed in dress, language, and attitude. It is worth noting that, although Tatum is speaking of black youngsters, plenty of evidence exists for other groups as well. For example, a Filipino American, reflecting on the formative years that led him to drugs and gang participation before his reform, stated:

> We lived in Cicero until I was about seven years old. I had assimilated into the White society there. . . . Then in 1976 my family moved to San Diego. . . .
>   . . . things were much different, because I didn't quite fit in so readily. . . . We were among the first group of Filipinos to move there. The majority White population was not tolerant of any minorities. This I got to experience from watching racial fights my brothers were involved in and seeing the words "Flips go home" spray-painted on the house of one of my best friends. . . .
>   I could not understand what was going on, because I felt that I was being rejected from a group that I had always belonged to. . . . That led to much confusion in my life. . . .
>   It was when I was around older generations of Filipinos, like my brothers and their friends, that I started noticing the differences between White and brown. These older Filipinos had been affected more by racial tensions than I had. When I was around them, I saw a real hatred for White people [Espiritu, 1995, pp. 182–185].

Regardless of the type of "other," the behaviors, including academic performance, often yield, in the third stage, to oppositional identity. Tatum explains that this is *not* inevitable, if schools and educators provide "an alternative to the cafeteria table" (Tatum, 1999, p. 71). Adolescents are eager for education that supports their search for identity. Tatum rightfully suggests that efforts should be made by all of us to nurture rather than impede that search. Constructive and informative curricula and other forms of alternative media (not throwing out the three Rs) can allow the adolescent a positive view of self and an alternative identity through the fourth, "immersion" stage of development. Allowing a child to delve into his or her own cultural history (not necessarily one of minority victimization) will permit self-definition and a sense of security that leads to the fifth and final stage of internalization. Tatum tells us that this stage is marked by a commitment to one's culture due to a positive racial identity, but it is also one that can transcend race (Tatum, 1999). Allowing an "other" the opportunity for a positive self- and group identity comes at no expense to white identity and is equally important to all "other" adults and children. Clearly, this is not likely to happen soon without the cooperation of "white allies," which is why Tatum encourages white role models to facilitate the actualization of this model in white society. To suggest this is both wise and useful. However, it will not come easily in a culture of white self-interest.

Summary

Most significant issues have protagonists and antagonists. In the case of American racism, even those who agree that it exists are divergent in their views about its degree, permanence, causes, and consequences. These deep philosophical differences suggest that it will be extremely difficult to achieve a social and political consensus about twenty-first-century racism. The various points of view discussed in this chapter, however, converge in their agreement that there is a long history of exploitation of minorities that has led to racial inequalities and bad feelings between the races. These individuals, whether social scientists, social commentators, journalists, or social critics, all view race relations as a crucial issue of twenty-first-century America. Not one among these various experts would argue that racism does not exist. However, they differ greatly in their assessments of the causes and prescriptions necessary to rid the United States of racism. It will benefit each American and, therefore, America to ask questions about racism and racialism within his or her own life. An important beginning is a fair and honest treatment of history, not only of segregation, discrimination, and isolation and their impacts but of how American leaders, political and academic, and the media shape our racial images. This may aid our understanding of how whites as individuals and as a national majority view minority citizens, including those of a different race, ethnicity, religion, and other walks of life. This will help us avoid vicious attacks, such as those repeatedly directed at innocent Arab Americans and Muslims during the United States' response to the bombings of the federal building in Oklahoma and New York's World Trade Center in the 1990s and, more recently, the deadly hijackings of commercial jetliners that were flown into the same New York towers and the Pentagon in 2001. Although the nuclear family is crucial to teaching hate as well as tolerance, we have come to better understand that our views are also shaped by our leaders. The concept of white advantage may also help explain why so much is taken for granted by the white majority and why they seem unwilling to embrace the "cost" of moving from unequal to equal housing, employment, and service access among the races.

As we noted, there are several perspectives on the narrative of American racism. None deny that racism exists, but their views on its origins and permanence vary greatly. We have added our perspective to these sociological narratives. In the next chapter, we turn to the topic of urban form and processes. This may come as a bit of a surprise in a book on race and inequality. However, we noted in earlier chapters that America's minorities are becoming more urban. We also noted that minority concentrations have become well established in U.S. urban centers. In fact, our major thesis is that racial inequalities are linked to places within urban settings. This arises obviously out of the history of urban settlement, to a degree. However, why these settlement patterns took their initial form and how they have changed and are likely to change are topics of urban geographic theory. Not surprisingly, more than one view exists. Racial segregation and discrimination result in racial isolation and spatial inequalities, which are nagging social and economic issues of the twenty-first century. One of the key issues will be the place of minorities, literally in geographic space and also in terms of work, recreation, and other places Americans play out their lives. As the U.S. population has changed, so has the complexion of urban space, expanding and being restructured. Imbedded in the competing theories of urban spatial restructuring are very different philosophical positions about how minority space evolved over time and especially what future panaceas may eradicate them. Practical solutions to existing urban problems will be difficult, especially if they must be framed during times of tension or crisis. To prepare for dialogue and action, it is crucial that we continue to create accurate national and local perspectives of the two deadly urban expressions of American racism: the interrelated elements of segregation/isolation and race-place inequalities. We need to carefully examine the geographic patterns that reflect inequalities in the distribution of housing quality, accessibility to services, and environmental hazards, as well as other indicators of life quality in urban America. It is equally important in policy debates to understand the diametrically opposed theoretical views as to why urban America is in its current spatial form and what changes are required to solve urban problems, especially those associated with race and place. The next chapter summarizes the competing views of urban spatial organization and their positions on urban solutions.

Chapter 4

Theories of Spatial Relationships in Urban America

Background to Theoretical Discussions

While U.S. minority settlements expanded during the twentieth century, urban America was being transformed from a set of highly centralized cities to metropolitan systems. Not only were metropolitan areas gaining larger populations; they were consuming greater amounts of territory as well. Even when population growth was modest, land consumption was often substantial. For example, in metropolitan Chicago, population growth between 1960 and 1980 was less than 5 percent, yet land consumption increased by approximately 50 percent. This urban-metropolitan transformation has been described as a shift from industrial to postindustrial form. Although this is generally accurate, there exists a far more complex microgeography that reflects capital investment, political decisionmaking, individual and group choices, and overt and covert forms of discrimination. The result has been the further separation of the rich and poor and of the white majority from minority populations. Visual distinctions between the aging "central cities" and their surrounding suburbs have become apparent.

Any conscious adult residing in a metropolitan area in the last quarter century had to notice radical landscape changes. The construction of inner-city public housing projects, disinvestment in central cities, and failure of downtown establishments, resulting in blank storefronts, occurred while expensive new suburban homes, strip malls, and industrial parks seemed to appear overnight in areas far removed from old downtowns. All of these events were nearly ubiquitous in metropolitan America. But few Americans questioned these developments or even pondered the changes in their neighborhoods.

Today, urban restructuring has become so commonplace that most Americans have come to expect growth and decline in the same communities. For urban scholars, however, such activities mask a complex set of processes that operate almost invisibly. They are controlled by decisionmakers who act either individually or collectively to reshape urban landscapes. The minority concentrations discussed in the preceding chapters are patterns that result from migration and segregation processes. Urbanists see these processes as operating within broader macrobehaviors. They espouse theories of spatial relationships that not only involve segregation and migration processes but also explain urban inequalities as consequences of political and economic systems.

The last chapter discussed sociological theories of racism at length to illustrate the divergent views. It is worthwhile to reflect a bit more on the nature of these narratives before discussing the geographic theories of urban spatial structure. The differences and similarities of the sociological viewpoints presented provide a framework for understanding the philosophical differences between the two viewpoints of the U.S. political economy and the urban structures that they produce, which are the topics of this chapter.

One of the themes of this book is that racial inequalities are linked to particular places. Urban America has taken on a spatial form that guarantees the racial isolation that contributes to our racial problems and growing international image of preaching justice while practicing injustice in our economy and living space. Racial inequalities are a threat to our future well-being as a nation. In Chapter 3 we noted the general view that racism is deeply imbedded in the United States' past. Viewpoints may conflict on its permanence but not its impact. There is clear disagreement as to its causes. Some argued that racism, not economic class, causes inequalities in urban America. Others maintained that class distinctions and the tensions they generate are the culprits that guarantee those inequalities. Chapter 3 presented the liberal viewpoints of Wilson (concentration of the urban poor, spatial mismatch, and social policy) and the conservative narratives of Hamblin (self-help through education and hard work) and Brown (self-help, more education, especially in technical areas, and separatism within the free-market economy). Although proposed methods for dealing with American racism differ greatly, the common ground among all of these authors lies in their belief that operating within the free-market system to find a solution to American racism and racial inequalities is possible. In short, they recognize the problems of racism and the inequalities that it causes but believe that capitalism and the mechanisms it offers to a free society can provide an adequate basis for creative solutions to these horrible ills.

This position stands in strong contrast to Marable's position, forwarded in Chapter 3. For Marable, the system is the problem. Free-market capitalism not only exploits the working class but has, as an inherent flaw, racism. The working class and underclasses, such as the chronically unemployed and unemployable, are weak and exploitable. They are controlled by consensus and coercion for the purpose of producing never-ending profits for the elite. Education is just another institutional mechanism manipulated by the elite for their benefit. To these general negatives, however, must be added racism. Marable sees blacks as having received a disproportionate share of coercion from capitalism's "iron fist of force," including "economically based" riots (when whites are pinched and manipulated to the commission of racist acts) and disproportionate and unfair punishments from a racist justice system. For Marable, one cannot find any solution to problems caused by a racist, capitalist system by working within it. The answer is to be part of a protracted struggle (not a violent revolution) to dismantle the capitalist free-market system.

Ideologies control the organization and use of space and, thus, the resulting visual city landscapes. The distinctly different sociological narratives presented in Chapter 3, therefore, have their counterparts in urban geographic theories about the spatial organization of the city or, more precisely, the evolution of the city into a metropolitan system in the United States during the nineteenth and twentieth centuries. Specifically, in the race-place connection of urban space and urban inequalities, two views emerged to explain the structuring and restructuring of urban space. These two explanations have the same general philosophical underpinnings as those prescribed above to sociological narrators of American racism. In short, one position holds that the American system is rightly driven by competition, innovation, and investment. It may have flaws but still is the best. Its flexibility permits the development of policy that can right its wrongs. The other viewpoint holds that the American political-economic system is inherently flawed by conflicts and contradictions, prohibits solutions to its problems, and therefore must be removed to allow the eradication of the social problems it created. Both viewpoints recognize the impact of the industrial era in creating a new urban form and the role of the information age in the restructuring of urban form and function. However, their theoretical explanations of the social and economic mechanisms behind the processes of urban change differ greatly. Although both viewpoints see space as a commodity under capitalism, their assessments of the intentions of the societal leadership that structures geographic space are very different.

Their proposed solutions for reducing racially segregated space and inequalities are substantially different. We classify the first theory as the free-market technological perspective of urban spatial organization and urban expansion. It generally asserts that the leading principles of laissez-faire economics, especially competition and investment, coupled with limited government intervention led to prosperity that will continue to generate a higher standard of living for Americans through better jobs, regular improvements in education-based skills, and constantly improving technology. These urban theorists use the same reasoning to explain the forces of competition for the most accessible land in the city center and, then, suburban-metropolitan formation by the process of decentralization (relocation from central city to suburbia). Thus, the evolution of urban spatial structure, which is rooted in Western capitalism's principles of competition and ability to pay for locational value, is viewed as "natural." Improving technology and increasing capital investment have led to new dimensions of urban space, making inner cities obsolete and unattractive compared to the locational attributes of suburbia (clean, open, easy access and good connectivity, relatively inexpensive land, etc.). Those with better education, skills, and concomitant earning power have access to the best residential locations in urban metropolitan space. The "system" provides all Americans with equal opportunity and access to the resources necessary to choose lifestyles associated with certain places in metropolitan America. Not surprisingly, when necessary, economic and social policies should emphasize investment, as well as technological and educational solutions to solve economic woes and racial inequalities. The philosophical similarity of the free-market technological view with the liberal and conservative narratives of Chapter 3 should be obvious.

Likewise, the second position, which we term the postmodern-Marxist perspective, relies in large part on the Marxist/socialist position that is similar to Marable's. Generally, the postmodern urbanists rely on Marxist explanations of the formation of industrial and postindustrial cities of urban America and their form (such as the creation and maintenance of ghetto and barrio spaces) and function (to maximize the financial interest of the elite) while attempting to offer a perspective on solutions different from those of hard-core Marxists and, of course, free-market supporters.

These two theories of spatial organization, one postmodern/Marxist and one free market, illustrate clearly the different beliefs about the roles of capitalism in shaping urban form and racial inequalities. They also suggest very different paths to potential fixes of American urban and racial problems. Both are rooted in macroeconomic beliefs that individuals react behaviorally to systemic conditions created by materialism. On one hand, capitalists say that it is the system of individual initiative and competition that not only creates the motivation for personal improvement and family security but sparks innovation and discovery leading to improved lifestyles and well-being. Under free enterprise, people work hard for success, and this leads to investment that produces economic growth and development. Individual success has meant not only more disposable income for luxury cars, vacations, and other amenities but spare cash to invest in the stock market, which drives future economic growth. Although this system may have disproportionately favored whites, opportunities are now open to and are being used by nonwhites as well.

Marxists, on the other hand, argue that, under capitalism, individualism and competition are tools of the elite. Worker is turned against worker in order to maximize control and extract as much capital as possible out of every worker. As a result, workers do not receive a fair share of income from their work. Further, racism is a tool of the elite. It breeds and fosters hatred that distracts workers from the real problems created by capitalism, while the elite profit. All workers lose under the bust cycles of capitalism, while the elite class protects its investments from losses, including by moving them around geographically.

Given the projected growth of all minorities in urban America and the likely debates that will occur in the coming decades, a basic understanding of these different perspectives on the organization of urban space is important for all Americans. How did ghettos emerge? Why does segregation persist? Why do inner cities contain expensive, gentrified neighborhoods as well as barrios? What policies have permitted the majority of federal housing projects to remain in the inner city, and why? What impact will future decisions have on the organization of urban space? Such questions are essential background for discussions of equity and for future policy initiatives. They are also important to debating some of the United States' most basic human problems. Review of competing theories encourages the consideration of multiple explanations of minorities' places in America's past and perhaps its future. A better understanding may also better prepare each of us to forge his or her own views of race rather than adopt a particular *ism*. In examining the two distinct positions, then, we do not propose to favor one over another. Rather, we wish to provide the reader different contexts for understanding a changing American urban system, including its racial inequalities, which reflect the nation's character and, beyond explanation, beg actions that will make a better urban America in the future.

The remainder of this chapter is divided into two parts. Each provides one of the theoretical arguments of the two approaches referred to above. Part I is a conceptualization of urban-metropolitan expansion in terms of technological improvements and an expanding free market. Part II examines the perspective that interprets the urban-metropolitan transformation as "restructuring" due to the nature of the capitalist system but adds a postmodern view that differentiates it from a purely Marxist explanation. The chapter concludes with a brief summary.

Part I: The Free-Market Technological View

Phase I: Pre–World War II Urban Expansion and Centralization

Growth and Change.   Shortly after independence, in 1790, the U.S. urban population was approximately 5 percent. The total populations of New York City and Philadelphia, the two largest urban centers, differed by less than 5,000 people (33,181 and 28,522, respectively). The growth of cities between 1790 and 1960 has been explained by transportation technology (sail-wagon canal, steam, railroad, and automobile) and industrialization (Borchert, 1967). During the period 1790–1840, the percentage of urban dwellers doubled, as the number of cities increased and Americans pushed westward to begin tapping the land's vast resources. It was during this period that black slavery built the southern agricultural economy and that Mexicans provided cheap labor for the agricultural expansion taking place in the American West (Chapter 2). Between 1840 and 1890 the percentage of urbanites more than tripled, to 35 percent. The U.S. Industrial Revolution had exploded, and European immigrants provided its cheap labor source. By 1920 more than half of all Americans resided in cities. By this time, European immigration had been halted by the quota system, but the American industrial city had already established its form. Thirty million European immigrants had entered the United States by 1920. Du Bois had already spoken of the special problems of the "negro districts" of northern cities (Chapter 2), and millions of Hispanics awaited their turn to enter urban America, but European immigrants and industrialization were the factors of change in the transformation of America's economy and living spaces.

Social Patterns of the U.S. Industrial City.   Factories became magnets, and America's towns became cities, and its modest-sized cities became much larger. Economic activities transformed New York City, Boston, Philadelphia, Chicago, Pittsburgh, Cleveland, and other communities. The locations of factories and institutional forces determined the locations of a range of other economic activities and of immigrant neighborhoods and ethnic ghettos of the period. Arriving poor and frequently penniless, most urban immigrants settled in neighborhoods adjacent to factories in which they became employed. For the Irish, Italians, and others, this meant residing in old, converted single-family units or in new, poorly constructed tenements. The deplorable conditions associated with these environments—high density, overcrowding, poorly lighted and poorly ventilated units with inadequate sanitation—were comparable to the conditions of late medieval Europe. Du Bois reported the conditions of northern black settlements in the early 1900s. Before then, immigrant slums caught the attention of social activists.

Before the close of the nineteenth century, New York City's "Lower East Side" had been transformed into bustling factory operations and a landscape of tenement slums. Such patterns became by-products of the American industrial city. Social activists became appalled by the living conditions of immigrants there. Among the most noteworthy was Jacob Riis, a police reporter who became outraged by the level of exploitation, despair, and ill health among slum dwellers. Riis's outrage at greedy industrialists and landlords led him to photograph daily life in the industrial city and then lobby for change. His 1890 publication, *How the Other Half Lives*, provided graphic details of the daily misery that ranged from hunger to starvation and from chronic health problems to the deaths of children residing in the tenement slums or living on the street. In the preface of a reprint of this volume, Charles A.

Madison noted that, though Riis had a "limited political perspective," he also had the ability to relate the harsh plight of a million-plus Irish, German, Jewish, and Italian slum victims to an important segment of the public:

> ... [Riis] fought for the elimination of slum conditions on New York's lower East Side more persistently and with greater effectiveness than any of the more conventional social workers and civic reformers of his day. ... [He] seared the conscience of prominent New Yorkers and forced reforms upon greedy landlords—among them men and organizations belonging to the highest social stratum [Riis, 1971, p. v].

Activists like Riis played important practical roles in changing tenement life. However, unlike the social activists of the day, late-nineteenth-century urban planning–oriented professionals took a very different approach to the new urban condition.

Explaining the American Industrial City. In 1893, when the Chicago World's Fair opened, a new brand of city thinker appeared on the urban scene. The "White City" exhibition at the fair was used to depict industrial cities of the future. As noted by Arthur Gallion and Simon Eisner (1986), the depiction of cities had little to do with the reality of the dirty, problem-ridden American city of the period but allowed the portrayal of an expanding industrial empire. This form of denial enabled planners to distance their thinking from the economic and social hardships created by the industrial city and to focus on idealized cities of the future. What followed were propositions for grand plans for city growth and beautification through the creation of monumental scenes reminiscent of earlier European cities (Gallion and Eisner, 1986). The practical realities of the cost of such designs gave way to a call for industrially and commercially based urban efficiencies, which became the tools of the era's new urban planners, architects, and engineers.

Around the turn of the century, the University of Chicago was founded. The "Chicago School" of urban sociologists emerged and were charged with understanding urban processes and problems. Urban geographers at Chicago soon joined in the search for understanding urban pattern and process. Both groups emphasized the spatial organization of land use within the American city and the function of cities. By the time Ernest Burgess (1925) offered the first explanation for American urban form and process, World War I had ended, the quota system had dramatically slowed European immigration, and the factory-based industrial city, with its transportation tentacles and differentiated social classes, was the dominant urban form. The industrial city was the center of a new urban universe.

At the heart of this urban and industrial "centrality" lay great competition. Competition for space and access to the center of activity resulted in disproportionate land values and positioned the highest bidder in the central intersection of urban communities. This location, termed the "central business district" (CBD), contained much more than the city's peak land values. The theater district, exclusive restaurants, financial center, and all significant cultural functions—the best the city had to offer—were all located there. Not far beyond this bustling center, however, lay warehouses and clear visual signs of neighborhood decline. In these areas resided the newest immigrants and the sections of the black ghetto.

Just as technology had created the factory magnet, it provided the early release mechanism for the wealthy seeking residential exclusivity away from the new urban form's negative aspects. The trolley and electric streetcar were the early devices that permitted the wealthy the opportunity to reside some distance away from their factory offices and still return daily to oversee their operations. Residential relocations coincided with economic expansion and the massive influx of European immigrants into the city center, often single males seeking the most inexpensive housing available next to the factories. Over time, social fluidity provided second- and third-generation families the opportunity to accumulate sufficient capital to buy a home in a better neighborhood.

It is not surprising, then, that Burgess's graphical representation of the American industrial city (Chicago but later generalized to other cities) incorporated elements of the visual landscape—factories, transportation lines, retailing, wholesaling, tenements, boarding houses, and single-family homes—with knowledge of theoretical concepts and processes of the period—competition for space, the impacts of immigration, the growth of a middle class, and transportation technology and its impact—into a framework to explain urban expansion. Burgess's ecological, or concentric zone, model was rooted in the concepts of physical science and his posited five principal zones, concentrically arranged. His thinking represented a free-market technology explanation because of its assumption that accessibility determines land value and its dependence on transportation technology to explain residential zonation. It also is an organic formulation, suggesting that each zonal district seeks outward expansion (needs to grow).

Among the model's concentric zones, the outermost one held the wealthy residents, who were there because of their ability to commute to and from the city center. This model has also been termed *ecological* because its residential and other zones are ecologically determined. Burgess linked particular functions and populations to circular zones. The CBD formed due to commercial interests' desire for maximum access. The zone of transition lay between a residential zone of "working men's homes" and the CBD. The transition zone contained mixed land use, including a high-density residential area containing rooming houses, slum dwellings, and manufacturing and commercial strips that yielded unattractive images and poor living conditions. Beyond the niche of working-class homes, which recognized social fluidity and the ability of second-generation European immigrants to purchase homes, lay other residential districts, ecologically derived and representing class structure. The outer ring, as noted above, was the location of the wealthy who departed the large, aging homes of the factory zone, which were converted to rooming houses. Implicit in this viewpoint is the notion of upward mobility among hardworking new Americans.

The conceptual longevity of Burgess's framework is somewhat surprising. This simplistic model of urban expansion became the basis of future ideas that attempted to capture the essence of an expanding urban society and city. Homer Hoyt's sector/wedge model (1939) used a similar technological and market perspective. He maintained that urban residential growth lacked the uniformity of Burgess's concentric zones and, instead, took the form of wedges of expansion. Transportation technology explained growth patterns of urban America. He argued that during urban expansion high-growth areas of U.S. cities followed major transportation arteries, while low-growth (or non-) sectors were without such crucial arteries. High-income residential growth not only was patterned, following transportation links, but was directed to high elevations and attracted to social and community leadership locations.

Another conceptualization of urban expansion was the Harris-Ullman multiple-nuclei model (Harris and Ullman, 1945). Unlike its predecessors, this model was proposed after World War II and benefited from decades of observations of additional urban growth. The Harris-Ullman explanation made clear that the era of the urban monocenter was over. Its authors explained by examples that urban expansion now started from a variety of nodes, including industrial districts and major shopping areas. Also, as a rule, particular urban activities attracted complementary functions, whereas others served as repellents to certain land uses due to their noxious characteristics. All of these conceptions of urban America involved static representations of an orderly set of function-based districts that emerged and expanded within a free economy. For Harris and Ullman, some of the newest nuclei were the locations of new technology and new investments and, as such, generated urban expansion in their surrounding geographies.

Social aspects of urban geography and city living were reduced to static patterns in these models. Tenements and ghettos were geographic patterns subsumed in ecological zones of transition. None of the models were rooted in empirical analyses of tenement or ghetto conditions, nor did they provide details of the lived experience of ghetto dwellers nor the impacts of racism. The American industrial city's large, ugly, and deplorable slums often experienced crime and other social ills that led to the popular notion that their unsavory European immigrant residents suffered from pathological behaviors. Even when they were studied in the middle of the twentieth century, social scientists applied the traditional explanations of the ecological model:

During three generations of sustained and heavy European immigration into the U.S., . . . congested ghettos of foreign immigrants assumed substantial dimensions within the residential structures of American cities. Most immigrants settled near the sources of unskilled employment and . . . the majority of newcomers concentrated on the margins of the emerging CBDs. The CBD provided the largest source of unskilled employment opportunities, and many of the adjacent residential quarters had been abandoned by their original residents . . . [Ward, 1968, p. 343].

In addition to the factors of accessibility, the streetcar network, the long workday, and periods of unemployment, David Ward (1968) reported a cultural dimension:

Group consciousness, as well as economic necessity or advantage, stimulated the concentration of immigration in the central tenement districts; for once established, the ghetto provided institutions and neighborhood life familiar to the immigrants [p. 347].

Ward cited cases wherein such ghettos, "once established, resisted or retarded the rate of any subsequent commercial claims," suggesting that, once a ghetto survived efforts of an invasion, it would persist and pass to newer immigrant groups, who, like their forerunners, had the promise of moving up and moving out. Thus, urban space was transformed in stages that gave rise to specific areas (zones), some stable, some not. These provided credence to Burgess's concept of a transition zone and broader explanatory framework, which indicated the potential for poor immigrants, through hard work and savings, to escape the poorer zone for the better adjacent zone of workingmen's homes.

It is important to note that, although this model treated the black ghetto as just another ecological niche, black social scientists of the era challenged the model's relevance to African-American settlement. As early as the 1930s, E. Franklin Frazier (1932) noted that, whereas Europeans were able to escape the zone of transition, blacks were contained by an artificial housing market that restricted their residential choices. Such limitations underscore the point made earlier that these models present a generalized view of urban expansion, often failing to explain the microgeography and the roles of ethnic and racial differences in the city's spatial reorganization, while emphasizing technology and social mobility.

In summary, unlike the social activists of the late nineteenth century, liberal and conservative professionals responsible for understanding and planning industrial cities followed models that reduced the industrial city's social and economic ills to either invisible problems or static patterns of adaptation and growth. These models valued the operation of the free-market system and its technology and incorporated associated concepts (competition, accessibility, land values, technology, etc.). They combined direct observation of the urban landscape with highly generalized knowledge of urban processes, especially immigration, social fluidity, and migration, within some of the concepts of natural systems.

Phase II: Post–World War II
Decentralization and Metropolitan Growth

The second period of urban expansion was dominated by decentralization of urban functions, the suburbanization of the United States. As the population continued to expand and urban migration increased after World War II, the land consumed by city life dramatically changed. Suburbanization, a reflection of a whole new American lifestyle, led to a new urban form that would dramatically affect the distribution of people, goods, and services. Since U.S. lifestyles and place are linked, the new American urban geography magnified the differences between societal haves and have-nots, particularly on a racial basis, and between the nation's inner and outer cities.

Suburbanization was well underway before World War II, especially in the Northeast. However, in the second half of the twentieth century, a variety of forces led to unprecedented urban expansion and the out-migration of central-city residents to a suburban ring of new communities. The United States emerged from WWII as a superpower capable of funding the rebuilding of Western Europe. It built strategic trade and defense alliances in both hemispheres that bolstered its superpower status. At the same time, its postwar domestic population expanded (creating the baby boom), the effects of which, when coupled with wartime pent-up demand for consumer goods, resulted in major industrial expansion and economic good times. It was during this period that white Americans and the businesses that served them moved en masse to suburbia. Like previous expansions, the wartime and postwar economic expansion required large amounts of inexpensive labor. In this period, Mexican immigration to the American West and the migration of southern poor blacks and whites to northern and western inner cities of industrial America served that purpose. As noted in Chapter 2, the Hart-Celler Act greatly changed U.S. immigration law and increased dramatically the numbers and cultural diversity of the U.S. Hispanic and Asian populations. The result was another transformation of urban America. Millions of minorities created ethnic enclaves, while others joined blacks and became ghetto dwellers. Hispanic barrios also expanded. White flight created the need for more suburban living space, and later the expanding black middle-class pushed out of the ghettos into newer segregated neighborhoods. Subsequently, many aspiring Hispanics and Asians, as the labor market's newest arrivals, sought inexpensive housing in the inner city, where they accepted the lowest level of work in the rapidly changing economy. The metropolitan region became both a census concept and popular usage for explaining a new urban form that had burst into rural America, establishing a new sphere of urban influence. Despite periodic recessions, the U.S. economy grew rapidly between 1940 and 2000, a period when the urban population grew from 56 percent to greater than 70 percent of all Americans. Urban sprawl became an ugly phrase to describe America's unplanned urban expansion.

A multifactor explanation was provided by free-market thinkers for the rapid decentralization of the United States' inner cities: transportation technology, growth in incomes, an expanding middle class with growing disposable incomes, and federal policies. These factors explained why inner cities were becoming depositories of the poor while white suburbia was becoming disproportionately young, educated, and wealthy. As the middle class sought a better living environment for their families, cheap land became accessible in suburbia. The middle-class population logically fled the congestion, crime, and industrial obsolescence of older inner cities. They were followed quickly by retailing and industrial enterprises. The technology that produced the automobile also produced modern industrial equipment and more efficient production space that could be located in industrial parks free of inner-city obsolescence and social ills. Economic growth and investment also provided the increasing opportunity to shop outside the central city's CBD, which had been the traditional home of the department store and related activities. This "natural" set of processes seemed as logical as the evolution of ecological zones.

Meanwhile, the "electronics revolution" was creating the need for "higher-order skills" and more education, while "high-tech" offices departed central city locations for "business and high-tech parks." In fact, the American economy was undergoing a transition from manufacturing to multifaceted services. All of this consumed large amounts of rural land, turning it into what became part of "postindustrial" metropolitan America. Each new nucleus became the focus of additional expansion, a magnet attracting more people and more business until some reached the status of "satellite," rather than "dormitory suburb," and eventually independent "edge city." As the number of nuclei increased, metropolitan areas consumed entire counties, even in areas that had very modest population growth. City living and a suburban lifestyle were being pushed further apart. The manufacturing jobs sought by new urban arrivals, especially black migrants, rapidly disappeared. In short, invisible walls and greater distances between "inner cities" and "outer cities" were constructed during the postindustrial urban-suburban transformation, which included the migration of employment to outer cities. A closer look at this transformation based on theories of economic expansion and technological change is helpful in explaining the free-market perspective of urban restructuring that created the metropolitan United States.

It was the relocation of economic activities and related employment opportunities that in large part explained the new model of urban expansion after

1945. The suburban explosion began with the inception of "bedroom communities," exclusive residential communities without commercial or governmental functions. "Bedroom" residents worked in the inner city during the day and commuted home to the suburb to sleep. Three additional stages of suburbanization followed "bedroom status," according to Truman Hartshorn and Peter Muller (1986). The decentralization of retailing and other activities during these stages not only transformed the American landscape but in some locations created true "outer cities" that competed strongly with their inner, "central" city counterpart (Hartshorn and Muller, 1986).

Decentralization occurred at an accelerated rate after World War II, at a time when the national economy was being transformed from manufacturing to services. For some time, the growing U.S. demand for office space provided some stability for inner cities by filling vacant retail buildings and creating new ones. This led to the recharacterization of the CBD, in some cases, as the "OBD" (office business district). Government and corporate headquarters provided employment opportunities in "downtowns" because suburbanites commuted to downtown high-rises for daily work and returned home to suburbia in the evening. However, not long into the postwar era, locational changes in corporate headquarters occurred, resulting in the regional relocation of many to new regional centers across the United States. At the same time, many corporate offices departed the older inner-city CBDs for new locations in suburbia (Semple and Phillips, 1982; Wheeler, 1985; Semple et al., 1985; Holloway and Wheeler, 1991). Other service employment followed. These relocations not only contributed to major changes in the urban spatial structure of the United States but dramatically influenced the location of additional employment opportunities. As a result, functional relationships between the inner and emerging outer cities changed.

As noted, Hartshorn and Muller (1986) suggested that suburbanization took multiple geographic forms and involved several stages. After the initial "bedroom" stage of dependence on central-city employment and retail functions, a suburb often evolved into the "independence" stage, which recognized its ability to stand alone from the central city as an employment center. Some of these newly independent suburbs evolved further by developing magnetic attractions promoted by developers, including open space, access to transportation links, and retail malls, as well as tax advantages, that resulted in more growth as other businesses relocated to the suburbs, including hotels and conference centers. Still other businesses sought affiliation with office parks, retail centers, and other service providers. As a result of this third, catalytic stage, such suburbs competed with central cities in specific ways, such as for some office space and specialized retailing. As the catalytic suburbs evolved into "suburban downtowns," the fourth stage, equal status with the central city, was achieved

The ability of some suburbs to compete effectively with their formerly dominant central city differentiates this period from others. This brand of suburb effectively competed in the provision of prime office space through the creation of high-rises and high-tech centers. They also became able to provide high-rent housing, thus appearing in every way as "complete downtowns" (Hartshorn and Muller, 1986). As a result, the overall set of urban-suburban relationships changed dramatically in a very short period of time. Burgess's urban monocenter was replaced by a complex set of competing centers that were arranged in a multifunctional and multinodal metropolitan region, most often with the old center as the weakest link in the region surrounded by a ring of competitive suburban downtowns.

Using the work of Hartshorn and Muller (1986), as well as that of Robert Cervero (1989), Thomas Stanback (1991) effectively argued that suburbanization had created a new set of relationships that created negative consequences for many older central cities. Clearly, the functional relations of the central city as dominant and magnetic economic node serving the suburbs no longer held in many U.S. metropolitan areas before 1990. By the end of the twentieth century, many suburbs had evolved into "agglomeration economies," once found only in central cities (Stanback, 1991). Many suburbs were no longer economically unidimensional and no longer provided large numbers of commuters to central-city jobs. In short, American urbanism had changed dramatically and the urban cultural landscape was again transformed by the growth and new functions of American suburbia. As suburbia changed from a labor provider to a competitor for jobs and employees, older central cities lost their tax bases. The obvious result was declining inner cities with growing "dependent populations" and fewer financial resources to care for the aging infrastructure. Among the dependencies were the disproportionately poor and minority citizens. Inner cities quickly became ill equipped to contribute to the twenty-first-century workforce and found themselves in the uncomfortable position of competing with diversified, highly attractive suburban downtowns (Stanback, 1991).

Stanback explained the "changing nature of work" in the new service economy and how it influenced the metropolitan economy. The greater emphasis on services, especially health and education but also producer services (those that are exportable as well as consumed within the country), meant new products and new production processes. Information provision and analysis, as well as decision and strategy making, are examples of the new basis for the growth in employment among the "intermediate services," such as finance, insurance, and real estate (FIRE) and government. Data became crucial to decisionmaking and the consumer-based marketing services of postwar America. The electronics revolution of the twentieth century made such services widely available and created a large number of new jobs. Technology that spawned this industry continued to develop exponentially, demanding a more highly educated workforce and influencing the locational choices of businesses. Thus, the higher unemployment rates of inner cities, disproportionately high for minorities, are due to structural changes in the economy and the relocation of business activities. Left behind are the "hard to employ" of the old central cities (Stanback, 1991, p. 6). It is this situation that led Wilson to apply the concept *spatial mismatch* to the plight of the ghetto underclass (Chapter 3); retail, manufacturing, and service employment moved to suburbia. Residing at a substantial distance from the new job locations, many of the inner-city poor and minority populations found themselves with too few resources to reach suburban jobs.

Muller (1981) and Stanback independently examined the suburbanization of economic activity and employment during the period 1960–1987. Using statistical records of suburban shares of total jobs, retail sales, and manufacturing employment, Muller revealed that by 1970 the average share of total jobs in suburbia had reached 47.6 percent; there had been an average gain of 10.6 percent from the previous decade in the large SMAs that he studied. He also found for the same period an average increase of greater than 15 percent in the share of retail sales employment in suburbia. The suburban share of manufacturing jobs in the ten-year period increased on average by about 13 percent, with all fourteen regions showing gains and seven of those realizing double-digit increases. (See Table 4.1.) Central-city job losses surpassed those of the previous six decades, while white-majority suburbs gained 29 percent of the blue collar jobs, and 67 percent of white-collar jobs relocated to the suburbs (Muller, 1981).

Stanback's data for the period ending 1987 confirmed the trends reported by Muller. He noted that one useful measure of the growth of employment in the suburbs was the increase in intrasuburban commuting, movement between the suburbs for the journey to work. This commuting type increased by 10 percent between 1960 and 1980, to a total of more than 25 million commuters (Stanback, 1991). Stanback reported that the suburbanization of employment continued in the period 1969–1987 (Table 4.1; Stanback, 1991). The annual rates of net overall employment changes for this period illustrated continued suburban gains over central cities. These gains were greater in every case but Columbus, Ohio, and half of the central cities in Stanback's study experienced very modest gains, or some loss, for the period.

The most common suburban industrial form became the industrial park, which, like retailing, served as a new nucleus for further metropolitan growth. A significant impact of these locational shifts in employment was on journey-to-work travel patterns, which are the topic of Chapter 9. Initially, suburbanites traveled from the outer cities to inner city for employment. However, as the polycentric metropolitan form evolved and more employment shifted into the outer cities, the white majority's journey to work became either a short-distance commute within a suburb or required trips between suburbs in the outer ring of metropolitan regions. The journey to work expanded for inner-city residents as the multiple nuclei of metropolitan

TABLE 4.1   Suburbanization of Employment in Selected U.S. Metropolitan Areas

	Percent change in suburban share of total jobs, 1960–1970	Employment: rates of change for city, 1969–1987	Employment: rate of change for Suburbs, 1969–1987
New York	7.1	–0.2	2.6
Chicago	15.3	0.4	4.0
Philadelphia	14.8	–1.2	2.5
Los Angeles	6.5	2.2	5.7
Atlanta	–	2.1	5.9
Boston	6.7	0.5	2.5
Cincinnati	–	1.1	3.6
Columbus	–	2.6	1.7
Dallas	5.6	3.7	6.3
Detroit	18.1	–1.0	3.2
Minneapolis	17.5	2.5	2.9
Pittsburgh	–0.3	0.2	0.6
St. Louis	18.7	–1.7	2.9
Washington, D.C.	18.7	0.6	4.3
Average	10.6	–	–

SOURCE: 1960–70 shares of total jobs are calculated from Muller, 1981, p. 121; 1969–87 rates of change are taken from Stanback, 1991, p. 8.

expansion pushed farther and farther away from central cities. The spatial mismatch for inner-city job seekers held two costs. Relocated suburban jobs meant minimum access to job openings in distant locations and, for those inner-city residents fortunate to secure a suburban job, longer, more costly daily commutes.

Summary of the Free-Market Technological View.   The considerable historical period of U.S. urban growth and development prior to World War II was marked early by pioneer spirit, rugged individualism, and risk taking. Coupled with this spirit, technological innovation transformed the United States from a series of eastern colonies to a nation of growing small towns and cities that continuously changed the location of the American frontier. The Industrial Revolution quickly transformed the American economy into a global industrial power. Industrial cities became the center of a new U.S. power base and created a new urban form. Factories became the magnets for European immigrants and then for aspiring racial minorities. Part of the new urban form included European ethnic ghettos and "negro districts," which were the places of severe poverty and pestilence. Although social activists lobbied for improvements in such environments, a new class of urban thinkers—planners, academics, architects, and engineers—focused on different urban concerns, planning new efficient cities and explaining urban patterns and processes. The ecological model of the city became the focus of free-market thinkers in academia and planning, explaining urban growth and expansion through the application of the natural concepts of physical science. Particular social concepts, social fluidity and the moral character of the system, became part of organic explanations that persisted for another generation.

Suburbanization started prior to World War II but accelerated greatly afterward, begging explanation and creating new planning concerns. Suburbanization was explained by free-market thinkers as part of the natural order of things in a free economy. Restructuring and relocations occurred as population and economic benefits increased due to the growth of the economy. Private investment, not periodic government spending and intervention, was seen as the backbone of the free-market economy. Investors carefully choose the projects that pay the highest returns. Individual entrepreneurs and corporations must be sensitive to the economic forces that can result in profit or failure. The free-market vision of metropolitan growth argues that urban expansion is the logical outcome of economic forces to which a free society responds. More growth and more disposable income lead to higher aspirations for all economic classes, the desire to improve living space, personal pleasure, and financial security.

In a capitalist society, it is natural for corporations to seek better locational strategies, including access to well-trained workers and an attractive physical setting close to a full range of services. As a result, agglomeration economies developed and sustained themselves by competing with old downtowns. Their development is well balanced, attracting retailing, high-value housing, clean industry, and broadly based services to meet workers' needs. Thus, a variety of free-market forces have yielded a new post–World War II metropolitan landscape wherein urban functions and employment have relocated to maximize efficiency and environmental quality. Spatial reorganization under free-market conditions has resulted in different lifestyles in different locations. Unfortunately, due to a changing, technologically dependent service economy, skill requirements are ever more demanding but result in higher wages. Taken together, the forces of restructuring and urban expansion predictably have created places of wealth and places of poverty. But there is hope. Periodic government intervention in the form of federal and state programs is designed to rebuild inner-city places, to make them more attractive to business and industry. Yet other programs are designed to improve the welfare and employability of those left behind through training programs designed to teach skills that are in demand. The unemployed can become employable. Many such programs are devised for targeted areas of the inner city. The government has also created programs designed to assist young inner-city students to succeed in school and aspire to higher education. These are the building blocks for a better, more productive life in a fair society. The free-market system has sufficient compassion to help all Americans achieve a decent lifestyle in an increasingly equitable society.

Part II: A Postmodern-Marxist
Explanation of Urban Growth and Restructuring

Chapter 3 presented Marable's position on the "iron fist of capitalism" and its consequences for all Americans, especially blacks. His view maintained that the capitalist elite exploit workers in order to unfairly extract capital that generates continuous profits for themselves. Labor and space are commodities exploited under capitalism. Individual greed leads to depersonalization of markets and people and to a large range of exploitive actions.

It is fairly easy to see how Marxists could use the victimization of minorities reported in Chapter 2 as examples of capitalist exploitation. Beyond slavery we can certainly describe as exploitive the victimization of Mexicans, using their cheap labor to expand agricultural lands and then forcing them home during economic downturns, and the abusive treatment of the Chinese in California, using their labor to build the transcontinental railroad and various industries and then restricting their locations and movements while prohibiting additional Asian immigrants, including their spouses. The treatment of European immigrants living in Lower East Side New York is more of the same. Marxism would predict the government's actions in such cases to be either complacent or contributory, unless sufficient social pressure required a short-term appeasement action. When racism can be used to turn one group of workers against another group, such as workers' attacks in California on the Chinese, it serves the purpose of redirecting anger away from the system that caused the problem in the first place.

Urban space plays a primary role in the Marxist explanation of urbanization and suburbanization. Theories of spatial relations under capitalism have been forwarded by Marx and Friedrich Engels and by some leading urbanists of the twentieth century (e.g., Harvey, 1973). Others have accepted some of the Marxist explanations but stress views that allow for social and political action short of rebellion to change the negative consequences of a capitalist economy. One of the most recent alternatives to the technological free-market framework was forwarded by an urban and critical social theorist, Edward J. Soja. He suggests a postmodern position that incorporates Marxist explanations of urban space but departs from the Marxist solution.

A Postmodern-Marxist View of Urban Patterns and Processes
Soja believes that Marxism offers useful insights into the processes of industrialization and the creation of industrial city spaces. For Soja (2000), industrial city patterns are not due to mass migrations into bulging urban centers. Rather, urbanization in this period of industrial city formation involved new spatial processes that involved a metamorphosis of people and the urban landscape. Process, pattern, and human relationships required changes. The drastic alterations in production processes, away from hand labor toward

machine labor, and a new dependence on an industrial labor force required a new system of controls, both for disciplining labor and for maintaining social and spatial cohesion. The capitalist nation emerged for that purpose and linked state, region, and urban center, creating the centralized control of production (Soja, 2000).

Soja criticized the theoretical underpinnings of the ecological model of urban expansion and its derivatives. He dismissed their "simplistic notions" in the application of physical concepts and accepted the Marxist position that, once the "bourgeoisie" gained control of the industrial city, "the dense inner city became the home of the working class and still another vital component of industrial capitalism, . . . the 'reserve army' of unemployed and casual laborers" (p. 80). The capitalist industrial city indeed contained a CBD and a zonation of classes. However, within the ring of the working-class laborers operated new spatial processes. Intentional urban slums were the result of the spatial planning of capitalists, who desired them as forms of social control. In short, space was not only a commodity to be bought and sold under capitalism. It was a tool for capitalists seeking to control a new industrial labor force created by capitalism. The zone of working-class neighborhoods adjacent to the factories permitted social control. The location of the "reserved army" nearby served as a labor threat to the workers and as a reserve pool of labor when economic booms necessitated their use.

Soja also acknowledged the macroeconomic cycles of capitalism—the boom-and-bust periods, decades of high growth rates followed by low- or no-growth periods, that erupt into crisis and efforts to return to higher growth rates. Economic restructuring occurred in phases of U.S. economic expansion and recession, including the economic boom associated with the rise of large corporations, monopolies, and imperialism just before the Great Depression. These also included the "Fordist-Keynesian" phase of capital development, which involved mass production, mass marketing, and mass consumption on one hand and suburbanization and an increasingly large federal role in welfare and market stimulation on the other. Soja's position accepts institutional and government regulation as an explanation for bridging capitalist crises, such as when production exceeds demand. It also suggests that production and demand become linked through particular systems. Fordism, described as methods of industrial organization and a labor system, became tied to both mass production and the limited skills of early European immigrants to the United States, resulting in high levels of both production and consumption (Knox and Pinch, 2000). The government's role is key. This was expressed by Paul Knox and Steven Pinch (2000), who described the key timing and the Keynesian principle:

> After the Second World War, however, there emerged a system which, for a quarter of a century, seemed to create a relatively harmonious relationship between

production and consumption. This period is often called the "long boom" or Golden Age of Fordism. Underpinning this time period was a government policy known as Keynesianism. . . . [Keynes] argued that governments should intervene to regulate the booms and slumps in times of recession to create more effective demand for private goods and services . . . the economy was greatly stimulated by government spending on the interstate and intra-urban highway systems. These new roads enabled urban dwellers to decentralize out of inner-city areas into surrounding low-density suburban areas. This resulted in greater distances between home, work and centres for shopping and therefore greatly boosted the automobile industry. The construction industry was also kept busy building new suburban dwellings . . . [p. 34].

These authors also note Harvey's contention that suburbanization amounted to a change in a capital investment pattern that benefited the elite in two ways. One, mass consumerism (materialism), amounted to a fetish that was meant to be a material display of wealth. The second advantage involved the fact that the average American accumulated debt, which made him or her complacent, thus contributing to the stability of the capitalist system (Knox and Pinch, 2000; Harvey, 1978).

By the 1970s, the United States faced global and domestic problems that resulted in national economic crises and near disaster for many cities. An oil embargo, combined with double-digit inflation, increasing global competition, labor unrest, increasing production costs, and failure to adequately reinvest at home, led to financial crises. Unemployment rose, tax receipts fell, deficit spending became a habit by the 1980s, and some cities faced bankruptcy. These crises led to urban restructuring efforts. Since then, according to Soja, major changes in urban form have occurred, and the urban form has induced additional changes in human and institutional behaviors. Specifically, capital-induced suburbanization led to government-sponsored "urban renewal" efforts. Further, urban restructuring took on many forms and was uneven over geographic space, time, and scale. The result is a set of complex urban patterns that vary place to place in the United States.

To get a clearer understanding from a Marxist perspective of how urban space became organized under capitalism and then was reorganized, it is worthwhile to summarize some of Harvey's views, especially as they relate to ghetto formation and housing problems spawned by the capitalist system. Neil Smith also provides a Marxist interpretation of gentrification processes after urbanization began.

A Marxist View of Urban Spatial Structure and the Ghetto.   In discussing ghetto formation in American cities, David Harvey contrasted the approach of the Chicago School with the framework of Engels. He argued that the descriptive theory of land use presented by Burgess and others was flawed by its emphasis on ecological and social concepts (adaptation, competition, etc.) and by reasoning that linked the "moral order" of society to that model. Harvey believed that the lack of an economic context for this ecological model led to ignorance of the "social solidarity" that the free market system created. Harvey noted Engels's much earlier explanation for urban-ecological zonation and found it "far more consistent with hard economic and social realities" (Harvey, 1973, p. 133). For Engels, social solidarity had nothing to do with the "moral order" and everything to do with the economic system. The inescapable "miseries of the city were an inevitable concomitant to an evil and avaricious capitalist system" (Engels quoted in Harvey, p. 133). The spatial organization of the city, including ghettos, resulted from the system of market exchange and, according to Engels, kills the weak individual.

... the brutal indifference, the unfeeling isolation of each in his private interest becomes the more repellent and offensive, the more these individuals are crowded together in a limited space.

The dissolution of mankind into monads, of which each one has a separate principle, the world of atoms, is here carried out to its utmost extreme. ... Hence it comes too, that the social war, the war of each against all, is here openly declared ... people regard each other only as useful objects; each exploits the other, and the end of it all is, that the stronger tread the weaker under foot, and that the powerful few, the capitalists, seize everything for themselves, while to the weak many, scarcely a bare existence remains ... [Engels, quoted in Harvey, pp. 131–132].

The impacts of individualism and personal initiative are exactly opposite those recognized by the free-market perspective. In this case, individualism is seen to breed unhealthy competition and results in exploitive behavior. Under capitalism, technology is the tool manipulated by the industrial elite and is used not to create new, better-paying jobs for workers nor social equality and justice but, rather, greater efficiencies and higher profits for the few. Education, like technology, is a tool of the elite. As such, it does nothing to improve the living conditions of the poor, who are mere objects used to facilitate the desires of the wealthy.

This form of Marxism sees conventional theory as serving the interests of capitalists. For Marxists, its only value lies in identifying what must be destroyed. Harvey summarized conventional urban land-use theory and critiqued it for its ability merely to identify mechanisms that are problems created by capitalism. The mechanism of competitive bidding is an example. Accessibility and centrality explain businesses' willingness to bid high for land in the city center. Centrality is the key to industrial and commercial success because location provides maximum accessibility to necessary goods, services, and employees and thereby maximizes potential profits. There are, however, other cost considerations for residential space. With increasing demand for industrial labor in the city center, Harvey argued that the poor, unable to pay transit cost related to urban expansion, have to reside on expensive downtown land, which can be achieved only through crowding into rooming houses that reduced the per-person cost of rent (Harvey, 1973). The wealthy, in contrast, because they have surplus resources, can afford transit costs and therefore can locate in the outer city when they desire to do so. They also can afford to relocate in the city center by enforcing their "preferences over a poor group because . . . [they have] more resources to apply either to transport costs or to obtaining land" (p. 135). Thus, under capitalism, the wealthy have complete locational choice and the power to exercise it whenever they wish.

Given the suburbanization of employment, logically the poor should follow employment to the suburbs. Harvey argues that they could not because of the existence of control mechanisms imposed by the wealthy. Mechanisms such as "exclusive residential zoning" served to control the location of the poor and racial minorities, keeping them out of exclusively white high-income neighborhoods. Finally, Harvey noted the contradictions of inherently flawed capitalism that led to the inevitable failure of liberal policies, including subsidized transportation, "black capitalism," and urban renewal, all rooted in erroneous assumptions.

For Harvey, then, conventional theories and solutions that arise from this economic system are worthless for social justice purposes. Theories (including classical economist Richard Muth's) predict that the disenfranchised and poor will reside in residential space that is unaffordable to them. This is no more than "an indicator of the problem" (the results of competitive bidding for land) (Harvey, 1973, p. 137) and suggests the necessity of revolutionary action:

> Our objective is to eliminate ghettos. Therefore, the only valid policy with respect to this objective is to eliminate the conditions which give rise to the truth of the theory. In other words, we wish the von Thunen theory of the urban land market [according to which, land is allocated through competitive bidding] to become *not* true. The simplest approach here is to eliminate those mechanisms which serve to generate the theory [Harvey, p. 137].

Another basic control mechanism Harvey discussed is scarcity, which he maintains is used to control prices in a capitalist economy. If the availability of a resource is controlled such that it appears unavailable but in demand, then an inflated, controlled price can be maintained for the product or service. According to Harvey, scarcity is required for a capitalistic economy to function and, thus, must be eliminated to bring an end to the capitalist economy. The challenge of its destruction lies in dealing with all of the institutions that support it.

In an advanced productive society, such as the United States, the major barrier to eliminating scarcity lies in the complicated set of interlocking institutions (financial, judicial, political, educational, and so on) which support the market process [Harvey, 1973, p. 140].

Harvey applies the same analytical framework to understanding the poor housing quality of ghettos and extends the argument that social policy rooted in capitalism must fail. In this case, it is rent that explains the contradictions within the capitalist free-market system. Why, in the same ghetto neighborhoods, are high rents paid for inferior-quality housing and overcrowded quarters, while residential units stand vacant and abandoned there? The answer is geography—location within the capitalist space economy. Harvey notes that high rents in the ghetto do not result in high landlord profits. Rather, the explanation lies in the contradictions of the capitalist economy. A flaw in the economic system is the culprit that leads to this apparent disconnect and causes inevitable tensions. In the free market the business sector must maximize returns on investments. There are also tax-base necessities for local governments. These lead to the necessity of rents corresponding to locational expectations, or as Harvey states it, rents must be "consistent with location" (Harvey, 1973, p. 140). We are back to competitive bidding and its consequences, which include high rent for poor quality, crowded housing, and abandonment. According to Harvey, Engels predicted an impasse in treating housing problems in capitalist economies and argued that the tensions these problems create inevitably lead to production declines and other negative outcomes. Harvey quoted Engels as follows:

The growth of the big modern cities gives the land in certain areas, particularly those which are centrally situated, an artificial and colossally increasing value; the buildings erected on these areas depress this value, instead of increasing it, because they no longer correspond to the changed circumstances. They are pulled down and replaced by others. This takes place above all with workers' houses which are situated centrally and whose rents, even with the greatest overcrowding, can never, or only very slowly, increase above a certain maximum. They are pulled down and in their stead shops, warehouses, and public buildings are erected [Engels, quoted in Harvey, 1973, p. 142].

Harvey then adds:

This process (which is clearly apparent in every contemporary city) results from the necessity to realize a rate of return on a parcel of land which is consistent with its location rent. It does not necessarily have any thing to do with facilitating production [p. 142].

Harvey, like Engels, addressed the issue of social ills generated by poor-quality housing and the living environment it provides. He sees the bour-geoisie's policy responses as self-serving and of no significant impact on the poor. In fact, Harvey noted, Engels used the Haussmann method to describe capitalist motives and outcomes: Capitalists simply move the societal prob-lem around geographically and praise themselves in the process for cleaning up a social ill. Harvey again relies on the words of Engels to capture the process that he believes operates in the free-market system:

> . . . the result is everywhere the same; the scandalous alleys disappear to the ac-companiment of lavish self-praise from the bourgeoisie on account of this tremendous success, but they appear again immediately somewhere else and of-ten in the immediate neighborhood! . . . The breeding places of disease, the infa-mous holes and cellars in which the capitalist mode of production confines our workers night after night, are not abolished; they are merely *shifted elsewhere!* The economic necessity that produced them in the first place produces them in the next place also [Engels, quoted in Harvey, 1973, p. 143].

It is clear from Harvey's presentation that the ghetto and other poor working-class neighborhoods cannot be improved by investment. It may grow the national economy and create better technology, but this does not benefit the masses. The system has no intention of improving the plight of the working and lower classes. Rather, workers are commodities to be controlled and manipulated for the purpose of profits. No amount of education and technology can heal a system that is inherently flawed by contradictions that result from its mode of production and use of space. Harvey, then, sees as a necessity the rejection of the very ideas that the system produces, including the notions that investment will improve technology and education and somehow level the playing field for all Americans in the future. Such are the self-serving statements of the power elite, who control the masses through so-cial and economic mechanisms that benefit the few. One of these mechanisms, as noted earlier, is the restriction of living space by the nation's poor, disen-franchised, and minority groups. Social and spatial mechanisms are the tools of the haves used to control and manipulate the have-nots. This is the race-place connection for Marxism. Social policy arising from the evils of capital-ism will never solve the problems they create. If the playing field is to be lev-eled and the ghettos eradicated and if urban America's social injustices and inequalities are to be eliminated, then the answer lies in a "commitment to revolutionary practice" (Harvey, 1973, p. 146).

A Marxist Explanation of Suburbanization and Gentrification.   Earlier, we briefly noted Harvey's explanation of suburbanization. The Marxist frame-work also was offered by Neil Smith (1986) to explain U.S. suburban patterns and urban gentrification efforts since World War II. He noted that the "limited class struggle" since the Cold War has resulted in capitalism's "free hand in structuring and restructuring space" (p. 356). Smith linked the urban restructuring efforts of the 1970–1980 period to the global economic crises of the 1970s and argued that, when the industrial sector suffers decline in profit rates due to such crises, it logically moves capital to the built environment (same argument as Harvey, 1978). Since profit rates are higher from investments in construction during such times, there is a "cyclical movement of capital," in this case, back to the inner city. Smith argued that the action is rooted in the "timing of the rent gap" and, rather than being accidental, is an "integral part of capital accumulation related to the boom and bust cycles that create crises" (p. 346). Postwar decentralization in the form of suburbanization, then, resulted from the growth of capital and the desire to maximize profits. Urban restructuring of selected inner-city locations, he explains, resulted from the changes in "ground rent structure."

> The outward movement of capital to develop suburban, industrial, residential, commercial, and recreational activity results in a reciprocal change in suburban and inner-city ground-rent levels. Where the price of suburban land rises with the spread of new construction, the relative price of inner-city land falls. . . . This results in what we have called a rent-gap in the inner city between the actual ground rent capitalized from the present (depressed) land use and the potential rent that could be capitalized from the "highest and best" use (or at least a "higher and better" use), given the central location. This suburbanization occurs in consort with structural changes in advanced economies. . . . Where it is allowed to run its course at the behest of the free market, it leads to the substantial abandonment of inner-city properties. . . .
>
> At the most basic level, it is the movement of capital into the construction of new suburban landscapes and the consequent creation of a rent-gap that create the economic opportunity for restructuring the central and inner cities. The devalorization of capital in the center creates the opportunity for the revalorization of this "under-developed" section of urban space [Smith, 1986, pp. 23–24].

For Smith, urban restructuring is also influenced by government actions. Government intervention is designed to assist the elite, in this case by assuming all early risks through federal expenditures that guarantee a "comfort" level for additional private investments in a range of restructuring efforts. The result of these processes is very uneven development patterns that highlight the winners and losers in urban America. One result identified by Smith is that American inner cities contain both ghettos and "bourgeois playgrounds" that contribute to class struggles (Smith, 1986). This explanation, like Harvey's observation of high-rent crowded housing standing next to vacant and abandoned housing in the ghetto, suggests that apparent contradictions exist

within the free market that allow the poor, especially minorities, to suffer unnecessarily due to greed.

The Postmodern Departure from the Marxist Framework

In the preface to a recent text, *Postmetropolis: Critical Studies of Cities and
Regions*, Soja (2000) explained that his focus is on what has changed the
most and is most different about contemporary urban process and pattern.
He termed his approach "eclectic postmodern" and added that, while this
perspective benefited greatly from Marxist principles, it was influenced also
by the varied approaches of critical studies. Soja's self-defined approach includes the intentions of producing useful knowledge that can make the world
a better place while promoting political action that leads to eradicating inequalities between the races, social classes, and genders.

Soja applied Marxist reasoning to explain urbanization's evolution in the
context of the "industrial capitalist city." Like Harvey and Smith, Soja rejected the ecological and transportation-technology arguments for decentralization, finding the Marxist argument more logical and cogent. He saw inequalities, spatial and racial, as outcomes of an unfair system. He agreed
with the Marxist position that the journey to work became an important cost
and equity issue as suburbanization continued through the 1960s and 1970s,
because of the ability of city institutions to manipulate location and infrastructure to the ruling class's benefit. Soja cited Harvey's work in describing
the inevitability of inequalities due to the nature of the capitalist urban-
industrial process and the inability of public planning to rectify this reality.
He agreed with Harvey that the urban capitalist system requires both pro-
tecting previous capital investment in urban centers and destroying it when
necessary to create a place for new accumulation (Harvey, 1973). Results favor the elite and cause other groups to be disenfranchised and marginalized.

Although he accepted the leading principles of Marxism, Soja also argued that a "more complex" set of processes operated during the era of
massive urban restructuring. He maintained that these processes resulted in
complex urban patterns and processes that are difficult to analyze due to
incomplete urban theory. This unwillingness to assign all urban spatial patterns to Marxist theory contributes to postmodern, eclectic argument (Soja,
2000). He noted, for example, that the simultaneous processes of "deterri-
torialization," the lessening of sentiment toward place, and "reterritorial-
ization," the creation of new places, are occurring and that they "are producing human geographies that are significantly different and more
complex from those we have recognized in the past" (Soja, 2000, p. 152).
Soja separated himself from the traditional left and right by anchoring his
postmodern concern with "improvements in the here and now" (p. 283).
Within the context of inequalities, which have intensified in recent decades,
he differentiates his views from both traditions.

In terms of systemic inequalities, Soja's critical analysis of Los Angeles included a chapter on the "Fractal City." His use of this concept was based on his belief in its utility for describing the "restructured social mosaic, . . . the combined and interactive spatiality and sociality of the postmetropolis" (p. 283). Soja examined various aspects of inequality among racial and ethnic groups in Los Angeles since its tremendous transformation from a WASP-dominated population to the mosaiclike "ethnic quilt" of the 1990s, including income polarities, ethnic niches in the labor market, and residential space. Related to his self-defined purposes and the position that he claims differentiates postmodern, cultural critiques from other approaches, Soja intended to provide knowledge that is useful and action oriented. He argued that the polarities of black-white and rich-poor and other issues, especially within the context of political action, are too limited and fail to achieve social justice. Rather, "adaptive strategies" are necessary for successful action. These include a "new cultural politics" that will focus "around more cross-cutting and inclusive foundations of solidarity, collective consciousness, and coalition building" and that "most effectively combine the oppressions of class, race and gender" (Soja, 2000, p. 279).

Soja's message was that documented inequalities demand policy. However, because counterforces have such power and social justice movements have been so disjointed, effective policy has been difficult to achieve. His "new cultural politics" suggests confronting equity issues not by fostering individualized struggles but rather by searching out collective issues and creating effective "spatial struggles" on a regional and local basis. His discussion closes with hope based on a particular brand of political activism:

A third group of activists, also feeling abandoned by the established order, has responded not by withdrawal or reactionary violence but with reinvigorated efforts to assert the power of local and non-governmental community movements and a more progressively insurgent civil society. Out of these developments, slowly but surely, there is emerging a more spatially conscious network of creative resistance and redirection with regard to the new urbanization processes, an active practice of a progressive cultural politics of place, space, and region that consciously crosses and disrupts existing boundaries of class, race, gender, and locality to deal with the specific injustices and inequities embedded in the restructured urban-regional milieu [Soja, 2000, pp. 406–407].

Thus, Marxism blended with a postmodern framework creates a view of urban restructuring and the human enterprise that is very different from that of free-market technologists. It characterizes the free-market, capitalist approach as purely exploitive and driven by profit for capital accumulation. The control and use of space are crucial within this theory of spatial relations. To ensure that profit continues at high rates for society's elite, capitalists protect investments and then, at critical junctures, move them around geographically in the form of urban restructuring. They also deliberately maintain a reserved labor pool through controls that lead to an unemployed subculture, the paupers. Minorities and women are also marginalized in the same process. Race-place and class-based inequalities persist because capitalists require that it be so. The hope of women and minorities, like the working class and the poor, lies in changes in the capitalist enterprise through collective action that avoids violence. For postmodernist followers like Soja there is hope through the construction of a new cultural politics within a spatial framework. However, only if we are aware of the flaws inherent in capitalism and the misery it creates can we desire actions necessary for change in the here and now.

It is very clear that these two perspectives differ greatly on the nature and role of capitalism in the expansion of urbanism and in the treatment of the working-class poor, the unemployable, and racial minorities. They also differ in their views of racism and how it can be cured. Perhaps more important for the purpose of this chapter, they view the nature and use of urban geographic space very differently. The free-market proponents see geographic space as a commodity, having positive and negative attributes that attract or repel buyers. Initially, centrally located space provided advantages for businesses that competitively bid for its use. As urban centers expanded, space and its friction of distance was something to be overcome by technology, which permitted the wealthy to move away from congested centers to outlying areas. With postwar suburbanization, outlying spaces were filled because of their positive attractions (once found in inner cities), accessibility to transport links and related business (spatial affinity), prestigious sites, nearby high-rent neighborhoods, and the economic advantages related to relatively inexpensive property and taxation. In addition, the government provided subsidies of various sorts for particular projects that reduced costs. Thus, it was a "natural" process that households and businesses fled to suburbia, eventually resulting in competing suburban downtowns and a metropolitan system characterized by older cities in trouble and a ring of thriving suburban centers.

The postmodern-Marxist viewpoint differs greatly from the free-market one. From the Marxist point of view, space is not something with attributes but, rather, a tool of the elite. People were herded and deliberately retained in the city center in early industrialization as a control mechanism to maintain a new labor force and a reserve labor pool. The result is ghettoization. Other capitalist tools of social and spatial control take many forms. The control offered by exclusionary zoning, for example, restricted minorities and the poor from certain places. Space, like most things, is totally within the control of the elite, who because of their superior resources can at any time select the space they wish to use and value. In the period of decentralization, the power elite decided to place capital in suburbia, but at any time they can and do move capital around to serve their economic needs. This is why gentrification goes on in certain periods and not in others, as well as in certain places and not others. Even when postmodernists argue that complex urban processes complicate the understanding of the contemporary urban system, they do not take issue with the fact that the capitalists control what is invested where. They also agree that capitalism, by design, exploits the working class and controls geographic space for the purpose of profit.

Beyond the location of capital investment and space, however, lies a major difference in perceptions of people and the role of the individual in society. The free-market approach places great emphasis on the individual, his or her talent and contribution to society. From this point of view, the individual matters in that individual initiative, which is sparked by competition, means something. Namely, rewards come to those who work hard, are intelligent, and invest wisely. The wealthy get wealthy and stay wealthy because of individual abilities and actions. Further, in the capitalist system, anyone can succeed because everyone has the equal opportunity to do so. Those who are born to disadvantage can use government support to improve their economic situations. The free-market approach also, therefore, places great emphasis on the importance of developing technology and educating the workforce. The poor, the ghetto dwellers, and others who are not doing well, can improve their lot through persistence, hard work, and education. The government offers them assistance to do so. Minorities of all colors have succeeded and left behind poverty and inner-city ghettos. These are role models to be emulated.

For the Marxist, there are only two kinds of people under capitalism, the elite (exploiters) and everyone else (the exploited). Capitalists have only one goal, the accumulation of profits. They abuse the working class through various control mechanisms that are supported by the institutions of the free-market system. Individuals are turned against one another, forced or inspired to compete for survival. Racism emerges and is maintained under this economic system as another control mechanism. The problem lies, then, in the mode of production, which treats labor (people) as a commodity. People are depersonalized and have no value except to produce profits for the wealthy. Citizens work out of self-interest or to survive.

Finally, it is not surprising that free marketers and Marxists see very different solutions to U.S. race-place problems. The free marketers call for more investment, more technology, and a better-educated workforce to ease racial tensions and to improve the economy for all Americans. They also suggest that government intervention should occur on an as-needed basis, a last resort. They argue that life has already improved for most Americans, including minorities, and will continue to do so if we just do the right things. More economic development will further reduce racism and ghetto living, and perhaps eliminate it entirely. For Marxists, government itself is the problem because it represents the elite. Government policy under capitalism will not benefit the working class and poor. Postmodernists separate themselves from Marxists at this stage and suggest a different type of politics, such as Soja's cultural politics, which emphasizes hope for changing the here and now.

Perhaps the different explanations of the government's roles in shaping urban policies and the different assessments of policy effectiveness on segregation and uneven development best characterize the gulf between the two perspectives. Clearly, policies that will deal effectively with housing and employment discrimination and that improve living conditions in minority concentrations are badly needed. We will have more to say about policy in Chapter 10.

Chapter 5

Minority and Nonminority Concentrations

Differentiating Between Race-and-Place-Based Inequalities in Urban America*

Introduction

In previous chapters, we have touched on the long history of black, Hispanic, and Asian settlements across the United States and the discrimination that each group has endured. We have also suggested that racism led to the segregation of U.S. minorities. Segregation in housing and discrimination in the workplace are believed to be the main culprits in the evolution of racial inequalities of all types. Varying assimilation patterns have been suggested as determinants of the high levels of segregation observed among these groups. However, the existence of minority concentrations in various parts of the country, especially in urbanized areas, is not solely the result of slow assimilation rates. It is also an outcome of the conscious efforts of institutions and individuals to separate themselves from other people who are different on the basis of color, class, ethnicity, or other sociological dimensions. Some groups are also separated from employment sources and services that they may require or desire in their neighborhoods.

Segregation, like racism, is sometimes viewed as a "natural" process; it is just what people do and have a right to do. Unfortunately, such a view is considerably naive and ignores racism's profound impacts on and long-term consequences for American society as a whole. In the 1960s, the protests, civil disobedience, riots, and finally, federal intervention via civil rights laws signaled an attempt to tackle some of these problems. However, such laws have generally

---

*This chapter is coauthored by Blair Tinker, University of Virginia.

failed, for a variety of reasons, to stop the discriminatory behaviors that continue to keep segregation in place. In this chapter, we will examine the relevance of segregation to equity issues and the resultant outcomes in urban America, including at the beginning of the current century. The chapter is divided into four sections: (1) segregation, including the policies designed to redress it, and the differential attitudes toward governmental intervention; (2) supportive evidence from several empirical studies to confirm some of the spatial inequalities of group segregation; (3) a brief review of studies that document the changes that are currently taking place within minority concentrations; (4) an analysis of forty urbanized areas to visualize and statistically identify variables that best differentiate the minority concentrations from the white-majority urban subregions in the United States. This analysis offers new insights into the multicultural, multiracial nature of U.S. cities at the close of the twentieth century by focusing on Hispanic and black concentrations in urban counties.

Segregation

Public Policy and Segregation

Different opinions exist with regard to the impact that public policy has had on changing segregation in the United States. Policymakers often defend their actions by citing laws aimed at decreasing segregation and housing discrimination. Cases in which public policy has decreased segregation have usually come in the form of equal housing legislation. For example, the Home Mortgage Disclosure Act (HMDA) and the Community Reinvestment Act (CRA) are two key pieces of anti-discrimination legislation that have been implemented in the past. Unfortunately, however, some of these public policies have also been blamed for directly increasing segregation. Public housing projects and upward mobility programs are two areas that have received a large portion of the blame from minority leaders and public policy makers in recent years. Many of these programs focus on removing a select few individuals or families from the "ghetto" and integrating them into nicer, usually "white" neighborhoods. Although the program usually does give some minority families a better environment and improves integration in some areas, some blacks have complained that they feel cut off from the rest of black society. Many leaders also feel that these programs ignore the larger problems of the "ghetto" and succeed only in siphoning off the more educated and ambitious minority residents, leaving the rest behind and thus continuing long-term segregation (Neuman, 1994).

Public housing has also received a share of the blame for continuing high levels of segregation. Historically, such housing projects have been located in racially segregated areas. Local officials determine the placement of high-density, authority-owned, high-rise residential buildings. More often than not, the desire to keep the voting white public's favor dictates that these projects be located in previously demolished "ghetto" areas, rather than in economically sound "white" areas. In fact, public housing–authority designation depends on a locale requesting such a designation, which is not likely to occur in white suburbia. Thus, the segregating effects of public housing are dramatic. The housing projects contribute not only to existing minority segregation but also to concentration of poverty (Dreier, 1991; Massey, 2000; Neeno, 1996; W. J. Wilson, 1996).

White Attitudes and Segregation

When examining issues related to segregation, it is necessary to include the attitudes of the white public and their role in creating racial dichotomies in U.S. society. Several studies in recent years have examined the impact of residential segregation patterns on accessibility to potential employment, housing choice, and quality education, and whites' attitudes and opinions toward segregation and governmental efforts to integrate the races. For example, in a study examining the difference in primary and secondary school segregation between 1968, 1980, and 1988, Steven Rivkin (1994) found that the school district policy played a very small role in school segregation rates. Rather, Rivkin attributed most of the segregation present in the schools to residential segregation patterns. This implies that, even when school districts change policy in an attempt to increase integration, areas with high residential segregation will continue segregating their children at school (Rivkin, 1994; Ferguson, 2000).

Given that white attitudes toward minorities do play a significant role in how segregated a minority group will be, it is promising to know that Farley and Frey (1993) found that black segregation had decreased in most of the metropolitan areas that they studied. They attributed part of this decline to changing white attitudes. Using the concept of a "tipping point," or the number of minorities who enter a neighborhood before a white resident leaves, they found that white flight was decreasing. Results of interviews conducted with whites in 1976 and 1992 indicated that, for whites to feel uncomfortable, the number of blacks in a neighborhood had to be significantly higher in 1992. The tipping point seemed to increase, as well. Despite these improvements, Farley and Frey (1993) are quick to point out that blacks are still very highly segregated in U.S. communities. Howenstine (1996), however, argued that decreased black segregation in Chicago was not due to changing white attitudes nor improved black social mobility. Rather, he contended, out-migration of whites coupled with the in-migration of Hispanics explained the lower segregation rates.

Bobo (2000) has characterized post–civil rights era racial attitudes as improved in some ways but clearly divisive. He summarized a number of recent trends in attitudes and racial relations that, for example, indicate "positive changes in attitude toward principles of equality and integration" (p. 273). However, he also noted the gap, sometimes an increasing one, between black and white beliefs and attitudes regarding such things as institutional discrimination (such as by banks) and perceptions of community race relations, where the proportion of blacks rating race relations as "poor" was double that of whites (p. 285). Bobo cited a number of studies that support the findings reported in earlier chapters, namely, that middle-class blacks are becoming increasingly disillusioned with white attitudes and behaviors related to racism. Bobo concluded that a new American "free market ideology of racism" may have taken hold. It is more subtle than the old, pre–civil rights era form but perhaps as dangerous to future race relations. The new ideological attitude moves us no closer to racial equality, because, like its predecessor, it rejects the "common humanity" among the races:

> . . . the tenacious institutionalized disadvantages and inequalities created . . . are now popularly accepted and condoned under a modern free-market or laissez-faire racist ideology. This new ideology incorporates negative stereotypes of Blacks; a preference for individualistic, and rejection of structural, accounts of racial inequality . . . [Bobo, 2000, p. 292].

Institutional Racism, Discrimination, and Segregation

The long histories of government and private-sector efforts to maintain racial segregation, as noted earlier, are well documented. The 1968 fair housing laws were landmarks that made redlining (drawing a geographic boundary around neighborhoods that are not loan worthy due to "risk" factors) an illegal act. Despite this fact, housing discrimination continued unabated in an effort by banks and realtors to minimize risks and maximize profits through discriminatory practices such as steering (guiding buyers to "acceptable neighborhoods") and redlining (Bullard, Grisby, and Lee, 1994a; Massey and Denton, 1988). Under pressure, the U.S. Congress passed the Home Mortgage Disclosure Act (HMDA) in 1975 and the Community Reinvestment Act (CRA) in 1977. Generally, these were designed to expand the area covered by the Federal Housing Act (FHA). Specifically, HMDA was designed as a tool for the public to help determine whether financial institutions were serving community needs and to disclose potential discriminatory lending practices. Lending institutions, including banks and credit unions, are required to file reports about home-improvement and home-purchase loans, including applications. Those reports reflect the type of loan; financial institution information; applicant information, including location, race, gender, family size, marital status, and disability status; and loan activity, indicating whether the loan was approved or denied.

The CRA was also designed to assist the public with loan information on lending institutions. This was to help determine whether financial institutions were serving through reinvestment the communities that chartered them. Despite all of these efforts, discrimination continued in the post–Civil Rights Movement era.

Several studies of banking practices in the 1980s and 1990s examined the continuing practice of redlining. In Boston, for example, Mayor Raymond Flynn took office in 1983 and tried several programs to encourage growth in some of the city's poorer areas, including a "linkage" policy that required developers to supply money to housing funds in the areas surrounding their offices. Unfortunately, the policies initiated had little effect on the overall working of the banking system in Boston. Dreier noted the lack of economic rationality involved by bankers:

Lenders seemed to have more confidence in (and made lending easier for) speculative market-rate condos in the suburbs than affordable housing in Boston's neighborhoods, even though the delinquency rate was much higher for the upscale housing [Dreier, 1991, p. 19].

Flynn ordered an evaluation of the city's banking institutions by the Boston Redevelopment Authority (BRA) to determine if any racial disparities in mortgage acceptances and denials had occurred. At the same time, the Federal Reserve Bank was conducting a similar study of its own (see also Carr and Megbolugbe, 1994).

The studies showed similar results. The Federal Reserve study reported that white neighborhoods received 24 percent more loans, and the Flynn study showed whites getting three times as many. Both of the studies controlled for spurious variables that could have affected the results, the main difference being that the BRA study did not include government-insured loans because they did not pose any risk to the banks issuing them. The BRA also included a brief study on the number of bank branches in the white and black areas, finding that minority areas had fewer banks per capita and therefore were being underserved (Dreier, 1991, p. 21).

Other studies reported similar findings in other parts of the United States. A study of Detroit loan activity revealed similar elevated denial rates for blacks (Zack, 1992) and Squires and Velez (1996) uncovered similar trends in their study of the Milwaukee metropolitan area. What made the latter study especially interesting was the fact that, while it found black neighborhoods had high denial rates in comparison with white neighborhoods, the highest rates were found in the integrated neighborhoods. This includes areas that are not only predominantly black-Hispanic, but also those that are black-white and Hispanic-white. Their findings reinforce the concept that racially integrated neighborhoods are transitional and, therefore, somehow unstable and undesirable. As

Squires and Velez (1996) noted, this is "using the effects of past discrimination to serve as the justification for current and future discrimination in mortgage lending and the provision of financial services generally" (p. 1205). This is related to Dymski's opinion (1995) that discrimination will not disappear because personal bigotry is decreasing. Because of past personal discrimination, lenders now feel justified in practicing rational and structural discrimination on the basis that the minority neighborhoods in question have low housing values and are in disrepair. This generational equity is a real concern.

Finally, a large-scale study also was performed by Avery, Beeson, and Sniderman (1996), who examined HMDA records in their entirety to determine if racial biases existed within lending institutions. They did indeed find differences in loan denial rates for mortgages, refinancing, and home improvements between white, black, Hispanic, and Asian applicants. They also found that the location of the housing played a role in the denial rates and that discrimination likely occurred on a case-by-case basis as well. Overall, they concluded that, although the evidence was highly suggestive, the use of HMDA data alone could not determine if racial discrimination was occurring, because of the inability to control for extenuating circumstances and credit history.

Insurance Information Provision and Redlining

There are reports that similar types of activities occur within the insurance industry as well. Although there is disagreement regarding redlining in the insurance business, issues such as equitable provision of information to all racial/ethnic groups have been raised frequently. For example, the application of a 103-question telephone survey to two hundred black and Hispanic residents in five inner cities (Houston, Los Angeles, Miami, New York, and Washington, D.C.) allowed researchers to conclude that, although 96 percent of respondents had not been turned down for insurance, 50 percent felt that minorities are discriminated against when buying insurance (Smith, 1995). Beemer (1995) argued that insurance redlining in general did not occur but that the minority community's perception was that it did. He attributed much of this to the lack of advertisement by insurance companies in ethnic and racial neighborhoods. This is a very important point: Even if there is no actual insurance redlining, the fact still remains that minority communities are not supplied with adequate information and options when it comes to the purchase of insurance (Beemer, 1995). This is another type of inequality, involving procedural equity.

Another study, performed by the National Fair Housing Alliance, revealed a discrepancy in both price and service quality between black and white callers to local insurance agencies. Agency personnel supposed they could identify the callers' race by their name, voice, phone exchange, and address. The results of the study showed that the white callers were quoted $216 on average for coverage, whereas black callers were quoted $371. On top of this discrepancy, there were issues of service quality; white callers were given information on discounts and free quotes, whereas black callers were given none of this information and were generally not provided with quotes unless they had made an agreement to do business with the company (Smith, 1995).

Such findings help explain a variety of housing inequalities among American racial/ethnic neighborhoods. Massey, though acknowledging the white majority's increasing tolerance of minority neighbors in the last quarter century, noted that the white majority also retains negative attitudes and stereotypes about minorities that perpetuate the inequalities caused by segregation and isolation (Massey, 2000).

Minority Equity Issues

We introduced the term *equity* in Chapter 1 to refer to the fair distribution of risks, costs, services, and benefits across population groupings and spatial entities. Forced segregation and concentration of minorities often are accompanied by racial disparities in the distribution of services and benefits that subsequently result in spatial inequities. Such disparities include a wide range of conditions, including but not limited to employment, education, recreation, assets, and health (Kingston and Nickens, 2000; Massey, 2000; Oliver and Shapiro, 2000). There is perhaps no other area in which segregated minorities are so disadvantaged as in housing. Housing involves questions of both social and generational equity. Nonwhites often pay higher prices than whites for the same housing quality and sell property for less than the original value, resulting in lower assets. The effect can be viewed as a minority tax. Von Furstenburg, Harrison, and Horowitz (1974) reported that nonwhites spent between 40 and 70 percent more than whites for housing of similar quality. F. J. James and Tynan (1986) noted that Hispanics received less real-estate advice than others, especially in terms of information about housing affordability. L. Gordon and Mayer (1991) found that, when housing costs available to whites and nonwhites were similar, the housing quality differential favored whites and disfavored nonwhites. This inequality is passed from generation to generation because laws remain unenforced at certain times and in certain places (procedural equity).

Another characteristic that is more prevalent today than in the past is the association between joblessness and poverty in segregated minority neighborhoods. Historically, poorer neighborhoods had more poorly paying jobs. Today, the scenario is that poor neighborhoods have no jobs at all. This is Wilson's argument: Joblessness and poverty have become intertwined, creating drastic psychological effects on those who live in this type of environment. The psychological effects of joblessness, isolation, poverty, and despair are overwhelming, and their effects can be especially dramatic in the life of a child. What is important is that isolation, whether caused by Wilson's mismatch or Waldinger's ethnic employment niches, diminishes the chances for segregated children to experience positive environmental stimuli.

A popular idea among social scientists is that social isolation has negative impacts on life choices. Kempen (1997) concluded that residents in "poverty pockets" have an increasingly negative outlook that is strengthened by reduced access to jobs, social isolation, stigmatization, and limited access to social citizenship rights. In addition to having diminished access to services, people in isolated communities are found to have weak social networks (strong social ties to other communities outside their neighborhoods). Black males living in poor neighborhoods have reduced access to social and economic resources due to their weak social network (Tigges, Brown, and Green, 1998). This does not negate Steinberg's position, mentioned in Chapter 3; rather, it reinforces it (segregation via racism creates the environment that negatively influences children), thus clarifying the outcomes of the severe segregation and isolation caused by racism.

However, as demonstrated in previous chapters, segregation and inequalities also have an impact outside the inner-city ghetto, where "black culture" certainly cannot be blamed for lack of progress. Tienda and Li (1987), for example, explored the possible relationship between race, education, minority concentration of the labor market, and the potential earnings of males between the ages of sixteen and sixty-four. Their analysis contained not only the three variables in question (ethnicity, education, and minority concentration) but also a series of control variables. Their general findings support findings of anger and rage among middle-class and professional minorities (Cose, 1993). Overall, white males had the highest average income, followed by Asians, then Hispanics, and finally, earning the least, black males. Education levels also played a role in comparative annual earnings between the races. It was found that a much higher income differential existed among the highly educated than among the poorly educated. In other words, a poorly educated black man may earn the same amount as a poorly educated white man, whereas a black college graduate can expect to earn less than a white college graduate does. This seems to be a clear impediment to upward mobility.

The same study also revealed that the earnings differential between educated whites and blacks increased in highly concentrated minority areas. This was not true for Asians and Hispanics, however: Although their income levels varied with education, there was no significant difference in regard to minority concentration. In short, the study indicates that blacks were more disadvantaged than either Asians or Hispanics in 1980. The researchers believed that, through increased assimilation, many Hispanics and Asians may have closed the income gap, whereas this prospect seemed much less likely for blacks. Similar findings, such as Fainstein's (1993), illustrated income and other inequalities for African Americans as compared to whites of similar socioeconomic class and level of education, regardless of socioeconomic status (SES). Finally, J. P. Smith (2000) reported significant wage differentials for both Hispanics and blacks when compared to whites.

Other forms of minority- and place-based inequities do occur. Public services available to nonwhites are often of lesser quality and/or are more poorly maintained than those available to whites. This leads to lower satisfaction levels among blacks for public services than those among whites. Weir (1997) described the services that are most important to escaping poverty and having a good-quality life—including education, recreation, a library, and crime control—as having "deteriorated markedly" in the central city because they must be provided locally, but local officials have cut budgets that support them (p. 224).

It has been shown that spatial segregation influences service provision and therefore impacts quality of life, especially in the health care sector. Many studies demonstrate that minority access to quality health services is minimized by differential location of facilities away from inner cities and low-income neighborhoods (Collins and Hawkes, 1997; Kelley, Perloff, Morris, and Wangyue, 1993). There is also a generational equity concern: Poor health of adults leads to poor health of children (Williams, 2000).

Unlike most equity studies, which focus on a few communities, Frazier and James (1998) statistically analyzed eighty urban counties in the United States to test for inequalities between areas of minority concentration (AOMCs) and white-majority areas in the same central city and county. They demonstrated that AOMCs nationally not only have lower incomes, pay higher proportions of their incomes for rent, and experience more crowding than their white-majority counterparts but also have lower housing values (resulting in the black, or minority, tax) and receive fewer home mortgage dollars per capita than white areas. The same analysis also demonstrated that minority concentrations have less access to health care, certain government services, and several commercial services, including banks and real estate offices.

Frazier, James, and Tinker (1999) also examined the differences in HMDA denial rates from 1992 to 1995 between the AOMC and the white-majority areas of the surrounding central city and central county. The analysis was based on two counties, Cook County, Illinois, and Milwaukee County, Wisconsin. Some of the graphics are reproduced as Figure 5.1. The AOMC, recall, contains all races and is compared to the central city (minus the AOMC) and the urban county (minus the AOMC and central city). Figure 5.1(a) reveals that for Cook County, Illinois, black denial rates, after declining between 1992 and 1994, increased substantially for all three urban subregions between 1994 and 1995. The amount of home mortgage dollars loaned within the average AOMC was far less than in the other areas. Black denial rates increased more rapidly for blacks living in the AOMC than for the other racial groups for the four-year period. Further, there are major discrepancies in loan denial rates of blacks among the three subregions. The highest average denial rate for blacks in the period was in the AOMC (53 percent). This finding illustrates the plight of blacks living in Areas of Minority Concentration; one of every two applications was denied. Blacks also had the highest loan denial rates in all three areas in Cook County.

Figure 5.1(b), which reports the same types of data for Milwaukee County, Wisconsin, further supports the plight of minorities seeking loans in all three types of urban subarea. For both Cook and Milwaukee Counties, the home mortgage denial rates for blacks and whites in each subregion were higher in the last year (1995) than the first year (1992). Asians consistently experienced a decline in loan denial rates between the years 1992 and 1995 except in the central city. The percentage of loans denied were always higher in the AOMC than the central city and in the remainder of the central county for all racial groups. These results underscore the connection between race and place, on one hand, and the inequalities they represent, on the other.

Changing Minority Concentrations: The Growth of Hispanic Populations and Black-Hispanic Settlement Patterns

We noted in Chapter 2 that several actions by the U.S. government have led to increasing numbers of ethnically diverse Hispanics, especially in urban America. The implications of this recent growth and the varying location preferences of different Hispanic ethnicities seem clear. There are Hispanic settlement patterns that differ from those of other minorities, and patterns within the Hispanic community are diverse. Further, some Hispanic populations are moving into former or current African-American neighborhoods. This has led to (1) the study of differences between the various Hispanic subgroups in terms of settlement patterns and segregation levels and (2) studies of black and Hispanic residential patterns. Massey and Denton's (1988) is among the first group of studies. The authors examined segregation rates, measured against the index of dissimilarity, among Puerto Ricans, Cubans, and Mexicans, using 1980 census data. Their research confirmed that there were significant differences in segregation rates among the three Hispanic subgroups. All three of these groups had established their own settlement patterns throughout the 1960s, and these remained constant through 1980. Out of the three groups, the Mexican population exhibited the lowest levels of segregation from white society. As Ortiz (1996) noted, residential segregation was relatively new for Angeleno Mexicans in the 1960s, when they experienced only "moderate segregation." By the 1970s, however, their segregation increased due to immigration. By 1990, Hispanic segregation rates were high in both Chicago and Los Angeles, where large numbers of Mexicans contin-

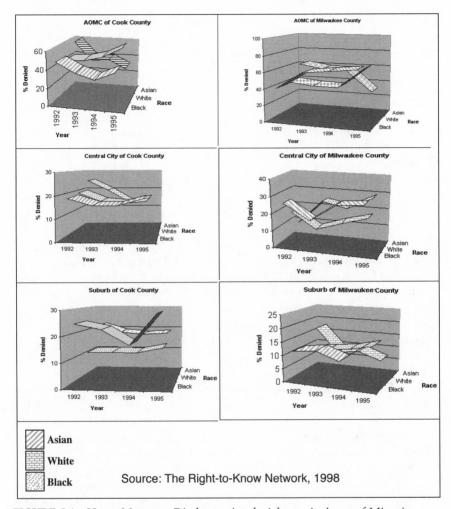

FIGURE 5.1   Home Mortgage Disclosure Act denial rates in Areas of Minority Concentration (AOMCs), central cities, and suburbs, 1992–1995, of (a) Cook County, Illinois, and (b) Milwaukee County, Wisconsin. Source: Right-to-Know Network, 1998.

ued to enter. Wherever Mexicans came in contact with blacks, Cubans, and Puerto Ricans, their segregation rates were quite high (Denton and Massey, 1989). Further, as time passed, they were increasingly likely to be exposed to other Mexicans and Hispanics (such as Salvadorians) and less likely to be in contact with whites (Ortiz, 1996).

Cubans have very high rates of segregation from Anglos. This is especially true in the two metropolitan areas that have the bulk of Cuban immigrants,

New York and Miami. Like Mexicans, Cubans have been highly segregated from blacks, but unlike the Mexican population, Cubans have lower segregation levels from Puerto Ricans in areas like Florida where Cubans are the majority but higher levels in areas around New York, where Puerto Ricans are the majority. In general, Cubans have been very segregated from Mexicans. Denton and Massey (1989) believe that this high level of Cuban segregation is voluntary, based on the fact that most Cubans choose to reside in the ethnic enclaves of South Florida. This appears to be true even in cases where the U.S. government has attempted to relocate the incoming Cuban immigrants (Haverluk, 1997).

Out of the three Hispanic subgroups, Puerto Ricans experience the highest levels of segregation from Anglos. Conversely, they demonstrate the lowest levels of segregation from black society. This is attributed in part to many Puerto Ricans' low SES and their African-American ties (Massey and Denton, 1989). Although Puerto Ricans are culturally distinct from blacks, their parallels in status, segregation, and discriminatory treatment have resulted in not only shared living space with blacks but their equation with blacks, including the existence of a Puerto Rican "underclass." Rosenbaum (1996) reported aspects of Puerto Ricans' extreme disadvantages related to social and procedural equity, including their proportions living below poverty status and on public assistance. She noted the links between housing discrimination, including redlining and abandonment, and segregation patterns. Supporting the notion that geography matters, others also have reported the causes of Puerto Rican segregation within an equity context (Rivera-Batiz, 1994; Santiago and Galster, 1995).

Hispanic Assimilation

A few scholars have also examined the varying rates of assimilation within Hispanic communities. For example, Farley and Frey (1993) revealed that Mexican and Cuban immigrants were the fastest to assimilate, much faster than their Puerto Rican counterparts. Assimilation also occurred more rapidly in the Sunbelt states, while lagging considerably in the Northeast and Midwest. Assimilation also seemed to play a role in segregation. Whereas the West and Southwest had the lowest segregation scores, the list of most-segregated areas included New England, Pennsylvania, and Chicago.

Segregation and assimilation are also affected by the rate of Hispanic population growth. Although areas in the South and Southwest have the lowest segregation scores, these areas of high growth are where segregation scores are increasing the most. Haverluk (1997) has attempted to define an immigration model that accounts for the varying degrees of Hispanic segregation and assimilation. His model, unlike the traditional colonial model, argued that assimilation hinges on the type of Hispanic community. He suggested that, in the case of the "new" Hispanic community, where the dominant culture has always been Anglo and Hispanics are an immigrant population, pressure to assimilate is very high. It is the Hispanic culture in these communities, including language, that fades the fastest (Haverluk, 1997). In the opposite situation, where Hispanics have always been dominant, assimilation does not occur. In the final case, where the dominance of one culture in the community has been discontinuous, at some point the Hispanic culture yielded to the Anglo culture and assimilated.

Hispanic populations also have different settlement patterns depending on SES. Clark and Mueller (1985) explored three hypotheses pertaining to the SES of different Hispanic populations in Los Angeles and Orange Counties. In the case of the first hypothesis, there was a strong association between SES and residential location. Namely, Hispanics living within the central city had a much lower SES than those Hispanics living in the suburbs. The authors also determined that there were far fewer native-born Hispanics in the suburbs than within the central city, where the Hispanic population was predominantly foreign-born.

Results of the second hypothesis uncovered a strong association between the Hispanics' SES and mobility. Clark and Mueller concluded that Hispanics who were moving to the suburbs had a much higher SES than those who were moving within the city limits. The tests also concluded that Hispanics moving to these counties from other areas were divided by SES when it came to their final residence. Higher-SES Hispanics moved into suburban areas, whereas lower-SES Hispanics found their way to the central city. The last hypothesis demonstrated through the index of dissimilarity and the index of exposure that Hispanics in the suburbs were more spatially assimilated than their inner-city counterparts. Neither cultural nor political assimilation was included in these measures, though it was demonstrated that the number of Hispanics who spoke English was higher in the suburbs than in the central city, which shows some cultural assimilation (Clark and Mueller, 1985).

Not all researchers share this notion of Hispanic mobility, however. Betancur (1996) used a qualitative view of Chicago to argue that the assumptions of the ecology model do not fit the case of Hispanic settlement. The ecology model posits a settlement structure that is dependent upon minority mobility in the form of increased SES and then assimilation into white society. This integration into white society opens an area for additional minority in-migration and the process continues. Betancur argues that any mobility experienced by Chicago's Hispanics was very limited; it did not represent any upward mobility but rather reflected the dominant white culture's "flight" behavior (Betancur, 1996).

Domination of Latino culture in Chicago dates back to the early 1900s, when poorly educated Mexican workers were brought North for unskilled labor (Betancur, 1996). Due to their poor economic situation and discrimination by whites, the choice of housing for Mexicans was greatly limited. They were forced to take housing that European immigrants found unsuitable, and were usually forced to pay inflated rents by opportunistic landlords. In the 1960s, incoming Puerto Ricans faced similar constraints and often ended up clustered together in the poorest neighborhoods near the Mexicans. In contrast to the ecology model, poverty and isolation, not upward mobility, characterized these neighborhoods. The Hispanics in these neighborhoods did not integrate into white society as other researchers, such as Massey and Mullan (1984), indicated they would. Instead, any movement was restricted to the areas immediately surrounding the neighborhood (Betancur, 1996).

The apparent Hispanic integration in some areas of Chicago is explained as the first stages of white flight. The appearance of integration exists because Hispanics and whites are found in the same tracts for a brief period before white turnover occurs. Betancur argues that the situation of Hispanics in Chicago is very similar to that of blacks, with Hispanics often acting as buffers between black and white society. Nowhere does it appear, in the qualitative sense, that Hispanics in Chicago are assimilating into white society as the ecology model would predict (Betancur, 1996).

As noted earlier, Angeleno Hispanics also were increasingly less likely to experience contact with whites. Further, Ortiz (1996), when speaking of the Mexican-origin population of Los Angeles, concluded that they "are likely to experience persistent working class status, which means exposure to labor-market conditions that are currently unfavorable and probably will not improve" (p. 252). Not only is the socioeconomic progress of Mexican immigrants and Chicanos slow, but "the immigrants of the 1980s are doing worse than their counterparts of the 1960s . . . the traditional saga of hard work followed by rewards does not apply" (p. 274). Some other Hispanic groups, such as the Guatemalans and Salvadorians, earn even lower wages and are located in the informal sectors of the economy due to their precarious immigration status (Lopez, Popkin, and Telles, 1996).

Not only are Hispanics becoming more segregated (Farley and Frey, 1993); there appears now an economic bifurcation in their population that is associated with their segregation. This led Camarillo and Bonilla (2000) to suggest that American Hispanics are at a "crossroads." Although a Hispanic middle class has clearly emerged, another class—the large and growing "Hispanic underclass"—also has evolved, suggesting a future intensification of inequalities among Hispanics themselves.

A Comparison of Black and Hispanic Settlement Patterns

Although there are many different views concerning the exact process of Hispanic settlement, most researchers agree that the process of black settlement, although similar in many ways to Hispanic settlement, is not identical. Massey and Mullan (1984) believed that the degree and specifics of black and Hispanic assimilation differ significantly. They tested seven hypotheses between 1960 and 1970 using Western SMAs that had significant black and Hispanic populations. Their findings underscored the significant color-line difference for blacks versus Hispanics when entering an all-white neighborhood. They used a coding system that identified census tracts as either Hispanic or black and classified each as one of the following: establishment, invasion, succession, growth, displacement, or decline. A tract was considered established if the minority population exceeded 60 percent in both 1960 and 1970. A succession tract was one where the minority population was growing and the white population was declining. A growth tract was one with a growing minority and white population, and a displacement tract had a shrinking minority population and growing white population. Finally, a declining tract had both a shrinking white and minority population (Massey and Mullan, 1984).

The results of their tests confirmed that, although an increase in Hispanics' SES led to a greater probability of interaction with whites, the same did not apply to blacks. Results also revealed that, though the invading Hispanic group's SES and the distance from an ethnic enclave determined the amount of white turnover, areas of black invasion experienced nearly uniform succession regardless of the incoming black population's SES. Not only did black invasions lead to greater succession, the geographic spread of black invasions was more limited than that of Hispanic invasions. Hispanics were found all over the urban county, whereas blacks were generally limited to invasion tracts immediately surrounding the ethnic/racial neighborhoods (a finding that directly conflicts with Betancur's notion of a constrained Hispanic population). The constraint on black movement regardless of SES demonstrated that blacks are less able to convert an increase in SES into spatial proximity with whites. All of these factors lead to a black population that has a decreased chance of coming into contact with or assimilating into white culture. The study showed that, in these communities, Hispanics were better able to assimilate into white culture due to their increased chance of spatial proximity to Anglo society (Massey and Mullan, 1984).

Through such studies, differences between the settlement patterns of Hispanics and blacks become clear. It is also evident that Hispanic segregation depends at least in part on Hispanic assimilation and that this assimilation process differs from region to region and from one Hispanic culture to another. Because of these differences, it becomes important to determine whether the Area of Hispanic Concentration (AOHC) can in fact be treated as an individual entity and how its demographic characteristics compare to those of AOMCs and racially and ethnically mixed neighborhoods.

The Case of Chicago's Black and Hispanic Neighborhoods. Some research rightfully draws attention to the difference in black and Hispanic settlement patterns, emphasizing both segregation between the two groups and cultural distinctions. For example, Howenstine (1996) emphasized black-Hispanic hypersegregation in Chicago.

Chicago has experienced a declining population since 1990 due to white out-migration. However, an in-migration of Hispanics has resulted in highly segregated black and Hispanic neighborhoods. Chicago's two main black communities are located on the "Southside" and "Westside" and total approximately 1 million residents. Its white population is largely concentrated in the northwest, southwest, and gentrified areas north of the Loop. Its highly segregated Mexican population was described by Howenstine (1996):

> The Hispanic concentration west of downtown is comprised of two adjacent communities, both largely Mexican. The westernmost, with more than 80,000 people, is larger and faster-growing, having increased from 33 to 91 percent Hispanic from 1970 to 1990. Crowding in this largely Mexican community, combined with the rapid in-migration over the past twenty years, has affected settlement patterns citywide [p. 37].

Speaking of the same Chicago subareas, Wilson found very significant differences between black and Hispanic neighborhoods (W. J. Wilson, 1996). He reported that African Americans were more likely than Mexican Americans to live in ghetto areas of very high poverty; Mexicans were more likely to be in moderate-poverty neighborhoods. Wilson attributed this to both cultural and economic factors. Mexicans in the study were largely immigrants (85 percent first generation) who viewed work very differently from African Americans. What black men considered low-paying, long-hour jobs, available under hard conditions, Mexican immigrants embraced as an opportunity to, among other goals, avoid deportation (W. J. Wilson, 1996). This, of course, is viewed by some as a difference in "work ethic." Beyond this, however, the Chicago survey noted other major differences between these two groups and their neighborhoods, including housing, unemployment, and social and family structure. For example, whereas Chicago's Mexican children have a strong traditional, husband-wife family situation (75 percent), only 25 percent of black children experience the same. In 1993 nearly six of every ten black children lived with a single parent, while less than one-third (32 percent) of Hispanic children experienced the same. Nearly two and one-half times as many African-American children as Hispanics lived with a parent who never married. W. J. Wilson (1996) quoted a survey team member's observation of the two ghettos:

> Mexican immigrants living in Chicago poverty areas may well be residents of crowded and dilapidated buildings, but they are surrounded by small and local businesses, many of them owned and operated by persons of Mexican origin, and by Mexican-targeted social service agencies. Poverty-tract blacks are more isolated from jobs and from employed neighbors than are Mexican immigrants [p. 52].

Despite these neighborhood and cultural contexts, it is also true that circumstances sometimes result in shared racial/ethnic space, including by Mexicans and blacks. In Chicago, the familiar situation exists in which Hispanics are wedged between white and black neighborhoods. This has also led to a settlement structure of mixed black-Hispanic neighborhoods (BHNs), which according to Howenstine (1996) was due in part to black upward mobility into Hispanic neighborhoods. Thus, BHNs now occur for a variety of reasons and involve the mixing of Mexican Americans, as well as Puerto Ricans and others, with African Americans.

J. W. Frazier (1999) also examined Chicago neighborhoods but at a different scale, incorporating the racial/ethnic concentrations of AOMC, AOHC, and BHN. This framework does not suggest that all minorities are trapped in inner-city ghettos. It recognizes the suburbanization of blacks and the in-migration of Hispanics, including their mixing with African Americans in certain neighborhoods. Because methodology removed Hispanics (AOHCs) and mixed neighborhoods (BHNs) from Chicago's AOMCs, the latter were predominantly black neighborhoods. This allowed comparisons of racially concentrated areas to one another and to Cook County's white-majority areas. The results illustrated that the black minority concentrations all differed from the white-majority areas in important ways. However, Frazier's findings mirrored some of the key findings reported by W. J. Wilson (1996) and demonstrated that the inequalities exist between the different types of racially concentrated areas:

The AOMCs [predominantly black] differ from all other urban subregions in important ways. They have more crowding and poverty, lower housing values and incomes, and more of their residents pay a higher proportion of income as rent than their Hispanic counterparts. Blacks are also more likely to live in housing built before 1940 than Hispanics. . . . For health care and other services, including banks and real estate offices, black areas (AOMCs) fare worse than Hispanic areas (AOHCs). AOMCs also differ from BHNs . . . in important ways. They have more crowding and poverty, and lower median housing values and median household incomes [Frazier, 1999, p. 45].

It is this type of disaggregation that helps clarify the various conditions of different racial/ethnic neighborhoods. What must be remembered, however, is that the two racial-ethnic subregions studied contain two very different cultures with very different histories. The black community reflects a hundred years of inequalities in social, segregation, and procedural equity contexts, brought on by discrimination. In the next section we provide empirical analyses of differences between minority concentrations and white-majority areas of selected urban counties, first cartographically, so that visualizations of geographic differences are clear, and then statistically, to test hypotheses.

Differences Between Minority
Concentrations and White-Majority
Urban Subregions: An Empirical Analysis

Cartographic Analysis

In order to visualize some of the equity issues discussed above, we created 3-D maps of selected socioeconomic and housing attributes. In each case we compare the census tract value of a variable with the same variable's county mean value. Thus, the higher the 3-D spike, the greater the deviation of the census tract value from the county average value. In this section, we limit our displays to Alameda County (Oakland), California, and Monroe County (Rochester), New York. Each of these counties contains a large central city and a racially mixed population. Both also are parts of metropolitan areas of more than 1 million people.

We selected two variables for visual comparison of AOMCs (containing all minority groups) and AOHCs (30+ percent Hispanic concentrations) with the white-majority areas of Alameda and Monroe Counties. The variables are the unemployment rate and the percentage of residents living below the poverty level. Figure 5.2 contains maps of Alameda County, California. Figure 5.2(a) illustrates the distribution of the differences in 1990 between the Alameda County average unemployment and the individual census-tract unemployment rates. This visualization clearly reveals the disproportionate share of relatively higher unemployment within the central city of Oakland and within the AOMCs (dark) of Alameda County. Figure 5.2(b) illustrates the same patterns for AOHCs, although inner-city Hispanics appear to experience less-striking unemployment disparities with the County than the minorities residing in the AOMCs (largely blacks).

We also provide poverty maps for Monroe County, New York, as Figure 5.3. Two of the striking differences between Monroe and Alameda Counties include the compactness of Monroe's central city, Rochester, and the containment of minority concentrations within the central city. These are probably due to the differences in timing and magnitude of urban expansion. As a result of the central city's high concentration, Rochester's patterns are visually striking. Figure 5.3(a) and (b) show the highly concentrated poverty in Rochester in 1990, with the greatest differences between the county average and individual census-tract poverty values occurring in both types of minority concentrations.

These visualizations help dramatize the substantial social-equity differences in two urban counties between minority and nonminority populations. We return to a statistical approach in the next section by applying an analytical framework to the BHN and other minority concentrations using a national sample of urban counties.

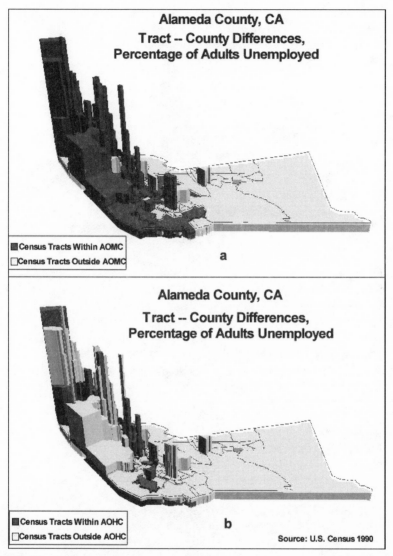

FIGURE 5.2   Differences between countywide and census-tract unemployment rates in Alameda County, California: (a) Areas of Minority Concentration (AOMCs); (b) Areas of Hispanic Concentration (AOHCs). Source: U.S. Census Bureau, 1990.

Statistical Analysis of Inequities Among Racial/Ethnic Groups in Urban Subregions

The Sample Urban Counties.   Two major considerations guided our selection of sample counties. First, we needed to minimize our data collection and

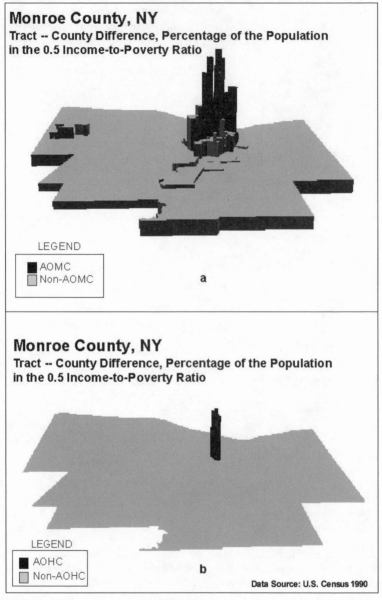

FIGURE 5.3   Census tract–county differences in percentage of Monroe County, New York, households earning annual income less than 50 percent of county poverty level: (a) Areas of Minority Concentration (AOMCs); (b) Areas of Hispanic Concentration (AOHCs). Source: U.S. Census Bureau, 1990.

manipulation efforts. Second, our hypotheses required counties that contained a relatively high number of Hispanics to permit the existence of AOHCs and BHNs. These considerations led us to the use of Frazier and James's sample (1998) of eighty urban counties as our universe. From these eighty, forty emerged as usable in the analysis. A list of the sample urban counties appears as Appendix A.

Fifteen of our sample forty counties are located in the northeastern United States, eleven are located in the West, eleven in the Southwest, and three in the South. Regarding population size in 1990, sixteen exceeded one million residents, another eighteen contained between one-half million and one million people, and six had populations of less than one-half million persons.

As to racial distributions, only three of the forty had Asian populations that exceeded 20 percent of their total populations; all three were in California. Ten of the forty had Hispanic populations exceeding 20 percent of their totals; four were in California, three in Texas, and the remainder were in separate states. Twelve of the forty counties had African-American populations that were at least 20 percent of their total population. Only New Jersey had more than one (two) that met this threshold.

As a group, the AOMCs of these forty counties contained nearly 12 million people (11.8 million). The combined AOHCs held slightly more than 5 million persons (5.2 million).

The Hypotheses
We proposed five null hypotheses to test for differences in urban subregions. The statistical analysis and findings associated with each hypothesis are presented below.

Differentiating the Urban Subregions: Hypothesis 1.   The first hypothesis dealt with differentiating the types of minority concentrations from each other and from the white-majority regions of their urban counties. The null hypothesis is that there is no difference between any of these urban subareas. The primary focus of the analysis was to determine whether the minority areas in question (AOMC, AOHC, BHN) are indeed distinct place entities when compared to the other urban regions (central city, urban county) and to one another. Once this was accomplished, we proceeded to address the other hypotheses that dealt in detail with the minority areas.

Stepwise discriminant analysis was the main tool used in determining the veracity of the first hypothesis. Thirteen variables entered into the discriminant analysis, generating four discriminant functions. Three of the functions were highly significant and accounted for almost 100 percent of the variation. The fourth function, because of its minimal significance, is not discussed.

The first function explained 78.5 percent of the variation in the model, while the second and third functions accounted for 14 percent and 7.4 percent, respectively. The strength of the analysis, as indicated by Wilks's lambda, led us to reject the first null hypothesis. Descriptions of the first three significant functions are useful for understanding the basic differences in our urban subareas.*

The "Black Housing and Unemployment" Function

The first function is the most powerful of the three (explaining 78.5 percent of the variance and having a canonical correlation of 0.743). This function, which compares the largely black AOMC to the other four urban subregions, shows the importance of housing characteristics and unemployment in differentiating these areas. Although thirteen variables were entered into the first function, it can be termed the "black housing and unemployment" function because of the strength of these variables: number of households, population, crowding, year structures were built (prior to 1940), and unemployment. This function indicates that the largely black AOMCs have relatively lower populations and fewer households than the other urban subregions, including other types of minority concentrations and the nonminority regions. Finally, they suffer higher rates of unemployment than the other urban subareas. This finding is in keeping with results of other studies that illustrate the magnitude and persistence of black unemployment rates (Boston, 2000). Our results indicate their importance on a race-place basis. The next most significant variable after those five is income-to-poverty ratio (the percentage of households earning less than 50 percent of the county's poverty level), which suggests that the black AOMCs suffer from greater poverty ratios than people residing in the other urban subregions of the county, including other minority concentrations. The standardized coefficients for all thirteen variables for the first three functions appear in Table 5.1.** We will discuss individual variables in more detail when we discuss sample means.

The "Hispanic Socioeconomic" Function

Several of the variables that were relatively important in function 1 also showed high coefficients in the second function, which differentiated the AOHCs from all other subareas. Function 2 is termed the "Hispanic socioeconomic" function. In this function, the crowding variable had the highest value, followed by unemployment and then the total population. Both the income-to-poverty and year-built variables also had an impact on the distinc-

---

*The classification results in this discriminant analysis were quite acceptable, with approximately 60 percent of the original cases correctly classified by function. It is important to bear in mind that the racial variables representing the percent who are Black and Hispanic in each tract were left out of this discriminant function. A second discriminant analysis was also run, using random samples of each of the groups so that group sizes were equal (two hundred tracts each). The results of the second discriminant analysis did not differ from the findings listed here.

**Other, subsequent analyses use standard coefficients but, due to space limitations, are not included here.

TABLE 5.1   Discriminant Functions that Differentiate the Urban Subregions (standardized coefficients)

| | Function Number | | |
	Black	Hispanic	BHN
Crowding	0.622	0.781	–0.175
No diploma	0.007	–0.119	0.239
Income to poverty	0.265	–0.229	0.277
Median housing value	–0.068	–0.059	–0.042
Median income	–0.111	0.055	0.406
Median rent	0.067	–0.145	–0.061
Households	–0.594	–0.176	–1.27
Total population	0.493	0.334	1.327
Rentals	0.067	–0.122	0.197
Vacanies	0.105	–0.018	–0.093
Year built	0.279	0.243	–0.561
Grocery	–0.006	0.058	–0.122
Unemployment	0.335	–0.455	0.326
Discriminant stats			
Explained variance	78.50%	14%	7.40%
Canonical correlation	0.743		
Wilk's lamda	0.329		

tion between subareas. A complete discussion of the variables that differentiate the AOHC from the other urban subregions is presented below in the section utilizing *t*-tests to compare the AOHC to the other regions.

The "BHN Size and Socioeconomic" Function
The third and final significant function to be examined has five very prominent variables. In this case, crowding is only marginally important. This is not surprising, considering the fact that function 3 compares only the BHN to the central city and urban county. The total population and total number of households have increased in importance, each one having a coefficient of more than 1.20. The year-built and unemployment variables both have a large impact on the model, with coefficients of –0.561 and 0.326, respectively. In this third function, median income moves up in importance, with a coefficient of 0.406. We termed this function "BHN size and socioeconomic." The individual differences between the groups will be discussed below. However, we note the consistency of housing and economic variables in all three functions, which separate our minority concentrations from the other subareas.

To get a clearer picture of the differences between these five groups, mean tests were performed on all of the variables. A number of the service variables proved to be significant. However, a larger number of the socioeconomic and neighborhood characteristic variables were important in clarifying the differences. The four variables that played the largest role in the discriminant analysis were graphed to visualize relationships among the urban subregions (Figure 5.4).

Differences in Population Size Among the Urban Subregions

As mentioned above, total number of households and total population had a significant impact on the discriminant function. A pattern emerges in which the areas with the higher percentages of Hispanics have a greater population per tract. The AOMC area has the lowest mean population, with the central city having the next lowest. A similar trend exists with number of households, the AOMC having the lowest number and the urban county having the most. In this case, however, the major dip in population occurs at the BHN, not the central city.

Housing and Socioeconomic Equity Differences

Although the population data show a clear distinction between the urban subregions in regard to neighborhood characteristics, they do not lend insight into any socioeconomic situations in these areas. The graph in Figure 5.4 depicts other variables that had a large impact on the discriminant analysis. The percent of housing units built before 1940 was chosen as a variable because it was thought to represent the general state of the housing stock as determined by age. The graph shows the AOMC with an elevated percentage of older housing units and the urban county with a greatly reduced percentage.

The next variable, the percentage of crowded housing, has an even more obvious pattern when displayed graphically. Figure 5.4 shows the stark difference between the nonminority areas, central city, and urban county on one hand and the minority areas (AOMC, AOHC, and BHN) on the other. The mean levels for crowding in both the central city and urban county are much lower than their minority counterparts. Also visible is the obvious upward trend toward crowded housing as one moves from the AOMC into the AOHC and then to the BHN. In this case, it appears that the integrated neighborhoods have the most crowded housing.

Mean unemployment levels also contributed significantly to all three discriminant functions. The central city and the urban county have significantly lower unemployment rates than any of the minority areas. This finding probably lends credence to Wilson and others who point to the lack of job opportunities in association with racial/ethnic areas (W. J. Wilson, 1996). In this case, it appears that the AOMC faces the highest unemployment rates, followed by the BHN and then the AOHC. The importance of this graph is that it shows that unemployment and the percentage of black residents go hand in hand whereas the urban county, which is largely white, has an unemployment rate approximately 4 percent lower.

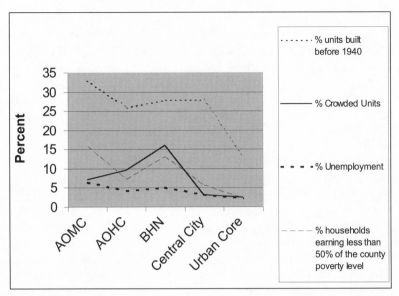

FIGURE 5.4   Comparison of forty sample cities' subregions across the four most significant means-tested variables

A common corollary to unemployment, of course, is poverty, and Figure 5.4 shows how the income-to-poverty variable is distributed throughout the sample counties. The graph emphasizes the trend of AOMC hardship seen thus far. The AOMC displays the highest proportion of households that earn less than 50 percent of the county poverty level. As the percentage of black residents decreases, the degree of poverty also declines.

Through this analysis, it is acceptable to reject the first null hypothesis and assert that these five urban subregions are indeed different based on this study's criterion variables. The results not only show that differences exist between these five race-based regions but also depict an urban setting that contains two broad race-based categories. Our results lead us to state that there exists within these forty urban areas minority and nonminority populations that are not only place based but distinctive by their housing and socioeconomic equity.

Differentiating the AOMC from the Other Urban Subregions: Hypothesis 2. Since it is clear that different statistical regions make up the urban landscape and that these regions are at least in part defined by race, the next step is to determine what some of the specific differences are and between which groups they exist. The discriminant analysis has already given strong evidence to support the idea that minority areas are differentiated from the other subregions, but a closer examination of *t*-test results sheds light on the conditions faced by residents of the AOMC, AOHC, and BHN.

AOMC versus AOHC

The AOMCs and AOHCs have significant differences in all four of the neighborhood-characteristic variables. The results, as expected, show that the AOMC has a significantly higher percentage of black residents, whereas the AOHC has a significantly higher percentage of Hispanics. The AOHC also has a larger number of households and more people than the AOMC. All of the six variables representing housing attributes showed significant differences between the AOMC and AOHC. The discrepancy between the vacancy rates in these two areas is more than 2 percent in favor of the AOHC. Most of the other housing variables show a similar trend; the AOMC is almost always in poorer condition that the AOHC. The exception to this is the high level of crowding experienced by the AOHC.

Other equity differences between the AOMCs and AOHCs include high levels for both unemployment rate and median household income, showing differences between these urban subregions which could elevate the AOMCs' income-to-poverty ratios over those of the other subregions. Some of the problems AOMC residents face could be linked to their poor educational level. Of all of the urban subregions under study, the AOMCs have the highest percentage of people over age twenty-five who do not have a high school diploma (16.4 percent). Their concentration in geographic space reflects not only the impact of segregation but the serious barrier involved in solving the host of problems Wilson described among the "underclass."

The only service variable that proved to be significant in comparing AOMCs to AOHCs was the difference in the number of chain grocery stores per 10,000 people. Although the difference may seem small, it is statistically significant and probably reflects the lack of large grocery store chains within Areas of Minority Concentration as demonstrated by Tettey-Fio (1999). This lack of large chain stores in these areas is usually made up for by the preponderance of small, privately owned groceries, which often charge higher prices for products than grocery chain stores. Evidently the AOMCs are even worse off in this regard than the AOHCs by having fewer chain groceries. This issue of access to particular services by those residing in minority concentrations is examined in more depth in Chapter 9.

Table 5.2 summarizes the findings of the AOMC-AOHC comparison. It shows that the AOMC tracts are much worse off than those of the AOHC in terms of socioeconomic and housing equity. There are also differences in the neighborhood variables, but little difference in service per capita among numerous services examined.

AOMC versus BHN

This section examines the differences between the primarily black AOMC and the mixed BHN. The results for this hypothesis show that, once again, the AOMC is somewhat worse off in regard to the variables used in the test.

TABLE 5.2   AOMCs and AOHCs Compared

After comparing primarily black AOMCs to primarily Hispanic AOHCs, the following con-
clusions can be made:
The AOMCs have:
- Lower median housing values
- Higher monthly rent
- More vacant housing units
- Older housing units
- More rental and fewer owner units
- A lower median income
- Higher unemployment
- Fewer grocery stores
The AOHCs have:
- More-crowded housing units

Community: The AOMCs contain a greater percentage of black residents and are larger
and contain more households than AOHCs. The AOHCs have a larger number of Hispanic
residents.

TABLE 5.3   AOMCs and BHNs Compared

When comparing primarily black AOMCs to mixed black-Hispanic BHNs, the following
conclusions can be made:
The AOMCs have:
- Lower median housing values
- Higher proportion monthly income to rent
- More vacant housing units
- Older housing units
- Greater proportion of adults without high school diploma
- A higher unemployment rate
- Higher income to poverty
The BHNs have:
- More crowded housing
- More rental and fewer owned units
- Fewer Hospitals
- Fewer schools

Community: The AOMCs have more black residents, more households, and a larger
population, whereas the BHNS have more Hispanic residents.

However, the discrepancy is not as distinct as the differences between the
AOMC and AOHC. The results appear in Table 5.3.

All four of the neighborhood variables proved to be significant when comparing the AOMC to the BHN. As would be expected, the AOMC contains a
greater percentage of blacks than the BHN. Conversely, the BHN contains
a much higher percentage of Hispanics (almost 60 percent) than blacks. The

BHN also has a greater average population per tract, as well as a greater per-tract number of households. Not only are there more people per tract in the BHN, but they live in more crowded housing than their counterparts in the AOMC. There is also a greater tendency for BHN residents to rent rather than own their units. The housing stock within the AOMC is significantly older, as demonstrated by the greater percent of units being built before 1940. This older housing stock is more likely to be vacant than the newer housing located in the BHN. Even though the housing is older and more likely to be vacant, the AOMC residents are spending a significantly greater percentage of their income on rent. It may be that Hispanics living in the BHNs have invaded formerly black areas with hopes of moving to better neighborhoods when their socioeconomic status improves.

Three out of the four socioeconomic variables tested were significant. The percent of people without a high school diploma is 2 percent higher in the AOMC than in the BHN, which is likely reflected in the increased level of unemployment in the AOMC. Although the difference in median income between these two areas was not significant, the number of people in poverty (income to poverty) in the AOMC is 3 percentage points greater than in the BHN.

There were two service variables that were significant between the AOMC and BHN. The AOMC has both more hospitals and more schools per capita. This may be a function of blacks living in older housing in the older neighborhoods that contain more hospitals and schools because of their location near the central business district. One of the shortcomings of our analysis is that we merely measure services per capita at this stage, thus providing no evidence of quality or access related to schools or medical care. We modify this approach in the case studies in subsequent chapters. Despite this shortcoming, however, as with the comparison between the AOMC and AOHC, it becomes clear that the AOMC and BHN are two distinct entities. Unlike the AOMC-AOHC comparison, the AOMC-BHN comparison shows that the AOMC fares worse in the majority—though not in all—of the equity indicators applied.

AOMC versus Central City

The results of the equity differences between the AOMC and the central city are summarized in Table 5.4. All of the demographic variables and two of the service variables have significant differences between the primarily black AOMC and the largely nonminority section of the central city.

The AOMC and the central city differed on all four of the neighborhood variables. The population of the AOMC was on average 450 persons lower per tract than that of the central city. This equates with fewer households as well, the AOMC showing 1,200 per tract, whereas the central city displayed more than 1,600. As would be expected, the percentage of blacks in the AOMC is significantly higher than in the central city. In fact, the AOMC has

TABLE 5.4   AOMCs and Central Cities Compared

When comparing primarily black AOMCs to primarily nonminority central cities, the following conclusions can be made:
The AOMCs have:
 • Lower median housing values
 • More income paid in monthly rent
 • More vacant housing units
 • Older housing units
 • More crowded housing
 • More rental and fewer owned units
 • A higher unemployment rate
 • More uneducated people
 • Less income
 • More people in poverty (income to poverty)
 • Fewer outpatients care centers
The Central Cities have:
 • Fewer grocery stores

Community: The AOMCs have more black residents, fewer households, and a smaller population, whereas the central cities have more Hispanic residents.

a black population approaching 75 percent, whereas that of the central city is barely more than 8 percent. The number of Hispanics also differs between the two areas. Even with an overall population that is much smaller, Hispanics still comprise 10 percent of the central city, whereas blacks, a much larger minority, only constitute 8 percent. This may be an indication of the Hispanic population's heightened ability to assimilate.

The housing situation in the AOMC is significantly worse than that in the central city. The AOMCs' residents live in more crowded conditions, pay more of their income in rent, live in older housing units with less value, and are more likely to be renting the unit rather than owning it. The AOMC vacancy rate is also 4 percent higher than that of the central city. These results support some of the earlier findings of Frazier and James (1998).

AOMCs fare no better when considering the socioeconomic variables. The AOMC has a greater number of uneducated people, who also have a lower median income. This is especially troublesome since we have already demonstrated that AOMC residents pay more of their income toward their monthly rent. The high unemployment rates in the AOMC translate into greater levels of poverty, as expressed by the income-to-poverty ratio, than in the central city.

Two service variables showed high levels of significance: the number of grocery stores, of which the AOMC had more than the central city, and the number of outpatient care facilities, which showed the reverse trend. It is safe to conclude from this test of the AOMC and the central city that these two areas are vastly different.

AOMC versus Urban County

Every variable except number of grocery stores, including all the housing and socioeconomic variables, placed the AOMCs at a distinct disadvantage to the urban counties. Overall, the combined results proved not only that the AOMC and other minority concentrations are definable urban subregions but also that major housing, socioeconomic, and service variables are important to understanding the equity distinctions between them that are the legacies of segregation and isolation.

Differentiating the AOHC from the Other Subregions: Hypothesis 3.

AOHCs versus BHNs

The third hypothesis involves a comparison of the Hispanic-oriented AOHCs (30+ percent Hispanic population) and the racially/ethnically mixed neighborhoods, or BHNs. The null hypothesis is that no differences exist. In this case the results are quite powerful. The BHNs faced worse conditions on all of the variables tested.

Two out of the four neighborhood-characteristic variables were significant in the comparison of AOHCs and BHNs. Although there was not a significant difference between these two subregions in regard to the number of housing units or to total census-tract population, the racial percentage showed variations. The mixed regions, BHNs, contain a higher percentage of Hispanics than the corresponding AOHCs. In fact, the census tracts in the mixed-race BHNs had a Hispanic population that accounts for 64 percent of the total population, whereas the AOHC tracts had only 45 percent Hispanic population. This is not surprising when the heightened immigration and assimilation rates of Hispanics as compared to blacks are taken into account. It is likely that the AOHCs represent areas where Hispanics have assumed residence after leaving the higher minority concentrations of the BHNs. Perhaps the AOHC Hispanics have left the poorer conditions of the BHNs for the better conditions of the more Anglo AOHC neighborhoods, which may serve as a buffer between the highly concentrated black and Hispanic populations of the BHNs and the predominately white AOMCs and nearby all-white areas of the urban county (Howenstine, 1996).

Four of the six variables representing housing in these two areas show differences (Table 5.5). The BHNs' residents pay a greater proportion of their income for rent and live with more crowded housing conditions than residents of the AOHCs. The housing that is within the BHNs is also older and less likely to be owned by the inhabitants. These features, coupled with a lower median housing value, imply that BHN residents have more housing problems and concerns than the AOHC residents.

BHN residents also face considerably more socioeconomic problems than people residing in the AOHCs. The BHNs exhibit signs of poverty and hard-

TABLE 5.5   AOHCs and BHNs Compared

When comparing primarily Hispanic AOHCs to the mixed black/Hispanic BHNs, the
following conclusion can be made:
  The BHNs have:
    • Lower median housing values
    • More income paid in monthly rent
    • More vacant housing units
    • More crowded housing
    • More rental and fewer owned units
    • A lower median income
    • Higher unemployment
    • Lower educated levels
    • More people in severe poverty

Community: BHNs have more black and Hispanic residents.

---

ship on all socioeconomic variables analyzed. Households and individuals living in BHNs are more likely to be unemployed, and even in the case of employed households, the median annual household income was lower than that of the AOHCs by about $6,000 per year. Lower incomes and joblessness lead to a heightened level of poverty, as expressed by the percentage of the population with an income less than 50 percent of the poverty level (13 percent within the BHNs and 8 percent within the AOHCs), and, according to Wilson, greater family dysfunction (W. J. Wilson, 1996). A higher proportion of uneducated persons reside within the BHNs than in the AOHCs, which may be contributing to BHN residents' lower socioeconomic status.

All of these variables combine to create a living environment in the BHNs, where blacks and Hispanics share city space, that indicates significantly greater hardship than that experienced in the AOHCs, where Hispanics are likely assimilating into white-majority neighborhoods.

AOHCs versus the Central Cities

The results of the comparison of means between the AOHCs and their central cities are opposite those from the comparison of AOHCs and BHNs. As compared to their central cities, the variable means for the AOHCs indicated poorer conditions in socioeconomic, housing, and service equity.

When examining the neighborhood characteristics, we found no significant difference in the number of households, even though the AOHCs have somewhat larger populations. Of course, AOHCs have a greater proportion of Hispanics than the central-city census tracts, but they have 5 percent fewer African Americans than the central cities. In short, they are areas containing upwardly mobile Hispanics moving into white areas.

The housing units of the AOHCs are more crowded as compared to the central city (Figure 5.4). The housing units there also have a lower median value, as well as lower ownership rates. Although the vacancy rates in the AOHCs are higher than in the central city, the percentage of those spending more than 35 percent of their income on rent is considerably lower in the AOHC (27 percent) than in the central city (47 percent). In fact, the AOHCs have the lowest mean value for this variable out of all five of the subregions. This may be due to household size.

All of the socioeconomic variables proved to be significant between these two subregions. In all cases the central city fared better than the AOHCs. In the AOHCs, the level of educational attainment is lower, there are more people in poverty (income-to-poverty ratio), and the unemployment rate is higher. The most striking of the socioeconomic characteristics is the discrepancy between the median household incomes of the two urban subareas, which was approximately $5,300.

The central city also has significantly more hospitals and schools per capita than the AOHCs, though the same limitations of interpreting access and quality apply here and in all of the service analyses at this scale.

AOHCs versus the Urban Counties

As with the comparison between the AOMCs and the urban counties, the results of the AOHC-versus-urban-county comparison provided significant findings. Most of the AOHCs' variables did not compare favorably with those of the urban counties. A greater proportion of AOHC households pay 35 percent or more of their incomes for rent as compared to other urban race-based regions. When health care provision is considered, the AOHCs have fewer dentists per capita than their urban-county counterparts. Socioeconomically speaking, the AOHCs had a worse position on all variables with the already noted exception of percentage of income paid to rent.

Differentiating BHNs from the Other Urban Subregions: Hypothesis 4.   The fourth hypothesis deals with the differentiation of the mixed-minority BHN from the rest of the urban subregions. The null hypothesis is that no differences exist. At this point, the BHNs have already been compared to the AOMCs and AOHCs in the second and third hypotheses; now they will be compared to the central cities and the urban counties.

BHNs versus Central Cities

All but one variable (number of houses built before 1940) was significantly different between these two groups. The BHN, of course, contains a relatively high proportion of black and Hispanic residents. The BHN also has a greater population per census tract, even though on average it has fewer households per tract than does the central city (130 fewer).

All the other housing variables were significant in explaining the equity differences between these subregions. The BHN is marked by greater amounts of crowding and a higher percentage of rental units and vacancies but a lower median housing value as compared to the central city. A lower proportion of the BHN residents did, however, pay less of their incomes in rent (9 percent less). Out of all the socioeconomic variables, not one of them favored the BHN over the central city.

The numbers of outpatient clinics and hospitals are both significantly lower in the BHN. The central city also has more schools per capita than the BHN. Although the significance of the real-estate variable (0.072) did not meet the generally accepted 0.05 cutoff, this significance certainly suggests a difference between the numbers of real estate services in these two subregions.

BHNs versus Urban Counties
There were many differences between the BHN and urban county as well. This pattern of relatively large inequities between minority areas and the largely white central city and urban county in our previous tests holds true here. The results clearly reveal that the hypothesis should be rejected; the BHN is significantly different from the urban county.

Summary of the Race-Place Connection in Urban America
The results of the empirical analyses provided thus far, though not surprising on a race basis, clarify the race-place connections of urban American at the close of the twentieth century. First, wherever African Americans are segregated in large numbers, they fare very poorly. The AOMCs, which exist in the "inner city" and as enclaves elsewhere in urban counties, are distinct from all other race-based areas within their communities because of wide discrepancies in socioeconomic, housing, and service equity. Inequalities, as we have indicated in earlier chapters, are due to social, generational, and procedural problems tied to segregation and isolation. The consequences are visible in much of the American urban landscape and are strongly supported by the statistics employed in our analyses.

Where African Americans share living space with Hispanics (BHNs), probably in an effort to flee the "underclass ghetto," conditions are only slightly better than in the primarily black AOMCs, and these BHNs are far worse off when compared to their white-majority central cities and suburbs (urban counties).

Areas of Hispanic Concentration outside the BHNs likely reflect the ability of some Hispanics to cross the "color line" and integrate with whites, even if only on a temporary basis, in neighborhoods that serve as buffers between blacks (in AOMCs and AOHCs) and white-majority neighborhoods. Because these areas are previous white strongholds and now represent areas of Hispanic "upward mobility," they fare better than the other minority areas. However, when equity comparisons are made with nearby white-majority areas (central cities) and urban counties outside the central city, the equity of Hispanics fades dramatically.

We now turn to the other race-place connections by comparing inner- and outer-city minority concentrations and white-majority areas.

Outer-City and Inner-City Differences: Hypothesis 5.   In previous chapters, we made two observations about minority status and settlement. First, as minority status improved, some minorities moved out of the ghettos to better environments but were still restricted, resulting in segregation and minority concentrations. Second, we noted that, despite improving their status, minorities faced two problems due to discrimination and segregation. One is that, despite similar education, they earn less than their white counterparts (Fainstein, 1993; Cose, 1993). The other is that minority incomes buy less housing (i.e., the "black," or minority, tax). This, in part, leads to the middle-class and professional rage felt by African Americans (Cose, 1993). Given the continued segregation outside poor ghettos, the improved incomes and housing values relative to poorer inner-city ghettos (minority concentrations), and restricted housing available to minorities in the outer cities, we should expect to find minority concentrations of two types:

1. Inner-city minority concentrations that contain the least attractive values for indicators of equity. These include AOMCs (largely African American), AOHCs (high proportions of Hispanics), and BHNs (mixed African American and Hispanic), all located in the county's central city; and
2. Outer-city minority concentrations that contain indicator values that are higher than those of their inner-city counterparts but lower than those of the white majorities living in the county outside the central city.

In the first case, using the same variables tested in previous sections, we evaluate the differences between the predominantly black AOMCs of the inner, central city and the county's black outer-city AOMCs. Our results show that the inner-city versus the outer-city African-American areas were not different in terms of services per capita, with two exceptions. Inner-city AOMCs had fewer doctors and outpatient facilities per capita than AOMCs located outside the central city. With regard to socioeconomic and housing indicators, inner-city AOMCs as compared to outer-city AOMCs had more crowding, more persons with little education, higher proportions of income paid to rent, older housing units, higher unemployment, and lower median incomes and housing values. Regarding annual household incomes, the 1990 median income of inner-city AOMCs was $19,711, as compared to the $29,521 of outer-city AOMCs; inner-city AOMCs' median housing value was $60,276, versus $92,900 for outer-city AOMCs. Clearly, these differences reflect the "two minority worlds" frequently mentioned in the literature. We therefore reject the fifth hypothesis.

In the second case, we examined the equity status of the outer-city minorities (BHNs, AOHCs, AOMCs) and white majorities living outside the central city but in the urban county. It is reasonable to expect that the most affluent whites reside there. We used the same variables to test for differences. There were no differences in services per capita. At least in urban-county locations outside central cities, all types of minority concentrations and white-majority concentrations had equal services per capita. Again, we do not suggest equal access nor equal quality exists; rather we indicate that there are no differences in the number of service establishments per capita. The same was not true for housing and socioeconomic status.

Table 5.6 reports the variables with significantly different means between each type of minority concentration and white-majority area located in the urban county (outside the central city). BHNs and white-majority subregions differed in terms of BHNs having higher crowding and unemployment but lower income and housing values. The results were identical for AOHCs as compared to white-majority areas in the urban county's outer cities. It is noteworthy that Hispanic and BHN concentrations did not differ from the white-majority areas on the basis of poor education (no high school diploma), income-to-poverty ratio, age of housing, or proportion of income paid to rent. However, these minority subregions had significantly lower housing values and annual incomes than the white-majority areas. Regarding median housing value, the average AOHC tract value was $109,416, whereas the corresponding values for the average BHN and white-majority tracts were $93,927 and $146,859, respectively. Thus, the average AOHC census tract had a substantially higher median housing value than the BHN but dramatically lower value than the white-majority tract. The same was true for annual household incomes, which were $31,910, $25,872, and $42,926, respectively, for the outer-city AOHC, BHN, and urban county.

The AOMCs, or majority–African American concentrations, in the outer cities had the lowest housing values of any concentration and had annual incomes only higher than those living in the BHNs. The values for the average AOMC tract were $92,900 (median housing value) and $29,521 (annual household income).

It seems quite clear from these findings that the color line indeed exists and that important equity differences occur between these race-based outer-city urban subregions. African Americans indeed lived in "two different worlds" in 1990. However, regardless of how much "better off" black suburbia was as compared to inner-city black ghettos, relative to white America, black America suffered major inequalities wherever it was concentrated and segregated. It is also true that, wherever Hispanic America is highly concentrated or is mixed with black America in segregated urban subregions, its lack of equity relative to white-majority areas is strikingly obvious. In the final section of this chapter, we use selected data estimates for the year 2000 to update the

TABLE 5.6   Housing Variables for Minority Concentrations in Outer Cities versus
White-Majority Outer Cities in Urban Counties, 1990

	Central-city BHNs vs. outer white cities	Central-city AOHCs vs. outer white cities	AOMCs vs. outer white cities
Crowding	X	X	X
Median Housing Value	X	X	X
Median Household Income	X	X	X
Housing built prior to 1940	Not signif.	Not signif.	X
Unemployment	X	X	X

X denotes significant at 0.05 level of confidence.
SOURCE: U.S. Census Bureau, 1990.

analysis at the turn of the century. It must be remembered that the 2000 U.S.
Census data at this scale were not released until mid-2002. Despite this, it is
informative to use the few data elements available as estimates to update our
analysis.

Minority Concentrations and Equity Differences: The 2000 Update of Race-Place Connections

Availability, quality, and cost are considerations in purchasing data estimates.
We utilized two commercial databases to update our 1990 analysis on a
census-tract basis. These were purchased from CACI Marketing Systems, a
reputable international firm. One database was composed of racial population estimates for the year 1998. The second database, the socioeconomic
one, contained estimates of household income, median housing value, net
worth, number of rental units, total number of housing units, and vacancy estimates for 2000. Some data available in the 1990 census simply were not
available on an estimation basis. For example, ethnicity (as opposed to black,
white, etc., race data) is available only in the decennial census, as is crowding.
Available estimates for household net worth, however, allowed us to expand
our approach for 2000. Oliver and Shapiro (2000) have noted that wealth is
an important dimension for the analysis of racial stratification and disparities. Estimated net worth permits the addition of this dimension to the race-
place analysis. We joined both of these databases to our original database,
which also contained 1998 services data, for analysis. Where appropriate, we
normalized these data.

   We examined two general issues associated with our 1990 findings. The
first issue had to do with the minority concentrations themselves. First, we
used the 1998 race data to test the stability of minority concentration tracts

from 1990 to 1998. That is, would minority concentration tracts in 1990 remain minority tracts in 1998? We also wanted to establish whether new minority concentrations were emerging. Second, we wanted to test for equity differences between our urban subregions using the data estimates to establish whether some of the equity differences of 1990 persisted to 2000. We discuss these two issues separately below.

AOMCs and AOHCs: Boundaries and Minority Concentrations, 1990–1998.
Regarding the stability of the 1990 minority-concentration census tracts, almost without exception any tract designated AOMC or AOHC in 1990 remained a minority tract in 1998. Less than 1 percent of the tracts in our sample of forty urban counties lost their 1990 minority designation by 1998. There were changes, but these involved 1990 AOMC tracts becoming AOHC tracts in 1998, an indication of a rapidly increasing Hispanic population. The second question associated with the boundaries of minority concentrations is addressed by Table 5.7, which is a tabulation of new minority-concentration tracts by region. The table reports the average changes in the minority concentration tracts between 1990 and 1998 in the urban counties. Using the race estimates, new AOMC and AOHC designations were created for each of our sample forty urban counties. The table shows that the average number of new AOMC tracts in 1998 was nineteen, whereas the number of AOHC tracts increased by an average of thirteen. However, the table clearly reveals the significant variation by region in the United States. The greatest number of changes occurred in the West and South, which in our sample included only urban counties in California, Texas, and Florida. The 1998 changes reflect the heavy influx of immigrants into those areas, as well as the generally increasing concentrations of all minority populations in urban space in those three states' urban counties. The average California urban county in our sample realized an increase of forty-three AOMC census tracts, which included minority races and Hispanics. The average California county gained on average twenty-one new AOHC tracts. Sometimes these new tracts were part of AOMCs (thus, they were BHNs), and sometimes they were independent of the AOMCs.

In the case of Alameda County, California, 1990–1998, both AOMCs and AOHCs expanded dramatically during the period. Alameda County is a very racially and ethnically diverse and complex set of communities. The changes occurred inside and outside the city of Oakland. Also, the expansion of minority concentrations included two processes—contagious expansion from existing centers and leapfrogging to the county's outer cities. (*Leapfrogging* refers to a geographic pattern of settlement that results from migrants moving from their previous locations to an outlying area some distance away rather than to an adjacent location.) Finally, although Hispanic concentrations were modest in 1990, their expansion was significant between 1990 and 1998. They appear both to have spread in a linear fashion along the Oakland eastern city limits in

TABLE 5.7   Average Increase in AOMC and AOHC Census Tracts by U.S. Region, 1990
to 1998

	AOMC tracts	AOHC tracts
West (California)	43	21
Southwest & Mountain	9	16
East	6	6
Midwest	17	6
South (Florida & Texas)	33	39
Sample Means	19	13

SOURCE: U.S. Census Bureau, 1990 and CACI Marketing Systems, 1998.

a southeastern direction and to have leapfrogged into the county's southwestern sections.

Not surprisingly, Table 5.7 indicates that our sample urban counties in the Southwest and Mountain region gained on average a higher number of AOHCs than AOMCs. Cities in Arizona, New Mexico, Nevada, and other states have well-established Hispanic populations and are gaining new Hispanic immigrants every year. The increase in the average number of AOMC census tracts for our sample urban counties was nine. The sample counties gained an average of sixteen new AOHC tracts. This change reinforces the trends reported in Chapter 2; minority populations are urbanizing, or are being segregated, into minority concentrations.

In the East, our sample counties averaged six new AOMC and six new AOHC tracts. In the Midwest, our urban counties gained an average of seventeen new AOMC tracts by 1998 and six new AOHC tracts. These averages are based on a wide variety of experiences among the sample communities and, therefore, are somewhat misleading. Just as location influenced the changes in California, Texas, and Florida, size of existing minority population, size of urban county, and other factors contribute significantly to local experiences. For these reasons we illustrate one more case below.

Large midwestern cities such as Chicago, Cleveland, Detroit, and Milwaukee have a relatively long history of African-American settlement. As a result, blacks were the dominant and highly segregated minority population by 1990 for Wayne County, Michigan, which contains Detroit. Hispanic migration, though evident in some midwestern cities early in the twentieth century (see Chapter 2), was still modest by 1990 as compared to that of African Americans. As a result, the midwestern urban counties in our sample gained an average of seventeen new AOMCs between 1990 and 1998 but gained an average of only six new AOHCs (Chicago and Cook County contributed disproportionately more than other areas in the Midwest).

In 1990 a large number of minority concentrations existed in Detroit and were dominated by blacks; only five AOHC tracts existed in inner-city Detroit then. However, according to 1998 estimates, AOMC and AOHC tracts expanded beyond their 1990 boundaries. In the case of African Americans, it appears that new black-dominated minority-concentration tracts emerged in northwestern and central Wayne County. They also emerged on all sides of the 1990 AOMC borders, suggesting expansion through contagion and invasion processes. In the case of Hispanic minority concentrations, the number of tracts increased from five to seventeen. The newly emerging concentrations involved a greater number of Hispanics moving into neighborhoods previously dominated by blacks but also into a few tracts that were white-majority in 1990. All AOHC tracts in Detroit are adjacent to each another.

These examples illustrate the likely spatial impacts and regional variations of the increasing minority populations in urban America discussed in Chapter 2. Minority concentrations exhibit no single pattern of growth. Their magnitude and content will vary regionally and locally. However, it is equally clear that major expansion of minority concentrations is occurring throughout the United States. As a result, minority dominance is replacing white majorities in particular places. Sometimes blacks and Hispanics are mixing in neighborhoods, often for relatively short periods until Hispanic succession replaces black dominance. Other times black populations are moving away from the ghetto to other places. Sometimes minorities move to neighborhoods that are adjacent to minority areas, and other times they are involved in leapfrogging, indicating the emergence of new enclaves away from old ones. Whatever the spatial process, it seems apparent that the geographic concentration of minorities continues, even as a real expansion occurs. We now return to the second issue—the perpetuation of inequalities among race-based places.

Persistent Equity Differences Between Minority Concentrations and White-Majority Subregions, 2000. It should be noted that newer urban counties, including those that have recently been added to our forty SMAs, are very likely even more affluent than their older central urban counties and their corresponding central cities. Accordingly, the equity differences between minority concentrations and these new metropolitan counties would be much more severe than those reported in our analysis. Put differently, we might well expect less of a difference between minority concentrations and the white-majority regions in the older central counties than we would if we were comparing minority concentrations to the more dramatically suburban counties within their own SMA. Even though central counties may increasingly resemble their inner-city neighborhoods, we are confident that in relative terms the inequalities reported in previous sections have stood the test of time. We tested for the mean differences between our subregions as they existed within the urban county in 2000.

Our results support the persistence of race-place inequalities in 2000. The AOMCs remain distinctly different from all of the other subregions on a statistical basis when socioeconomic variables are considered. There were only two cases in which the socioeconomic variables were not significantly different between the AOMCs and the other subregions (median net worth in AOHCs and median household income in BHNs). In the other cases, socioeconomic inequalities persisted. The average median housing value of AOMCs in 2000 was $84,950, which was the lowest of any subregion: BHN, $96,000; AOHC, $116,000; central city (CC) $146,000; central county (CO), $161,000. The same is true for median household income and for net worth. When per-capita services are considered, the AOMCs did not differ significantly from any of the urban subregions, including the white-majority areas, in our updated analysis. This finding makes no claim regarding the quality or cost of such services and what inequalities they may generate.

AOHCs are significantly different from and better off than the mixed-race BHNs on all indicators in 2000, with the exception of services. For example, the average net worth of a household in an AOHC is more than $25,000 higher than that of an average household that resides in a BHN. The socioeconomic equity of AOHC households, however, continued to pale in comparison with an average household in the white-majority areas, where household incomes, housing values, and net worth substantially exceeded those of the AOHCs.

Results for BHNs and the white-majority areas of the central cities and urban counties, like the AOMCs and the AOHCs, indicated that the BHNs remained distinct from the other urban subregions, specifically the white-majority areas of the central cities and urban counties, both in socioeconomic and housing equity issues. There were no significant differences between the regions on the basis of services per capita.

Overall, then, the 2000 data estimates substantiated the persistence of inequalities between minority and white-majority places.

Outer City Differences Between Minority Concentrations and White-Majority Subregions, 2000. In this part of our updated analysis we compared only the racially based urban subregions that existed outside of the central city, in the urban county's outer communities. Our results indicate that, for 2000 data, the outlying AOMCs and AOHCs are not significantly different. The AOHCs have somewhat better numbers for median household income, housing value, and net worth, but these differences are not statistically significant.

Results for the AOMCs and BHNs in the outer cities do, however, indicate significant differences but only on the basis of three socioeconomic variables. The largely black AOMCs have higher median household incomes and average net worth than the BHNs. It is noteworthy that despite these differences, their median housing values are different by less than $1,000.

The results are quite different when the outlying AOMCs' mean values are compared to those of the other white-majority urban subregions. In this case, the white-majority median housing value ($161,062) is more than $65,000 higher than that of the AOMCs. Similarly, the median annual household incomes differ significantly, by more than $10,000. Household net worth differs by nearly $80,000 in favor of the white-majority areas. Significant differences between AOHCs and BHNs on one hand and white-majority areas of the outer cities on the other also remained in 2000. Not surprisingly, the AOHCs located in the outer cities of the county are less well-off than their white-majority-area counterparts by significant margins as measured by the same socioeconomic indicators applied before.

Finally, BHNs are also significantly different from the white-majority areas of the urban counties. They fared less well on all socioeconomic indicators.

This updated analysis of race-place inequalities demonstrates the persistence of outcomes related to racial segregation and isolation, as well as the strength of our minority-concentration concepts. This chapter has illustrated that minority concentrations vary in magnitude, content, and location on a regional and local basis. They reflect inequity in urban America. This underscores the need to conduct microanalyses on a case study basis to determine the nature of racial distributions and equity differences on a local basis. We will pursue this case study approach in the next several chapters.

Summary

Equity issues cannot be examined with any authority without first understanding minority settlement form and evolution and contemporary immigration patterns. These lead inevitably to discussions of isolation, segregation, discrimination, and racial inequalities on a race-place basis. In this chapter, we have relied on the findings from previous investigations to document the multiple impacts of segregation on minority groups. We have also used empirical data to illustrate that one of the spatial outcomes of segregation is the existence of at least five distinct urban subregions. Our findings also demonstrate that minority-concentration subregions differ a great deal in terms of socioeconomic, housing, and service equity when compared to each other and especially when compared to the white-majority subregions across forty U.S. urban counties containing significant African-American and Hispanic concentrations. Several general patterns emerged that support the notion of two American societies, one the white-majority haves and the other the nonwhite have-nots. Beyond this often disputed pattern, however, a clear distinction emerged among the have-not minority concentrations themselves. The specific differences noted are as follows:

- The white-majority urban tracts were better than all the other regions in regards to all demographic variables and all service variables, with the exception of grocery stores.

- The central-city white-majority tracts usually fared better than the minority areas on most accounts, including demographic and service measures.
- The BHN tracts fell on the lower end of the spectrum, usually between the AOHC and AOMC tracts, in terms of socioeconomic and housing equity and services per capita.
- The AOHC compared well against the other minority areas, usually coming out ahead of both. In some respects, the AOHC was similar to the central city. However, in general, the white-majority areas had better services per capita and a higher level of socioeconomic status.
- And in almost all cases, the AOMCs had lower services per capita, as well as a lower socioeconomic status. The one exception to this was the case of grocery stores, where the AOMC displayed the largest number of stores per person, which is not necessarily a positive indicator (Tettey-Fio, 1999).

It seems quite clear from these findings that the color line indeed exists and that important equity differences occur on a complex race-place basis. African Americans indeed live in "two different worlds" when one examines ghettos versus outer-city minority concentrations. However, regardless of how much "better off" black Americans are as a group, relative to white America and its white-majority neighborhoods, black America suffers inequalities wherever it is concentrated or segregated. Hispanic concentrations fare better than black concentrations. It is also true that, where Hispanic America is highly concentrated or is mixed with black America in segregated urban subregions, its lack of equity relative to white-majority areas is strikingly obvious. It is important to note that all of these findings were based on sample counties and data estimates. However, there is little reason to believe that the race-place inequalities revealed here will change with more up-to-date information. We believe that the findings reported here will, unfortunately, stand the test of future research.

Chapter 6

Deconstruction of Emerging Racial Mosaics

Equity Issues Where Asian Americans Mix with Other Minorities in Alameda County, California

Introduction

We have developed a number of themes in this book. Among them is the increasing racial/ethnic diversity that is spreading throughout the United States. We also have emphasized the separation of the races by legal, institutional, and other means and the resulting inequalities on a race-place basis in urban America. In the last chapter, we demonstrated the range and magnitude of the inequalities between whites and minority concentrations and between minority areas themselves. We also illustrated that, when African Americans and Hispanics mix in certain proportions (as in BHNs), they are substantially less well-off than the white majority and differ from other minority concentrations as well. This raises a related issue about places where different types of racial mixing occur. Since racially mixed neighborhoods, whether permanent or not, are likely to characterize a significant part of urban America during this century, it is worthwhile to explore how various racial mixtures differ from one another on an equity basis now and in the future. To do so will require a deconstruction of existing residential mosaics in places that are racially heterogeneous. In this chapter we are particularly interested in examining areas where Asians mix with other racial groups.

Southern California in the 1990s may serve as a lens for viewing racially diverse residential patterns that will characterize other urban counties in the future. As one of the world's most complex racial mosaics, Southern California offers one model for understanding the evolutionary processes of residential development and the related equity patterns. Perhaps more than anywhere else, Asians in Southern California are a key part of the evolving urban form. This region offers some leading principles regarding the type of mixed-race and minority concentrations that have emerged under the conditions of extreme immigration for more than three decades.

We have two purposes in this chapter. First, we take advantage of some of the key research already conducted on this region, because it informs us about inequalities, debunks a leading myth about Asians, and provides a basis for examining our case study. The second purpose is to perform a case study in the West Coast region, specifically in Alameda County, California, not only because it contains a racially mixed population but also because of its well-documented history of race relations, which helps explain its contemporary residential patterns.

Below we review some of the important research on this broader region, its racial trends and growth, and its use in the debunking of an Asian myth and then raise questions about the nature of places where Asians mix with other races. To address these questions, we use the same data applied in Chapter 5 to analyze the inequalities present within Alameda County's racial/ethnic mosaic.

Increasing Racial Diversity:
Some Trends and Issues in Southern California

The Los Angeles region, famous for its phenomenal, sprawling growth since the 1960s, contains five counties and more than 33,000 square miles; it is nearly twice the size of New York City (Waldinger and Bozorgmehr, 1996). Once dominated by "eastern" whites who migrated from other states, this area changed dramatically after 1960. African Americans trickled into the region beginning in the late nineteenth century, but their more serious influx occurred during World War II and continued thereafter. The African-American population's most important period of growth occurred between 1960 and 1990, when the black population doubled in the area. During the same period, a record number of Hispanic and Asian immigrants also came to the region, due largely to the policy changes brought by the 1965 Hart-Celler Act (Waldinger and Bozorgmehr, 1996). Its provisions allowed entry of immigrants with needed skills and family ties and resulted in more than 7 million new immigrants in California in the 1980s alone. Both Hispanics and Asians came from diverse ethnic backgrounds. The largest numbers of Hispanics were from Mexico (66 percent), El Salvador, and Guatemala, while immigrant Asians were Chinese, Asian Indians, Koreans, Vietnamese, Cambodians, Laotians, and Hmongs. The Asian population entered in two general waves. Waldinger and Bozorgmehr (1996) noted that the first wave, dominated by Chinese, Asian Indians, and Koreans, was of a highly educated, professional nature and included doctors, nurses, pharmacists, engineers, and students, whereas the second wave, led generally by uneducated and unskilled immigrants from Southeast Asia (Vietnam, etc.), contained political refugees and "boat people," who found economic survival a challenge. The researchers noted that immigrants of the second wave settled in LA's inner-city neighborhoods, swelling poverty rates in some places to 11 percent by 1990 (Waldinger and Bozorgmehr, 1996). In 1970 Los Angeles's Asian population was less than a quarter million, but by 1990, 1.3 million Asians were counted among the totals, making Asians nearly one of every ten Los Angeles residents.

By 1990 the Los Angeles region contained an incredibly diverse range of racial and ethnic groups and economic polarization. These issues led James Allen and Eugene Turner to take up the concern of racial equity (1997). These researchers employed ratios for selected indicators (educational attainment, occupational status, income gap, and home ownership) to compare the differential status of the various racial groups that make up the region's cultural mosaic. The ratios for educational attainment, based on the completion of high school and of a four-year college, showed a large black-white gap at both levels for men and women in 1960. Generally, however, by 1990 the education gap narrowed slightly, but the already wide gap between men at the college level actually widened. Not surprisingly, similarly large education gaps (at the high school and the college level) existed between whites and nonwhite Hispanics (even larger for Mexican immigrants), for men and women. For Asians, however, the ratios were remarkably different. Categorically, the education gap favored Asians. On the surface such numbers supported the notion of Asians as the "model minority."

Cheng and Yang (1996) have suggested that this model (and myth) was created during the civil rights era to combat the challenge of minority blacks against majority whites. It paints Asians as good, hardworking people who, despite their suffering through discrimination, harassment, and exclusion, have found ways to prosper through peaceful means. Thus, Asians overcame many obstacles through strong cultural and family values, foremost among them being perseverance, pride, patience, and a very high regard for education. As Cheng and Yang (1996) noted, the model ignores the anger and rage experienced by a wide range of Asian ethnics (Lagunda, 1995) and, as important, ignores the reality of the entry of "boat people" and female Asians with dramatically less education and skills than earlier Asian immigrants and who work for less than others to become established in the labor force. These researchers offered empirical evidence to debunk this model-minority myth. Evidence from labor, household income, and wage statistics supported their contention not only that Asian success varies by ethnicity but that Asians receive less than equal financial rewards for similar skills and work as compared to their white counterparts. The authors' "fatal criticism" of the model is that Asian "ethnic groups do not seem to be progressing at comparable rates, no matter how hard they try" (Cheng and Yang, 1996, p. 324). They noted the "double burden" of many Asian Americans who must invest time "to learn the ropes" of employment, often at lower-than-market wages and then, after acquiring the requisite skills, must face persistent discrimination that results in less than equitable compensation as compared to white Americans. Another result of this situation is substantial economic differentiation among Asians that has led to class distinction and residential segregation among them (Wong, 1999, 2000).

Similar issues were raised by Allen and Turner's analysis (1997), which noted that better education ratios for Asians were due to the incipient education base of the first Asian immigration wave and did not translate into better-paying jobs. Their analysis was based on an occupation gap measure (the proportion of jobs occupied by a minority group in high-status versus lower-status jobs). The white-collar, or high-status, jobs included professional and management positions with administrative and executive responsibilities. Apart from Chinese women, all minority groups, men and women, had lower ratios for this indicator than their white counterparts in the 1960s. By 1990 the occupational gap narrowed in all categories except Mexican immigrants and Chinese women (both had poor English and low education levels). Despite this general narrowing of the high-status occupations gap during the thirty-year period, the relative median income gaps widened in the same period. Apparently, the access to high-status jobs did not translate into anything near income equity for Asians and other minorities. Allen and Turner noted that even the relatively high incomes of Japanese men by 1990 could be attributed to executive positions temporarily filled by male visitors. Clearly, the lack of convergence between occupation and wages reflects white advantage and control of the labor force between 1960 and 1990 in California.

Finally, Allen and Turner analyzed home ownership rates for the same thirty-year period. On one hand, they found that African-American rates were stable, but Hispanics experienced a widening of the already existing negative gap with whites. Asians, on the other hand, realized gains in home ownership that did much to close the Asian-white gap between 1960 and 1990. In fact, they reported that home ownership in the region was higher for the Japanese and Chinese groups than for whites. Despite this and perhaps because of the economic polarization and ethnic diversity among Asians, Allen and Turner found that Asians had a definite pattern of segregation among themselves. Despite this intraracial segregation, there has been evidence of racial mixing among ethnic Asians in some parts of Southern California. This has led some to believe that residential separation of the races is due to economic rather than racial factors. In fact, increasing racial diversity and stable, or even increased, home ownership rates among some racial groups has led to the hope for a more integrated set of residential neighborhoods in Southern California, a true racial mosaic. However, Clark

(1996; also see Clark, 1998) has cautioned researchers against accepting this neighborhood-level "multiethnicity model." His analysis of ethnic mixing and racial segregation at various scales of geography in the LA region led him to warn against disposing of the succession model in favor of multiethnicity. He believes that rapid demographic change due to immigration has blurred the succession process. Clark pointed to particular racial trends at the neighborhood level to make his case.

> Tracts that were almost all-white stayed all-white. In contrast, tracts in the 20 to 40 percent minority range were very likely to become more minority (Hispanic or Asian) but, as predicted from the demographic changes, also less black. . . . Perhaps more significantly, of the sixty-four tracts that met the 20 percent criterion [20 percent of at least three different groups] in 1980, only twenty-two maintained a stable mixed structure in 1990. Again the analysis suggests caution in abandoning old models of succession and in accepting descriptions of large-scale multiethnic integration as stable [Clark, 1996, pp. 133 and 134].

Clark concluded that the 1990 patterns of multiethnicity may well be transitory. He expects such patterns to be reversed—"swept away by the effects of continuing large-scale immigration" (p. 137)—resulting in ethnic majorities' replacing the multiethnic mix.

In summary, the Los Angeles region experienced substantial change between 1960 and 1990, especially in the racial and ethnic mix of its population. Hispanics, largely Mexicans with modest or low skills, entered the region in enormous numbers. Asians became Los Angeles's third largest racial group. Some Asians came with considerable education and skills, others with very limited skills and small promise. As a group, Asians had relatively high levels of education as compared to all other groups during the 1960–1990 period. Although initially lagging behind whites in filling professional and high-status jobs, they managed to close the occupational gap in a generation. However, despite these occupational gains, they received less compensation than whites for their work. Despite this, the Asian group closed the equity gap with whites in terms of home ownership, whereas blacks and Hispanics saw no gains. Also, despite some evidence of multiethnic residential mixing, there is reason to be cautious before dispensing with the succession model that predicts a single racial majority in a neighborhood.

For many, like Allen and Turner (1997), racial and economic polarization, combined with segregation, is a long-term problem. The immigration process has greatly impacted the Los Angeles region, with as yet unclear results for mixed-race neighborhood stability. Despite full knowledge of their long-term impacts, evidence of segregation, economic polarization, and discrimination persists in Southern California, as they have elsewhere in urban America. This led Allen and Turner (1997) to conclude, unfortunately, that

1990s California is "a collection of ethnic societies" rather than a multiethnic melting pot (p. 259).

These findings can be used as leading principles as we explore the nature of other multiracial communities in an attempt to understand their residential patterns. They lead to questions about equity in racially mixed places. For example, how do multiracial neighborhoods in which Asians mix with whites, Hispanics, and African Americans compare? It seems obvious that Asians, when mixing with whites at the neighborhood level, assimilate with whites by being of similar socioeconomic status. However, what is the nature of black-Asian and Hispanic-Asian neighborhoods, even if transitory, as Clark cautions us, and how do they compare on various equity measures? Further, how do these areas compare to majority-black and BHN areas? We address this question in the next section, after discussing experiences of minorities in Alameda County. First we examine the roles and experiences of the Chinese. Then we report the change in the fate of Asians in Alameda County when African Americans came there in substantial numbers. Each minority story is important for a clearer picture of race relations and for understanding how the current racial mosaic has been shaped, socioeconomically and geographically.

The Making of a Racial Mosaic:
Alameda County, California

White-Chinese Racial Tensions, 1850–1940

By the time California was admitted to the United States in 1850, Hispanic California was already changing due to the lumber industry and Gold Rush, which attracted white and Asian transplants to the region. By the late 1800s, Alameda County had grown to include 8,927 residents. Oakland's future growth was sealed in 1870, when it was selected as the western terminus of the newly completed transcontinental railroad. Its population had risen to 10,500 by 1870; the county then boasted 24,237 people. The breaking of bulk at the rail terminus led to an economic boom that continued to boost the local population (Bagwell, 1982). Factories sprang up almost overnight; lumber, breweries, and canneries flourished. In addition, Alameda County, rich in fertile soil, became a diverse agricultural region with central city Oakland providing the processing and shipping (Bagwell, 1982). With the Gold Rush and early economic development came ethnic and racial diversity. By 1860 nearly 40 percent of the county's population was foreign-born, and a small number of African Americans came as employees (porters) of the Pullman Company. The Chinese came for gold but found employment building dams and working for the railroads. Important parts of Alameda County's economy came to depend on and preferred Chinese labor, including agricultural canning and the shipyards (Ma and Ma, 1982). Unlike African Americans, whose housing was segregated early, Asians in 1870s Alameda County were highly dispersed (Bagwell, 1982). This, however, was soon to change.

An economic downturn in the 1870s led to lower wages and unemployment in California. Angry whites blamed Chinese workers for their economic hardships, and in 1882 the first Chinese Exclusion Act became law. This prohibited other Chinese, including the wives of those present in the United States, from entering the United States. Economic hard times waxed and waned for the remainder of the nineteenth century, but Chinese bashing continued for decades. Anti-coolie clubs and the Workingmen's Party took control of the Oakland-Alameda area and provided economic harassment that, coupled with legal and physical attacks, crippled Chinese initiative and violated their basic freedoms. The Chinese of Alameda County, like those of other communities, were subjected to riots, beatings, mass firings, and isolation. Accompanying the anti-Chinese feelings and harassment was the demand for the destruction of Chinatown. In fact, Oakland's Chinatown was relocated several times. Also, local and state politicians joined the cry for Chinese exclusion (Cummings and Pladwell, 1942), and the California state constitution permitted (until 1890) the removal or segregation of the Chinese people by municipality (S. C. Miller, 1969). Together, these forms of restriction, harassment, and violence shaped the Chinese experience for a generation and led to a reduction of their population by more than 1,000 in Alameda County between 1880 and 1890, about 25 percent of their 1880 total. This situation changed dramatically in 1906.

The San Francisco earthquake and fire of 1906 resulted in the displacement of thousands of people, including nearly 4,000 Chinese (a number higher than Alameda's total Chinese population in 1890) who entered Oakland that year (Ma and Ma, 1982). Many became long-term Oakland residents and, due to local restrictions, were forced to reside in an expanded "Chinatown." For the next decade, the general economic health resulted in growth, but barriers kept the Chinese from leaving the crowded Chinatown. At a time when the Chinese were benefiting from a better economy, the "whites only" specifications of local zoning and neighborhood regulations forced separatism that segregated the Oakland Chinese into the city's Chinatown (Ma and Ma, 1982). What today is sometimes presented as an example of Chinese unity and choice was, in fact, place dictated by law.

Economic hardship followed the Chinese through the early 1900s by way of lower wages and unemployment during downturns in the California economy. The racism that led to the Chinese Exclusion Act in 1882 also provided the impetus for the 1924 National Origins Act, which limited new Chinese immigrants to about one hundred persons per year. In the late 1930s, as the general economic conditions in the state and nation improved, Chinese Americans in Alameda County, as in other places, were still restricted from buying homes in most neighborhoods. This was due to real-estate agents and developers' racist convictions that racial invasion of a neighborhood led to racial succession and then, inevitably, to the devaluation of that neighborhood (Abrams, 1971).

Thus, up until World War II, the Chinese of Alameda County, though contributing much to its early prosperity, were the scapegoats of racists during economic bad times. Once discrimination was set in motion in Alameda County, it persisted. Chinese lived in forced separation from Euro-American whites, despite the fact that they had worked hard and earned the financial status to leave inner-city Chinatown for better housing. Regulated by state and local laws, the Chinese were denied access to white neighborhoods until World War II erupted, when a new scapegoat would free them. In short, social, procedural, and generational equity issues were a significant part of Chinese-Asian history in this region until World War II.

White-Black Tension and Asian Prosperity, World War II to the Present

World War II not only resulted in an economic boom for California but also signaled the beginning of a new attitude toward selected Asian ethnic groups. The suffering of Japanese Americans is well documented. During the war, however, Chinese and other Asian ethnic groups in California saw their stock rise among Euro-American White–operated businesses. Much of California's initial economic impetus came from federal government spending that fueled wartime expansion:

> A decade before, the total expenditures of the federal government for fiscal year 1930 had been less than $3 billion. In the period between 1940 and 1946, the federal government spent about $360 billion . . . $35 billion of this was spent in California. In the fiscal year 1945 alone, the federal government spent $8.5 billion in California [Bagwell, 1982, p. 34].

These investments, and private spending, led to the growth of other industries as well, including military bases, shipbuilding, and food packing. Asian labor and skills were needed for an exploding economy that suffered labor shortages. As a result, the war years yielded growth in California that swelled its population by more than 2 million.

Not surprisingly, the sheer number of new people resulted in problems, including shortages in housing and consumer goods. Beyond this, however, there were problems due to race and gender. The labor shortage forced women into former male employment niches. Further, African Americans and Asians moved into jobs previously dominated by White males. White-dominated Alameda County responded to these racial groups in different ways. The Chinese, for example, although scorned in earlier decades, had been visible in the region for a long time and, as important, had been viewed by at least some as preferred workers. African Americans, in contrast, though also in the region for some time, had very small numbers and were less visible. Further, they had worked in only a very few employment niches. During the war years, the small African-American population swelled dramatically due to the thousands migrating to California from the eastern United States. These new arrivals were segregated into black neighborhoods in inner-city Oakland. During the war years, the African-American population grew eightfold, totaling more than 37,000 by 1945, and by 1950 reached 50,000 (Bagwell, 1982).

This likely resulted in the same situation noted in Chapter 2, namely, the local white population feeling overwhelmed by the sheer volume of new African Americans into a region formerly dominated by whites. The result was the same—the enforcement of color-line inequalities. Restricted by the local housing market and becoming the scapegoats for wartime problems, African Americans were paid less than others and were hired for mainly unattractive jobs. Bagwell noted the white-black racial tensions due to whites blaming blacks for food and housing shortages and other problems for which blacks certainly held no ultimate responsibility. Black reactions to white accusations, criticisms, and harassment caused the tensions to worsen. Bagwell (1982), noting the mistreatment of African Americans, also cited the negative reactions to blacks by the local press, including the accusation that black newcomers were to blame for "stirring up the good niggers" (p. 240).

Some Asian Americans still may have suffered from the spillover effect of the anti-Japanese sentiment of the war years, but generally speaking, non-Japanese Asians gained greater acceptance from whites than did the newcomer blacks. The improved socioeconomic status that Asians achieved during the war continued into the 1950s. As a result, the acceptance of Asian Americans increased, and their status improved. Thus, the Chinese and other Asians were permitted to leave Oakland's Chinatown for other Alameda neighborhoods. As Ma and Ma (1982) observed, laws and patterns during and after World War II changed significantly:

... laws which restricted Chinese immigration and the rights of Chinese Americans began to fall. The most important of these changes was the repeal of the Chinese Exclusion Act. ... Chinese immigrants were finally allowed to apply for American citizenship. In addition, the California State Legislature repealed the provision of California's constitution forbidding the state to employ Chinese in 1944. Many other obstacles to free and equal employment were removed during the war years as the country found it needed the services of the Chinese immigrants and their Chinese American descendants [pp. 84–85].

In 1948, the United States Supreme Court ruled the restriction neighborhood covenants unconstitutional ... [p. 90].

These actions stimulated Chinese population growth between 1950 and 1960 from 6,500 to 7,500. These numbers pale, however, when compared to the influx of African Americans. Unfortunately, Alameda County whites seemed to have reacted to blacks in Oakland virtually in the same way as eastern whites did in New York and other cities.

Although the Asian population increased between 1940 and 1960, it was, as noted earlier, the two waves of Asian migration, the first linked to the 1965 Hart-Cellar Act, that dramatically increased Asian diversity and size in California. Alameda County was no exception. Obviously, an increased Asian population occurred during a period of rapid expansion of the Hispanic (largely Mexican) population as well. Both came on the heels of the great influx of African Americans during and after World War II, resulting in an increasingly racially diverse Alameda County.

A Profile of Contemporary Alameda County

Alameda County experienced only modest population growth (3.2 percent) during the 1970s due to the combined factors of increasing housing prices and recession (Alameda County Planning Department, 1996). However, from 1980 to 1990 the total population increased by nearly 16.0 percent, to nearly 1.3 million. This period was also one of substantial racial and ethnic change. The County's Asian/Pacific Islander population doubled, while its Hispanic- and African-American populations increased 39 percent and 13 percent, respectively. The white population increased by a scant 3 percent in the same period. In 1990 whites were a very modest 53 percent majority population in Alameda County, whereas African Americans were the largest minority, at 17.5 percent, and the rapidly growing Hispanic community, of which 66 percent were of Mexican origin, accounted for nearly 14 percent of the county's total population. The Asian population, originally dominated by the Chinese, had diversified with the arrival of large numbers of Koreans, Japanese, and Vietnamese, as well as the relatively new Cambodian and Laotian populations. By 1990 the Asian/Pacific Islander group represented nearly 15 percent of the county's total population. The significance of immigration to Alameda County will likely continue in this century. One forecast suggests that all minorities combined will represent nearly 60 percent of the county's residents by 2010 (Alameda County Planning, 1996).

By 1990, the racial/ethnic profiles of the county and the city of Oakland were strikingly different. The largest discrepancy between the two distributions involved blacks. About 43 percent of Oakland's population was black in 1990—about double the percentage of blacks residing in the county. Whites, in contrast, accounted for slightly more than one in every four Oakland residents (28 percent) in 1990, whereas they constituted a majority in the county. Asian and Hispanic proportions were virtually the same for the city and the county (about 14 percent).

Race and poverty are closely connected in this region. The regional income and poverty statistics reported for the Bay Area, Alameda County, and Oakland underscore the impact of Oakland's large minority and immigrant populations. Oakland's median household and median family incomes in 1990 were much lower than those of the county and Bay Region, the smallest gap being about $10,000 in annual household income. The gap, of course, is wider when Oakland is compared to the wealthier nine-county Bay Region, whose $48,532 median family income in 1990 was almost $17,000 higher than Oakland's. The poverty rate differences were equally significant and reflected both Oakland's inner city and more widely distributed poverty within the entire city as compared to other parts of Alameda County and the broader region. Oakland's 18.8 percent poverty rate exceeded that of the Bay Region by more than 10 percentage points in 1990 and exceeded the County's by more than 8 percentage points. These proportions probably mirror comparable gulfs between most U.S. central cities and their respective counties and regions. However, they underscore the equity arguments made earlier and, given the racial mix of minorities in Oakland, substantiate the need to raise questions about inequalities between various minority groups and between places where they mix.

In 1990 slightly more than one-third of all Oakland households qualified for federal low-to-moderate-income status. When race is considered in Oakland, it appears that poverty affected all minorities disproportionately as compared to whites. Nearly two-thirds (64 percent) of all Hispanic households qualified for poverty status in 1990, whereas six of ten African-American households had the same status. Asian/Pacific Islanders were not far behind in 1990, with a 59 percent poverty rate. The problems suffered by Oakland's poor are noted in the city's *Consolidated Plan,* which reported not only the relationship between minority status and poverty but the links between homelessness and housing needs and between race and housing problems (City of Oakland, 2000). It stated that nearly half of Oakland households experience housing problems and that racial groups are segregated into residential neighborhoods of lesser and greater needs. It also identified the lack of quality housing data by race but stated unequivocally that the housing problems encountered by all minorities are similar and include cost, crowding, and deterioration. The plan notes that, despite the city's racial and ethnic diversity, racial concentrations are evident and contribute to economic polarization and housing problems. It reported, for example, that "Whites are concentrated in the hills and above MacArthur Boulevard" and that Hispanics are concentrated in places like Fruitvale. In addition, it provided descriptions of inner-city examples of combined Asian and African-American concentrations, including descriptions of Asians in the formerly all-black San Antonio area. The economic polarization of Los Angeles noted by Allen and Turner obviously also is present in Alameda County, as are discriminatory bank lending patterns and other forms of discrimination that affect fair housing choice.

> Patterns of racial clusters and segregation are readily identifiable, suggesting that discrimination continues to be a serious problem and an impediment to fair housing choice [City of Oakland, 2000, p. 105].

By design, consolidated plans emphasize needs related to poverty. They say little about equity outside the HUD-defined low-to-moderate-income geography. As demonstrated in earlier chapters, inequalities spread across the geographic and socioeconomic landscape when minorities are present. Therefore, it is necessary to examine the racial patterns of Alameda County beyond its poverty zones.

Figure 6.1 is a map series of racial distributions in Alameda County in 1998. Figure 6.1(a) represents the distribution of the county's white population in 1998. The pattern is obviously in keeping with the description of the Oakland *Consolidated Plan*. The census tracts containing the greater proportion of whites are those to the north and west of central-city Oakland and in municipalities located to the east, far from the downtown. Figure 6.1(b) represents the distribution of African Americans. They are highly segregated in two separate sections of Oakland, one in the North and West Oakland areas that spills over into Chinatown and the other centered in the Elmhurst area. Both are poverty zones (City of Oakland, 2000). The black population mixes with Asian and Hispanic populations within these highly segregated neighborhoods. They mix in other areas as well, including with Asians—for example, in neighborhoods outside the Oakland inner city, where black social status changes from poor to middle class.

Figure 6.1(c) represents the Asian distribution in Alameda County. Obviously, there are Asian concentrations in inner-city Oakland, such as in Chinatown. However, as this map shows, Asians have decentralized substantially due to the factors cited earlier in this chapter and now boast a much wider geographic distribution than African Americans. Even though Asians represented about 15 percent of Alameda County's population in 1990, they appeared as more than one-quarter of the population of numerous tracts in various parts of the county, including Berkeley, Alameda, Freemont, Hayward, and Oakland. As a result, they are mixed with whites and Hispanics, as well as with African Americans, in various neighborhoods throughout the county. Although Asians have been mixed with all races, some newcomer Asians have mixed with an inner-city, poor black population in various proportions. For example, in largely black Central Oakland and West Oakland, Asians range from 11 percent to 20 percent of the total population, whereas in San Antonio they are as much as 40 percent of the total population. Asians and blacks reside in integrated neighborhoods, however, outside these inner-city neigh-

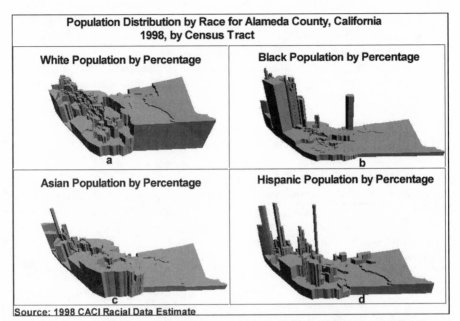

FIGURE 6.1   1998 population distribution by race, Alameda County, California
(by census tract): percentage of population that is (a) white; (b) black; (c) Asian;
(d) Hispanic. Source: CACI Marketing Systems, 1998.

borhoods as well. Whether such neighborhoods are transitory and will finally
succumb to succession, as Clark suggested for Los Angeles, must await future
analysis of the 2000 census. For now, it is quite clear that various forms and
types of mixing occurred in the 1990s.

Figure 6.1(d) is a map of the Hispanic population distribution in Alameda
County in 1990. The Hispanic distribution across Alameda County is more
like that of Asians than of African Americans. Two-thirds of all Alameda
County Hispanics are Mexican, many of them light skinned. This likely explains why they have been more successful than their African-American counterparts in assimilating into a wider range of racial/ethnic neighborhoods
across Alameda County. Despite this, and like blacks and Asians, Hispanics
are also geographically concentrated in places like Fruitvale and in inner-city
Oakland, where a disproportionate number of minorities are trapped in
poverty. As noted earlier, many Hispanics reside in BHNs with blacks, such as
in Central East Oakland (City of Oakland, 2000). Unlike African Americans,
however, Hispanics have spread into numerous neighborhoods outside Oakland, where they mix with races of diverse socioeconomic status. They may
also occupy buffer areas that separate African Americans and whites. Whatever the case, Hispanics, like other Alameda County minorities, have complex distributions that include mixing with all racial groups.

This complex pattern of racial mixing in Alameda County clarifies the limitation of the HUD-defined AOMC (Chapter 1) for such complex multiracial communities. Given the Alameda County pattern, it is necessary to deconstruct the AOMC concept into a more complete classification in order to make some general conclusions about equity concerns in a multiracial environment.

Equity Issues in a Multiracial Environment

The Multiracial Census Tract Designations
We noted above that major class distinctions exist within all of Alameda County's racial distributions (e.g., poor Asians and wealthy Asians). Elsewhere it has been claimed that one of the largest black middle-class populations in the United States resides in Oakland (Bagwell, 1982). In addition, we have demonstrated the complex set of racial distributions that include the mixing of all races at some level within the county. With this in mind, we developed a classification of census tracts according to the presence of two or more races. Our interests were in comparing various racially composed areas, specifically those places where minorities mix in some proportion. For this analysis we are not concerned with areas that are predominately white and have no secondary race of any magnitude. For example, if a tract contained some small mix of Asians, blacks, and Hispanics that was overwhelmed by a white population, we chose to exclude it from our classification and analysis. In fact, we focused on places where Asians mixed with the other races in some meaningful proportion and compared these areas to each other and to other nonwhite race areas. Our race-based classification of census tracts follows.

1. *White-Asian* areas (N = 60) are census tracts in which at least 10 percent of the total population was Asian in 1990 and the combined Asian and white populations exceeded 90 percent of the total tract population. The proportion of Asians in these tracts varies greatly. For that reason we did a means test on two subgroups, one a set of tracts with less than 15 percent Asians and the other with more than 15 percent Asians. Using the same socioeconomic and housing variables tested in Chapter 5, we found no significant differences between the group means. Thus, since no differences existed, we use the full set of white-Asian tracts as one of our racial areas to be compared to others. The distribution of these areas can be viewed in Figure 6.2.
2. *Hispanic-Asian* areas (N = 24) are tracts that contained this two-race combination in a proportion that exceeded all other combinations. Sometimes the Hispanic total exceeds the Asian. Other times the opposite is true.

3. *Black-Asian* census tracts (N = 37) are combinations based on the same criteria as Hispanic-Asian tracts: When the black and Asian populations combined represent the largest population, they are classified as black-Asian. Either race can be the larger of the two in any given tract.
4. *Black-Hispanic* census tracts (N = 15) are comparable to the BHNs studied in Chapter 5. However, Hispanics are a majority in only four census tracts in Alameda County and are more widely distributed on a census tract basis as compared to some of the urban centers studied in Chapter 5 (such as Cook County, Illinois). Further, considering African Americans, although there are numerous tracts in Oakland with a black majority, most of these majority tracts also contain significant numbers of Hispanics and Asians. Given this, our Alameda County BHNs are more black than Hispanic. Any census tract that was 50 percent black and at least 15 percent Hispanic was classified as BHN.
5. *Mixed-race* census tracts (N = 81) are those that combine three minority groups, or two minorities and the white population, in such a way that each of the three represents at least 10 percent of the total population and the combination has not been classified as any of the other four classes (see above).

A Two-Tract Comparison of the Mixed-Asian Areas

All the preceding classifications have some within-group variation. For example, we know that not all black-Asian census tracts have high poverty rates, nor are they populated only by those working in low-income occupations. Such differences within groups could be tested statistically, but that is not our purpose. We wish only to offer a few examples of census tracts for the mixed-race areas to illustrate some of their diversity and to caution the reader not to overinterpret our statistical results. We randomly selected two tracts to represent each of the types of areas designated by our racial classification described above. Table 6.1 provides profiles for the three types of area classifications that involve Asians mixing with the other races. The two black-Asian tract profiles illustrate that a range of socioeconomic levels exists in areas within the same classification. In one case (tract 4081) in Oakland, black middle- and professional-class households coexist with Asian households. The other black-Asian tract, also in Oakland, is not as well-off in terms of socioeconomic status. The differences between the two census tracts are obvious. The 1990 median incomes were separated by nearly $42,000, and the median housing value by nearly $270,000. One tract had a higher percentage of unemployment and a higher proportion of uneducated residents than the other. Not surprisingly, there was a difference in employment patterns as well, as reflected in the statistics related to employment in professional and executive positions.

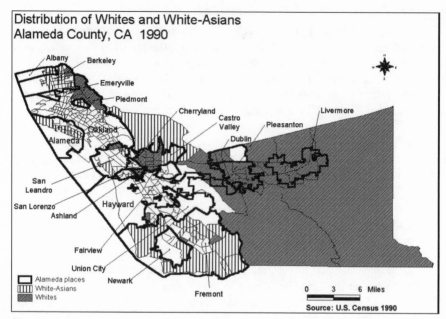

FIGURE 6.2   Distribution of white and white-Asian census tracts, Alameda County, California, 1990. Source: U.S. Census Bureau, 1990.

Table 6.1 also presents two 1990 profiles of Hispanic-Asian census tracts. Although within-group differences are obvious, they are not comparable to the differences displayed between the two black-Asian tracts. One of these Hispanic-Asian tracts is in Hayward, the other in Union City. Finally, Table 6.1 also reports the 1990 profiles for two white-Asian tracts, one in Alameda and one in Hayward. Again, within-group socioeconomic status differences are obvious, but the differences between the two tracts are less pronounced than those of the black-Asian areas.

We believe that the differences within these groups are important enough to warrant caution when interpreting our subsequent findings. However, despite these within-group differences and our caution, we also believe that significant differences will occur between the classes of our racially defined areas and are worthy of attention. In short, in our implicit hypotheses, we expect that the white-Asian areas will fare better than any other racial area type due to the obvious historical advantage of white-dominated areas. By associating with whites we believe that Asians will benefit from white advantage and from their incipient educational advantage. Perhaps less obvious is the advantage of Hispanic-Asian areas over other areas. Specifically, we expect the Hispanic-Asian areas to fare better than the remaining area types, largely due to the inequalities suffered by African Americans. Put another way, wherever

TABLE 6.1   Socioeconomic and Racial/Ethnic Profiles of Selected Census Tracts,
Alameda County, California, 1990

	Black-Asian Tracts		Hispanic-Asian Tracts		White-Asian Tracts	
	Oakland	Oakland	Hayward	Union City	Alameda	Hayward
Tract Number	4054	4081	4382.01	4403.31	4279	4328
No high school diploma (%)	24.1	4.4	22.8	17.3	7.0	9.6
Unemployed (%)	5.8	1.4	2.4	4.5	2.6	1.1
Exec.-prof Employees (%)	19.3	52.0	13.2	18.3	26.4	31.5
Median housing value*	$80K	$351K	$160K	$234K	$282K	$328K
Blacks (%)	35.1	31.8	7.4	8.3	2.9	3.3
Hispanics (%)	17.8	4.0	32.6	29.5	7.8	10.9
Asians (%)	38.3	18.4	22.0	34.0	13.6	17.3
Median income*	$20K	$62K	$31K	$45K	$33K	$328K
Chinese (%)	22.2	12.5	0	3.3	1.9	5.5
Filipinos (%)	2.6	0	15.0	15.1	7.6	3.2
Japanese (%)	0	2.5	1.0+	1.0+	1.0+	5.4
Koreans (%)	1.0+	1.0+	0	1.0+	0	1.0+
Vietnamese (%)	6.6	0	1.6	3.8	0	0
Cambodians (%)	4.1	1.0+	0	0	0	0

*Rounded.

SOURCE: U.S. Census Bureau, 1990

blacks combine with other races, we expect those areas to suffer the most and have the least equitable position. The logic of our position rests on historical facts presented earlier in this chapter and previous chapters. Most Chinese and other Asians came to Alameda County after World War II, after the local white culture had "warmed up" to their inclusion in American society. Although a black middle class has emerged, blacks as a race are still saddled by a long history including not only the enslavement of their ancestors by white Americans but the mistreatment of their friends, families, and themselves since arriving in Oakland during and after World War II. In short, not only did the attitudes of the receiving white majority change toward Asians, as we noted earlier, but blacks replaced Asians as scapegoats for economic and social problems in the county. As a result, African Americans generally inherited the negative status, restrictions, and inequalities that came with scapegoating and have not recovered.

Even though many recently arriving Hispanics are poor Mexicans seeking a better life, other, second-, third- and younger-generation Hispanics likely have moved to Alameda County suburbs, where they live in better conditions than their inner-city counterparts. For this reason, we expect the Hispanic-Asian areas to be better off than the BHNs but worse off than white-Asian areas. Given our findings in Chapter 5 however, and the locations of the Alameda County BHNs—generally in the city of Oakland—we expect the black-Hispanic neighborhoods to be the least well-off of the county's racially mixed neighborhoods.

Inequalities in Alameda County's Racially Complex Areas

Our methodology for the remainder of this chapter is the same as that employed in Chapter 5. Our tests use exactly the same socioeconomic, housing, and service variables, except the tests of means are those of the racially complex (mixed) areas defined above. We also tested for mean differences in median household income and median housing value, using 2000 data estimates. We included the black-majority areas in our tests because they serve as a minority baseline (see results of Chapter 5) against which all the mixed-race areas can be compared.

White-Asian Areas.   The results of our tests comparing white-Asian areas to each other racially defined area type, not surprisingly, show that the white-Asian and black-majority areas differed significantly on every socioeconomic and housing variable (except number of pre-1940 houses) tested (see Table 6.2). They also were different on all service ratios. The median housing values for the two areas were separated by nearly $150,000, and the 1990 income figures differed by more than $20,000. These findings, of course, mirror the race-place results of Chapter 5, which found that the biggest differences in the forty-urban-county study were between white and black areas.

Surprisingly, the white-Asian versus black-Hispanic area comparisons, while yielding virtually the same general patterns, revealed an even greater disparity in median housing value (nearly $200,000) and a similar income disparity, about $18,000. Three of the four results related to services indicate potential inequalities between the two area types for dentist, doctor, and bank ratios in favor of the white-Asian areas. We remind the reader that the black-Hispanic areas can be either black- or Hispanic-dominated areas but contain a high proportion of each.

Differences between white-Asian and Hispanic-Asian areas are less dramatic but still significant, specifically for unemployment, education, crowding, and percentage of housing built prior to 1940. The differences in income and housing amounted to about $9,000 and $110,000, respectively, in favor of the white-Asian areas.

When white-Asian and black-Asian areas' means are compared, again, dramatic differences are revealed: All socioeconomic and housing variables (except

TABLE 6.2　White-Asian versus Minority Areas Mean Difference Between Socioeconomic, Housing, and Service Variables by Racially Mixed Neighborhood Types

Variables	White-Asian vs. Black	White-Asian vs. Black-Hispanic	White-Asian vs. Hispanic-Asian	White-Asian vs. Black-Asian	White-Asian vs. Mixed-Race
Unemployment	.001	.002	.01	.004	–
Income-to-poverty ratio	.001	–	–	.001	.05
Median Household Income	.001	.001	.04	.001	.03
Education	.001	.002	.002	.001	.001
Population	–	–	–	–	–
Crowding	.001	.01	.001	.001	–
Median Housing Value	.001	.001	.001	.001	.001
Rentals	.001	–	–	.001	–
Vacancies	.001	.02	–	.013	–
Units built prior to 1940	–	–	.002	–	–
Dentists	.02	.05	–	–	–
Doctors	.05	.05	–	–	–
Pharmacies	.01	–	–	–	–
Banks	.034	.047	.01	–	
Black	.001	.001	.001	.001	.001
White	.001	.001	.001	.006	–
Hispanic	–	.021	.001	–	.001
Asian	.001	.001	–	–	.005
Median housing values	$271,711* vs. $122,107	$271,711* vs. $78,633	$271,711* vs. $161,450	$271,711* vs. $131,902	$271,711* vs. $203,449
Median household income	$44,311* vs. $21,535	$44,311* vs. $26,113	$44,311* vs. $35,345	$44,311* vs. $22,015	$44,311* vs. $38,267

*Still significant using 2000 data estimates.

housing age) were significantly different between the two areas. There were no differences in services ratios. The mean household income of the white-Asian areas exceeds that of the black-Asian areas, by about $22,000, as does the median housing value, by approximately $140,000.

The smallest number of significant differences occurs between white-Asian and mixed-race areas. No service differences existed, and the two areas differed only on four variables. Unemployment rates and the proportion of rental housing were both higher in the mixed-race areas. Income and housing values also favored the white-Asian areas, the former by approximately $6,000 and the latter by $68,000.

Clearly, then, areas where Asians have assimilated with whites in Alameda County reflect contemporary white advantage and are similar to the findings of Chapter 5 for white-majority areas. Such areas, regardless of location, stand in stark contrast to areas characterized as nonwhite multiracial. The magnitude of the differences is greatest between white-Asian and black-majority areas and between white-Asian and black-Hispanic areas. Finally, when comparing white-Asian areas to the other race-based areas using 2000 data estimates, the differences in income and housing value appear to persist a decade later. Although our findings meet our expectations, we find the quantifiable differences in equity in Alameda County sobering.

Black-Asian Areas.   When the black-Asian areas are tested against the black-majority areas, no significant differences emerge. This is likely due to the argument we made earlier, namely, that the tracts representing these areas are polarized, containing both poor and the middle class. The mixing of these classes likely results in averages that neutralize the real differences that occur within each area type. When such averages are compared, no significant differences are apparent.

The test results for the black-Asian versus Hispanic-Asian areas show that clear differences exist in favor of the Hispanic-Asian areas. Although no service differences were apparent, the majority of socioeconomic- and housing-variable means were significantly different. Among these factors, median household income and housing value favored the Hispanic-Asian over black-Asian areas by about $13,000 and $30,000, respectively. Hispanic-Asian areas also experienced lower crowding rates as compared to black-Asian areas.

Black-Asian areas also are significantly different from black-Hispanic areas in important ways, based on the results of our tests. Black-Asian areas had more people living in poverty and a greater proportion of housing units built prior to 1940 than the black-Hispanic areas. These two areas also had significantly different incomes and housing values. The income of the black-Hispanic areas was about $4,000 higher annually than that of the black-Asian areas. However, the median housing value of the Asian-black areas exceeded the black-Hispanic areas' by over $50,000. It is fairly clear that the black-Asian areas contained the extremes of which we spoke earlier—namely, highly concentrated poor and un-educated Asians who are recent immigrants (the data for some of these tracts supports this by the concentration of Vietnamese, Laotian, Cambodian, and other recent immigrants), who joined other poor minorities, especially blacks, in inner-city Oakland; and a second group, Asians who have attained middle-class or professional status and are mixing with middle-class blacks in other tracts (thus, the $131,902 median housing value), even if only on a temporary basis (Clark, 1996). A better classification, in the future, would differentiate this area type on the basis of recency of immigration for the Asian population.

The mixed-race areas were statistically better-off than black-Asian areas as measured by the mean differences of all socioeconomic variables, including median household income (+$16,000) and median housing value (+$70,000). In summary, black-Asian areas were not statistically different from black-majority areas but differed significantly from all of the other three racially mixed areas under consideration. Of the other three areas, only the black-Hispanic areas appear to have a lower level of well-being than the black-Asian areas, based on our results.

Hispanic-Asian Areas. The results for Hispanic-Asian areas against the two remaining minority areas, the black-majority and mixed-race areas, showed significant differences. The black-Asian areas differ from Alameda County's black-majority areas on most of the factors tested, including two service variables—dentist and pharmacy ratios.

In all cases, the black-majority areas suffer greater social inequalities as compared to Hispanic-Asian areas. Although the income and housing-value differences are generally less dramatic than those revealed in our earlier comparison of minority areas, they are nonetheless significant and amount to nearly $14,000 for the income variable and about $40,000 for housing value in favor of Hispanic-Asian areas.

Summary
This brief analysis crystallizes some of the inequalities that existed between areas where racial mixing had occurred in Alameda County by 1990. They reflect both social and generational equity issues. These are summarized as follows:

1. White-Asian areas, which contain census tracts with a white majority but an Asian presence at various levels, are likely areas of Asian assimilation into white residential areas. This notion is supported by Figure 6.2, which illustrates that two of the largest areas of white-Asian census tracts are adjacent to the predominately white areas of Alameda County and also tend to be along the county's border. These white-Asian areas were substantially better-off than any minority or racially mixed area in our classification, as measured by a number of socioeconomic-status and housing indicators. Inequalities were particularly pronounced between white-Asian and black-majority areas and between white-Asian and black-Hispanic areas, where service ratios were also statistically different.

2. Black-Asian areas, which contain various combinations of the two races, do not have better levels of socioeconomic status and housing values than black-majority areas. No significant differences in service ratios emerged, either. We noted the shortcomings of not differentiating black-Asian areas on the basis of recent immigrants.

Black-Asian areas are clearly less well-off than Hispanic-Asian areas, where second- and third-generation minorities share space with other groups, including whites. Where three races mix to form complex racial areas, they too fare better than black-Asian areas as measured by all variables except service ratios.

In our analysis, black-Asian areas fared better than only the black-Hispanic areas, which supports our hypothesis that, where African Americans mix with other races, the result is negative from an equity position.

3. Hispanic-Asian areas, which are census tracts containing more of these two racial groups than any other racial combination, fared better on socioeconomic and housing indicators than the black-majority, black-Hispanic, and black-Asian areas. They also had better service ratios for dentists and pharmacies than the black-majority areas.

It seems clear from the above that major inequalities exist between a variety of minority and racially mixed areas in Alameda County. The Oakland *Consolidated Plan* is correct in stating that race, poverty, and housing problems are strongly interrelated. Beyond this, however, it is equally clear that major inequalities of various kinds also exist on a race-and-place basis. Enormous differences in well-being occurred in 1990 in places where races mix in various ways and in varying proportions. In most cases, the inequalities in income and housing value remained in 2000, based on the data estimates.

We believe that there is sufficient statistical verification to accept our first three hypotheses. The fourth hypothesis must be rejected. The greatest differences occurred between white-Asian areas and all other minority and racially mixed areas. White-Asian areas enjoy better socioeconomic, housing, and service levels than the other areas in question. Many Asians appear to benefit due to their association with white advantage and white attitudes, which permitted their assimilation into predominately white areas. As in other urban counties in the United States, black-majority and black-Hispanic areas compare unfavorably to all other areas. Blacks and Hispanics do best when they mix with Asians without one another. Hispanics have similar experiences to Asians when they mix with other groups. Hispanics figure poorly when mixing with blacks, and far better when they mix with others, specifically Asians and whites (in the racially mixed areas of our classification). Asians appear to do best when assimilating with whites and Hispanics.

Chapter 7

Indicators of Environmental Inequities and Threats to Minority Health in Urban America

Introduction

Research dedicated toward a better understanding and elimination of racial/ethnic disparities in the United States must extend well beyond residential segregation, accessibility to jobs and services, and other issues addressed in the preceding chapters, to include concerns of environmental justice and equity. Over the last two decades, a growing body of literature has established that there are significant disparities in the distribution of environmental hazards relative to the demographic characteristics of population subgroups, particularly in urbanized communities. Neighborhoods of color, low-income residents, and the working class are faced with higher rates of exposure to environmental pollutants from a wide variety of sources such as industrial and chemical manufacturing plants, waste facilities, Superfund sites, and hazardous-material accidents. They are also the least likely to benefit from effective risk reduction and remediation programs or the prompt enforcement of environmental regulation (Anderton, Oakes, and Egan, 1997).

The higher rates of exposure to environmental hazards translate into a greater likelihood of adverse health outcomes and, consequently, wider and more persistent disparities in health indicators, an issue of primary concern now expressed by the Centers for Disease Control. For example, blood lead levels for poor and minority children especially in metropolitan areas are consistently higher than their counterparts' in suburban and rural environments (Margai, Walter, Frazier, and Brink, 1997). These groups also have a greater incidence of low birth weight, respiratory ailments, and certain kinds of cancers that have been causally linked to environmentally induced risk factors (Institute of Medicine, 1999; Weiss and Wagener, 1990). Such deleterious outcomes, whether perceived or real, warrant a comprehensive and thorough investigation of the causative mechanisms of environmental inequalities, as well as the consequences and implications for race relations in the twenty-first century.

The purpose of this chapter is twofold. First, we examine some of the theoretical and analytical studies conducted in recent years to identify the processes and landscapes of environmental inequities. This review is based on a proposed framework that integrates the different perspectives into a conceptual model of environmental equity. In the second half of the chapter, a case study approach is utilized for two counties in New York State to provide supportive evidence of environmental inequities as well as illustrate the use of spatial analytical tools in validating these claims. The chapter ends with a discussion of remedial strategies and directions for future research on this topic.

A Conceptual Model of Environmental Equity Research

Empirical research on environmental equity has evolved over the last several decades from descriptive accounts to more detailed quantitative analysis of risks and exposure patterns in low-income and minority communities. Researchers working in different urban settings such as Houston, Boston, Los Angeles, Cleveland, Chicago, St. Louis, and Detroit have identified a broad range of processes, factors, and ineffective governmental policies that account for environmental inequities. Some studies have addressed these problems from a historical perspective, whereas others have focused on contemporary contexts involving the current distribution of hazards relative to disadvantaged groups. A convenient starting place for examining these studies is a proposed conceptual framework that incorporates three major dimensions of environmental equity: (1) process equity (2) outcome equity, and (3) response equity.

The notion of process equity relies on the causal factors and mechanisms that have contributed to the present-day landscapes of inequality. It includes historical processes such as industrialization, urbanization, migration and demographic shifts, housing developments, as well as institutional forces. The second component, outcome equity, focuses on the environmental indicators and the present-day disparities among population segments, particularly the proximal relationships between the hazards and disadvantaged groups. Previous researchers restricted environmental equity studies to only these two areas, process and outcome (Cutter, 1995; Scott, Cutter, Menzel, Ji, and Wagner, 1997). However, the additional dimension proposed here, response equity, is also an integral part of environmental equity investigations. It incorporates all of the policy responses by governments and the efforts made by the public and various organizations to identify and address these problems.

The relationships among the three components are depicted in Figure 7.1. These proposed relationships are based on linkages established earlier in the pressure–state response framework adopted by various organizations to deal with urban environmental problems (Organization for Economic Cooperation and Development, 1997). In general, the proposed framework suggests human choices, decisions, institutions, and activities such as industrialization, urbanization, siting, and agglomeration (processes) all contribute to the current distribution of environmental risks and disproportionate exposure among population subgroups (outcomes). Communities may respond to these outcomes through various approaches, such as the implementation of new environmental policies, grassroots activism, and legal and compensatory activities (responses). The last may act as feedback to minimize or eliminate the urban-environmental processes and alleviate the outcomes in existing communities. In the next three sections, various components of the model are discussed in detail, using previous research findings, to illustrate the complexity of these factors and the interactions between them that give rise to environmental inequalities in urban America.

Process Equity

As indicated earlier, studies of process equity address the dynamic and causative mechanisms of environmental inequities, specifically, the historical processes and factors that have contributed to current landscapes of inequalities. The investigations typically revolve around the fundamental question, Which came first, the people or the hazard? That is, were the hazardous facilities intentionally located in preexisting disadvantaged communities, or did low-income and minority populations migrate into the hazardous areas after the facilities were sited and, subsequently, the high-risk communities evolved? As with most studies of causation, it has been difficult to establish a comprehensive list of contributory factors or a chronology of events that best explains these outcomes. Instead researchers, often working in different situational contexts, have provided several arguments and, sometimes, conflicting evidence that point to one or more of the following processes:

1. Siting discrimination
2. Neighborhood changes or institutional forces and market dynamics
3. Racialization or immigration processes

Siting Discrimination. The siting of hazardous waste sites, landfills, toxic storage and disposal facilities (TSDFs), and other noxious land uses (all of which are typically referred to as "locally unwanted land uses," or LULUs) has fueled most of the debate on process equity. In evaluating historical siting decisions, some researchers claim that, more often than not, the communities that are unfairly targeted by polluting companies are those that pose minimal or no opposition to the siting process. For example, Walsh, Warland, and Smith (1993) noted that industry consultants typically focus on certain characteristics of target communities, such as the socioeconomic status of the residents, their level of education, degree of organization, level of discontent, and the presence or absence of a local supporter of the proposed project. Communities targeted

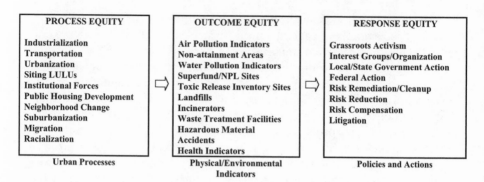

FIGURE 7.1   The three dimensions of environmental equity

in the past have been identified as "least resistant" either because most of the residents are economically disadvantaged, with lower educational attainment, or perhaps, because most are politically uninvolved.

Other researchers have investigated the role of race and ethnicity in the LULU siting decisions. For example, Bullard (1983) presented evidence to substantiate the strong relationships between race and facility siting. His research, based on historical siting decisions in Houston, Texas, concluded that minority communities were unfairly targeted. Yandle and Burton (1996) suggested a counterexplanation to siting discrimination, however. Based on the analysis of past demographic data, they concluded that race was not a factor in siting decisions. They compared the ethnic and economic characteristics of communities at two different times: (1) time of siting of the hazardous waste facilities and (2) several years later, during the 1990 census. The results revealed that, at the time of siting, hazardous wastes were more likely to be placed in poor white communities. In 1990, however, only poverty remained significant; there was no discernable shift to nonwhite communities, though the authors acknowledge a positive relationship between nonwhite populations and poverty in these communities. They inferred that perhaps a third variable, population density, was responsible for the observed distributions, since political objections to siting decisions were likely to be weaker in rural, sparsely populated communities than in densely populated areas.

Hamilton (1993, 1995) also explored the role of race, income, and political power in the siting and expansion of noxious facilities. Contrary to Yandle and Burton, he concluded that host communities often had a higher proportion of nonwhite populations. He examined three potential factors that explain the observed patterns: (1) intentional discrimination, (2) differences in willingness to pay, and (3) community participation. The last was the most significant factor. Specifically, the collective action of community members, through actual voter turnout, played an important role in determining the likelihood of site expansion. A subsequent study by Hird and Reese (1998) confirmed the role of political mobilization in explaining the uneven distribution of polluting facilities across the country.

Market Dynamics, Neighborhood Changes, and Community Evolution. Aside from the siting process, a variety of social, economic, and institutional forces are responsible for the contiguous distributions of disadvantaged neighborhoods and polluting industries. The dynamics of the housing market, neighborhood development, and institutional mechanisms are perhaps the most powerful and enduring factors. Been (1994) examined the role of market dynamics in the distribution of LULUs in Houston, Texas. Using historical data, she traced the neighborhood changes following the siting of LULUs. She concluded that the presence of LULUs often led to a decline in property values. Consequently, the demographics of the neighborhoods changed, with an increase in poverty levels and minority residents. Another investigation, in South Carolina, showed that once again, these noxious facilities were located prior to the emergence of residential neighborhoods (Mitchell, Thomas, and Cutter, 1999). The investigators concluded that the dynamics of the housing market, as well as state and regional migration patterns, are responsible for the inequities that currently characterize the host communities. In evaluating similar relationships between the housing market and environmental risks, Gayer (2000) revealed that environmental risks were greater in neighborhoods with low-priced housing, suggesting further that polluters considered such characteristics when making siting decisions.

The recurring theme emerging from the preceding studies is that market forces do in fact precipitate changes within the neighborhoods regardless of whether they occur before or after the siting of LULUs. Perhaps the most exhaustive analysis of these changes is provided by Liu (1997). In an attempt to develop an analytical framework of environmental equity dynamics, he incorporated four major theories of neighborhood change: (1) the classical invasion-succession model that is congruent with Burgess's ideas (1925) presented earlier in Chapter 4; (2) the neighborhood life cycle model; (3) push and pull factors; and (4) institutional forces. Using the invasion and succession model, Liu (1997) contended that racial and ethnic changes are analogous to ecological processes in which "competition, conflict and accommodation characterize the relationships among different social groups" (p. 646). Thus, the expansion of blacks into new neighborhoods, coupled with white flight, is a natural transitional process that may not necessarily be linked to the presence of environmental disamenities in these communities. In articulating this point further, Liu borrowed his conception from the neighborhood life cycle model, which proposes that neighborhoods are like families undergoing different stages of a life cycle, starting out with residential development and followed by transition, downgrading, thinning out, and finally, renewal. In explaining these processes, Liu argued that the two major determinants of structural changes in neighborhoods or host communities are age and density. Liu insisted that the deterioration may have nothing to do with LULUs in the host communities. He conceded, however, that the aging process can be accelerated by the siting of LULUs in a given neighborhood.

A similar perspective of neighborhood succession is shared by others (G. Daniels and Friedman, 1999; Hurley, 1997; Krieg, 1995). For example, using historical data for the Greater Boston area, Krieg (1995) contended that environmental inequities exist in American cities and may have been partially caused by the historical processes of industrialization and urbanization. He maintained that polluting industries were present long before the high-risk neighborhoods emerged. As in the life cycle model, he concluded that a treadmill effect based on preexisting industries, falling land values, and low-income housing decisions is responsible for bringing the toxic facilities and the poor and minorities together.

The push and pull model also has been adopted by some researchers in an attempt to identify additional causal mechanisms of environmental inequities. As in most studies of migration, pull factors are the desirable attributes of a community that attract new residents, such as ethnic homogeneity, new housing developments, urban renewal, gentrification projects, jobs, and availability of services and other amenities. In contrast, push factors are neighborhood deterrents, such as aging housing stock, crime, unemployment, the absence of community services, and environmental hazards. Among these push factors, hazardous and noxious facilities are perhaps the most concrete and easily identifiable deterrents that initiate out-migration and depreciation of property values (Liu, 1997). Adeola (1994) introduced the term *community property degradation* or *devaluation* (CPD) to characterize the impact of noxious facilities in minority communities in Louisiana. Unfortunately, these studies have failed to point out that noxious facilities may be push factors for the wealthy but not necessarily for disadvantaged groups. Specifically, low-income or minority residents with limited choices may be unable to relocate, despite the deplorable conditions in their host communities. As made evident in previous chapters, there are institutional barriers, such as lending discrimination, that may influence mobility decisions for these groups.

This notion of environmental push factors is further supported by a comprehensive study that examined the relationships between environmental hazards and internal migration flows (Hunter, 1998). The study was conducted nationwide at the county level to determine whether communities with the greatest environmental risks were likely to *push* residents out to less risky areas. Among the independent variables used were environmental indicators such as air and water quality, hazardous waste facilities, toxic releases, and proposed Superfund sites. The results confirmed that the presence of environmental hazards was likely to reduce the number of in-migrants into a county, in effect serving as a deterrent to migration. This was particularly apparent in counties with poor air quality. In predicting out-migration rates, the research disclosed that, contrary to expectations, counties with high levels of environmental risk were *less likely* to lose residents. Attempted explanations for the observed patterns are consistent with some of the institutional barriers presented in previous chapters. Hunter (1998) suggested that the presence of structural and economic barriers may limit the movement of the residents out of polluted areas. She also noted that the lack of environmental awareness may partially explain why residents do not move out of risky environments.

Neighborhood changes and evolution can also be brought about by financial institutions and other establishments located in the community. Banks, investment companies, insurance companies, real estate agencies, and other service-oriented businesses all play a critical role in the economic viability and stability of a given community with or without a LULU. The decisions made by these companies, as well as their active involvement in community affairs, influence the actions taken by individual residents and smaller investors. On one hand, an institutional decision to move out of a neighborhood with a LULU may be misinterpreted, may lead to a loss of confidence in the market by small investors, and may result in neighborhood decline. On the other hand, the decision to stay is likely to induce economic growth and increase spatial agglomeration by attracting and retaining new businesses (Liu, 1997). Unfortunately, over the last few decades, some minority neighborhoods have suffered from withdrawal, disinvestment, and out-migration of financial institutions into the suburbs.

Perhaps even more important are the policies and land-use planning decisions made by governmental institutions. As Pulido (1996) noted, "urban environmental racism is as much about planning and land-use as anything else" (p. 379). This becomes most evident when one delves into the past practices of local planning agencies, the establishment of zoning regulations, the siting of public housing developments, and federal policies such as Titles I and VI of the Federal Housing Act. Through these historical investigations, a number of researchers have succeeded in proving that the decisions made at various levels of government may have significantly contributed to the iniquitous landscapes. For example, Krieg (1995) blamed Boston public officials for siting low-income housing in deteriorated areas to make use of cheap land values. In evaluating the situation in Houston, Bullard (1994b) argued that, from the early 1920s to the late 1970s, all of the city-owned landfills and eight garbage incinerators were located in black communities. A more recent study in Commerce, a large industrial city east of Los Angeles, arrived at similar conclusions (Boone and Modarres, 1999). The presence of several polluting manufacturing facilities within the vicinity of Latino neighborhoods prompted the investigation. The analysis revealed that the zoning decisions, made by the Los Angeles County Regional Planning Commission in the 1920s and 1930s, were largely responsible for the development of this hazardous community.

Residential Segregation, Racialization, and Immigration Processes.   Finally, a thorough review of the causative mechanisms of environmental inequities within metropolitan areas cannot be complete without addressing residential segregation, racialization, and international migration patterns. All of these are dynamic and complex processes that have further compounded the disparate outcomes in environmental exposure among population subgroups. Even though these processes have been adequately discussed in the other chapters, a few points must be noted here. First, there is no question that American cities are today a patchwork of highly segregated communities, as evidenced by new expressions such as "ethnic quilt," "hypersegregation," "demographic balkanization," and "American Apartheid." Second, U.S. international immigration rates were relatively high in the twentieth century and are likely to remain unabated into the new millennium. We noted that, for a variety of reasons, immigrant groups tend to cluster in specific locations within cities to form ethnic enclaves such as Chinatown or Little Haiti. These communities are often located in working-class neighborhoods adjacent to manufacturing plants or with easy access to transportation services. Furthermore, such neighborhoods often reflect not only the industrialized structure of the community but also low-income families with evolving ethnic identities and perhaps little or no involvement in the political process. Using the same arguments presented earlier about siting decisions, it is no surprise to find that these neighborhoods are often the most polluted areas in metropolitan America. Further evaluations of environmental inequities in these neighborhoods therefore require historical analysis to chronicle the development of these hazardous communities—how and why they became what they are today. Pulido (2000) researched the impacts of these processes within ethnic neighborhoods in Los Angeles. In comparing the plight of Latinos to African Americans, she observed the linkage between the barrio and nearby industry:

> Latinos have always lived close to industry. . . . Latinos' contemporary exposure cannot be understood outside of industrial and immigration shifts. . . . Their exposure is a function of their class and immigrant status as well as their racial position [p. 378].

Her research findings underscored the joint effects of continuously active processes of immigration, residential segregation, racialization, and industrialization in the transformation of some ethnic and immigrant neighborhoods into high-risk communities.

In summary, the studies of process equity reviewed so far and their related findings endorse the need for conducting historical investigations not only to identify the causes but also to chronicle the stages of environmental degradation. Some would argue that documenting the histories or the timing of the siting of these noxious facilities is unnecessary. But, as Shrestha

(1997) argued, unless we understand the historical reality of these problems, we cannot reverse the outcomes: "the past and present inform each other and coexist together. While the past feeds the present, the present mirrors the past" (Said, quoted in Shrestha, 1997, p. 711). It is therefore imperative that we uncover these historical experiences in order to fully grasp the social, economic, and institutional forces that brought us to this point. In the next section, we examine the outcomes and indicators of environmental inequality.

Outcome Equity

Unlike the historical factors and mechanisms of environmental inequity, the outcomes are concrete and, for the most part, readily apparent as one drives through low-income and ethnic neighborhoods of metropolitan America. Blight, smokestacks, air plumes, soot, abandoned waste sites, and noxious odors are all perceptible scars of environmental pollution that mark the urban industrial landscape. Several studies have used proximity-based measures to analyze the spatial distribution of these physical indicators of pollution relative to the demographic attributes of the surrounding communities. The most commonly used environmental data are based on fixed facilities, such as the Toxic Release Inventory (TRI), Superfund National Priority List (NPL), and toxic storage and disposal facilities (TSDFs).*

Some of the earliest contributions to the outcome equity literature can be traced to the work of the U.S. General Accounting Office (1983) and the United Church of Christ's Commission for Racial Justice (United Church of Christ, 1987, updated 1994), followed by others. Such studies revealed inequitable environmental outcomes in low-income and minority communities. These preliminary findings also stimulated further research on inequitable outcomes, using a considerable amount and variety of data. However, over the years, the debate shifted from a simple documentation of quantifiable environmental indicators to methodological issues of spatial scale, sampling, and measurement. Some studies were criticized for the use of aggregate spatial data, poor sampling methods, and inappropriate definitions or measurement of terms such as *proximity* or *host communities* (e.g., Cutter, 1995).

---

*Superfund sites include thousands of contaminated waste sites across the country, such as abandoned warehouses, industrial facilities, processing plants, and landfills. About 1,200 of these hazardous waste sites have been placed on a National Priority List (NPL) for remediation and cleanup. The program is part of the Comprehensive Environmental Response, Compensation and Liability Act (CERCLA) that was first established in 1980 by the federal government. Toxic Release Inventory (TRI) is a database with records of all manufacturing facilities that release or transfer toxic chemicals. Along with other criteria, all facilities that produce more than 25,000 pounds, or use more than 10,000 pounds, of chemicals during a given year are required to report the amount of toxic chemicals they released by environmental media (air, water, land, and underground).

More recent analyses of outcome equity have explored the use of different spatial units of analysis and application of stringent statistical methods. For example, to minimize the errors associated with aggregate spatial units such as counties or zip codes, some studies have been conducted at census tract and block group levels. Burke (1993) examined the relationship between Toxic Release Inventory (TRI) facilities and the socioeconomic characteristics of residents in Los Angeles. Her study showed strong relationships between the number of TRI facilities and the percentage of minorities, lower per-capita incomes, and lower population densities. Holm (1994), in contrast, found no relationship between TSDFs and low-income and minority communities at these levels. Rather, a linkage was observed between these facilities and areas with high population densities. Anderton et al. (1994) also conducted their study at the census-tract level and found no significant differences in the racial composition of the tracts with TSDFs and those without such facilities. In evaluating the effects of spatial scale, however, the study revealed that an association between race and the location of TSDFs exists at more aggregate spatial levels. The opposite finding was revealed in another study by Carroll (1995), where inequities were noted at block-group levels in Erie County, New York.

Improvements in the statistical analysis of the environmental data can also be seen over the years. The research by Mohai and Bryant (1992) was among the first to provide a proximity-based measure of environmental equity. Using two random samples of residents within the Detroit area and those within 1.5 miles of TSDFs, proximity was analyzed as a function of two variables, race and income. The results showed that race was the best predictor of location of waste facilities in the Detroit area. Polluck and Vittas (1995) offered a more accurate measure of proximity to waste facilities by calculating the distance (in miles) between each census-block group and the nearest TRI facility in Florida. They measured the relative importance of racial, economic, and occupational characteristics of residents at the block-group level. The results showed that, although occupational and housing variables accounted for most of the variance in proximity to pollution, race was still a dominant predictor of inequity, particularly in African-American neighborhoods.

Overall, the results generated from studies of outcome equity provide conflicting evidence of inequities in low-income and minority communities. These inconsistencies exist for a number of reasons, including the spatial scale at which the data were analyzed, the type of facility examined, and the analytical tool used to evaluate the research questions. Nearly all of the investigations, however, rely on proximity-based measures of chronic pollution hazards from fixed facilities such as TSDFs, Toxic Release Inventory facilities, and Superfund NPL sites. None of the studies have inquired about communities that are frequently affected by accidents involving hazardous materials. Some may argue that such accidents are random, uncontrollable events and therefore may not exhibit any discernable clustered or inequitable pattern. However, two studies indicate otherwise, with implications that environmental inequities may likely exist in the areas where these pollution accident sites occur (Chakraborty and Armstrong, 1996; Glickman, 1994). Both studies bring attention to a possible correlation between chemical disasters and inequities. Our case study will expand on this idea and evaluate the spatial pattern, distribution, and health impacts associated with exposure to such accidents. The data, however, will be based on records of actual incidences involving the release of toxic chemicals, not on hypothetical or potential accidents as evidenced in the previous studies.

Response Equity

The final component of environmental equity involves actions by the public and various levels of government in response to concerns about environmental inequities. Response equity is analogous to the environmental justice (EJ) movement, which is primarily geared toward risk reduction, compensation, and increasing governmental efforts to correct the perceived and observed differences in exposure to environmental hazards. It includes government efforts to enforce environmental laws and develop new, long-term strategies that will mitigate the impacts of pollution in high-risk communities. It also involves actions by grassroots activists, interest groups, and national organizations in engendering public awareness about environmental discrimination and challenging siting decisions and inequitable impacts of preexisting LULUs in hazardous communities. The ultimate goal of all of these efforts is to ensure the fair treatment of all groups in environmental decisionmaking regardless of race, ethnicity, national origin, or economic status. In this section, we will examine the federal programs developed in recent years to tackle these problems. Next, the efforts made by individual states are reviewed, and their performance so far in correcting the disproportional impacts of these hazards is evaluated. This is then followed by a discussion of the challenges and accomplishments of activist groups and other organizations in seeking environmental justice.

Governmental Responses to Environmental Inequities. Governmental efforts to address environmental inequalities include a wide range of strategies. Capek (1993) categorizes these efforts into four areas: (1) developing laws to protect residents from pollution, (2) enforcing laws that prevent adverse health impacts from polluting facilities, (3) developing mechanisms for assigning culpability to polluters, and (4) redressing the injustices through targeted remedial action and resources. A review of federal policies reveals that, unlike housing and other social policies, environmental justice (EJ) legislation is relatively recent, having emerged only within the last decade. Perhaps the first visible sign of federal acknowledgment of the problems of environmental inequalities was through the establishment of the Office of Environmental Equity in November 1992 (later renamed the Office of Environmental Justice). The office was established within the U.S. Environmental Protection Agency (EPA) to serve as a focal point for addressing EJ issues as well as coordinating public outreach and educational programs. Following a series of investigations and preliminary reports, a more comprehensive program was established by the Clinton administration to broaden the scope of EJ policies across all federal agencies. This was achieved through the enactment of Executive Order 12898 in 1994. The major objectives of this mandate were threefold:

- To focus federal agencies' attention on the human health and environmental conditions in minority and low-income communities, with the goal of achieving environmental justice
- To foster nondiscrimination in those federal programs that substantially affect human health or the environment
- To give minority and low-income communities greater opportunities for public participation in, and access to public information on, matters relating to human health and the environment.

A number of states across the country have also acknowledged the disparate outcomes of environmental pollution in various communities. A study by B. Hacker (1994) at the Center for Policy Alternatives (CPA) showed that, since 1993, several states have proposed legislation that call for the identification, assessment, and remediation of high-impact areas. However, some states have been more successful than others in passing and implementing these laws. For example, in 1993 Arkansas passed Act 1263, which prohibited the construction of high-impact solid-waste management facilities within twelve miles of existing facilities. The basic intent of this law was to prevent the agglomeration of waste management facilities, since several studies, including those reviewed earlier, had indicated that low-income and minority communities were more than likely to be the involuntary hosts.

During 1993, the states of Louisiana, Michigan, Tennessee, and Virginia also enacted legislation that addresses EJ concerns. Louisiana's Act 767 authorized the state's Department of Environmental Quality to develop guidelines to prevent water pollution and its discharge into publicly owned treatment facilities. More important, it required the establishment of new strategies to promote public awareness and participation, particularly on EJ-related matters. Michigan's Resolution 662 was more of an acknowledgment of the problem than an attempt to address it. Agencies in various states are now required to address these issues, especially in areas of significant impact.

In 1994 Florida passed comprehensive legislation (Act 1369) to evaluate the scope of the EJ problem across the state and propose a series of actions. A commission was set up to conduct a scientific investigation that covered a range of issues including a list of targeted sites, demographic and economic profiles of these areas, and a review of the existing data, methodologies, statutes, and policies for dealing with the problem.

While some states, such as Florida, have been successful in implementing comprehensive programs, others have failed to pass even the most rudimentary programs aimed at public protection. In reviewing these legislative efforts, however, certain geographic commonalities are apparent and noteworthy since they underscore some of the geographic themes presented earlier in this chapter. For example, several state programs focus exclusively on controlling the *siting* of new polluting facilities. Others have proposed or implemented programs that seek to systematically identify *host communities* or delineate high-impact areas on the basis of *environmental, economic,* and *racial or ethnic attributes.* These legislative efforts basically reinforce our position, taken earlier in this book, that race and place are perpetually intertwined and must be tackled together. As expected, there are wide disparities in the language and criteria used to delineate the affected areas. For example, the buffer zones for delineating host communities vary from five miles, in New York's legislation, to twelve miles, in Arkansas's.

All of the noted differences among states reflect two things. First, they reflect the relative recency of the legislative efforts to tackle these problems. Second and perhaps more important, they reflect the absence of a federal mandate or comprehensive plan that provides guidelines for states to follow in designing and implementing their own EJ programs.

Group Activism and Response to Environmental Inequities.   While federal and state governments have continued to grapple with the development of feasible risk reduction and remediation policies, several activist groups and organizations have evolved around the country. Some of these groups are affiliated with national environmental organizations and interest groups, such as the National Toxics Campaign (NTC), Greenpeace, and the Sierra Club. Other organizations, such as the United Church of Christ (UCC), Southwest Organization Project, and Public Interest Research Group (PIRG), have sponsored EJ conferences or assisted in the dissemination of research findings.

A number of researchers have documented the general characteristics of the grassroots organizations, their struggles, tactics, accomplishments, and failures (e.g., Greenberg, 2000). Bullard (1992) provided an excellent reference for detailed characteristics of these groups, particularly in African-American communities. Drawing from earlier investigations by others, he identified some of the salient attributes of the grassroots movement, including:

- A focus on equity
- An emphasis on the needs of the community and workplace as the primary agenda items

- Attacks that extend well beyond the toxic contamination issue itself to include remedial action on other inequities such as housing, transportation, air quality, and even economic development
- Use of citizen lawsuits instead of relying on legislation and lobbying
- Reliance on self-taught "experts" who acquire new skills in areas where they previously had little or no experience
- Reliance on active members rather than dues payers from mailing lists
- A focus on democratic ideology that is similar to the civil rights movements and women's movement of the 1960s
- Use of a "protest infrastructure" that is already in place based on residents' prior affiliation with civic clubs, neighborhood associations, community improvement and empowerment groups, and an array of anti-poverty and anti-discrimination organizations.

The availability of these community resources has assisted several groups in weaving together effective campaigns against corporate polluters in their neighborhoods. These campaigns are nonetheless faced with formidable tasks since they are going against institutions and establishments that are formally entrenched in the communities. Using case studies from the Carver Terrace neighborhood in Texarkana, Texas, Capek (1993) documented some of the obstacles that grassroots activists frequently encounter, among them racial barriers:

> Grassroots groups mobilized against toxic contamination generally have less access to political, legal and scientific resources than do their opponents . . . racial and ethnic barriers are also significant; the gulf between the neighborhood residents and city hall is typically greater for racial minorities [p. 7].

Despite these challenges, some groups have been successful in blocking the construction of LULUs or seeking remedial action in their communities. Strategies used by these groups include litigation, protest marches, press conferences, letter writing campaigns, and direct encounters with public officials or the polluters (Capek, 1993). For example, Walsh et al. (1993) examined two siting disputes involving incinerators, with different outcomes. They concluded that the successful anti-siting campaign depended on several factors, including the timing of the protests and an early framing of the protest ideology to appeal to the wider public.

Existing hazardous communities have also been successful in acquiring compensation packages using tactics similar to those described above. For instance, the situation in Texarkana, Texas, was resolved through a federal buyout program and subsequent relocation of the residents away from the Superfund site (Capek, 1993). Boerner and Lambert (1995) also report on other kinds of compensation packages that have been adopted by communities.

Some concerns have been raised about compensation packages and other economic trade-offs, especially on moral grounds. That is, paying people (especially, the disadvantaged) to expose themselves to environmental health risks is morally irresponsible (United Church of Christ, 1994; Bullard, 1992). Others have argued, however, that compensation packages are "just" and at least attempt to equalize the imbalances created by the unfair distribution of environmental hazards (Boerner and Lambert, 1995). They contend that such remedies are more effective than the governmental strategies presented earlier, because they offset some of the disproportionate environmental costs without altering the racial and socioeconomic composition of the affected communities. However, it is also important to point out that, even though compensation alleviates the immediate concerns of the residents, it does not necessarily deal with the root cause of the problem or the underlying processes responsible for the existing inequalities. At best, a compensatory package is superficial or should be viewed as a Band-Aid to a problem that is likely to repeat itself. In contrast, effective governmental strategies, if implemented and properly enforced, would not only hold the polluters responsible but penalize them through the payment of heavy fines or other mechanisms. The funds that are retrieved can then be used to permanently correct the hazardous problem and prevent its recurrence.

Overall, it is apparent from our discussion in this first half of the chapter that three issues are at stake when dealing with environmental inequalities: processes, outcomes, and responses. The literature reveals much research over the last two decades to uncover these processes. In the next section, a case study will be presented to illustrate firsthand the complexity of the problem as it has unfolded in urban America.

Evidence of Inequitable Outcomes in Monroe and Suffolk Counties, New York

Environmental inequities are multifaceted; they originate from different sources and are manifested in various ways in urban America. As indicated earlier, most studies have focused on outcomes arising from routine emissions from LULUs such as TRI facilities, Superfund sites, or TSDFs. The primary purpose of this empirical study was to deviate from this norm and, instead, delineate the spatial pattern and distribution of nonroutine hazardous materials accidents and assess the inequitable impacts on low-income and minority neighborhoods in two counties in New York State. Hazardous materials incidents are accidental releases of toxic substances from either fixed facilities or transportation. Unlike routine emissions, these accidents are unintentional spills or releases into the air, land, or water bodies that can potentially result in serious public health consequences for workers and residents in surrounding communities. During the last few years, there have been up-surges in the numbers of accidents reported in the United States. More than 23,000 accidents involving toxic releases were recorded between 1993 and 1995: on average about 20 accidents a day or nearly one incident per hour (Phillips and Gray, 1996). Further evaluation of the locational patterns show that approximately one in every six Americans now resides in a zone that is vulnerable to accidents involving hazardous materials. Densely populated urban centers such as Houston, Los Angeles, Chicago, Baton Rouge, and Cleveland are most at risk from the potential impacts of these incidents (Public Interest Research Group, 1998).

Study Area Profiles

The study was conducted in New York State, which lies within the Northeastern Corridor of polluting industries and hazardous-materials accidents in the United States (Cutter and Ji, 1997). Two counties within the state, Monroe and Suffolk, were selected for detailed analysis at the census-tract level. Their selection was based primarily on the relatively high frequency of hazardous accidents reported in recent years (see Figure 7.2[a]); more than thirty incidents were reported in each county in 1997.

The inclusion of both counties also provided adequate spatial representation of urbanized counties within the state. Monroe County, which is located upstate in the Finger Lakes region, has a population of approximately 713,968. It is part of the Rochester metropolitan area, the state's third largest urbanized region. As shown in previous chapters, its minority population is highly segregated. Suffolk County, in contrast, is more representative of downstate New York. It is part of the Nassau-Suffolk metropolitan area, with a population of more than 1.3 million. In 1998 Suffolk County was the twenty-second most populous county in the nation, with a population greater than that of twelve states (Suffolk County Planning Department, 1999). It is also slightly more urbanized than Monroe County, with a larger proportion of high-income and minority populations. Also, unlike Monroe County, where African Americans are still the dominant minority group, in Suffolk County, Hispanics now constitute the largest minority group, with roughly 8 percent of the total population.

Both Monroe and Suffolk Counties are home to a variety of industries, many of which generate, utilize, or store hazardous materials. They are also characterized by a high degree of transportation connectivity (as evidenced in Figure 7.2[b]). Both counties face moderate to high risks for accidental spills from both transportation and industrial operations (Figure 7.2[a]).

Monroe County represents a classic example of the complex interplay of historical urban processes, demographic shifts, suburbanization, industrial and retail expansion, and other growth processes discussed earlier. The largest employers are based in the city of Rochester. They include Eastman

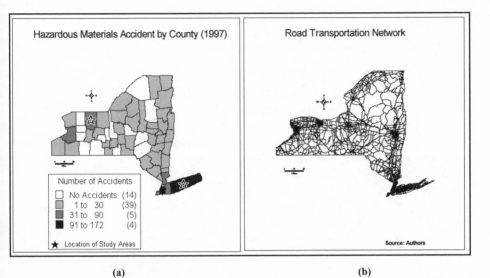

(a)   (b)

FIGURE 7.2   Environmental profile of Monroe and Suffolk Counties, New York: (a) number of hazardous-materials accidents by county; (b) New York State road transportation network

Kodak, Xerox, and Bausch and Lomb, all of which have historically dealt with a variety of optical photographic and imaging products and chemicals. New, high-tech industries have recently emerged but are situated along arterial lines, such as the Thruway Industrial Park, or confined to industrial parks in the suburbs, such as the University Park and John Bailey High-Technology Park. Most of the old manufacturing companies remain in the northwestern quadrant, the CBD, of the city of Rochester. This area has been experiencing "severe blight, deterioration, disinvestment, poverty, and drug-related crime" (Department of Planning and Development, 1999). Our research shows that, unfortunately, the Areas of Minority Concentration (AOMCs) are also situated in this part of the city.

A recent environmental report card for Monroe County shows that, although there have been significant achievements in several environmental quality indicators, the annual number of reported hazardous-materials accidents has continued to increase. Between 1992 and 1995 the highest number of emergency events in upstate New York occurred in Monroe County (Health Action, 1999). The Eastman Kodak Company's Kodak Park (KP) was responsible for many incidents. This, however, comes as no surprise, given the facility's size and scale of operations. It is the largest photographic product manufacturer in the world and the largest industrial facility in the United States. KP is located on more than 1,300 acres and extends four miles through Rochester into the town of Greece. The chemical that is primarily used by this facility is methylene chloride, a potential carcinogen (Health Action, 1999). Even though recent trends indicate a decline in emissions, this facility continues to accidentally release more than 2 million pounds of this chemical routinely each year.

Residents in Suffolk County also face risks of exposure to hazardous chemical releases. Suffolk County is located on Long Island, east of New York City. Until recently, employment opportunities were largely based on defense-related industries. One of the major employers, and also a significant source of environmental pollution, is the Brookhaven National Laboratory (BNL). This facility was established in 1947 and is one of nine national laboratories administered by the U.S. Department of Energy. It is a very extensive facility, located on 5,300 acres of land north of the Long Island Expressway.

In 1989 the BNL site was placed on the EPA's Superfund National Priority List (NPL), primarily because of significant environmental contamination related to past operations and handling of toxic substances. Specifically, twenty-nine "areas of concern" were identified, consisting of the hazardous waste management facility, the sewage treatment plant, former and current landfills, potable wells, cesspools, and radioactive-waste storage tanks (Brookhaven Science Associates, 2000). Most of these areas were contaminated with radioactive elements, volatile organic compounds, and heavy metals such as copper, zinc, and aluminum. Even though the site is currently undergoing mandated cleanup and remediation, administrators also have to contend with occasional releases of nonroutine hazardous materials associated with current operations. Fortunately, most of the contaminants are confined to the BNL property, and access to this area is restricted. But it is not always possible to confine contaminated air and water, which, depending on the hydrological and atmospheric conditions, can and do disperse into surrounding neighborhoods. In fact, recent investigations have linked these releases to groundwater contamination since the facility sits directly atop an aquifer. Our research, however, will focus on the atmospheric dispersion of the contaminants and the potential impact on surrounding communities.

Data Collection

Environmental Data.   The environmental data on accidents involving hazardous substances were acquired from the Emergency Response and Notification System (ERNS), which is self-reported data managed by the EPA. This national database is used to inventory and record all information pertaining to accidental releases of oil and hazardous substances from both fixed facilities and transportation. The information includes the location of the spill, the amount of chemical released, the polluted media (air, water, land, or groundwater), the number of deaths and/or people injured or evacuated, the amount of property damage, the cause of the accident, and information pertaining to the discharger. As with most self-reported data, there are some concerns with reliability, particularly with underreporting of the occurrence and severity of accidents. The EPA, however, has a follow-up program, the Accidental Release Information Program (ARIP), to verify all of the information regarding fixed facilities. Transportation accidents are also recorded in the Hazardous Materials Information System (HMIS), managed by the U.S. Department of Transportation (DOT). Both data sources (ARIP and HMIS) are useful for corroborating the information provided in the ERNS system.

In 1997, according to ERNS records, a total of 1,127 incidents were reported in New York State. About 48 percent of them were associated with fixed facilities like Kodak Park in Monroe and the Brookhaven National Laboratory in Suffolk County. Roughly 30 percent were linked to transportation, and the remaining 22 percent of the cases were from unknown causes. An evaluation of the environmental media affected during these incidents showed that roughly 56 percent of releases were water related, 30 percent occurred on land, and 8 percent were releases into the air. The chemicals that were frequently reported include hydrocarbons, such as gasoline, propane, and ethylene glycol, and potentially more corrosive and dangerous substances such as chlorine and ammonia.

Demographic Data. The most recent demographic information for the two counties consisted of detailed 1990 socioeconomic, ethnic, and housing indicators collected at the census-tract level. Three variables were selected to measure the economic conditions within the tracts: median household income, percent below the poverty level, and percent unemployed. The degree of urbanization and the percentage of residents involved in manufacturing and construction activities were also included. Housing conditions were evaluated using the median housing value, median rent, and the percentage of owner-occupied housing. The ethnic composition of the tracts was based on the percentages of the population that are white, African American, Hispanic, Asian, and Native American. Other demographic variables included the proportion of residents eighteen years and older without a high school diploma and the proportion of vulnerable residents such as the elderly (age sixty-five and older) and young children (under five).

Analysis and Results

Data analysis was performed in a sequence of four major steps. The first involved a dispersion modeling approach to delineate impact zones (or "footprints") of previous accidents. This required a thorough examination of the entire environmental database over a ten-year period (1987–1997). All of the accidents that occurred within Monroe and Suffolk counties during that period were reviewed. As commonly suggested, the worst-case incidents in each county were selected for detailed analysis using the ALOHA (Areal Location of Hazardous Atmospheres) program. This is a computer modeling package that is distributed by the National Safety Council (NSC) in cooperation with the EPA and the National Oceanic and Atmospheric Administration (NOAA). It was specifically designed for emergency planning and response to accidents involving the release of hazardous materials. Based on local weather conditions and the type and amount of chemical that is released, the program can delineate the area over which the hazardous material is likely to disperse into the atmosphere. A detailed discussion of dispersion modeling concepts and program applications can be found in the User's Guide (National Oceanic and Atmospheric Association and U.S. Environmental Protection Agency, 1995).

Following input of the data, the program generated different footprints for each accident scenario. A footprint is the geographic shape and size of an impact zone (such as a plume) for a specific substance at a specific time, given local wind speed and direction. For our study, the maximum threat zone ranged from 150 yards to 3.2 miles. As expected, the footprints confirmed that the fate and transport of each chemical accident are unique and likely to generate a unique impact zone within a surrounding community. Given the variations from one incident to another, we decided to use the average footprint size of 1.4 miles as the basis for delineating the generalized impact zone around all incidents that occurred in the two counties in 1997.

The second stage of the analysis involved a detailed evaluation of the accident sites in Monroe and Suffolk Counties, using the generalized impact zones delineated in the preceding step. As indicated earlier, more than thirty accidents involving hazardous materials were reported in each county in 1997. These accident sites were successfully located by x, y coordinates and the data sent into a computer mapping program for cartographic analysis. A 1.4-mile buffer was then established around each site as the impact zone within which the population was at greatest risk from the harmful health effects of the accident. This data layer was then overlaid on the demographic map of each county to illustrate some of the proximal relationships between the impact zones and selected demographic variables within the two counties. The map of Monroe County is shown as Figure 7.3 and illustrates that the percentage of African Americans in the northwestern quadrant of Monroe County is significantly above the state average. This area also appears to have witnessed a disproportionate number of hazardous accidents in 1997. The same race-place pattern occurred for Hispanics and hazardous accidents in Suffolk County in 1997. However, great care must be exercised in interpreting such maps since they are merely visual patterns that have yet to be subjected to statistical analysis. It is also important to note that more than two incidents were reported at some locations. Thus, the number of accidents portrayed on a map does not necessarily add up to the total number of accidents reported in that county in 1997.

In order to isolate the demographic profile of high-impact areas, a spatial query was performed to identify and select all tracts lying inside or overlap-

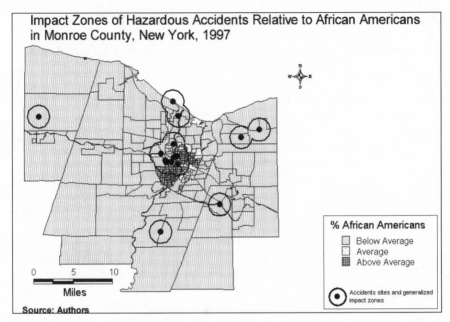

FIGURE 7.3   Hazardous materials–accident impact zones in relation to areas of African-American concentration, New York, 1997

ping the area within a 1.4-mile radius of each accident site. The 1.4-mile-radius buffer zones were designated as high-impact areas, and all others were characterized as low-impact areas. The population characteristics (size, age, structure, racial and ethnic composition) of the buffer zones were then computed. Additional calibrations involved the economic and housing indicators of all these areas. At the conclusion of the process, the data profiles for each county were merged and later exported into a statistical package for analysis.

Having isolated the attributes of the high- and low-impact areas, the third phase of the analysis was mainly geared toward statistical comparison of these areas using a preliminary test (independent samples *t*-test) and a more advanced technique (discriminant analysis). Among the economic indicators, the most significant factors were census tracts' median household income, poverty, and the degree of urbanization (see Table 7.1). As expected, the results showed that the more urbanized areas were likely to fall within the high-impact zones. Similarly, high-impact tracts had a larger proportion of families below the poverty line than the low-impact areas. There were no differences in the percentage employed in manufacturing or construction within the two groups of areas. Among the housing indicators, the median housing value was the only significant variable. The areas of high impact were characterized by cheaper housing, a finding that is congruent with other investigations such as Gayer (2000). The analysis of racial and ethnic characteristics showed that African Americans and Hispanics were more likely to reside in the high-impact tracts. The proportion of whites, however, was significantly lower in the high-impact areas. Other demographic factors such as education and age were important indicators, as well. Specifically, there were more young children in the high-impact tracts, and the proportion of residents with minimal education (eighteen years and older without a high school diploma) in these areas was also significant.

Statistical analysis provided supportive evidence of racial, ethnic, and economic differences between the high-impact and low-impact areas. Ten variables that were significant in the preliminary statistical analysis were incorporated into the procedure. The use of the stepwise procedure resulted in a more efficient and parsimonious model with a single linear function that maximized the group differences. The three variables associated with the function included poverty, the proportion of Hispanics, and the proportion of whites. The structure matrix revealed that the differences between the high and low accident-impact areas are best characterized by the prevalence of residents below the poverty line, Hispanics, and nonwhites. The standardized coefficients, representing the relative contribution of each variable in explaining the group differences, showed that poverty provides the best explanation for the variation between the two areas.

The final analytical step involved sensitivity analysis to determine the stability of the research findings. A series of radii was constructed around the accident sites for comparative analysis. These zones were established within radii of 0.5, 0.7, 1.0, and 2.0 miles from the accident sites, respectively. For each radius, the sequence of analytical steps previously outlined was followed, and a separate discriminant analysis was performed using the categorized impact zone as the dependent variable (see Table 7.2). The two variables that emerged as consistent indicators of tract differences were poverty and the proportion of Hispanics.

Summary

Overall, the results of the empirical analysis, as well as some of the previous investigations reviewed earlier, provide ample evidence of environmental inequities in urban America. These inequities are not just limited to routine emissions from industrial and waste facilities. They could also arise from nonroutine releases of toxic chemicals. Within a half mile to two miles of most hazardous accidents, one is likely to find a significant proportion of low-income residents, Hispanics, and nonwhites. Is this merely a spatial coincidence? If so, why is this pattern repeated when using other environmental indicators such as air quality, landfills, incinerators, Superfund sites, and

TABLE 7.1 Statistical Comparison of High- and Low-Impact Areas for
Hazardous-Materials Accidents (census tracts in Suffolk and Monroe Counties)

| | Mean | | t-test |
	Low impact (N=278)	High Impact (N=218)	
Median household income	$45,124.60	$40,392.01	2.97[c]
Families below poverty (%)	5.52	11.68	–6.131[c]
Manufacturing	8.89	9.32	–1.067
Construction	2.95	2.73	1.766
Percent urban	86.53	93.55	–2.748[c]
Median housing value	$147,079.86	$129,762.07	2.687[c]
Occupied housing	90.12	92.33	–1.522
Children under 5 (%)	6.74	7.72	–4.047[c]
Elderly (65+) (%)	11.83	11.56	0.37
No high school diploma (%)	13.21	17.47	–5.129[c]
White (%)	87.0	80.93	2.82[b]
African American (%)	8.79	13.65	–2.628[b]
Hispanics (%)	3.97	8.39	–5.564[c]
Asian American (%)	1.67	1.58	0.430
Native American (%)	0.29	0.22	1.221

[a]Significant at p = 0.10
[b]Significant at p = 0.05
[c]Significant at p = 0.01

TABLE 7.2 Sensitivity Analysis of Low- and High-Impact Areas for Hazardous-Materials
Accidents (stepwise discriminant analyses using variable buffers)

Buffers around accident sites	Variables entered	Removed	Stepwise statistics Wilks lambda	Canonical correlation
0.5 Miles	% Hispanics % Children (< 5 yrs) % African American % Families below poverty		0.898*	0.319
0.7 miles	% Hispanics % Children (< 5 yrs) % African American % Families below poverty	√	0.898*	0.320
1.0 miles	% Hispanics % Families below poverty % Whites		0.881*	0.344
2.0 miles	%Families below poverty % Hispanics % Whites		0.870*	0.292

*Statistically significant at p < 0.01
√ Removed in subsequent iterations

water quality? Alternatively, why is the pattern repeated at other scales or in different situational contexts, such as Boston, Houston, Los Angeles, Cleveland, Detroit, Buffalo, St. Louis, and several other settings in metropolitan America? Our research was guided by a conceptual framework proposed at the beginning of this chapter. The results of our investigation confirmed that the disparate outcomes of environmental pollution reflect the history of these urban areas, institutional characteristics and decisionmaking, demographic processes, as well as the presence of ineffective and/or failed governmental policies and practices. We will address the implications of these findings for public policy in Chapter 10.

Chapter 8

Retail Structure, Accessibility, and Inequalities in Areas of Minority Concentration

Introduction

Our discussion and empirical analyses in previous chapters have substantiated the negative impacts of residential segregation on U.S. minorities. Some of the reported disparities, such as poor access to quality housing at a fair price or the disproportionate exposure to environmental hazards, have been quite obvious and, therefore, have received more attention. Other racial and ethnic disparities have been less apparent but, nonetheless, have dramatically affected the lives of millions of minorities on a daily basis. For example, minority populations reside in locations that were once busy with commerce and industry but are now virtually empty, with high levels of unemployment. Significant changes in retail structure occurred during the last few generations, leaving many "inner cities" devoid of department stores and other important retail activities. Such losses have created a mismatch in accessibility, such that the locations of Areas of Minority Concentration (AOMCs) are now truly disadvantaged in terms of proximity to specific retail establishments, services, and convenience goods such as groceries, hardware, and home improvement merchandise. In this chapter, we explore the underlying processes that are responsible for the disparities in access to goods and services and the implications for minority households. We begin by examining the present distribution of certain retail functions relative to minority concentrations. Next, we present some definitions of accessibility based on other researchers' previous investigations. After defining accessibility in quantitative terms, we use empirical data to examine two urban counties by comparing the relative access of minority and nonminority neighborhoods to grocery stores, discount department stores, and home improvement centers. Additional results are presented to document the differential pricing of goods in certain neighborhoods and also to illustrate the out-shopping behavior of minorities in urbanized areas (the number of shopping trips outside the trade or market area of the shopper's neighborhood or closest stores). The chapter concludes with a discussion of future trends in the distribution of retailing structures in metropolitan America.

Urban Restructuring and the Location of Selected Retail Functions

A detailed review of the transformation of the postindustrial city was presented earlier in Chapter 4. Retailing was one of the catalysts of the evolution of the polynucleated metropolitan form. As an integral part of modern American society, retailing takes on distinctive locational patterns. Retail patterns reflect historical urban growth processes that have evolved over time. During the period of urban centralization, retailing was the most identifiable characteristic of the central business district (CBD). However, after World War II substantial changes took place in the retail industry. These were precipitated by a growing national economy, higher disposable household incomes, highway improvements, new investment strategies, easy access to cheap land, and residential relocation.

According to the advocates of the technological free-market position, the push factors associated with the inner city also contributed to retail relocation. By the mid-1950s, the form and functions of the retailing industry had changed to conform to consumer preferences and behaviors that were tied to the decentralization of high-income families and new suburban lifestyles (Muller, 1981). At first these changes led to the emergence of only a few suburban retailers, but eventually they exploded into the creation of large shopping centers. This new retailing phenomenon diffused rapidly throughout the United States, and by the late 1960s, the regional shopping center had become the dominant form of retailing, drawing to it parasitic stores and, often, new housing developments. In its wake it reduced many CBDs to "nondepartment store" status. The loss of these retail anchors in the inner city killed smaller retailing outlets that once relied on the consumer traffic for survival. Small shopping centers, initially in the form of open-air strip malls, emerged outside the old urban core and became magnets for the growth of other functions, including residential land uses. Ghosh and McLafferty (1991) summarized this postwar retail transformation:

> i) a shift of retail activity from the central city to the suburban and exurban areas; ii) the development and rapid growth of planned shopping centers; and iii) the rise of corporate ownership and increased market concentrations in retailing [p. 253].

More recently, a fact sheet produced by the International Council of Shopping Centers (2000) confirmed that by the year 2000, roughly 95 percent of the 44,360 shopping centers in the United States were strip malls.

Although the early suburbanization of retail activity varied in structural morphology, the new retail centers commonly included banks, grocery stores, and some form of general merchandising. Real estate, banking, financial services, and health services also decentralized, leaving neighborhoods of older central cities sometimes devoid of key retail functions. As mentioned earlier, associated with the postwar period were the introduction, subsequent growth, and diffusion of shopping centers as the new wave of retail establishment. Shopping centers varied in function and scale and started at the lowest levels, with neighborhood convenience centers and community centers. At the intermediate scale, they were regional, fashion/specialty, and power centers. Macro shopping centers included the superregional, theme/festival, and outlet centers with trade areas covering 5 to 50 miles. This retail innovation had a slow start and was characterized by a reluctance of major retailers to adopt initially because of the uncertainty associated with new ideas. Once the initial doubts were overcome, however, the diffusion process accelerated in the 1960s as shopping centers became the dominant suburban retailing form. At first, this change was not embraced by the large retail chains with higher-order goods. Thus, the early shopping centers were generally small and dominated by commercial strips. Within two decades, however, developers introduced regional shopping centers with large catchment areas. The concept of one or more large department stores serving as anchors was introduced. Malls became defined by their numbers of anchors and square footage.

Muller (1981) examined both the expanding trade areas and centralizing force of the regional shopping centers. He equated them to "convenient all-purpose places to go" and suggested that "suburban lives were increasingly organized around them" (p. 125). Due to competition and the slowing of the retail boom, suburban malls reached a saturation point by the 1990s; additional changes occurred in retail structure and location. Developers reacted to these changes by de-emphasizing the role of planned shopping centers and reverting to, or reinventing, the smaller, strip power centers. Invariably, these operations were dominated by a few large stores (power tenants), including discount department stores like Wal-Mart and Target, warehouse clubs such as Sam's, and category killers, such as Best Buy, which offer a large selection of merchandise at low prices. The retail landscape, in its return to outdoor locations that target special socioeconomic groups, had apparently completed a full cycle by the 1990s.

Today, these power centers are among the latest establishments in retail development and provide an alternative to the regional malls and other types of retail shopping centers. Another relatively recent addition to the retail structure involves the home-improvement center, which is designed to be a one-stop shop for both local developers and home owners doing housing improvements. Examples of such chains are Lowe's and Home Depot, which typically locate in or near strip retail centers.

This reverse trend in retail size and corresponding structure illustrates that the shopping center phenomenon has completed a full cycle. Today's smaller suburban malls have limited trade areas and appeal to specific socioeconomic

groups who patronize specialty goods stores. The most recent direction in retail development now involves designing the retail environment, both physi-
cally and psychologically, for target populations.

The structural and locational attributes of grocery stores have also evolved
over the last several decades. During the period of suburban expansion, chain
stores were established, and most of the new stores were located in or near
emerging malls. Later, the grocery megastore emerged and diversified its merchandise to include a pharmacy, a florist, a barber, video games, and other
merchandise to attract shoppers who wanted variety and one-stop shopping.
Another model offered by chains was to strategically locate in a "neighborhood" to serve both urban and suburban populations. Initially, these were
relatively smaller stores designed to "cover the market." For example, chain
grocery stores were located to serve smaller neighborhoods or communities in
both urban city and suburban markets. These stores tended to provide food
and other convenience items to residents. This location process allowed chain
stores to be competitive in every segment of the market. However, as the
megastore emerged, such chains were forced to upgrade the smaller stores to
include more variety and merchandise offerings. As a result, many stores in
the less profitable urban areas were closed. The most recent and perhaps
dominant trend is for the discount department stores (such as Wal-Mart) and
club/warehouse stores (such as Sam's Club) to sell groceries.

In sum, retail establishments, including discount department stores (or general merchandise stores, GMSs), grocery chains, and home-improvement centers, have undergone several changes over the last several decades. All of
these trends have resulted in a new pattern of retailing in metropolitan America. Overall, the bulk of such changes and developments during the last quarter of the twentieth century involved locating in growth areas or just outside
the central cities, to the detriment of inner cities. It is therefore no surprise to
find blank storefronts and abandoned strips in the inner cities despite the continued, and often unsuccessful, efforts by government agencies to sponsor
projects aimed at commercial redevelopment, gentrification, and luring people in large numbers back into the CBD.

At issue in this chapter is what inequities, if any, have emerged for minorities as a result of this continuing transformation. Before addressing this question, we turn to a review of various measures of accessibility.

Retail Distributions: Defining and Formulating "Accessibility"

Analysts and planners have long grappled with the concept of "accessibility."
In lay terms, we often wish to understand how "easy" or "difficult" it is to get
from point A to point B. We understand that sheer distance is an impediment,

but other factors also impede our ability to reach point B. Also the attraction of B itself helps determine how much we are willing to sacrifice to get from A to B.

The concept is simple enough when used in dialogue. However, as noted by others, it "... is a slippery notion" when one is "faced with the problem of defining and measuring it" (Sathisan and Srinivasan, 1998, p. 78). This difficulty has led to many definitions in the literature (Allen, Liu, and Singer, 1993; Miller, 1999; Weibull, 1980). We maintain that accessibility essentially measures the potential of interaction between places. It involves the attraction that place A exerts on place B (and its residents) based on measurable factors, such as population, store size, and so forth. The measure of effort to overcome spatial separation between two places is described as "relative accessibility"; when an assessment of effort to overcome separation between many places is derived, we use the term "integral accessibility" (Allen et al., 1993). These terms become relevant when we discuss differential accessibility among the AOMC, AOHC, central city, and urban counties of our study areas. Talen (2001) summarized the factors related to differential accessibility as "urban form, organizational rules, citizen contacts and race" (p. 469). In short, the level of accessibility for one place is related to its overall level of equity as compared to other places. Talen (2001) illustrated this empirically for school accessibility in forty-eight school districts in West Virginia.

Accessibility can be evaluated using a measure of distance, time, or cost. Proximity is also a surrogate for accessibility due to the difficulty of quantifying the concept. Accordingly, Song (1996) specified numerous measures of accessibility, including: (1) average commuting distance, or time in measuring residential accessibility; (2) normalized average travel time to all destinations within an urban area; and (3) locational potential, determined by the surrounding area's cumulative opportunities. Earlier, Hansen (1959) derived a gravity-based accessibility measure based on an exponential distance-decay function. Yet others have defined accessibility as the attraction of location offset by the negative exponential function of distance.

Because accessibility is so complex as an operational concept, many studies have evaluated accessibility functions. Ingram's study (1971) reviewed four distance functions: average distance function, reciprocal function, negative exponential function, and the Gaussian function. Also, using analytical and graphical methods, Guy (1983) evaluated seven different measures of accessibility. These included the shortest distance indexes, the cumulative opportunities index, four gravity-based indices, and the Gaussian index. In evaluating accessibility to job opportunities, Song (1996) applied empirical data to assess the levels of performance of these measures. He tested nine frequently used alternative accessibility measures to determine the best measures of accessibility. He utilized a population density formulation for each accessibility measure to empirically test the performance of each model, drawing on the criterion of maximum explanatory power for a standard regression model.

His first measure was based on the Euclidean distance from the point of interest, the CBD, as a location for job opportunities. The second and third measures were gravity-based, and the fourth and fifth used the exponential distance-decay function and the Gaussian function, respectively. Measures 6 and 7 were based on the cumulative opportunity accessibility measures. The final two measures, 8 and 9, were derived from average distance and weighted-average distance functions, respectively.

Song demonstrated statistically that the gravity-based accessibility measure, the fourth measure, based on the exponential distance-decay function, was superior to all the others. His findings supported the work of Ingram (1971) and Guy (1983). His study used Guy's formulation to measure welfare and retail accessibility of residents in the inner city and outer city of Portsmouth, United Kingdom (UK). The formula is as follows:

$$A_i = \sum S_j \exp[-1/2(d_{ij}/d^*)^2]$$

where

A_i is a measure of access to shopping opportunity for block group i,

S_j is the size of store j in thousands of square feet,

d_{ij}, the distance from block group i to store j,

d^*, the point of inflexion at a predetermined distance from i.

It must be noted that d^* is set to reflect the distance threshold at which a shopper is willing to travel to acquire the good in question.

The preceding formulation will be used in this study to derive a measure of accessibility to grocery, discount, and home improvement chains by minority and nonminority block groups. In setting d^*, for grocery stores, one mile will be used, whereas for discount and home improvement stores, three miles and five miles, respectively, will be used. Our rationale for these criteria is based on the automobile-dependent culture of the United States and the minimum-radii of circular primary-trade-area boundaries for the grocery chain store in a neighborhood convenience center and for discount and home improvement stores in community, regional, and power centers (International Council of Shopping Centers, 2000).

Unlike some of the other studies (Sathisan and Srinivasan, 1998; Wang, 2000), we will not employ block-group population as an indicator. Rather, we will use store size because attractiveness is what draws the customer to a store. Stores that are the most attractive are also the most accessible. Accordingly, we will generate statistics that illustrate "how easy or difficult it is to get to a store." These statistics will then be used to compare minority and nonminority concentrations in our study areas. Our implicit null hypothesis is that no difference in accessibility occurs between minority and nonminority concentrations. The corollary is that no inequities exist.

Accessibility and Equity

The Data

Three data sources were utilized to display and analyze retail locations, population attributes, and accessibility. Retail chain locations, including grocery store chains, discount department stores, and home improvement centers, were initially taken from the Pro-Phone CD 2000 database for the United States. The original data were modified in two ways. First, we verified and added locations through the corporate Web pages and direct conversations with corporate representatives. Second, we conducted fieldwork in Monroe County, New York, and Lehigh County, Pennsylvania, to confirm the accuracy of our retail data.

The 1990 U.S. Census of Population and Housing was also utilized to define the AOHC and AOMC boundaries for the study areas. The specific procedures for acquiring the data have been detailed in previous chapters. We used Topologically Integrated Geographical Encoding and Referencing (TIGER) maps to construct the street networks that were the basis of our network analysis, which measured accessibility from each block-group type (minority and nonminority concentrations). Block-group boundaries were also taken from TIGER. Finally, we utilized ESRI's Arcview Network Analyst to conduct the network analysis.

Study Areas

As noted in preceding chapters, the size of minority populations and minority concentrations vary by history, size of metropolitan area, and other factors. We selected two study areas on the basis of the following requirements: (1) We sought one relatively large and one relatively small urban county so that differences due to population and city or county size might become apparent in our test. (2) Racial mix was required. We sought communities that had concentrations of both Hispanics and blacks, as previously defined in this text. And (3) urban counties had to be close enough to allow for fieldwork to verify the retail distributions and minority concentrations.

Based on the requirements, we selected Monroe County, New York, which contains the city of Rochester. Monroe County had a population of 713,968 in 1990 and was part of an SMA that exceeded 1 million people. Its minority population included 84,530 blacks and 24,731 Hispanics. The Hispanic population is dominated by Puerto Ricans (17,789) but also contains Mexicans (1,207) and Cubans (1,168), among others. The black and Hispanic populations are highly concentrated within Rochester's "inner city."

Lehigh County, Pennsylvania, which contains Allentown, had a 1990 population of 291,130. Of this total, only 6,977 were African American and

14,954 were Hispanic. This is likely one of the few eastern urban centers in which Hispanics outnumber blacks. Puerto Ricans alone outnumber blacks by roughly 10,821 persons. There are also 710 Mexicans and a mix of many Hispanic groups in very small numbers. As in the case of Rochester, minorities are highly segregated in the "inner city."

Previous chapters demonstrated that Monroe County's AOMC and AOHC were located in the central city of Rochester and these minority concentrations differed from other white-majority areas of Monroe on the basis of socioeconomic attributes, including unemployment and poverty. Negative characteristics and white flight likely explain why most chains fled the inner city.

Inner-city areas with high concentrations of minorities have lower standards of living as reflected in socioeconomic variables. There also are differences in the age and quality of housing units between minority and nonminority concentrations. It is not surprising that the center city is dominated by rental units. Tracts in the areas of Rochester's minority concentrations contain some of the highest proportion of rentals. This fact, along with supporting documentation regarding other socioeconomic and housing conditions in inner-city Rochester (in the minority concentrations in particular), helps explain the locations of new facilities and the exodus of retail chain stores outside inner-city Rochester.

Lehigh County, although much smaller than Monroe County, reflects the same patterns of differential well-being between minority concentrations and nonminority concentrations of the city and county. The income, poverty, and other socioeconomic characteristics of these areas in Lehigh County clearly support our general findings that minority concentrations are less well-off in socioeconomic status, housing quality and value, and general well-being than their nonminority counterparts.

Selected Retail Distributions in Monroe and Lehigh Counties
Up to this point we have assumed that retail chains of various types have abandoned the central city, resulting in a lack of access by minorities to competitively priced goods. In this section, we provide mapped locations of three types of chain stores in the two study areas: grocery, GMS-discount, and home-improvement stores.

Monroe County, New York.   Not a single large grocery chain exists within a minority concentration. Figure 8.1 illustrates that only seven chains are located within the city limits, whereas twenty-four are in other towns of Monroe County. Figure 8.2 illustrates the pattern of discount department stores, such as K-Mart and Wal-Mart, in Monroe County. Again, not a single chain has located within a minority concentration. In fact, all stores are outside the city limits of Rochester, though one is on the border of the city and its AOMC. Figure 8.3 is a map of home-improvement chains in Monroe County,

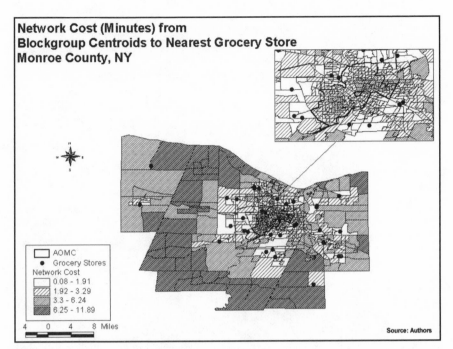

FIGURE 8.1   Network cost in minutes from block-group center to nearest grocery store, Monroe County, New York

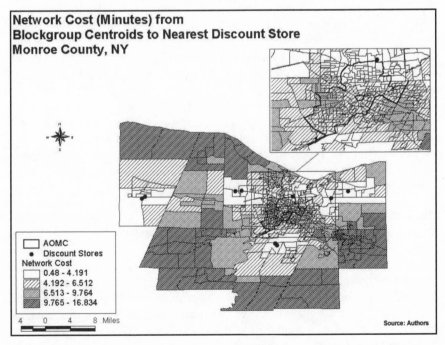

FIGURE 8.2   Network cost in minutes from block-group center to nearest discount store, Monroe County, New York

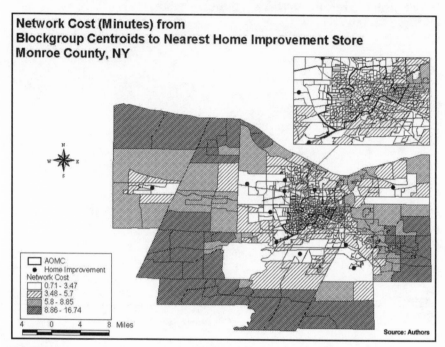

FIGURE 8.3   Network cost in minutes from block-group center to nearest home-improvement store, Monroe County, New York

including the well-known Lowe's and Home Depot. As in the other two cases, no chain is located in a minority concentration, and nearly all are outside the city of Rochester.

At this juncture, we note that we do not imply any racially motivated decisions on the part of any single corporation, nor a conspiracy. Rather, accepted locational principles have been applied within a capitalistic framework to maximize profit and minimize risk. The unfortunate result is a retail pattern that is likely to disadvantage those least able to afford the cost of travel to secure necessary goods.

Lehigh County, Pennsylvania.   As noted earlier, Lehigh County is a smaller urban county within which lies the small city of Allentown. The distributions of grocery, GMS–discount department, and home improvement chain stores in this county are quite similar to the general patterns described for Monroe County. In the case of chain grocery stores, the minority concentrations in this county are better off than those in Monroe. Three chain stores are located within or on the edges of the minority concentrations. Another six grocery chains are located outside the Areas of Minority Concentration but within the city of Allentown. Eleven stores are located outside Allentown in the county of Lehigh. Only two GMS–discount department stores are located within Lehigh County. Neither is located in the city nor within its minority concentrations.

There are only four home improvement chains in Lehigh County: Three are in the county outside the city, one is within the limits, and none are in minority concentrations. These patterns clearly reflect the national retail patterns discussed earlier in this chapter. With the exception of grocery chains, urban size seems to have little impact on the three retail distributions. It seems equally clear that residents of minority concentrations are disadvantaged due to unequal access to these retail necessities. Longer times and farther distances to travel translate into real financial costs and quality-of-life issues. We now turn to more concrete measures of accessibility and their use in evaluating racial and ethnic inequalities in pricing and distribution of retail establishments.

Accessibility and Equity: Euclidean and Network Distances Between Block Groups and Retail Stores

Three analytical approaches were used to compute the degree of accessibility between the block groups and retail stores in each county. The first involved the computation of Euclidean distances from the center of each block group to a store location. A second approach used was one of time cost across a network from a block group to a store. A third method was based on the accessibility index developed by Guy (1983). For both the Euclidean and network calculations, the minimum distance and time to the nearest store and the sum of all distances from each block group to every store in the county were determined. The nearest Euclidean distance provides a sense of the shortest possible distance a consumer needs to travel to a store. And the sum of the Euclidean distances is the shortest possible total distance to all the stores. The sum of the distances measures the relative access to all the stores. This sum is often normalized for average distance of a block group to a store within the system as a whole.

The cost of traveling the network is based on the types of roads in the network and the varying speeds on these segments of the network. The cost is measured in time (minutes) and indicates how long a consumer needs to go from the target block group to a store. This time becomes a surrogate for access because it provides a frame of measurement for comparing consumers from one block group against those of the other. The minimum travel times from the block group to the store through the network are calculated using a path-time search algorithm.

The types of roads that characterize the various segments of the network are identified based on the highway classification codes and are assigned average speed limits based on a pooled consensus of students from various regions of the country. The search for the best path involves the computation of time on each segment and then a search for the shortest or minimum time between the block group and a particular store. The sum of the times among all block groups and all the stores renders a general idea of areal accessibility. Basically it provides a way to judge a block group's relative access to the system of stores in the county in question.

There are, however, some dangers in treating accessibility measures as definitive indicators of equity. First, in the gravity formulation, the assumption that "attractiveness will draw" is like saying "build and they will come." In short, attractiveness and the ability and cost to travel are two very different things. An alternate explanation is that a grocery chain store's large size and attractiveness does not mean that an inner-city resident can afford to reach it. However, accessibility formulations that average the distance between a block group and all stores in a network can also be deceptive. Nonetheless, these measures do provide some indication of equity, but only in raw travel and distance, not in a household's ability to pay or to make choices under limiting conditions. For example, unemployed households may behave differently from employed households. Further, accessibility, as measured by our models, may be less important than pricing differentials between stores. For these reasons, we caution the reader not to overinterpret the results presented below. Following the presentation of the findings, we will report some previous research findings that are related to out-shopping behavior and pricing differences in Monroe County.

The Accessibility Model Findings: Grocery Chain Store Accessibility

The maps generated by different accessibility measures for Monroe County grocery chain are presented as Figures 8.1–8.3. The maps of the nearest Euclidean and network distances between block groups and stores (Figures 8.1 and 8.2) suggest that the AOMCs and AOHCs are relatively inaccessible to grocery chain locations in Monroe County. However, Figure 8.3, which reports the average network cost of each block group, illustrates the opposite, suggesting that minority concentrations are relatively well situated with reference to chain grocery stores. This measure reflects the problem discussed earlier. It examines the total distances between one block group and all stores in the network, divided by the number of stores. This creates a scenario wherein the block group appears closer to a particular store within the system due to averaging. In fact, in the case of Monroe County, not only are all the grocery chain stores outside the AOMC boundaries, but in some cases, they are literally across town.

In this study, the most appropriate measure, despite its assumptions about attractiveness, is Guy's accessibility index. The accessibility index distribution pattern is similar to that of the network cost of access for Monroe (Figure 8.1). It clearly indicates the relatively poor access of AOMC and AOHC residents to chain grocery stores in Monroe County.

Guy's accessibility measure for Lehigh County is based on the analysis of grocery chain stores and suggests that the distribution is identical to that of network cost (Figure 8.4). This map indicates differential access not only within the county and within the city of Allentown but also within the minority concentrations themselves. Specifically, the Hispanic concentrations, which consist chiefly of recent Puerto Rican immigrants, enjoy better accessibility to chain grocery stores than the eastern section of the AOMC, which is largely African American. It is also noteworthy that our fieldwork revealed the existence of a number of Hispanic markets offering better-quality produce within the AOHC, whereas nothing similar existed in the African-American section of the AOMC. This is in keeping with Boston's findings regarding the decline in black-owned food businesses (Boston, 2000). On the whole, the general accessibility via a street network in Allentown appears good, certainly better than some of the AOMCs in Rochester. We believe that this is, in part, due to Lehigh County's small size and the compactness of the central city and its retail form.

When we examine the accessibility patterns for discount department stores, clear differences emerge between the two study areas. In the case of Monroe (Figure 8.2), using Guy's index, we found the AOMCs and AOHCs have relatively less access to such stores than other Rochester areas. In the case of Lehigh, however, accessibility differences again exist within the minority concentrations themselves. The western, largely Hispanic area has better access than the eastern, black section of the AOMC. In fact, the Hispanic areas have among the best accessibility measures. Overall, the accessibility via the street network is good in the small, compact central city.

Finally, we examine accessibility to home improvement centers for these two counties. The results are once again similar to the network cost of access (Figure 8.3). In the case of Monroe, the Rochester minority concentrations enjoy moderate accessibility to chain home improvement stores, although none are located within the AOMCs or AOHCs. The minority concentrations, by Guy's measure, have less access than areas of Rochester that are generally west and south of AOMCs but have better access than some of the urban neighborhoods east of the minority concentrations. Again, this measure does not address dollar cost and ability of inner-city households to travel to these locations.

The accessibility to chain home improvement stores for Lehigh County block groups mirrors the results for grocery and discount chains. Accessibility is generally good, and the Hispanic concentrations have somewhat better access than blacks, who constitute the bulk of the AOMCs.

Together, these results generally support the contention that minority concentrations have less access to key retail functions than their white-majority counterparts. However, some accessibility differences exist within the minority concentrations. The most striking differences in our study involve the

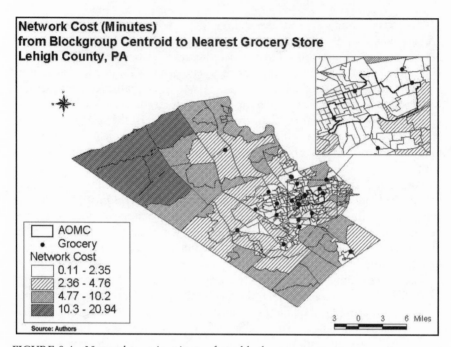

FIGURE 8.4   Network cost in minutes from block-group center to nearest grocery store, Lehigh County, Pennsylvania

generally greater accessibility enjoyed by Hispanic concentrations in Allentown. What cannot be exactly determined at this point is why Hispanics have better access. Is it the accident of settlement? Is it perhaps partly due also to the compact urban form of Allentown? Also, network analysis cannot adequately address individual behavioral choices regarding out-shopping behavior, nor the prices that households pay for goods purchased at different locations. A brief review of some shopping behaviors of Rochester AOMC residents and the results of a pricing study will provide some insights into the situation.

Overall these results illustrate that there is a degree of service deprivation in Areas of Minority Concentration. This translates into our primary theme of equity in access to resources, amenities, and services given race and place.

Out-Shopping Behavior and Differential Pricing in Grocery Stores
Investigation by Tettey-Fio (1999) of shopping behavior among AOMC residents in Rochester, New York, revealed that out-shopping was common among minority residents. Respondents shopped for groceries at eight chain store locations in the city. Two of the eight captured 80 percent of the minority patronage. Nearly 40 percent of all of the minority households inter-

viewed spent their entire grocery budget at a chain store. Of interest, however, was the fact that nearly half of those interviewed indicated that they spent at least 20 percent of their budget at minimarkets or convenience stores in their neighborhoods—a trend that likely reflects the need to purchase convenience items more frequently than out-shopping permits. About 20 percent of the residents shopped only once or twice per month, and 54 percent shopped four times per month or less. These findings may also reflect the inconvenience and costs associated with out-shopping trips. Overall, however, the findings underscore the importance of neighborhood grocery stores for minorities and the limitations associated with performing only network analysis to establish inequalities in retail access.

Tettey-Fio's analysis (1999) also clarified the nature of pricing differentials among the minority concentrations, the central city, and urban-county minimarkets and convenience stores. In purchasing similar brand items in stores in all three locations, the survey revealed that the average prices were higher in the AOMCs than in city or county locations. Tettey-Fio also compared the pricing of sixteen items purchased in AOMC markets with those in a well-known upscale chain in Rochester. The results showed that the aggregate bill for these sixteen items was highest in the AOMC and lowest at the upscale chain store. This led to the conclusion that clear pricing differentials existed, both by individual item and by aggregate bill, between the urban subregions and between chain and minimarket locations. These underlying price disparities contribute to frequent out-shopping behavior by minorities and further underscore the cost disadvantage for AOMC residents. Thus, in addition to our general finding of poorer accessibility for AOMC residents, there are other disadvantages and costs associated with minimarket and convenience store purchases by the residents who buy goods regularly in their neighborhoods.

Future Retailing in Inner Cities

It seems clear from the discussion in this chapter that segregation on one hand and retail decentralization on the other has not only had catastrophic impacts on urban economics but led to accessibility and price-differential problems for minority concentrations. These disparities, combined with other notable inequalities over the past generations, continue to further stress the resources and patience of minority populations in many urban centers. Attempts to remedy these inequalities, particularly in retailing, depend on the return of establishments and reinvestment in the inner cities.

As early as the 1980s, Epstein (1981) called attention to the fact that more than 24 million inner-city minorities constituted a potentially strong consumer market for food and merchandise:

The growing power of non-Whites in America has affected virtually every area of the nation's life—government, education, and business; yet, nowhere could it possibly have as much effect as in the marketplace for food and services [p. 155].

Despite this growing potential, Areas of Minority Concentration and inner cities have continued to host very few chain stores, resulting in a limited variety of brands and sizes, lower-quality merchandise, and generally higher prices for goods and services (Alwitt and Donley, 1997; B. F. Hall, 1983; Nayga and Weinberg, 1999).

Over the last ten years, however, some analysts and nonprofit organizations have pushed for a return by retailers to the central city. For example, Hendersen (1995) noted that the vacuum created by the disinvestment of urban retailing in the central city has accelerated full-scale cutthroat competition in the suburbs that has resulted in rapid saturation of the suburban market and stagnant or declining revenues over time. Weighing the risks of doing business against the potential profits to be made in the inner city, some retail companies have ventured into the central city, with excellent results. Hendersen stated further that retail business is undergoing revival in blighted neighborhoods, and even in areas where crime remains a problem, business is still picking up. Another analyst, Porter (1995), has advocated wealth creation strategies as a way of generating economic opportunity in the inner city to accelerate retail growth. He chose this approach over government investment in social programs. Based on his empirical research, he found companies that do retail chain businesses in the inner city not only were profitable but often discovered such locations to be among the most profitable. Porter has seen the return of businesses as the main catalyst to inner-city development and strongly suggests development strategies based on the wealth generation motive as an initial step to lift the inner city from its economic depression.

Clearly, the recent call for businesses to return to the inner cities has come at a time when there is convergence between retail chain supply and inner-city demand. Retail opportunities among inner-city minorities now seem to be among the prime frontiers to be harvested, initially perhaps by the brave. Regardless, the retail decision to reenter the inner city should not be misconstrued as altruistic. Just as decentralization was for profit maximization, the only consequence for retail planners is the potential "green" of untapped minority markets. K-Mart has ventured into inner-city Detroit in its new urban program. Hendersen (1995) and Porter (1995) have documented the return of stores to inner-city Detroit, Los Angeles, Newark, and parts of New York City. It is too early to say whether these few examples are on the front wave of a new retailing process. If they are, they are certainly likely to encourage other investors into the inner cities and, with time, help minimize the significant disparities in access and pricing of goods and services for minority residents.

Chapter 9

Commuting and Locational Access to Employment in Urban America

Ethnic and Racial Disparities in Three Cities*

Commuting and Employment:
The Spatial Mismatch Hypothesis

The preceding chapter examined the restructuring and redistribution of retail establishments in urban America and the subsequent impacts on minority access to chain stores and quality merchandise. A related concern revolves around employment opportunities and whether racial/ethnic minorities in American cities suffer greater job accessibility constraints than do nonminorities. This issue moves us beyond the discussion of employment discrimination to one of disadvantage in access to the job market and in the cost of travel once a job is secured. Accessibility has been at the crux of the spatial mismatch hypothesis that was originally formulated by Kain (1968). The hypothesis proposes that the suburbanization of jobs and the resiliency of racial residential segregation have led to a spatial mismatch whereby inner-city residents, primarily racial/ethnic minorities, face difficulties in reaching the growing employment opportunities in suburban centers. A situation in which members of a group experience more difficulty in getting to work is not compatible with equitable access.

There have been different approaches to testing the spatial mismatch hypothesis and unequal access to jobs. Many studies depend on unemployment

---

*This chapter is authored by Ibipo Johnston-Anumonwo, State University of New York–Cortland.

and earnings data, whereas others examine differential access to employment using commuting data. Although scholars have found evidence both for and against the spatial mismatch of minority workers and jobs, many of the studies on commuting find that minorities, especially African Americans, spend a longer time for their work trips than white Americans. Yet some research indicates no differences between black and white commuting distances (P. Gordon, Kumar, and Richardson, 1989).

Part of the reason for mixed evidence about racial/ethnic disparities in work trip lengths stems from key shortcomings in the analyses, namely, the tendency to exclude workplace location in measuring employment accessibility, inadequate control for ethnic and racial differences in the locational and socioeconomic factors known to influence work trip length, and the failure to acknowledge the role of gender in commuting. Empirical inquiries that correct for these shortcomings are necessary when comparing the work trips of racial/ethnic minorities with those of nonminorities to detect any form of inequity. Evidence on the nature of ethnic/racial inequities in access to employment is especially relevant for informing analysts and policymakers about the impact of past and continuing employment suburbanization on the socioeconomic well-being of the urban minority population.

Equity and Access to Jobs

If members of ethnic/racial minority groups experience constrained transportation and locational access to work, this constitutes a significant form of inequity because they could thereby be excluded from being full functioning members of society. Young (1990) cites unemployment and other conditions that deny useful participation in life as forms of social injustice, because the people affected are confined to lives of social marginality (Young, 1990). According to Young, marginalization functions in such a way that the labor system cannot or will not use some people, and they are therefore potentially subjected to severe material deprivation. Furthermore, the material deprivation that marginalization causes is certainly unjust, especially in a society where others have plenty (Young, 1990). W. J. Wilson (1996) explains that the high poverty rates in American inner-city black neighborhoods are due to the rapid growth of joblessness. From a locational perspective, the length of the separation between home and workplace is an indicator of access to employment; hence commuting data are appropriate for testing equitable job access.

Unambiguous specification of the existence and nature of ethnic/racial commuting disparities is a necessary prerequisite for a better understanding of the locational cost constraints faced by minority workers. Also, establishing the existence of unequivocal ethnic disparities in workers' geographical access to employment will better inform scholars on the long-standing debate about the validity of a spatial mismatch. Yet some factors that are likely to be relevant in accurately investigating ethnic/racial differences in locational access to employment have often been neglected in many past studies.

First, depending on the measure of locational access to employment that is used, varying patterns of racial work trip parity or disparity may be observed in empirical studies. Although Kain's original hypothesis (1968) is explicit about the impact of residential and work locations on differential access of blacks and whites to jobs, few studies have looked at residential and work locations jointly. Appropriate measures of the influence of home-work separation are (a) suburban work location and (b) the travel time between home and work. Second, in addition to the intrametropolitan distribution of employment opportunities vis-à-vis residences, the length of the work trip is also influenced by many socioeconomic factors, such as mode of transportation, income level, and occupation. Racial/ethnic differences in these variables have to be taken into account. Third, few studies on commuting have examined racial/ethnic differences among women, which is a curious omission given the clear gender differences widely reported in the commuting literature.

Since many previous empirical studies have not necessarily investigated this combination of issues, the objective of this chapter is to closely compare the work trips of minorities and of nonminorities in three different cities to see if there is any difference. Commuting data are used to investigate whether Latino- and African-American male and female workers experience greater job access difficulties in the three cities. The questions examined are, Do Hispanic white men and women have longer commutes than non-Hispanic whites? Do black men and women have longer commutes than white men and women? Does lack of access to private automobiles affect the work trip times of ethnic minorities? If so, when private auto use is held constant, there should be no difference in the work trip times of minorities and nonminorities. We should also expect little or no ethnic/racial difference in commuting length among auto users of similar socioeconomic status. Finally, we could test if the workplace location vis-à-vis the residence is responsible for any difference. These questions are examined for separate subcategories of male and female white non-Hispanic, Hispanic, and black workers. Any observed ethnic differential in access to work among otherwise comparable groups of workers suggests racial/ethnic inequity.

The chapter is organized into three main sections starting with a review of the systematic theoretical knowledge about commuting and employment, as well as brief descriptions of the three study areas and the data sets chosen for the analyses. Next, the results of the three case studies are reported. The chapter ends with a discussion of the implications of the findings for Areas of Minority Concentration in the urban United States.

Commuting and Access to Employment

U.S. Metropolitan Commuting

Americans make far more nonwork trips than work trips, but the journey to work is still a large component of total travel. According to the 1995 Nationwide Personal Transportation Survey (NPTS), a survey of all trip purposes, trips for which the purpose is work or work related constitute about one-fifth of all trips in the country (U.S. Department of Transportation, 1999). Central aspects of the work trip are the origin and destination, the travel mode, and the commute length.

Four major types of journey-to-work flows characterize contemporary U.S. urban commuting patterns. They are the suburb-to-suburb flow, suburb-to-city flow, city-to-city flow, and reverse commuting (i.e., city to suburb). Over one-half of the work trips in metropolitan areas are suburb-to-suburb flows. This rapidly growing trip type is largely by automobile and comprises a broad mix of professional, blue-collar, clerical, and sales workers as a result of the growing variety of suburban jobs, as noted in Chapter 4 (Hartshorn, 1992; Stanback, 1991). Much of the suburb-to-suburb journey takes place on expressways since few public transit routes serve outlying suburban locations. Suburb-to-city flows are trips originating in suburbs and ending in the central city, especially the CBD. Affluent white-collar workers constitute the majority of these work trips. City-to-city trips are work trips within the central city. This involves workers across all income groups, but many are low-skilled workers and use public transit. Reverse commuting accounts for the smallest fraction of the four work trip flows. These are trips that originate in the central city and end at suburban locations. This work trip is typically slow and circuitous and is patronized by blue-collar employees, many of whom are minority workers (Hartshorn, 1992).

The automobile has remained the dominant work-trip mode in the United States. In 1980, 84 percent of metropolitan workers used an automobile (car, truck, or van), and only 8 percent of work trips occurred by transit. According to the NPTS, in 1995 about 76 percent of the total U.S. population generally traveled to work by automobile, with suburban residents being even more likely to depend on a car. From the 1990 census, only 6.5 percent of metropolitan commuters used public transportation for their work trip (U.S. Census Bureau, 1993a). Lastly, in 1990, the average travel time for the work trip in the United States as a whole was 19.7 minutes, but by 1995 it had increased to 20.7 minutes (accompanied both by an increase in average miles traveled by 11.6 miles and average speed—33.6 miles per hour—in 1995) (U.S. Department of Transportation, 1999). The mean travel time of metropolitan workers was 23.2 minutes in 1990.

Demographic Differences in Metropolitan Commuting

The journey-to-work literature is filled with documented evidence of the factors that affect commuting time, key among which are transportation mode, income, and occupation. Public transit users spend a longer time than private-automobile users (Cubukgil and Miller, 1982; Fox, 1983; U.S. Department of Commerce, 1982). Since minorities are more likely to use public transportation, their work trips are expected to take a longer time than those of nonminorities. High-income workers and workers in male-dominated occupations, such as professional and managerial jobs, have longer work trips than other workers (Dubin, 1991; Hanson and Johnston, 1985; Madden, 1981; Pisarski, 1987). Since minorities are more likely than nonminority whites to have lower-paying jobs, this racial difference in workers' socioeconomic status could contribute to racial differences in trip lengths.

Holzer (1991) provided a comprehensive review of the literature on the spatial mismatch hypothesis. Most studies find that more ethnic minorities than nonminority whites use public transportation and that African Americans, especially, have longer commuting times (Alexis and DiTomaso, 1983; Ihlanfeldt, 1992; Karsada, 1990; U.S. Department of Commerce, 1982). The conclusion of P. Gordon et al. (1989), however, differed substantially from the conclusions of most researchers who have analyzed commuting data. They found that nonwhites traveled shorter distances in nine out of fifteen work trip comparisons and that nonwhites had longer travel times than whites irrespective of central-city or suburban residence, but the authors interpreted these findings as insufficient evidence that minorities commute longer. Although P. Gordon et al. examined differences based on place of residence, their study (like many others that control for residential location) did not examine differences between commutes to suburban or central-city work locations, because their database did not contain information on workplace location.

It is very clear that the use of public transit increases commuting time (McLafferty and Preston, 1996; Taylor and Ong, 1995); but longer travel times may also be due to traffic congestion, a reality in inner-city neighborhoods. Most of the minority workers in U.S. metropolitan areas reside in the central cities, while most white workers reside in suburban locations. Also, higher proportions of Hispanics and blacks than of non-Hispanic whites work in the central cities. Any accurate test of the possibility that Hispanics or blacks endure longer trips than non-Hispanic whites, therefore, has to take into account travel mode as well as residential and workplace location.

An early study by Alexis and DiTomaso (1983) alluded to the effects of transportation and location on employment access, but the study did not include precise locational measures. A fairly comprehensive study of Detroit by Zax (1990) focused explicitly on commutes and considered residential location as well as workplace location. Zax found that African Americans who commuted to CBD workplaces lived closer to the workplace than did their white counterparts, but his findings on racial differences in commutes to a suburban workplace led him to conclude that residential segregation constrained African Americans. Both Dubin's finding (1991) that suburban employment is far more beneficial in reducing the commuting times of white workers as compared to black workers and Ihlanfeldt's finding (1992) that African-American workers who out-commute from central-city residences to suburban jobs have longer commutes concur with Zax's conclusions.

Gender is also a relevant factor in commuting. Gender differences in commuting are widely reported in the literature: women, particularly white women, have shorter commutes than men, whether the trip is measured in units of distance or time (Hanson and Johnston, 1985; Hanson and Pratt, 1995; Johnston-Anumonwo, 1992, 1997a, 1997b). Other studies document gender differences in residential locations, with minority female-headed households facing more constraints because they are more likely to have dependent children (Bullard, 1990; Leigh, 1989).

However, many early geographic gender studies did not integrate race and ethnicity (see Sanders, 1990, for a critique), and in the early discourse on the spatial mismatch hypothesis, few scholars considered the possibility of significant differences based on gender. Despite the increased labor-force participation of women in general, and the historically high labor-force participation of African-American women in particular, many studies excluded female workers (e.g., Kasarda, 1990; Hughes and Madden, 1991) or did not differentiate African-American and white female workers from the respective male workers (e.g., P. Gordon et al., 1989). The studies that examine differences in commuting across race and sex groups show that for both sexes being black is associated with longer commute times (e.g., McLafferty and Preston, 1991, 1997). Analyses of differential access to jobs should therefore incorporate gender and ethnic differences in socioeconomic factors and in the intrametropolitan locations of housing and jobs.

Minority Status and Differential Locational Access

As demonstrated in previous chapters, ethnic and racial residential segregation in U.S. metropolitan areas is for the most part pervasive and unyielding. According to a *USA Today* analysis (1991) of 1990 census data on the percentage of each race or ethnic group living in cities, suburbs, and rural areas, blacks and Hispanics were far more likely to live in central cities than in suburbs or rural areas. Almost six of every ten (57 percent) blacks lived in central cities, while nearly 27 percent lived in suburbs. For Hispanics the proportions were 51 percent living in central cities and 39 percent living in suburbs. For white non-Hispanics, only 24 percent lived in central cities, while 50 percent lived in suburbs. In short, minorities, particularly African Americans, are still less likely than nonminorities to live in suburbs, though more African Americans do live in suburbs than in the past.

In fact, the widely reported relative increase in African-American suburbanization since the sixties (Long and DeAre, 1981; Stearns and Logan, 1986) has prompted some scholars to examine differential access in suburban settings. For example, Joe Darden (1990) found that access to suburban housing was primarily a function of race, irrespective of the professional status of individuals. Others have confirmed that African Americans in suburbs live in segregated enclaves (see Chapter 5) and that black access to jobs is poor because of racial residential segregation (Schneider and Phelan, 1990). These studies on differential housing and employment highlight the importance of place-specific analysis in documenting a spatial mismatch of minorities and jobs, but they do not utilize any direct measure of locational access to employment such as commuting length.

It is important to point out that much of the research on the locational difficulties faced by African Americans usually tests for the impact of job access on employment opportunities by examining employment status and especially earnings. Some detailed empirical studies provide direct evidence of the impacts on African Americans' economic standing. For example, Ihlanfeldt (1992) found that, although most African-American low-skilled workers who out-commute from the central cities of Philadelphia and Detroit have considerable commutes, they generally do not earn more for working outside the central city. Hughes and Madden (1991) also found that increased commuting and/or housing costs associated with racial residential segregation adversely affect the economic status of African Americans. Although most studies tend not to find difficult access to jobs to be a major factor in black-white employment outcomes (finding instead that labor supply deficiencies and labor market discrimination impede African-American employment and earnings more than do locational constraints) many studies do find that African Americans face greater locational constraints than whites. This is another race-place connection.

More recent studies on commuting have updated our systematic knowledge about commuting by examining the 1990 Public Use Microdata Samples (PUMS), which include travel time to work. A shortcoming of many of these types of studies is that they suffer from varying degrees of omissions, including ignoring the significance of suburban commutes. As a result, the key findings of separate studies on commuting about the influence of specific variables are sufficiently important that these variables need to be synthesized together in more inclusive kinds of analyses. The next section will report on three case studies of ethnic and racial disparities in commuting among men and among women that take into consideration the factors that affect work trip time. But first is a general overview about the three study areas, Miami,

Detroit, and Kansas City, and a description of the data and variables used for the analyses.

Descriptive Summary
Data on the Study Areas

Of the three metropolitan areas chosen for this study, Detroit had the largest population: nearly 4.4 million in 1990. The Miami metropolitan area's population was about 1.9 million, and the population of the Kansas City metropolitan area was nearly 1.6 million (U.S. Census Bureau, 1993a). The three cities reflect different demographic, residential, and employment patterns.

In Miami the proportion of the population that was white was 73 percent. About one-fifth of metropolitan Miami's population (20.6 percent) was black in 1990. Miami remains one of the United States' metropolitan areas with the highest proportion of Hispanics. Almost half (49 percent) of the metropolitan population in 1990 was Hispanic (white or nonwhite). Minorities are more likely to reside in the central city. In the Miami central city, 62 percent of the population is Hispanic, and 27 percent is black (U.S. Census Bureau, 1993a). Thus, although the specification of Areas of Minority Concentration used in this book is at the census-tract level, the Miami central city approximates the notion of an AOHC (Area of Hispanic Concentration).

Detroit had a very small Hispanic population in 1990. Only 1.9 percent of the metropolitan area was Hispanic. Roughly 76 percent of the population was white, and 21.5 percent was black. Yet an overwhelming majority of the Detroit central city's population was black (75.7 percent). In this regard, the Detroit central city distinctly fits the idea of an AOMC, though the specification is not at the census-tract level. The Kansas City metropolitan area also had a very small Hispanic population—2.9 percent in 1990. Most (84.4 percent) of the metropolitan area was white. About 13 percent of the metropolitan area was black, and this proportion rose to 27 percent in the central city (U.S. Census Bureau, 1993a). The three study areas have varying levels of residential segregation.

The USA Today study (1991) of 1990 census data in 219 metropolitan areas provides segregation indices for the three metropolitan areas. Miami had a total segregation index of 58, Kansas City had an index of 67, and Detroit had an index of 83 (the highest in the country). These figures represent the percent of all minorities (blacks, Hispanics, and Asians) or white residents who would have to move from segregated neighborhoods in order to achieve residential integration in the respective metropolitan areas. An earlier report (in 1989) of a five-year study by researchers at the University of Chicago found that, in ten of the nation's largest cities, racial segregation was more pronounced in northeastern and midwestern cities, with Chicago being the most segregated followed by Detroit. Housing segregation retards minorities' economic and social outcomes (Cutler and Gleaser, 1997); hence it contributes to racial/ethnic inequalities.

Apart from residential patterns, there are also ethnic/racial differences in labor force characteristics in the three metropolitan areas, as presented next. Given the demographic composition of these cities, the comparisons in this chapter for Miami focus on Hispanics, whereas those for Detroit and Kansas City focus primarily on blacks.

Labor force participation of Hispanics in Miami was slightly higher than that of whites: 66 percent of Hispanics were in the labor force, versus 61 percent of non-Hispanic whites. Hispanic unemployment in 1990 was, however, 8 percent, whereas the corresponding unemployment level for non-Hispanic whites was lower—4.5 percent (U.S. Department of Commerce, 1993).

In Detroit and Kansas City, blacks participated less in the labor force than whites, and there are marked racial/ethnic differences in unemployment levels. In both metropolitan areas, black unemployment levels were much higher than white unemployment levels. Black unemployment in Detroit was nearly 21 percent, whereas white unemployment was about 6 percent. Black unemployment in Kansas City was approximately 13 percent, whereas white unemployment was 4.5 percent (U.S. Census Bureau, 1993a). These higher unemployment rates for racial/ethnic minorities are tantamount to marginalization as a form of social and economic inequity.

Along with labor force characteristics, the Census Bureau also provides summary data on commuting and vehicle availability by race and Hispanic origin. These data are provided as aggregate area-level data for entire metropolitan areas and subunits or by census tract. To provide a spatial illustration of the transportation profile obtained from one set of census data, two maps are produced from the 1990 census-tract data for one of the study areas—Detroit, Wayne County. Two measures of mobility are examined. These are one mode of transportation to work (bus) and the availability of automobiles. For example, in Wayne County, out of 822,620 workers, 649,839 drive alone, 96,558 carpool, and 38,481 take the bus, yielding county values of 79.0 percent, 11.7 percent, and 4.7 percent for these three mode types. The deviations of a tract's percentages from these county percentages are mapped for the bus-to-work mode and auto availability in relation to AOMCs and AOHCs in Figure 9.1.

Intersection of Transportation, Race, and Place: Detroit, Wayne County

The maps for Wayne County vividly show the overlap between race/ethnicity and transportation mode used for the work trip. Figure 9.1(a) illustrates the peaks of greater bus usage. There is a very stark preponderance of bus riders

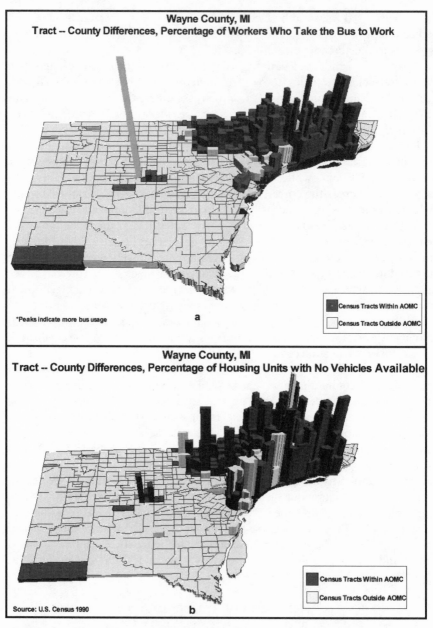

FIGURE 9.1   Wayne County, Michigan: (a) census tract–county differences in percentage of workers who take the bus to work; (b) census tract–county differences in percentage of housing units with no vehicle available. Source: U.S. Census Bureau, 1990.

in the eastern tracts (with the exception of one outlier tract). A very vivid west-versus-east dichotomy in bus usage is apparent. Compared to tracts outside of AOMCs, the census tracts within AOMCs (and also AOHCs) have higher percentages of workers who ride the bus to work. Figure 9.1(b) illustrates the relationship between vocation in Wayne County and access to a private vehicle. More specifically, it illustrates the race-place connection of auto ownership. Taken together, these maps support the disproportionate dependence on public transit by those residing in minority concentrations due to the lack of private car ownership. Clearly, many residents of minority concentrations in Wayne County depend on public transportation for their work trip.

The census data also indicate disproportionately fewer households in minority concentrations having more than one auto available, as compared to these living in nonminority concentrations. The data and maps on transportation patterns in Detroit conform to expectations of the interlocking nature of place and race in urban America.

We conclude with summaries of commuting data for all three study areas. According to the 1990 census, much higher proportions of minorities use public transit as their means of transportation to work in all three metropolitan areas. In Miami 5.3 percent of Hispanics (of any race) use public transit, as compared to 3.0 percent of whites (non-Hispanic). In Detroit and Kansas City, 11.3 and 10.3 percent of blacks use public transit as compared to only 0.7 percent and 1.2 percent of whites, respectively. The mean travel time for whites in Miami is a little less than the mean travel time of Hispanics (of any race). The mean travel time for whites in both Detroit and Kansas City is also slightly less than the time for blacks (U.S. Department of Commerce, 1993).

All these summary data are obtained from aggregate tabulations of the census data for metropolitan areas. But the range of factors necessary for a full understanding of ethnic/racial disparities in commuting requires that disaggregate data, which allow individual workers' socioeconomic characteristics to be identified, be linked with their locational and work trip attributes. PUMS data meet this requirement because they contain a diverse set of individual and household information as well as locational data for a relatively large number of workers in a given metropolitan area. Hence this is the data set utilized here.

Data and Measures

The database used for the analysis on access to employment in this chapter is the 1990 U.S. Census 5-percent PUMS for the Miami Primary Metropolitan Statistical Area (PMSA), the Detroit PMSA, and the Kansas City Standard Metropolitan Area (SMA). As noted earlier, much recent research on metropolitan commuting depends on the 1990 PUMS data because it allows an examination of large sample sizes for most metropolitan areas (U.S. Census

Bureau, 1992). The PUMS data, however, contain no detailed information on residential or workplace location within metropolitan areas. In order to protect respondents' confidentiality, locational information available in the PUMS is usually provided for very large geographical areas such as county or subcounty units. Typically, the locations obtained for respondents are simply central city versus non-central-city. An additional drawback that specifically applies to the analysis here is that in 1990 there was no place-of-work breakdown for the Miami PMSA. This situation made it impossible to conduct any place-of-work analysis for Miami using the 1990 PUMS data.

Travel time is the only measure of trip length provided in the PUMS. Information on distance is not collected in the census. It is instructive to note, however, that a study comparing measures of work trip distance and time concluded that "commuting time is more important to workers than commuting distance" (Dubin, 1991, p. 28). Travel time is the actual number of minutes spent traveling from home to work, as reported by the respondent. Apart from trip duration, the other variables included in the analyses are Hispanic origin, race, sex, transportation mode, area of residence, workplace location, income, and occupation.

Only white and black respondents (as specified in the census) who are sixteen years and older are selected. White respondents are then divided into Hispanic and non-Hispanic. Thus the comparisons are based on three ethnic groups: (1) white non-Hispanics, (2) white Hispanics, and (3) blacks. Two transportation modes are examined: private automobile and public transit. Residence and workplace locations are classified into two categories: central city or suburban (suburban locations are locations outside the census-defined central-city limits). Workers are classified as belonging to low- or high-income groups depending on whether their personal annual incomes were below or above $15,000. Workers' occupations are categorized into five standard Census Bureau designations: managers/professionals, sales/clerical/technical workers, service workers, craft workers, and industrial workers. Differences in travel mode are assessed using chi-square statistics (percentage differences). The ethnic/racial differences in travel time are assessed using the student t-test (two-tailed).

Case Studies

An Empirical Analysis of Miami: The Case of Hispanics. In this section the commuting of (white) Hispanics in metropolitan Miami is compared with that of whites (non-Hispanic). The sample sizes for the comparison groups are 10,440 Hispanic men, 6,930 white men, 8,223 Hispanic women, and 5,868 white women. As expected, more Hispanics (men and women) than whites use public transportation. Hispanic women in Miami are more dependent on public transportation than the other three groups—6.7 percent as compared to 3.6 percent for Hispanic men, 3.2 percent for white women, and 2.2 percent for white men (Figure 9.2[a]).

The dependence of Hispanics on public transportation may contribute to the slightly longer average journey-to-work times observed. The overall average travel time for Hispanic women is 24 minutes, whereas it is 22.8 minutes for white women. Among men, the difference between the two ethnic groups is very small (25.1 and 24.4 minutes), and it becomes insignificant once auto use is taken into account. Hispanic and white male auto users spend about the same time traveling to work in metropolitan Miami—about 25 minutes. Among women auto users, there is only a small difference (1 minute) in the time spent by Latina and white women.

Among Miami auto users, a small racial/ethnic difference in commuting time persists for low-income workers. Low-income Hispanic men spend 1.3 minutes longer than low-income white men; low-income Latina women spend 1.8 minutes longer than low-income white women. Among service workers, Hispanic men spend 1.6 minutes longer than white men, whereas Hispanic women spend 2.5 minutes longer than white female service workers. These findings for Miami illustrate that, even when socioeconomic variables such as income and occupation are taken into account, low-status Latino workers still spend more time on their work trips than their low-status white counterparts (though the difference in travel time is quite small).

Lastly, the analysis for Miami examines the situation for residents of the central city who use a private automobile for their work trip (Figure 9.2[b]). The pattern of relatively longer work trips for Latinos is clear. The difference between Hispanic men and white men is almost 4 minutes, and the difference between Hispanic women and white women is 2.7 minutes. The racial/ethnic difference in journey-to-work time is thus greater among residents of the central city (than the metropolitan area as a whole). By showing that ethnic disparity widens for central-city residents, this case study of Miami illustrates the role of both Hispanic ethnic status and central-city residence in commuting disparities. The findings suggest that, within Miami's central city, the residential patterns of Hispanic workers and white workers are sufficiently different as to contribute to differences in average journey-to-work lengths. The next section examines the case of blacks in Detroit.

An Empirical Analysis of Detroit: The Case of Blacks. In 1990 Detroit was the most racially segregated metropolitan area in the United States, with an overall segregation index of 83 and a black segregation index of 89. In other words, 89 percent of African Americans in Detroit would have to relocate their residences in order for the residential distribution of blacks and whites to approach the metropolitan proportion mix. The comparison groups for the Detroit PUMS analysis consisted of 32,360 white men, 4,560 black men, 25,150 white women, and 5,411 black women.

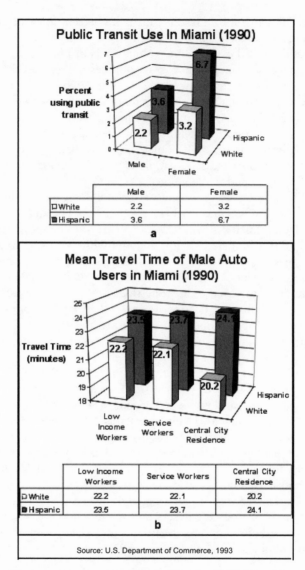

FIGURE 9.2   The journey to work in Miami, Florida, 1990: (a) public transit use; (b) mean travel time to work of male drivers. Source: U.S. Department of Commerce, 1993a.

In line with nationwide patterns, African-American men and women in the sample are more likely than whites to use public transportation. About 9.8 percent of the African-American men and 10.9 percent of African-American women in the sample use public transit, as compared to only 0.5 percent of

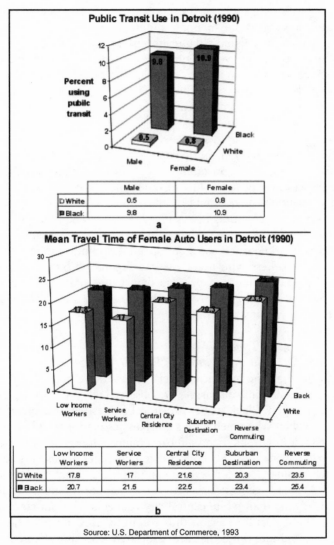

	Male	Female
☐White	0.5	0.8
■Black	9.8	10.9

a

	Low Income Workers	Service Workers	Central City Residence	Suburban Destination	Reverse Commuting
☐White	17.8	17	21.6	20.3	23.5
■Black	20.7	21.5	22.5	23.4	25.4

b

Source: U.S. Department of Commerce, 1993

FIGURE 9.3   The journey to work in Detroit, Michigan, 1990: (a) public transit use; (b) mean travel time to work of female drivers. Source: U.S. Department of Commerce, 1993.

white men and 0.8 percent of white women (Figure 9.3[a]). The observed difference in travel time between African-American male workers and white male workers in Detroit is, however, small and insignificant (0.6 minutes). But African-American women spend a longer time on average than white women—23.9 minutes versus 21.1 minutes. The racial/ethnic difference between women is reduced when automobile use is taken into account; black women auto users spend only about a minute longer than white women auto users. Among men, it is actually white auto users whose average travel time is 1 minute longer than the average time spent by black male auto users. One could conclude at this point that, in 1990, the racial differences in travel times among Detroit workers who use a car are negligible, but further subgroup comparisons reveal a different picture.

Comparing the Travel Time of Workers
with the Same Socioeconomic Status in Detroit

Based on the literature on commuting and on well-established racial/ethnic differences in wages, the low incomes and low-status jobs of African-American women and men should disallow long commutes. Yet, when low-income or service occupation is examined, low-income black women auto users in Detroit spend almost 3 minutes longer than white women, and black women service workers who use a car spend 4.5 minutes longer than white women service workers who use a car (see Figure 9.3[b]). Also black male service workers have a longer work trip than white male service workers. In short, minority workers of low socioeconomic status spend relatively longer times for their work trips.

Comparing the Travel Time of Workers
with Suburban Workplace Locations in Detroit

Although there are no significant racial disparities among Detroit central-city residents, racial/ethnic disparities are observed when the workplace is in a *suburban* destination. Black men with suburban destinations spend almost 2 minutes longer than white men with suburban destinations, and black women with suburban destinations spend almost 3 minutes longer than white women with suburban destinations. The longer commute times of blacks is equally apparent in the comparisons for reverse commuters, as black male and female residents of Detroit's central city who out-commute to suburban locations spend a longer time than white central-city residents who out-commute (Figure 9.3[b]). The results for Detroit thus confirm the existence of racial/ethnic differences in commute times that are associated with suburban employment location. Next is an analysis of black and white work trips in Kansas City.

An Empirical Analysis of Kansas City: Race and Place.   Kansas City is examined as an example of a less extreme metropolitan area than Detroit or Miami in terms of racial segregation or ethnic diversity. It might be considered an "average, middle America" metropolitan area. For example, the percentage of blacks in the Kansas City metropolitan area (12.8 percent) is similar to the percentage of blacks in U.S. metropolitan areas as a whole—13 percent (U.S. Department of Commerce, 1993).

The comparison groups for the Kansas City study are 14,201 white men, 11,971 white women, 1,192 African-American men, and 1,393 African-American women. The patterns of public transportation use in the Kansas City metropolitan area do indeed parallel the now familiar trend of higher African-American transit use. Whereas only 0.9 percent of white men and only 1.4 percent of white women use public transit, about 9.2 percent of the African-American men and 12.7 percent of African-American women do.

In spite of this disparity in the use of public transit for the work trip, the average travel time of black and white males in Kansas City approaches parity regardless of transportation mode. There is only negligible racial/ethnic difference among men. Among women, black women spend 2.3 minutes longer than white women do overall; but the racial difference among women auto users reduces to less than 1 minute. Thus it would appear that the disproportionate use of nonauto modes by African-American women in Kansas City accounts for their longer commutes as compared to white women. However, this explanation does not always apply, because even when access to a car is not a constraint, low-income black women actually spend a much *longer* time getting to work (20.5 minutes versus 15.7 minutes for low-income white women). In addition, there are also significant racial/ethnic differences in the commutes of men and women in Kansas City, based on whether they live in the central city of the metropolitan area and whether they work in suburban locations, as detailed next.

Among men who live in the central city, blacks spend a longer time on their work trips than whites (22.8 minutes versus 20.6 minutes), and among those who work in the suburbs, black men spend a much longer time than white men (26.7 versus 22 minutes). Among men who live in the central city but work in the suburbs (reverse commuters), blacks again have longer travel times than white men (30 versus 26.5 minutes).

Racial/ethnic differences in travel time are also observed among female workers who reside in the central city or who work at suburban locations. The most striking racial difference is that African-American women who work in suburban locations spend *over 6 minutes longer* getting to work than do their white female counterparts. But surprisingly, among female reverse commuters, African-American women spend just over one minute longer than white reverse commuters (and the difference is not statistically significant). Nonetheless, the results show that, in particular instances, both place and race are relevant factors in the observed differences of men's and women's commute times in Kansas City. That is, (1) if the residence is in the central city, there is a racial difference in trip length, and (2) if the place of work is in the suburb, there is a racial difference in trip length. Inner-city black residents are the ones with relatively longer commutes than whites; and blacks with suburban workplaces are the ones with relatively longer commutes than whites. These results on the role of suburban employment for

Kansas City's black workers' commute times are similar to those reported above for Detroit's black workers.

Summary and Conclusions

The three case studies show that many Hispanic workers in Miami and many African-American workers in Detroit and in Kansas City spend longer times getting to work than their white non-Hispanic counterparts. The most likely reason proposed for longer travel times for African Americans and Hispanics has usually been that members of these ethnic minority groups use more public transportation, a much slower mode of travel than nonminorities use. In line with this reasonable expectation, the results of the case studies show that a much higher proportion of Hispanic and African-American workers than white workers depend on public transit, a factor partly responsible for the somewhat longer commute times of minorities in the three study areas. When minority men and women do in fact use private vehicles, they spend about the same time as nonminorities. This tendency for racial/ethnic disparities in travel time to reduce or disappear among auto users led Taylor and Ong (1995) to suggest the importance of an "automobile mismatch." But differential access to private automobiles is not the main or only reason for the longer commuting time of Latino and African-American men and women. Both mobility and locational factors are important reasons for the racial and ethnic gap in travel time to work. Even when they use automobiles, Hispanics who live in Miami's central city and African Americans who live in Kansas City's central city have longer commutes than non-Hispanic whites who live in these central cities. Most minority and nonminority workers in the study areas do have similar travel times. However, it is the minority workers with locational or socioeconomic constraints who face longer commutes than their nonminority counterparts. In particular, traveling to jobs in suburban locations in Kansas City and Detroit results in longer commuting time for African Americans than it does for whites. If more jobs were available in central cities, there would be less need for suburban commutes. Alternatively, if African Americans had unrestricted access to suburban housing, the racial disparity in access to jobs might be alleviated. Based on the relatively small overall difference observed in the workers' commute time, the ethnic/racial difference in commute time may be expected to disappear as more minorities drive automobiles to work. If, however, employment opportunities continue to expand in suburbs and not in central cities, black workers, even those who use a car, face the penalty of longer commutes to suburban workplaces than do their white counterparts.

Discussion and Policy Implications for Areas of Minority Concentrations

Using travel time as a direct measure of locational access, the case studies in this chapter show the circumstances under which white Hispanic and black male and female workers spend relatively longer times getting to work than non-Hispanic white workers. One possible explanation for minority workers' longer travel times is that minority and nonminority workers live and work in different subareas of central-city and suburban locations, but the geographic units of analysis available do not allow an examination of this issue. The central-city neighborhoods in which Miami Latinos and Kansas City blacks live may be even more prone to traffic congestion or may lack direct access to high-speed freeways, as compared to the neighborhoods in which comparable whites live. Minority workers, male and female, may be traveling through busy inner-city neighborhood streets for a longer stretch of their work trips than are white workers. Going through congested inner-city routes with numerous traffic light delays could easily account for African-American workers' longer travel times in Kansas City or Latino workers' longer travel times in Miami.

Similarly, a data set with smaller area units for the workplace destination than the data used here may also reveal that whites and blacks have different work destinations *within* suburban locations. Evidence to this effect would raise the possibility of differential hiring of blacks and whites due to either differences in occupational qualifications or to employer discrimination. In fact, a qualitative study of employer hiring practices in suburban Detroit provided clear evidence of racial discrimination (Turner, 1997). The study linked findings about spatial mismatch with findings about the negative treatment and harassment of blacks in Detroit suburbs, both by the police and by white residents, to emphasize the multiple barriers facing African Americans in gaining access to employment opportunities in suburban neighborhoods. Also, an examination of more detailed data on workers' training, educational background, and precise job types may reveal racial/ethnic differences in the kinds of jobs that black and white workers take, and therefore differences in their work locations that lead to the differing work-trip times.

Another possibility may be that African Americans use older and therefore slower cars that make their commutes inefficient, but the database has no information on the age and mechanical state of workers' automobiles. Findings from the nationwide transportation survey do show that, when a low-income household has a car, it is likely to be quite old—eleven years on average as compared to eight years in other households (U.S. Department of Transportation, 1999). Nonetheless, it is clear that the work trips of many minorities are more time-consuming than those of nonminorities.

The time cost may appear minimal, but it is not trivial if one considers the cumulative time costs for the two-way trip, for example, on an annual basis. This has implications for minorities in particular and society in general. Spending more time than their nonminority white counterparts amounts to a cost borne by minorities. It could lead to lower motivation to seek employment, and for those employed it could mean more tardiness and absenteeism at work as well as poorer job performance. If these become factors in promotion decisions, this might mean fewer promotion prospects and lower economic gains for minorities. The goal of the analysis in this chapter is not to measure the labor force outcomes of locational constraints, but the findings on journey-to-work constraints show that, in the final analysis, these commuting inconveniences could easily translate into a race/ethnicity tax burden.

The findings about socioeconomic factors are noteworthy. In spite of the constraints, many low-income minorities, or those with service occupations in the study areas, still have longer commutes than do their nonminority counterparts. This suggests that race, not socioeconomic status, accounts for the commute lengths of poor minority workers. Not enough attention is paid to working-poor minorities or even to middle-class and professional minority workers. The overwhelming emphasis is on the unemployed, especially minority women who are on welfare. Yet the findings here indicate that many Hispanics and African Americans get to their workplace in spite of the odds and endure long commutes to low-income jobs. Compared to their white non-Hispanic counterparts, this situation is inequitable. But merely improving minority workers' access to low-status service jobs is not an acceptable policy goal. Instead, the findings here can inform policymakers about the need to recognize minorities' persistent efforts to get to work and reward such diligence with meaningful job opportunities. Indeed, the results for low-income African-American women especially are contrary to the stereotypical image of lazy dependent women and dispel the myth of the welfare queen.

Blacks and other minorities face transportation inequalities that reflect their lower socioeconomic status. People in low-income households are more likely than people in other income groups to use public transit in getting to work. According to the NPTS, a declining number of U.S. households are without automobiles, but this is not true across all population groups: 35 percent of African-American households do not have a vehicle. This is a significant constraint in light of research findings that indicate that a condition of employment was possession of an automobile in the household.

The maps on vehicle availability presented in this chapter for Wayne County confirm that the housing units in AOMCs and AOHCs disproportionately lack vehicles. A parallel racial/ethnic divide is obtained from data about minority households across all the three study areas. For instance, when one examines breakdowns by race/ethnicity, 7.1 percent of white households in metropolitan Detroit have no vehicles available, as compared to 15.1 percent of Hispanic households and 33.3 percent of black households. In the Kansas City metropolitan area, the percentages are 6.4 of white households, 11.9 of Hispanic households, and 24.5 of black households. The corresponding values for the Miami metropolitan area are 14.1, 14.8, and 25.4 percent (U.S. Census Bureau, 1993b). In short, both the aggregate and disaggregate data sources basically reinforce the conclusion about the restricted access of minorities to automobiles and, therefore, their greater reliance on public transportation for their journey to work when compared to nonminorities. Although vehicle ownership is not necessarily a prerequisite for work (especially in large metropolitan areas that have transit alternatives), access to an automobile is still a significant issue for many minorities seeking employment, particularly where most jobs are in the suburbs.

For reverse commuting, a commute flow in which minorities are disproportionately represented, the evidence suggests that the transportation system is not providing adequate access to job opportunities. Neither freeways nor public transit serve this movement well. Those traveling not by automobile but by public transit often have to ride downtown first and then transfer to an out-bound vehicle, which adds to the inconvenience (Hartshorn, 1992, p. 179). Inadequate access amounts to inequity. Clearly, the spatial mismatch of workers and jobs contributes to minority unemployment. Since the seventies, deindustrialization and decentralization have led to a restructuring of the U.S. metropolitan employment base (see Chapter 4). Employment restructuring is manifested in a significant increase in service jobs and a marked growth in suburban job opportunities. For example, 60 percent of new jobs created in the Chicago metropolitan area were located in the northwest suburbs of Cook and Du Page counties, in which African Americans make up less than 2 percent of the population (Wilson, 1996). Many of the new suburban jobs across American urban areas have been entry-level, low-skilled, or service jobs. With so many jobs, particularly service jobs, found in suburbs and a large fraction of welfare recipients living in central-city locations, the relevance of a spatial mismatch of jobs and workers remains current.

Although this study has concentrated on auto users, it does show that African Americans in Detroit and Kansas City are much more likely to use public transit and Hispanics in Miami are also more likely than non-Hispanics to use transit. The Wayne County maps are clear in showing the correspondence between Areas of Minority Concentration and restricted mobility. Further research is needed on public transit users to examine if there are place-specific factors that affect the mode choice of African Americans and Hispanics. For example, do the urban neighborhoods that minority workers reside in require having to pay higher parking fees than the neighborhoods of non-minorities, thus possibly reducing minority auto ownership? Are there ethnic/racial differences in the proximity to bus routes, such that Hispanics and African Americans spend a longer time between their homes and the bus stops than non-Hispanic whites? Another related possibility is the difference in the nature of the bus services in minority versus nonminority neighborhoods. If minorities have longer waiting times and/or more transfers to alternative bus routes, this would contribute to longer travel times. In addition, for bus riders, differences in working hours may translate to differences in the journey-to-work time if minority workers are more likely to work later shifts than nonminority workers, times when the frequency of bus services is reduced, thus raising a possible time-of-day penalty in minorities' commute times.

Many new entrants into the workforce may be less likely to find nine-to-five jobs but more likely to work at odd shifts and late nights. Welfare recipients often have no access to an automobile. Concerns of personal security are real when waiting for a bus late at night. This is especially true for women. The potential safety concerns of lack of a private automobile and dependence on public transit proved tragically real in the case of an African-American worker in Buffalo who was killed while trying to cross a suburban expressway on foot because the management of the shopping mall where she was employed made explicit decisions not to allow buses from the inner city to come to the suburban mall.

Finally, it is important to emphasize that the analysis on commutes in this chapter deals with those who are employed. It is not about individuals who are idle. Rather, what is presented is the commuting profiles of gainfully employed minority men and women vis-à-vis nonminority men and women. However, studies like this, based on commuting data, examine only those who have a work trip, thus excluding the unemployed (many of whom are unemployed most probably because of accessibility and other difficulties). But the focus on the journey to work enables an emphasis on the measures of access to employment that directly address mobility and locational constraints.

Using travel time as a measure of access to employment especially highlights the time burden that minorities bear. For instance, many of the significant travel time differences between minorities and nonminorities in the study areas range from 3 to 6 minutes for the one-way trip, yielding between 30 and 60 more minutes a week (or between twenty-five and fifty hours a year) that minorities spend getting to work than do nonminorities. The economic value of this lost time could be considerable. In addition to adverse impacts on economic returns, longer commuting times may also be associated with other indirect or hidden costs. The extra time spent commuting might mean time spent away from other tasks or away from home and family obligations, possibly generating tensions and discords in the family. Rogers (1987), for instance, links marital breakup and the increase in black female-headed families to the income and employment history of husbands. Thus, constrained work trips can impact the economic and social welfare of minority households in several ways.

Race and ethnicity remain relevant in differentiating the experiences of urban commuters. The findings from the three case studies about the remaining longer commutes of subgroups of minority workers indicate that analysts should not understate the importance of geographical access to the employment outcomes of Latinos and African Americans. It would be premature to abandon the role of place and race in analyzing the mismatch of workers and jobs. This conclusion rings as true today, at the beginning of the twenty-first century, as it did several years ago, when Alexis and DiTomaso (1983) grappled with the "elusive triad" of race, transportation, and employment. It is clear that race and place are connected.

Chapter 10

Racial Inequalities in Urban America

Retrospect and Prospect

Introduction

Throughout this book, we have examined the unfortunate realities of ethnic and racial polarization and the difficult challenges that confront the United States in the twenty-first century. We began by raising questions about the complexities of race, ethnicity, and racism in the United States and placed equity considerations within a spatial framework. Then we documented the ongoing changes in the demographic and racial composition of the nation and the subsequent redistribution of racial/ethnic minorities, particularly in the urbanized regions. We argued that, unfortunately, these emerging demographic patterns were being accompanied by persistent and unyielding disparities among the racial groups that were likely to deter the nation's progress toward peace and prosperity.

In examining the scope and magnitude of these disparities, we organized the book around two overarching themes. The first theme embodied the undeniable correspondence between race and place in American cities and the twin geographic consequences, racial segregation and isolation. These cities, we argued, are continually being transformed and restructured by urban, economic, and industrial processes, along with the resettlement and redistribution of residents following successive waves of immigration. The race-place theme provided the context for unraveling the unique aspects of the history of each of the dominant minority groups in these cities as well as narrating, from various sociological perspectives, their experiences with racial/ethnic prejudices and discriminatory practices. This theme also provided a useful framework to apply relevant concepts, such as Areas of Minority Concentration, that illustrate the geographic complexities of the evolving urban communities and their subdivision into multiple spatial units that are clearly distinctive by race/ethnicity and socioeconomic equity. Geographic space is organized by a set of principles, though there is disagreement regarding the intentions of those who apply such principles. Nonetheless, spatial relations and place matter where racial equity is concerned. One of the most important race-place connections in urban America involves the distribution of racial inequalities.

The second theme, equity, served as the basis for empirically investigating group disparities in the urban communities. The legacies of slavery and immigration processes have played, and continue to play, vital roles in shaping the United States' inequitable urban landscapes. The analytical findings established a physical record of inequities that is visible in the distribution of segregated neighborhoods and disparate outcomes in housing quality, environmental pollution, access to employment opportunities, and retail services. These findings are sobering and underscore the need to redress urban locational inequalities by developing effective policies and associated ideals that aim at a greater degree of equity and fairness across all population subgroups.

The purpose of this concluding chapter, therefore, is twofold. First, we want to outline the major theoretical and empirical perspectives that emerged from our work, in the hope that the findings will encourage others to think more critically about these problems and in the process develop new avenues of personal understanding of the issues. Second, it is customary to conclude works of social science with policy recommendations. Therefore, we will provide some suggestions that we hope would pave the way for initiatives that promote greater tolerance and racial harmony in the nation. However, we believe such suggestions are hollow if they fail to change the socioeconomic-political milieu of American daily life. This is a very tall order and, frankly, one about which we are not very optimistic.

Establishing Racial Equity and Social Change in America: Some Theoretical and Empirical Perspectives

The Urban Spatial Divide and the Plight of Minorities

Efforts to address the problems revealed in this book require a thorough understanding of the United States' increasingly diverse population, the emerging urban spaces, and the plight of the underrepresented groups in these communities. Specifically, researchers and policymakers alike must be cognizant of the unique backgrounds and experiences of minority groups, their neighborhoods, and their rapidly changing demographics in various U.S. cities. In the first part of this book, we documented these trends by providing a historical chronology of African Americans, Hispanics, and Asians, followed by their demographic projections to illustrate the likely changes in regional and metropolitan areas in the next quarter century. For blacks, this meant sketching their early movements from the South to New York City, Philadelphia, and Boston, first as a trickle and then in numbers that "overwhelmed" the local white majority. It also meant tracking the evolution of the national black ghetto system. For Hispanics, we examined their regional settlement patterns associated with the *entradas*, the expansion of the American West, and more recent trends in immigration policy. We also examined the regional patterns of Asian Americans, who now constitute the smallest but fastest growing minority population in the United States. Asians are also the most urbanized of any racial group, as well as overall the most assimilated minority. However, in some urban regions, they are highly segregated, and in others, nearly "invisible."

Although U.S. history in some ways is a history of immigration, the latest waves of immigration pose unprecedented challenges to a color-conscious society. The 2000 U.S. Census showed that about 14 million immigrants entered the United States in the 1990s, a level that exceeds all decades since the Great Depression. The bulk of immigrants in the 1990s came from Latin America, but a significant proportion also entered from a host of Asian countries. Editorials in the popular media have raised concerns about their potential impacts. A *U.S. News and World Report* editorial began:

> For the past six months, America has focused on the threats posed by strangers beyond our borders. But what about the danger posed by the strangers among us? We're talking not about terrorists but immigrants [*U.S. News and World Report*, 2002, p. 12].

Our analyses of the three dominant racial/ethnic groups revealed that, in the course of the next quarter century or so, they will continue to change the racial/ethnic mosaic of American cities, especially in terms of Areas of Minority Concentration. Detailed knowledge of the physical and socioeconomic attributes of these emerging neighborhoods is therefore a critical part of developing long-term policies that aim at improving the well-being of these urban residents.

In the first part of this book, we argued that the contemporary patterns of group segregation in urban areas and unequal treatment of minority groups within the larger society have largely been the result of a series of historical forces and policies based on racial/ethnic prejudices, myths, and stereotypes that have persisted across generations. We attempted to debunk some of these myths and called for a deeper level of understanding of each group.

We also presented different sociological narratives as evidence to substantiate the divergent perspectives on the nature of racism and its impacts and permanence within American society. Aside from the well-established sociological narratives, however, we concluded that a number of factors account for the origin and perpetuation of racism in the United States. The first set of forces, we argued, are couched within the socioeconomic-political milieu of the U.S. system. This system has always contained racial prejudice, based on white superiority and nonwhite inferiority, that placed American Indians, African Americans, Asian Americans, and Hispanic Americans in a subservient and expendable position. A second set of contributory forces involves the use, or more accurately, the abuse, of science and the media to characterize nonwhites as inferior to whites. Together, these forces have resulted in the depersonalization and dehumanization of minorities as objects and created a "class" that is differentiated from the dominant white society. The social images of racial identities are racialized constructions that occur not only in the abstract accounts of intellectual and political observers but in everyday life in American homes, neighborhoods, workplaces, and other locations based on who is and who is not present (Anderson, 1991). Everyday relationships of power in places at various scales create and reinforce racialized constructions of who there does or does not belong (Anderson, 1991). An overview of these contributory forces and related factors was offered in this book as part of an important historical lesson for understanding the roots of racism in order to tackle the contemporary problems that now prevail in urban areas.

Finally, in order to take corrective action toward racial inequalities, one has to know about the segmentation of urban geographic space, the factors that induce changes in urban space, and their impact on minorities. In Chapter 4, we presented different perspectives to help explain the expansion of U.S. cities during the industrial and postindustrial periods and the urban-economic processes that contributed to the segmentation of living space. These viewpoints were based on the free-market technological perspective and the Marxist and postmodern positions. Immigrants and minorities fueled the rapid expansion of the U.S. economy and became part of the urban pattern. However, as the city became a metropolis and then a metropolitan area, the living space was completely restructured, to produce a more complex urban form with balkanized spatial units reflecting capital investment, land use and political decisionmaking processes, individual and groups choices, and to some extent discriminatory practices and behaviors. The result is two urban worlds—the inner city and the outer city. The government, in particular, played an important role in shaping policies that led to cities' segregation and uneven development. The restructuring of urban space after World War II involved government spending and private-sector investment that contributed to the inner-city/outer-city dichotomy. The government policies involved tax reduction and other advantages for building new homes and factories in the outer city, while segregating, among other things, federally subsidized housing for the poor in the inner city. The federal urban initiatives of the postwar era included urban renewal, model cities, new towns, federal housing supplements, the Community Development Block Grant program, and a host of HUD programs, which were combined in the 1990s for reporting purposes into HUD's Consolidated Planning effort. The details, shortcomings, and criticisms of federal efforts are elsewhere documented (Neeno, 1996). A clear indication from most of the information provided is that federal programs developed to restore the inner city generally failed to adequately treat racial inequalities and did nothing to address the two inequitable urban spaces, the inner and outer cities.

To this picture of a decentralizing city must be added the federal investment in the 1956 Interstate Highway Act, which made daily commuting easier but also provided interchanges that would become the nuclei for more growth and expansion. This eventually led to what Hartshorn and Muller (1986) called "downtown suburbs." A 1979 study of federal policy impacts on urban-suburban patterns, funded by the U.S. government and the Kettering Foundation and published by the Rand Corporation, concluded that:

> ... It appears that the most important federal influence has been through housing programs. By subsidizing home ownership through income tax allowances and mortgage guarantees, the federal government has drawn middle and upper income households from the central city to suburbs where land prices have been lower and new units available.
>
> The income tax structure has, until recently, strongly favored investments in new structures rather than rehabilitation of existing ones. Grants to local governments for sewage systems and water treatment plans have subsidized suburban and new city development. At the same time, public housing projects and housing and building code enforcement have maintained those left behind in the older central cities in low income enclaves.
>
> The Interstate Highway System has played a major role in shaping patterns of residential settlement. Many areas in the South and West were opened up to economic development. Suburbs were extended many miles from the central business district, and even non-metropolitan areas served by an interstate highway grew in population. ...
>
> The fight against racial segregation has not proved effective. Although federal aid has increasingly targeted those cities containing disproportionately large shares of the nation's poor, racial and economic disparities between city and suburb remain large [Vaughn and Vogel, 1979, pp. 108–110].

This report explained decentralization trends in terms of "rapid automobile ownership since W[orld] W[ar] II, rising incomes, changing tastes, and technological change" but implied that government policies also contributed, if unwittingly (p. 108). The result was the creation of a disproportionately poorer inner-city population.

There are alternative viewpoints to the free-market technological position, as indicated earlier in Chapter 4, but mostly among academics such as Harvey, Smith, and Soja, who favor either the Marxist or postmodern perspective. They contend that the government itself is but a tool of the elite. It is the economic system itself that is the problem. It breeds injustice, including racism. No solution to urban problems that originates within the system is to be trusted. Most of the government's previous actions were intended to support the status quo. Federal policies and actions under capitalism are designed to benefit the elite and merely moved the problems inherent in capitalism to new and temporary places. Urban renewal programs purchased the bad "investments" of the elite that ended up as in empty storefronts and displaced minorities after tearing down their neighborhoods. The living standard of these minorities was not improved; rather they were moved with the inequalities they experience under capitalism to a new location. Such is the nature of the capitalist system, according to Marxists. No amount of technology and education can change its flaws and contradictions. As we noted earlier, in Chapter 4, however, postmodernists depart from some of what they believe is deterministic thinking and emphasize solutions different from Marxists, especially actions to improve contemporary living, such as Soja's cultural politics. Whereas Marxists believe empirical research on racial inequalities is unnecessary, postmodernists believe that such research is necessary to better inform theories and actions. The free-market camp also values empirical research to inform policy, but it believes that the magnitude of inequalities is overstated. It also believes that investment in technology-based education and job growth industries will eliminate existing inequalities. These different positions are likely to complicate the legislative process of deciding exactly how to go about eliminating the problems in our urban areas. Despite these differences, however, there is collective agreement on all sides that some action is needed to improve the well-being of disadvantaged populations in U.S. society.

We believe that a comprehensive overview of these processes and the underlying economic, social, and geographic components is necessary in order to be well informed about the current debates on group inequalities in these communities.

The Need to Validate the
Physical Record of Racial Inequalities

As with all planning and policymaking decisions, the development of long-term objectives to promote locational equity and social change must be guided by solid evidence of group inequities in our urban areas. In tackling these same issues, Cutter (1995) once argued that "we need better and more robust data to support inequity claims one way or the other, especially if those claims form the basis for litigation or public policy decisions" (p. 119). In the second part of this book, we attempted to provide such evidence by invento-rying, analyzing, and mapping the specific types and dimensions of group in-equalities in racially diverse communities. In Chapter 5, we used housing quality, socioeconomic, and services data from forty U.S. urban counties to evaluate the differences between black, Hispanic, and black-Hispanic neigh-borhood concentrations. We also examined the differences between the mi-nority concentrations and white-majority areas. The research findings pro-vided notable differences between the races both when each is a majority or dominant group in a place and when they share living spaces equally. Our re-sults confirmed that, on a national basis, real disparities existed in urban sub-areas, particularly in the communities with blacks and Hispanics. The persis-tence of these disparities was further illustrated by using updated information (2000 data) for both the expansion of minority concentrations and measures of equity.

The spatial inequities were also apparent in Chapter 6, but at a far smaller spatial scale than the analysis in the previous chapter. Here we focused on a local situation with a complex cultural mosaic. Our analysis was based on Alameda County, California, which contains a very large and growing Area of Minority Concentration. The racial/ethnic complexity in this community may well reflect the future distributions in other metropolitan communities where dramatic racial and ethnic changes are likely to occur in the coming decades. Different racial and ethnic groups coexist in this community in a variety of combinations and concentrations. Some neighborhoods are pre-dominately Asian or African American or white, while others are mixed neighborhoods, such as the familiar black-Hispanic, or Asian-white or Asian-Hispanic, among others. This case study provided the opportunity to examine equity issues as they have emerged within a particular mosaic. In particular, the dynamics of white scapegoating, first of the local Chinese population and then of the growing African-American population during World War II, crystallized the nature of prejudice and discrimination against two minority groups in two different periods of western U.S. history. This helps clarify that white prejudice and discrimination have known no re-gional exceptions in the United States. They may vary by time period and type but they are part of the fabric of U.S. history. Finally, Chapter 6 indi-cated the impact of post-1965 immigration on particular places and why the resulting local complexities require the case study approach. Furthermore, it illustrated the need for examining such issues not only at a national scale but also at a local level (Li, 1998).

In Chapter 7, we addressed a different type of racial inequality, namely, en-vironmental racism, within the context of urban pollution hazards. Since the preceding chapters had focused primarily on housing and other economic in-equalities, it was necessary to provide an overview of urban-environmental problems. Therefore, a conceptual framework of environmental equity was established using three major components of equity: process, outcome, and response. Examples were drawn from the literature to demonstrate components' relevance in understanding urban environmental issues. An empirical analysis was later performed using data from two urbanized counties in New York State. The data were used to delineate the spatial pattern and distribution of nonroutine hazardous-materials accidents and assess the inequitable impacts on low-income and minority neighborhoods. The analytical results confirmed that the neighborhoods at high risk for environmental pollution were inhabited mostly by low-income residents, Hispanics, and non-whites.

In Chapter 8, we explored the transformation of retail establishments and their redistribution in metropolitan America. The impacts of these changes on urban minority populations, in terms of proximity to the retail establishments and cost disadvantages, were evaluated using statistically formulated measures of accessibility. Empirical data were garnered for two urban counties, Monroe County in New York and Lehigh County in Pennsylvania. For each county, three measures of accessibility were computed between the block groups and chain grocery stores, general-merchandise discount stores, and home-improvement establishments. Various maps were presented to illustrate differential access between minority and nonminority block groups. Results from a previous investigation of out-shopping behavior and disparate pricing of goods in Monroe County were also presented to document additional inequities between minority and nonminority areas. Overall, the research findings confirmed that residents in the AOMCs were truly disadvantaged in terms of proximity to chain stores, the pricing of goods and services, and the availability of quality merchandise.

The final empirical study was presented in Chapter 9 to illustrate the demographic and gender differences in metropolitan commuting and access to employment opportunities for minority workers. The initial discussion in this chapter revolved around an ongoing contention that the suburbanization of jobs coupled with racial residential segregation had resulted in a "spatial mismatch," whereby inner-city residents, particularly ethnic minorities, faced difficulties in reaching the growing employment opportunities in suburban centers. However, we moved beyond the spatial mismatch on unemployment to illustrate the social and economic costs to minorities who *are* employed. We argued that unlike other commuters, the work trips of many minority residents typically began in the central city and ended at suburban locations. Such trips were heavily reliant on public transportation, which is generally slower and more circuitous than other modes of transportation. Thus, their trips are more time-consuming and expensive. To validate this claim, we presented data from three metropolitan areas—Miami, Detroit, and Kansas City—with different demographic, residential, and employment patterns. Access to employment opportunities within the three cities was evaluated using travel time as a proxy measure of trip length. The results showed that many

Hispanic workers in Miami and African Americans in Detroit and Kansas City spent longer times commuting to work than their white counterparts. The underlying causes for these disparities included their mode of transportation (the public transit system), the minorities' residential location (central cities), and the suburbanization of jobs.

Overall, there is enough empirical evidence in this book to substantiate the existence of a widespread distribution of racial inequalities in urban America and the contention that racial inequality is no longer only a black-white issue. Although our work has focused primarily on uncovering problems, it is important that future efforts be dedicated toward a common goal: closing the racial/ethnic divide by correcting these longstanding differences between the population subgroups. New initiatives must be developed to target the specific dimensions of inequity that have been uncovered by this study. From a policy-driven perspective, ideas must be expounded within a broad framework that seeks to simultaneously reduce these disparities while eliminating the anger, hostility, and distrust between the social groups. Following is a modest discussion of the kinds of policies that we deem important for shaping an improved American society that is rapidly changing from its historical position of white-majority domination to one best described as an emerging society of multicultural groupings.

The Need for a Broad Social Framework That Focuses on Place-Based Disparities

After nearly two centuries of racism, plus the record immigration of millions of poor in the 1990s, the United States finds itself with profound differences in well-being among its races and ethnic groups. Although black Americans have suffered the longest and hardest, others, including poor whites, Asians, and Hispanics, have joined their ranks. Given this mosaic, we agree with Wilson that there is a need for policies that are not race-based (W. J. Wilson, 1996). Rather, we encourage the development of policies that focus on the territorial variation of benefits and services across population groups. For example, given the universal role of income and wage differentials in determining access to services such as quality housing and to a low-risk environment, one of the policies that we endorse is ensuring full employment of individuals. This policy can be supported by automatic triggers that mandate federal spending for training and jobs for the unemployed on a place basis. Given the cyclical nature of the U.S. economy, when unemployment exceeds an established threshold, government-sponsored training programs should be automatically initiated to help restore full employment. Our discussion in both the theoretical and empirical chapters stressed the relevance of place in numerous aspects of well-being, including unemployment. Therefore, a policy that monitors full employment on a place basis with automatic triggers would help eliminate some of the locational inequalities that presently prevail in urban areas.

We also support a policy that favors a focus on housing-quality improvements that are linked to the training and employment opportunities specified above. Every American deserves access to quality housing. It is also apparent from previous studies that there is a definite need for vast upgrading of affordable housing in urban America. A comprehensive program exclusively targeted for housing improvements (not the Community Development Block Grant [CDBG] program that permits spending in a wide range of categories) would provide long-term employment prospects, especially in those places where employment and housing needs are greatest. From a training viewpoint, if job training is tied to the housing repair industry, this could address Holzer's concern about employment opportunities for those with limited incomes (Holzer, 2000) while improving the living conditions of millions of Americans.

Our research also clearly demonstrates that the lack of access to employment and services by those residing in Areas of Minority Concentration leads to greater costs than those of the white-majority areas. These costs are paid by those who are already employed. Many minorities travel longer distances to reach their places of employment and to purchase the necessities of life, such as food. Further, given welfare-workfare reforms, accessibility is of even greater concern for the working poor. The transportation problems of low-income minorities are multidimensional, including journey-to-work, shopping, and other travel-related activities.* Hodge (1986) reported the race-based inequalities related to urban transportation decisions, including projects that result in less bus service for poor minority households. Future policy must consider the social impacts of specific federal actions in construction projects and establish goals that expand modal choice for minority work locations while reducing travel times. Such policies must occur concurrently with efforts that return meaningful employment to inner cities and improve housing conditions. In the shorter term, it may be necessary to take the advice of Murakami and Young (1999) and establish federal programs that assist car ownership among the poor. The simple provision of transit service does not equate with the racially equitable access to necessities.

As Pastor (2000) recently noted, "Place matters" (p. 435). For this reason he and others, including HUD, have come to support "regional collaboration" linking vital places, including inner cities and outer cities. Among the promising ideas Pastor (2000) identified:

Federal incentives for mobilities should come in three areas—housing, transportation, and employment. Allocating low-income housing across the region (via scattered-site approaches and inclusionary zoning) and generating individual

---

*We gratefully acknowledge the insights and policy recommendations of our colleague Ibipo Johnston-Anumonwo, used in this section.

housing mobility are necessary to decentralize poverty and allow poorer individuals to connect to acquire new residential networks.

Generating transportation mobility is necessary to allow poorer job-seekers ways to connect to suburbanized employment. HUD's Bridges to Work program, for example, facilitates reverse commuting and is a flexible response to the problems of fixed-rail lines and bus patterns. . . .

Generating employment mobility should involve more than first-time placement. Although much attention has been focused on the jobless, an equally severe problem is that of the working poor—and it is one that is likely to worsen as ex–welfare recipients flood low-wage labor markets. New directions could involve public provision of continued training as well as efforts to increase firm-sponsored training. These could help those in low-wage, currently dead-end jobs to move up a career ladder. Part of this will also involve CDC [Career Development Center]–based job training and placement programs, the best of which seem to be deeply connected to their regional labor market [p. 460].

There are other hopeful signs. For example, integrated housing has been shown to benefit the employment prospects of nonwhites. Yet, we are also reminded by Massey (2000) that white attitudes and behaviors are still problematic. Despite research results indicating more lenient white attitudes toward blacks, Massey informs us that the majority of whites still "oppose the open housing law" and that their "tolerance for racial mixing is quite limited" (Massey, 2000, p. 413). For these reasons, he notes the necessary roles of the Departments of HUD and Justice in working together to ensure fair-housing enforcement. We believe that large financial penalties must be established for those guilty of housing discrimination. The same zeal applied to rid HUD programs of fraud in the 1990s will be required to eliminate this evil. Revenue collected from such penalties should be earmarked for additional enforcement of fair housing laws. Above all, adequate federal budgeting for enforcement is required.

Further, we maintain that new and existing programs must be of a much greater magnitude in order to address equity issues in other than a Band-Aid fashion.

Given the color line and its persistent impact, as well as recent immigration trends, a rather comprehensive action is needed to transform the emerging Areas of Minority Concentration into economically vibrant and healthy neighborhoods. As Zhou (2001) recently suggested: ". . . it is time to question the American faith in the inevitability of immigrant success. Children of immigrants, especially darker-skinned ones, may not fare equally well" (p. 238). Some researchers have cautioned against raising children in these areas. For example, Moffitt and Gottschalk (2001) recently indicated that Americans exposed to "risk factors" such as single motherhood, unemployment, poverty, lower education, and limited skills usually end up being dependent. Others have uncovered the negative impacts of poor environmental quality on children, particularly in utero and during their early childhood years (Kington and Nickens, 2000). These studies have documented the severe consequences of these inequities, including antisocial behavior, learning disabilities, juvenile crime and delinquency, and other social and economic costs. All of these findings underscore our concerns about the persistence of locational and racial/ethnic inequalities, which are likely to be passed on to future generations if adequate steps are not taken to correct them. We believe, therefore, that much needs to be done to address the long-term consequences of urban blight, segregation, unemployment, pollution, and other urban ills on young children and future generations.

One of our immediate concerns is the public health of the disadvantaged groups in environmentally hazardous communities. As indicated in Chapter 7, high exposure to hazardous chemicals translates into high hospitalization and mortality rates, particularly for respiratory ailments. Our findings, along with other investigations, show that the most frequently released chemicals from such incidents are chlorine, ammonia, acids, and volatile organic compounds (Cutter and Tiefenbacher, 1991; Hall, Haugh, Price-Green, Dhara, and Kaye, 1996). Of course, the potential health problems associated with exposure to such chemicals depend on the specific circumstances of the incident. It is generally agreed, however, that moderate to high exposure to these chemicals could result in acute health effects ranging from eye and skin irritations, nausea, and fatigue to respiratory ailments and, more seriously, death from asphyxiation (e.g., Kales, Polyhronopoulos, Castro, Goldman, and Christiani, 1997). Also, breathing or ingesting some of these chemicals over an extended period is likely to result in chronic health problems, such as lung disease, kidney or liver damage, reproductive dysfunction, birth defects, and cancer (Agency for Toxic Substances and Disease Regristry, 1998). Unfortunately, few studies have established the direct causal link between such exposures and the disparate health outcomes among racial and ethnic minorities. Efforts to do so have been hampered by data availability and sampling problems, such as the difficulties of conducting longitudinal studies and measuring, classifying, and reporting data on race, ethnicity, and other socioeconomic dimensions (Institute of Medicine, 1999).

Our research findings suggest a clear need for the reevaluation of the current emergency response and notification plans for dealing with hazardous incidents in urban minority concentrations. Even though all facilities are currently required to provide a Risk Management Plan (RMP) and outline the standard protocols that must be followed during an emergency, more needs to be done to prevent the recurrence of these events. The plans must be proactive, rather than reactive, to emergencies. Specifically, more emphasis should be placed on preventing rather than just responding to an emergency. Plans must start out with accident prevention as the top priority, and then follow with emergency incident management.

It is also important to recognize that, even with the best prevention plans, hazardous incidents, like other human-made, technological hazards, are inevitable. They are bound to occur sometime in a densely populated urban setting. And, as our records show, the high-risk areas are often populated by minorities. From a planning perspective then, our research methodology and the associated findings can be used by government officials and emergency response planners in at least two ways. First, the dispersion modeling approach can be used to prepare emergency evacuation procedures for specific communities. High-risk or -impact zones can be delineated using the historical records of incidents. Hospitals and emergency personnel will be better prepared for potential victims when they have detailed information pertaining to the demographic composition of those high-risk zones. Second, such information can serve as a valuable tool for preparing emergency notification and risk communication materials especially for immigrant and ethnically diverse communities. For example, in areas that are predominantly Hispanic, one may have to develop bilingual educational materials to alert the public to the potential health risks associated with exposure to the chemicals released during these accidents.

Finally, the idea of a nationwide comprehensive environmental-justice legislation, originally proposed by the Michigan State Senate, must be revisited. Our research has shown that environmental inequities are not just confined to a few neighborhoods, census tracts, states, or regions. They are rampant across the country; they are manifested in different ways and appear to be deeply rooted in our historical processes of urbanization, industrialization, racism, immigration, residential segregation, and land use practices and decisionmaking. The efforts of grassroots activists and organizations, though important in keeping the spotlight on this topic, can only go so far. Our review shows that these groups are often confronted with major obstacles, and at best, their success is felt only within local communities. We cannot, therefore, rely solely on these groups to bring about environmental justice at a national level. What is needed instead is congressional leadership and intervention to develop legislation that is broader in scope and yet flexible enough for states to adopt, and customize, to meet the specific needs of their local communities. It is through these bold steps that we can truly begin to redress these problems and permanently erase the significant and longstanding place-based disparities among population subgroups in the United States.

It is imperative that we decide, over the next few years, on the course of action to take, the kinds of government programs to sponsor, and ultimately, the quality of life we wish to encourage in these areas. We must confront the fact that social reconstruction required by centuries of neglect will carry a very large price tag. The costs of inaction will, however, be even greater. Unfortunately, the development and implementation of any course of action is likely to be strongly influenced by the philosophical viewpoints of elected and appointed government officials as well as advocates of various interests. In the next section, we will address these positions and discuss how they are likely to influence these proposals. We end the chapter with a candid discussion of what it is going to take to achieve social justice, change, and equity in American society.

Understanding the Role of the Institutional Environment in Shaping Policy

An essential part of developing initiatives that would bring about comprehensive social change in the United States requires some knowledge of the institutional environment and the ideological stance of government officials who shape policy decisions. In Chapter 4, we presented the viewpoints espoused by proponents of the free-market system as well as those of the Marxist-postmodernists. Clearly, the belief system that typifies American lawmakers and politicians is the technological free-market system. Although the political parties differ in their emphasis on *how* best to reach the solution to a given problem (for example, in 2001 they argued over the size and distribution of a federal tax cut but agreed that one was necessary), both leading parties endorse the view that a strong economy rooted in free enterprise, technology, and advanced education is the long-term answer to continued global leadership and righting the wrongs that have evolved in the American system. This will be accomplished by allowing the private sector to maximize profits and create new jobs. The wealth created by a free economy is sufficient to provide a safety net for their poor, their condition assumed to be temporary because they are momentarily displaced by the changing needs of a complex, technologically based economy. Federal and state programs, when necessary, provide short-term benefits, including training, that level the playing field for people and places disproportionately affected by change.

This belief system not only is the backbone of the existing U.S. political system but also permeates public consciousness through our educational system and the media. The majority of Americans believe that the American system is ethically, as well as economically, superior to other systems. An often-heard statement is "While not perfect, ours is still the best system in the world." This worldview helps guide individual and group behavior economically, socially, politically, and geographically. In this scheme, the individual (his or her rights, family, success, and satisfaction) comes first, though Americans can and do pull together as a group in times of crisis. Also imbedded in this belief system is the notion that things must always move ahead for the better, and the best way to get there is through education, technology, and investment. The free-market enterprise is therefore at the heart of the American democracy and it stimulates competition, innovation, and economic growth.

Evidence of the success of this viewpoint lies in the economic gains by high-tech industries at the close of the twentieth century. Major news services ran titles such as "Technology Hits Home Run: Growth Approaches 5 Million Jobs" (Gannett News Service, 2000) when reporting on *The Cyberstates 4.0: A State-by-State Overview of the High-Technology Industry,* an analytical study by the American Electronics Association (AEA) and NASDAQ. This report of the United States' economic future linked twenty-first-century high-tech growth to solving labor shortages and technology-based education. AEA President William T. Archey noted that unemployment rates were less than 2 percent in many high-tech industries at the beginning of the year 2000 and that education was the key to avoiding future high-tech labor shortages. The *Cyberstates* report noted that U.S. high-tech jobs surged to 5 million by 1998, affecting all of the United States and Puerto Rico. They were also the impetus for "invigorating" and "sustaining" U.S. state economies, particularly in the metropolitan areas. By the year 2000, the U.S. economy, having grown at exceptional rates during the 1990s, saw unemployment rates, including those for minorities, fall to historic lows. Nationally, a number of high-tech corporations joined Microsoft as "household names." In the 1990s, Intel added more than 40,000 new jobs, Oracle and Solectron added between 35,000 and 40,000 new positions, and CISCO and Dell increased employment by more than 20,000 jobs. Other high-tech employers added more than 10,000 jobs to their payrolls, including AOL and 3COM. Most of these private-sector jobs were very well paid. Two positive impacts beyond high wages were the increases to U.S. exports, which reached $181 billion in 1999 (up 85 percent from 1993), and the additional jobs generated due to the multiplier effect (service jobs to support these high-paid employees). These gains were touted as proof of a better high-tech future, equating to a better life for all Americans.

To return to the ideological stance of the lawmakers and politicians, it is fairly obvious that many believe that the long-term future of the U.S. economy is bright with significant improvements in quality of life for all individuals, regardless of race/ethnicity. However, we must also realize that we live in a new and rapidly changing global environment where information and high-tech equipment and services are the masters of future high-paying employment opportunities. Large wage differentials are going to exist, and one's knowledge and skills will determine the level of one's income. Since education is the future of the U.S. economy, it is also the factor that will determine one's economic position in life. American education, the argument goes, is open to all who are willing to work hard and have the intellect to grasp it. The bootstrapping through hard work characteristic of the early industrial age in the United States must be rediscovered and strengthened from preschool through higher education for the good of America's future. Technical fields are the most important to the new economy and must be stressed. Services that directly support this economy, especially financial services, will be valued. A broad spectrum of other services will be paid according to the knowledge, skill, and value they offer society. With regard to immigrants and minorities, the argument is that they too will benefit according to their contributions. Some immigrants, especially those who can immediately contribute to the high-tech sectors and important related fields, will benefit immediately. Native minorities will benefit from their level of education and related contributions to the economy.

In 2001, the beginning of this new century, the U.S. stock markets' nosedive resulted in massive devaluation, especially of technology stocks; reduction of workforces; and increasing unemployment. The already declining economy received additional shock waves from the terrorism and related actions of the September 11 attacks on the Pentagon and World Trade Center. Despite terrorism, the negative economic indicators, and investor fears, the free-market belief system remained intact. Its proponents argued that long-term economic prosperity, despite necessary adjustments, is viable. Technology and free enterprise will continue to change American society for the better, and as they do, more Americans will realize their dreams, and the United States will continue to rebuild its infrastructure and new living environments accordingly.

Racial Equity and Social Change: Prospects, Challenges, and Hope

Legislation that formulates the kinds of policy initiatives presented earlier is certainly essential to treating inequalities brought on by prejudice, discrimination, and neglect. It will be effective if the programs fund the most feasible ideas, provide respective incentives and disincentives for compliance and non-compliance, and provide adequate resources for monitoring and enforcement. Thus, although policy initiatives are crucial in achieving racial equity, they are insufficient to forge the social change necessary to make the policies work. Social justice will be achieved if, and only if, adequate social change is realized. The types of social change we speak of are radical and encompass a different outlook about what it means to be American in the new millennium. Social change must be guided by leadership but can be achieved peacefully only if the individual and collective white majority so wills it to be. Certainly all races must endorse the changes, but without the will of the white majority, adequate social change is not possible by peaceful means.

Earlier we noted Steinberg's conclusion (2001) that a racial backlash had occurred beginning during the Civil Rights Movement and resulted in a "retreat from racial justice and policy." This position, of course, is not shared by all observers. On the other side are those who push their nagging question: "Why, after spending billions of dollars on American inner cities largely occupied by minorities, has so little been achieved?" Their answer typically includes the claim that, despite the government's Herculean efforts, it is minorities themselves, their aberrant cultures, that stymie socioeconomic progress and equity. Minorities, especially blacks, fail themselves daily by succumbing to drugs, crime, laziness, and other negative aspects of their culture, which also include disregard for the nuclear family and education. Put simply, no amount of assistance can save a culture that refuses to take care of its own problems.

Those who agree with Steinberg's position maintain that government investments in inner cities have failed for at least two reasons. First, too much of federal investment has been misdirected to programs that broadly target and spend on infrastructure (streets, curbs, gutters, etc.) in low-to-moderate-income neighborhoods, because the law permits it. Second, federal expenditures have treated the symptoms, not the disease. Social programs provide subsidies to marginally boost the meager incomes of the poor. They do not treat the disease, which involves structural aspects of racial inequality, the lack of meaningful jobs, and fair access to them. Further, as long as public housing and Section 8 vouchers are locationally restricted, either de facto or de jure, the outcomes are the twin pillars of racism—segregation and isolation.

Steinberg dismissed the rise of the black middle class in recent decades as evidence of improving racial equity. He argued that a significant portion of that class was created by direct government employment and affirmative action policy, which is being dismantled in the backlash (Steinberg, 2001). He suggested that the "black job crisis" alone required 1.6 million new jobs at the beginning of the century to even approach racial equity (Steinberg, 2001). That number increases significantly when poor Hispanics and Asians are added to the picture. Steinberg noted that the 1990s offered an excellent opportunity for the United States to address structural racial inequalities by bringing African Americans and other minorities into labor's mainstream. He posed and answered the question related to that missed opportunity: "Why was the opportunity missed? To have acted otherwise would have required a level of commitment to racial equality that was lacking. It would also have required programs and expenditures for which there was no political will" (Steinberg, 2001, p. 195).

Steinberg explained the course of events beginning in the 1960s with the support outspoken segregationist George Wallace won from both northern and southern voters before the race riots and rise of the Black Panther movement (Steinberg, 2001). He also described Senator Moynihan's role in undermining the gains of the Civil Rights Movement, including providing the foundation for Nixon's efforts to demolish the War on Poverty, undermine school desegregation, and water down the 1970s Voting Rights Act. The King assassination was followed by rioting and then resignation, as former liberal voices of racial equality turned silent, or worse, retreated from earlier pro-racial-equity policies (Steinberg, 2001). It was in this context that a new liberal-conservative voice in Congress spoke to the need for black self-help and self-improvement, rather than supporting race-based policies to improve racial equity. For Steinberg, this amounted to "turning back" to pre–civil rights era attitudes of blaming the victim (Steinberg, 2001).

We believe that Steinberg's framework is accurate and clarifies the racial mood in the nation at the beginning of the twenty-first century. Further, we believe that global terrorism and the September 11 attacks on the United States have minimized the concerns for internal racial equity. They will reemerge sooner rather than later.

The complexity surrounding racial/ethnic relations in the twenty-first century has resulted, thus, in a number of distinct viewpoints regarding solutions to racial equity problems. West summarized three of them as liberal, conservative, and his own (West, 1993). The liberal view depends on the government as savior. The conservative argues that minorities are to blame for their own problems and must heal themselves. West's position is that minorities, in this case blacks, hold the keys to their own future. The solution to contemporary racism and racial inequalities lies in changes and actions by the black community. This position has had strong support from other minorities (e.g., Smiley, 2001). There can be little doubt that blacks and all minority peoples have a major role to play in changing the United States for the better, including confronting their own problems. However, racism is a national problem, and its expression and consequences are a national embarrassment. To be sure national policy is required to address the many ills detailed in this book. However, much more is required.

As urban America changes demographically and racially this century, a certain amount of social change is practically a given. Social, economic, and political changes will influence such things as regional political clout and racially based coalitions. They will also result in changes in the educational system and perhaps even in the workplace. However, in the absence of the kind of dramatic social changes of which we speak, segregation, discrimination, isolation, and their devastating consequences of racial inequalities will likely remain the Achilles heels of American racial progress in the twenty-first century. Existing policies like HUD's place-based CDBG program are popular because they offer great latitude in types of acceptable expenditures. In short, funds can be used almost in any fashion that can be justified as "benefiting" low- and moderate-income areas. Such programs are designed to focus reinvestment of public resources into neighborhoods that have the greatest need. The enterprise zone is another example of a place-based program. Both suffer from the basic problem of treating the symptoms of segregation without attacking its foundations. Both are designed to give our worst neighborhoods a better chance. However, such policies do nothing to create social changes that deal with the racism, segregation, and discrimination that cause racial inequalities in the first place. Further, such policies are not designed to treat the restrictions placed on the minority middle class that suffers from the same white advantage that has plagued the poor and the "underclass" (see Chapter 5). This is why racism has been defined as a "system of advantage based on race" (Wellman, quoted in Tatum, 1999, p. 7). In discussing white advantage, Tatum presented the benefits of white advantage unsought by an unsuspecting white woman, who, after some thought, came to the realization that white advantage indeed exists.

> . . . She did not ask for them [privileges], and it is important to note that she hadn't always noticed that she was receiving them. They included major and minor advantages. Of course she enjoyed greater access to jobs and housing. But she also was able to shop in department stores without being followed by suspicious salespeople and could always find appropriate hair products and makeup in any drugstore. She could send her child to school confident that the teacher would not discriminate against him on the basis of race. She could also be late for meetings, and talk with her mouth full, confident that these behaviors would not be attributed to the fact that she was White. She could express an opinion in a meeting or in print and not have it labeled as the "White" viewpoint. In other words, she was more often than not viewed as an individual and not as a member of a racial group [Tatum, 1999, p. 8].

For us, white privilege offers the most troubling challenge for necessary social change. White America typically takes its privilege for granted. In fact, many would argue it simply does not exist. However, whenever a privilege is challenged on an individual basis, it meets a cry of reverse discrimination. One of the reasons that affirmative action has been so controversial and unacceptable to white America is because it turns the tables, replacing white advantage with minority advantage. History does not offer many examples of those with power and privilege willingly relinquishing them or willingly sharing those advantages with "others." The white majority does, however, seem more willing to allow for minority improvements during good economic times such as the prosperous 1990s. For this reason, we believe that one prerequisite to social change is full employment. To be sure, the costs of social reconstruction will be very high. But the costs of not doing so will be higher. Americans must confront a simple question about themselves: Do liberty and equity go hand in hand in the American ethos? Are we perpetrating a fraud rooted in individual greed, where there is never enough wealth or consumption to satiate our individual appetites? If the answer to the first questions is "no," then our future is bleak. If the answer is "yes," then the second answer must be "no," and we must undertake the sacrifice that proves we are being honest in our answer.

Even if full employment is maintained, social changes related to racial equality are certainly not guaranteed. However, they stand a better chance under those circumstances because of greater white flexibility. Such an environment might also be more conducive to the other social changes that must occur if racial equity and harmony are to be achieved in the twenty-first century. Among the most difficult and challenging of those additional changes is a willingness by the white-majority culture to change its view to a new American culture that is less white and more inclusive. To do so does not necessitate casting off all of the American past that the white majority treasures. It does, however, require an honest recognition of the new and growing multicultural United States that is the future. It also necessitates overcoming fears and stereotypes that plague progress and eliminating the defensive posture of many of our politicians and educators, who fear a curriculum of inclusiveness because they believe that it threatens a national identity. The same fear comes from languages other that English being spoken. We should remember how many languages are spoken in a Europe that is busily and rapidly uniting.

We have demonstrated both the existence of multiple racial histories in the United States and the developmental needs of all people to create a positive racial identity that permits fondness, respect, and attachment to one's origins but allows for transcendence of race when complete. These diverse histories and identities necessitate change. Also, we must understand that a set of cultural histories need not be histories of victimization (although that story must also be told); rather, they can be histories that accentuate and celebrate the individual culture, instilling pride and identity, as well as the challenges and tribulations that make a culture stronger. Americans can report an accurate history and still keep both Columbus and Martin Luther King Days. Similarly, there is no reason to fear racial and ethnic celebrations and holidays of various sorts. We can learn that there is reason to respect and even celebrate such occasions. An example is Juneteenth. Every American should feel pride that American human bondage finally ended. We may experience different emotions about that ending but we can and should celebrate it together. Future American history certainly will be more complex than that of the past, but we argue that an inclusive American history must report and celebrate the successes and challenges of all of America's races and, in doing so, will provide the glue for a renewed United States that still will be held together by common goals and aspirations, as well as by mutual respect. In doing so, we will be creating future American history.

Also, on the topic of education, not only must curricular change occur at all levels, but all Americans need to become more critically aware of the purpose and impact of cultural messages, whether for advertising or for the "production of races." We should critically appraise all messages sent by all the media, questioning what is provided and how it might influence our perceptions of ourselves and "others." This too is an essential and challenging social change for this century. Information is power. It not only will affect racial relations but could influence our well-being in other ways.

In order to overcome the color line that was obvious to Du Bois at the beginning of the last century and is painfully present today, we must again undergo dramatic social changes. This will require an unprecedented engagement between and among America's races. American races must engage actively and regularly at schools, in the workplace, and in neighborhoods and other places that permit constructive dialogue. Such contact will provide the experience necessary for an understanding that color has been a psychological as well as physical difference imposed by nature and U.S. history. Until we truly interact with one another regularly, we cannot eliminate the physical and mental barriers created by our history and the geographic separation of inner-city and outer-city environments. This will be far from easy. Engagement means overcoming deep fears of potential failure, as well as the potential consequences of participation from a society not ready for racial harmony. The road will certainly be filled with hazards. Race relations in the United States have a horrible history, and *racism, oppression,* and other related terms are emotionally charged and bound to be misconstrued and misunderstood and to become the basis for sharp disagreements. Fear, anger, frustration, and rage will be very near to the surface of participants. Misunderstandings are guaranteed. But engagement is necessary for constructive discussions to occur and to achieve better understandings and solutions. Periods of peace and prosperity are preferable to periods of crisis for such interactions.

To have a broad impact, engagements must occur in various places—in neighborhoods, churches, schools, social clubs, and other places across the nation. This will require a committed, sensitive, and informed leadership—not one with all the answers but one committed to listening as well as speaking and, above all, committed to racial equity and racial harmony. It is difficult to predict where the seed for such engagement will originate. We are certain it will not be from politicians. Perhaps it will come from spontaneous coalitions at the local level, where Soja (2000) has suggested those new grassroots coalitions of "cultural politics," with a broader mission, will evolve. We hope such engagements are not rooted in racial crisis. Racism in the form of slavery created the only socioeconomic-political condition powerful enough to split this nation, to turn son against father and brother against brother in the Civil War. It would be the cruelest irony if the inability to stop racism and its oppression, which now has a much broader context and impact, emerged in the twenty-first century as an insurmountable wedge between Americans. Some will find this a ludicrous suggestion, while others, already speaking of the fear of race wars in the United States, will find it more meaningful. It should be clear to all that racial strife benefits no one but is a symptom of racism that must be addressed. Honest and peaceful engagement is necessary for future harmony and is preferable to explosive racial strife.

However, given American racial history, it is likely that some level of confrontation will occur before any serious efforts are made for peaceful and profitable engagement. Thus, those who favor equity will likely be forced to take unpopular but ethically important positions that run contrary to the white majority. We must move beyond appreciation of our racial/ethnic differences to clear positions that confront those who accept racial liberty but not racial equality. Political activism to support such positions will be necessary.

Our suggestions for social changes necessary for racial equity and racial harmony are a tall order for all Americans, but particularly for the white-majority, privileged classes. We have made suggestions that run contrary to short-term self-interest but that have long-term benefit for a renewed United States in the twenty-first century. Let us hope that Tatum's message (1999) of responsibility to her students is heeded wisely by all Americans:

> To say that it is not our fault does not relieve us of responsibility, however. We may not have polluted the air, but we need to take responsibility, along with others for cleaning it up. Each of us needs to look at our own behavior. Am I perpetuating and reinforcing the negative messages so pervasive in our culture, or am I seeking to challenge them? If I have not been exposed to positive images of marginalized groups, am I seeking them out, expanding my own knowledge base for myself and my children? Am I acknowledging and examining my own prejudices, my own rigid categorizations of others, thereby minimizing the adverse impact they might have on my interactions with those I have categorized? Unless we engage in these and other conscious acts of reflection and reeducation, we easily repeat the process with our children. We teach what we were taught. The unexamined prejudices of the parents are passed on to the children. It is not our fault, but it is our responsibility to interrupt the cycle [pp. 6–7].

Taking responsibility and participating are prerequisites for social change, but we must have the will to undertake them. Our inaction, like our action, will influence the quality of life for all our descendants in this century. What will the legacy of this generation be? Let us hope that our vision is clear and our commitment to a better future strong for all of America's races. They will be required in forging a renewed America, a nation different in important ways from twentieth-century America. We need to create a new human geography in our cities, one that truly reflects the America we like to portray—tolerant, respectful, fair, and equitable. That is the America of real hope, rooted not in sympathy for victims of racism but in a commitment to the provision of fairness and equity that will result in a better and stronger nation. It is indeed a tall order.

Appendix

Sample Urban
Counties Used in the Analysis

#	ST	COUNTY	#	ST	COUNTY
1	IL	Cook	30	OK	Oklahoma
2	TX	Harris	31	RI	Providence
3	CO	Adams	32	TX	Travis
4	CA	San Diego	33	PA	Delaware
5	AZ	Maricopa	34	NJ	Camden
6	MI	Wayne	35	NM	Bernalillo
7	FL	Dade	36	IN	Lake
8	TX	Dallas	37	NJ	Passaic
9	PA	Philadelphia	38	DE	New Castle
10	CA	Santa Clara	39	NJ	Mercer
11	CA	San Bernardino	40	PA	Lehigh
12	OH	Cuyahoga			
13	NY	Nassau			
14	CA	Almeda			
15	NJ	Essex			
16	TX	Tarrant			
17	CA	Sacramento			
18	NY	Erie			
19	WI	Milwaukee			
20	CT	Hartford			
21	FL	Hillsborough			
22	VA	Fairfax			
23	CA	San Francisco			
24	NY	Monroe			
25	MA	Suffolk			
26	CA	San Mateo			
27	MO	Jackson			
28	NV	Clark			
29	DC	District of Columbia			

References

Abrams, C. 1971. *The Language of Cities*. New York: Harper & Brothers.

Adeola, F. O. 1994. Environmental Hazards, Health and Racial Inequality in Hazardous Waste Distribution. *Environment and Behavior* 26: 99–126.

Agency for Toxic Substances and Disease Registry (ATSDR). 1998. *Toxicological Profiles*. Atlanta: U.S. Department of Health and Human Services, Public Health Services. http:www.atsdr.cdc.gov/toxfaq.html (accessed March 28, 2001).

Alameda County Planning Department. 1996. *Alameda County Profile*.

Alexis, M., and N. DiTomaso. 1983. Employment, Transportation and Race: In Pursuit of the Elusive Triad. *Journal of Urban Affairs* 5: 81–94.

Allen, B. W., D. Liu, and S. Singer. 1993. Accessibility Measures of U.S. Metropolitan Areas. *Transportation Research-B* 27B(6): 439–449.

Allen, J. P., and E. Turner. 1997. *The Ethnic Quilt*. Northridge: California State University, Center for Geographical Studies.

Alwitt, L. A., and T. D. Donley. 1997. Retail Stores in Poor Urban Neighborhoods. *Journal of Consumer Affairs* 31(1): 139–164.

Anderson, K. 1991. *Vancouver's Chinatown: Racial Discourse in Canada, 1875-1980*. Kingston: McGill Queens University Press.

Anderton, D. L., A. B. Anderson, P. Rossi, J. M. Oakes, M. R. Fraser, E. W. Weber, and E. J. Calabrese. 1994. Hazardous Waste Facilities: Environmental Equity Issues in Metropolitan Areas. *Evaluation Review* 18(2): 123–140.

Anderton, D. L., J. M. Oakes, and K. L. Egan. 1997. Environmental Equity in Superfund: Demographics of the Discovery and Prioritization of Abandoned Toxic Sites. *Evaluation Review* 21(1): 3–26.

Armas, G. C. 2001, March 21. Census Data Revealing U.S.'s Growing Diversity. Associated Press.

Avery, R., P. E. Beeson, and M. S. Sniderman. 1996. Accounting for Racial Differences in Housing Credit Markets. In J. Goering and R. Weink, eds., *Mortgage Lending, Racial Discrimination, and Federal Policy*. Washington, DC: Urban Institute Press.

Bagwell, B. 1982. *Oakland. The Story of a City*. Pamaron Way, CA: Presidio Press.

Bautista, V. 1998. *The Filipino Americans: From 1763 to the Present*. Farmington Hills, MI: Bookhaus Publishers.

Beemer, B. C. 1995. The Redlining Lie. *Best Review—Property Casualty Insurance Edition* 95(9): 49–53.

Been, V. 1994. Locally Undesirable Land Uses in Minority Neighborhoods: Disproportionate Siting or Market Dynamics? *Yale Law Journal* 103(6): 1383–1422.

Bell, D. 1992. *Faces at the Bottom of the Well: The Permanence of Racism*. New York: Basic Books.

Betancur, J. 1996. The Settlement Experience of Latinos in Chicago: Segregation, Speculation, and the Ecology Model. *Social Forces* 74(6): 1299–1324.

Blumstein, A. 2000. Race and Criminal Justice. In N. J. Smelser, W. J. Wilson, and F. Mitchell, eds., *America Becoming: Racial Trends and Their Consequences*. Volume 2. Washington, DC: National Academy Press, 21–31.

Bobo, L. D. 2000. Racial Attitudes and Relations at the Close of the Twentieth Century. In N. J. Smelser, W. J. Wilson, and F. Mitchell, eds., *America Becoming: Racial Trends and Their Consequences*. Volume 1. Washington, D.C.: National Academy Press, 264–301.

Boerner, C., and T. Lambert. 1995. Environmental Injustice. *Public Interest* 188 (Winter): 61–83.

Boone, C. G., and A. Modarres. 1999. Creating a Toxic Neighborhood in Los Angeles County: A Historical Examination of Environmental Inequity. *Urban Affairs Review* 35(20) 163–187.

Borchert, J. 1967. American Metropolitan Evolution. *Geographical Review* 5: 301–322.

Boskin, J. 1976. *Urban Racial Violence in the Twentieth Century*. London: Glencoe Press.

Boston, T. D. 2000. Trends in Minority-Owned Businesses. In N. J. Smelser, W. J. Wilson, and F. Mitchell, eds., *America Becoming: Racial Trends and Their Consequences*. Volume 2. Washington, DC: National Academy Press, 190–221.

Bowen, W. M., M. J. Salling, H. E. Kingsley, and E. J. Cyran. 1995. Toward Environmental Justice: Spatial Equity in Ohio and Cleveland. *Annals of the Association of American Geographers* 85(4): 641–663.

Brittain, J. C. 1997. Is Racism Permanent? Part I in C. Hartman, ed., *Double Exposure: Poverty and Race in America*. Armonk, NY: M. E. Sharpe, pp. 22–24.

Brookhaven Science Associates. 2000, July 20. Brookhaven National Laboratory. http://www.bnl.gov (accessed July 20, 2000).

Brown, T. 1995. *Black Lies, White Lies: The Truth According to Tony Brown*. New York: Quill William Morrow.

———. 1998. *Empower the People*. New York: Quill William Morrow.

Bullard, R. D. 1983. Solid Waste Sites and the Black Houston Community. *Sociological Inquiry* 53: 273–288.

———. 1990. Housing Trends in the Nation's Fourth Largest City. *Journal of Black Studies* 21: 4–14.

———. 1992. Environmental Blackmail in Minority Communities. In B. Bryant and P. Mohai, eds., *Race and the Incidence of Environmental Hazards*. Boulder, CO: Westview Press, pp. 82–95.

Bullard, R. D., E. J. Grisby, and C. Lee, eds. 1994a. *Residential Apartheid: The American Legacy*. Los Angeles: UCLA Center for Afro-American Studies.

———. 1994b. *Dumping in Dixie: Race, Class and Environmental Quality*. 2nd ed. Boulder, CO: Westview Press.

Burgess, E. W. 1925. Growth of the City In R. E. Park and E. W. Burgess and R. D. McKenzie, eds., *The City*. Chicago: University of Chicago Press, pp. 47-62.

Burke, L. L. 1993. Race and Environmental Equity: a Geographical Analysis in Los Angeles. *Geo Info Systems* 3(9): 44–50.

CACI Marketing Systems, Inc. 1998. Socioeconomic Data Estimates for the United States.

Camarillo, A. M., and F. Bonilla. 2000. Hispanics in a Multicultural Society: A New American Dilemma? In N. J. Smelser, W. J. Wilson, and F. Mitchell, eds., *America Becoming: Racial Trends and Their Consequences.* Volume 1. Washington, DC: National Academy Press, 103–134.

Capek, S. M. 1993. The "Environmental Justice" Frame: A Conceptual Discussion and an Application. *Social Problems* 40: 5–24.

Carr, J. H., and I. F. Megbolugbe. 1994. *The Federal Reserve Bank of Boston Study on Mortgage Lending Revisited.* Fannie Mae Office of Research.

Carroll, R. O. 1995. The Problem of Scale in Equity Research. *Middle States Geographer* 28: 1–8.

Cervero, R. 1989. *America's Suburban Centers: The Land Use–Transportation Link.* London: Unwin Hyman, Ltd.

Chakraborty, J., and M. P. Armstrong. 1996. Using Geographic Plume Analysis to Assess Community Vulnerability to Hazardous Accidents. *Computing Environment and Urban Systems* 19(5/6): 341–356.

Chan, A. B. 1982. *Gold Mountain: The Chinese in the New World.* Vancouver: New Star.

Cheng, L., and P. Q. Yang. 1996. Asians: The Model Minority Deconstructed. In R. Waldinger and M. Bozorgmehr, eds., *Ethnic Los Angeles.* New York: Russell Sage Foundation, 305–344.

Cheng, T. 1948. *Acculturation of the Chinese in the United States: A Philadelphia Study.* Dissertation. Philadelphia: University of Pennsylvania.

City of Oakland. 2000. *Consolidated Plan, 2000–2005.*

Clark, K. B. 1965. *Dark Ghetto.* New York: Harper & Row.

Clark, W. A. V. 1998. *The California Cauldron.* New York: Guilford Press.

_____. 1996. Residential Patterns: Avoidance, Assimilation, and Succession. In R. Waldinger and M. Bozorgmehr, eds., *Ethnic Los Angeles.* New York: Russell Sage Foundation, 109–138.

Clark, W. A. V., and M. Mueller. 1985. Hispanic Relocation and Spatial Assimilation: A Case Study. *Social Science Quarterly* 69: 468–475.

Collins, J. W., and E. K. Hawkes. 1997. Racial Differences in Post Neo-Natal Mortality in Chicago: What Risk Factors Explain the Black Infant's Disadvantage? *Ethnicity and Health* 2(1–2): 117–125.

Cooper, R. 1994. A Case Study in the Use of Race and Ethnicity in Public Health Surveillance. *Public Health Report* 109: 46–51.

Cose, E. 1993. *The Rage of a Privileged Middle Class.* New York: Harper Collins.

Cubukgil, A., and E. Miller. 1982. Occupational Status and Journey-to-Work. *Transportation* 11: 252–276.

Cummings, G. A., and E. S. Pladwell. 1942. *Oakland A History.* Oakland Historical Society.

Cutler, M., and E. L. Gleaser. 1997. Are Ghettos Good or Bad? *The Quarterly Journal of Economics* 112: 827–872.

Cutter, S. L. 1995. Race, Class and Environmental Justice. *Progress in Human Geography* 19(1): 111–122.

Cutter, S. L., and J. Tiefenbacher. 1991. Chemical Hazards in Urban America. *Urban Geography* 12(5): 417–430.

Cutter, S. L., and M. Ji. 1997. Trends in U.S. Hazardous Materials Transportation Spills. *The Professional Geographer* 49(3): 318–331.

Daniels, G., and S. Friedman. 1999. Spatial Inequality and the Distribution of Industrial Toxic Releases: Evidence from the 1990 TRI. *Social Science Quarterly* 80(2): 244–262.

Daniels, R. 1988. *Asian America: Chinese and Japanese in the U.S. Since 1850*. Seattle: University of Washington Press.

Darden, J. T. 1989. Blacks and Other Racial Minorities: The Significance of Color in Inequality. *Urban Geography* 10(6): 562–577.

_____. 1990. Differential Access to Housing in the Suburbs. *Journal of Black Studies* 21: 15–22.

_____. 2002. South Asians in Toronto: Residential Segregation and Neighborhood Socioeconomic Inequality. Paper presented to the Association of American Geographers, Los Angeles.

Davis, G. A., and O. F. Donaldson. 1975. *Blacks in the United States: A Geographic Perspective*. Boston: Houghton Mifflin.

Davis, W. M. 1909. *Geographical Essays*. Boston: Ginn & Company.

DeMott, B. 1997. Put on a Happy Face: Masking the Differences Between Blacks and Whites. In C. Hartman, ed. *Double Exposure: Poverty and Race in America*. Armonk, NY: M. E. Sharpe, 39–44.

Denton, N. A., and D. S. Massey. 1989. Residential Segregation of Blacks, Hispanics, and Asians by Socioeconomic Status and Generation. *Social Science Quarterly* 69: 797–808.

_____. 1988. Residential Segregation of Blacks, Hispanics, and Asians by Socio-Economic Status and Generation. *Social Science Quarterly* 69: 797–817.

Department of Planning and Development, Monroe County. 1999. *1995–2000 Consolidated Plan and 1999 Action Plan*. http://www.co.monroe.ny.us/ecodev/consolidatedplan.html (accessed July 20, 2000).

Dowdell, J., and D. Dowdell. 1972. *The Chinese Helped Build America*. New York: Simon and Schuster.

Dreier, P. 1991. Redlining Cities: How Banks Color Community Development. *Challenge* November-December: 15–23.

Du Bois, W. E. B. 1901. The Black North: A Social Study. New York City. *New York Times*. November 17 and 24 (also Philadelphia, Boston, and Some Conclusions in *New York Times*. December 1, 8, and 15, respectively). In J. P. Shenton and G. Brown, eds. 1978. Ethnic Groups in American Life. New York: *The New York Times*, Arno Press.

_____. 1944. Prospect of a World Without Race Conflict. *American Journal of Sociology* 49: 450–456.

_____. 1961. *The Souls of Black Folk*. New York: Fawcett World Library.

Dubin, Robin. 1991. Commuting Patterns and Firm Decentralization. *Land Economics* 67: 15–29.

Dymski, G. A. 1995. The Theory of Bank Redlining and Discrimination: An Exploration. *The Review of Black Political Economy*. Winter: 37–74.

Epstein, B. J. 1981. Ramifications of Observed Food Shopping Behavior in the Black Ghetto. *Papers and Proceedings of the Applied Geography Conference* 4: 55–146.

Espiritu, Y. L., ed. 1995. *Filipino American Lives*. Philadelphia: Temple University Press.

Fainstein, N. 1993. Race, Class, and Segregation: Discourses About African Americans. *International Journal of Urban and Regional Research* 17(3): 384–403.

Farley, R. 1977. Residential Segregation in Urbanized Areas of the United States, 1970: An Analysis of Social Class and Racial Differences. *Demography* 14: 497–518.

Farley, R., and W. Allen. 1987. *The Color Line and the Quality of Life in America*. New York: Russell Sage Foundation.

Farley, R., and W. H. Frey. 1993. Latino, Asian and Black Segregation in Multi-Ethnic Metro Areas: Findings from the 1990 Census. *Population Studies Center Research Reports* 93–278 (April): 1–34.

_____. 1994. Changes in the Segregation of Whites from Blacks During the 1980s: Small Steps Toward a More Integrated Society. *American Sociological Review* 59 (February): 23–41.

Feagin, J. R., and M. P. Sikes. 1994. *Living with Racism: The Black Middle Class Experience*. Boston: Beacon Press.

Ferguson, R. F. 2000. Test-Score Trends Along Racial Lines, 1971–1996: Popular Culture and Community Standards. In N. J. Smelser, W. J. Wilson, and F. Mitchell, eds., *America Becoming: Racial Trends and Their Consequences*. Volume 1. Washington, DC: National Academy Press, 348–390.

Fox, M. B. 1983. Working Women and Travel: The Access of Women to Work and Community Facilities. *Journal of the American Planning Association* 49: 156–170.

Frazier, E. F. 1932. *The Negro Family in Chicago*. Chicago: University of Chicago Press.

Frazier, J. W. 1997. Areas of Minority Concentration in U.S. Cities: Some Exploratory Hypotheses. *Research in Contemporary and Applied Geography* 22: 1–21.

_____. 1999. Defining Minority Concentrations as Urban Policy Tools. *Papers and Proceedings of the Applied Geography Conferences* 22: 37–50.

Frazier, J. W., and E. James. 1998. Differentiating Areas of Minority Concentration from Urban Counties: An Analysis of Demographic, Socio-Economic, and Services Differences. *Research in Contemporary and Applied Geography: A Discussion Series* 22(4): 1–26.

Frazier, J. W., E. James, and B. Tinker. 1999. Race and Place: An Analysis of HMDA Expenditures in Selected U.S. Communities. *Research in Contemporary and Applied Geography* 23(2): 1–21.

Fullilove, M. T. 1998. Comment: Abandoning "Race" as a Variable in Public Health Research: An Idea Whose Time Has Come. *American Journal of Public Health* 88: 1297–1298.

Gall, S. B., and T. L. Gall, eds. 1993. *Statistical Record of Asian Americans*. Cleveland: Eastword Publications Development.

Gallion, A. B., and S. Eisner. 1986. *The Urban Pattern: City Planning and Design*. New York: Van Nostrand Reinhold.

Gannet News Service. 2000, May 28. Technology Hits Homerun: Growth Approaches 5 Million Jobs.

Gayer, T. 2000. Neighborhood Demographics and the Distribution of Hazardous Waste Risks: An Instrumental Variables Estimation. *Journal of Regulatory Economics* 17(2): 131–155.

Ghosh, A., and S. McLafferty. 1991. The Shopping Center: A Restructuring of Postwar Retailing. *Journal of Retailing* 67(3): 253–267.

Glazer, N. 1999. On the Census Race and Ethnic Categories. In C. Hartman, ed., *Double Exposure: Poverty and Race in America*. Armonk, NY: M. E. Sharpe, 93–96.

Glickman, T. S. 1994. Measuring Environmental Equity with Geographic Information Systems. *Resources for the Future* 116: 2–6.

Gonzales, J. L. 1996. *Racial and Ethnic Groups in America*. Dubuque, IA: Kendall Hunt.

Gordon, L., and A. Mayer. 1991. Housing Segregation and Housing Conditions for Hispanics in Phoenix with Comparisons with Other Southwestern Cities. In E. D. Hutman, ed., *Urban Housing, Segregation of Minorities in Western Europe and the United States*. Durham, NC: Duke University Press.

Gordon, P., A. Kumar, and H. W. Richardson. 1989. The Spatial Mismatch Hypothesis: Some New Evidence. *Urban Studies* 26: 315–326.

Grant, D. M., M. L. Oliver, and A. D. James. 1996. African Americans and Economic Bifurcation. In R. Waldinger and M. Bozorgmehr, eds., *Ethnic Los Angeles*. New York: Russell Sage Foundation, 379–412.

Greenberg, D. 2000. Reconstructing Race and Protest: Environmental Justice in New York City. *Environmental History* 5(2): 223–250.

Guy, C. M., 1983. The Assessment of Access to Local Shopping Opportunities: A Comparison of Accessibility Measures. *Environment and Planning B: Planning and Design* 10: 219–238.

Hacker, A. 1992. *Two Nations: Black and White, Separate, Hostile, Unequal*. New York: Charles Scribner & Sons.

Hacker, B. 1994. *Environmental Justice: Legislation in the States*. Washington, DC: Center for Policy Alternatives (http://epa.gov/program/iniative/justice/ej-state.html).

Hall, B. F. 1983. Neighborhood Differences in the Retail Food Stores: Income Versus Race and Age of Population. *Economic Geography* 59: 282–295.

Hall, I. H., G. Haugh, P. Price-Green, R. V. Dhara, and W. E. Kaye. 1996. Risk Factors for Hazardous Substance Releases That Result in Injuries and Evacuations. *American Journal of Public Health* 86(6): 855–890.

Hamblin, K. 1999. *Plain Talk and Common Sense: From the Black Avenger*. New York: Simon & Schuster.

Hamilton, J. T. 1993. Politics and Social Costs: Estimating the Impact of Collective Action on Hazardous Waste Facilities. *Rand Journal of Economics* 24: 101–125.

———. 1995. Testing for Environmental Racism: Prejudice, Profits, Political Power. *Journal of Policy Analysis and Management* 14: 107–132.

Hansen, W. G. 1959. How Accessibility Shapes Landuse. *Journal of American Institute of Planners* 25: 73–76.

Hanson, S., and I. Johnston. 1985. Gender Differences in Work-Trip Lengths: Explanations and Implications. *Urban Geography* 6: 193–219.

Hanson, S., and G. Pratt. 1995. *Gender, Work and Space*. New York: Routledge.

Harris, C. D., and E. L. Ullman. 1945. The Nature of Cities. *The Annals of the American Academy of Political and Social Science* 242: 7–17.

Hartman, C., ed. 1997. *Double Exposure: Poverty and Race in America.* New York: M. E. Sharpe.

Hartshorn, T. A. 1992. *Interpreting the City: An Urban Geography.* New York: Wiley.

Hartshorn, T. A., and P. O. Muller. 1986. *Suburban Business Centers: Employment Expectations.* Washington, DC: Final Report for the U.S. Department of Commerce, EDA.

Harvey, D. 1973. *Social Justice and the City.* Baltimore: John Hopkins University Press.

_____. 1978. Labour, Capital and the Class Struggle Around the Built Environment. In K. R. Cox, ed., *Urbanization and Conflict in Market Societies.* London: Metheun.

Haverluk, T. W. 1997. The Changing Geography of U.S. Hispanics, 1850–1990. *Journal of Geography* May–June: 134–145.

Health Action, Division of Environmental Health, Monroe County, New York. 1999. Environmental Report Card. http://www.co.monroe.ny.us/health/environmental reportcard.pdf (accessed June 14, 2000).

Hendersen, A. 1995. Big Stores Return to the Mean Streets. *Governing* October: 29–30.

Henry, R. S. 1999. *The Story of Reconstruction.* New York: Konecky & Konecky.

Hird, J. A., and M. Reese. 1998. The Distribution of Environmental Quality: An Empirical Analysis. *Social Science Quarterly* 79(4): 693–716.

Hodge, D. 1986. Social Impacts of Urban Transportation Decisions: Equity Issues. In S. Hanson, ed., *The Geography of Urban Transportation.* New York: Guilford, 301–327.

Holloway, S. R., and J. O. Wheeler. 1991. Corporate Headquarters Relocation and Changes in Metropolitan Corporate Dominance, 1980–97. *Economic Geography* 67(1): 54–74.

Holm, D. M. 1994. Environmental Inequities in South Carolina: The Distribution of Hazardous Waste Facilities. Master's Thesis. Department of Geography, University of South Carolina.

Holzer, H. J. 1991. The Spatial Mismatch Hypothesis: What Has the Evidence Shown? *Urban Studies* 28: 105–122.

_____. 2000. Racial Differences in Labor Market Outcomes Among Men. In N. J. Smelser, W. J. Wilson, and F. Mitchell, eds., *America Becoming: Racial Trends and Their Consequences.* Volume 2. Washington, DC: National Academy Press, 98–123.

Howenstine, E. 1996. Ethnic Change and Segregation in Chicago. In C. C. Roseman, H. D. Laux, and G. Thieme, *EthniCity.* Lanham, MD: Rowman & Littlefield.

Hughes, M. A., and J. F. Madden. 1991. Residential Segregation and the Economic Status of Black Workers: New Evidence for an Old Debate. *Journal of Urban Economics* 29: 28–49.

Hunter, L. M. 1998. The Association Between Environmental Risk and Internal Migration Flows. *Population and Environment: A Journal of Interdisciplinary Studies* 19(3): 247–277.

Huntington, E. 1921. The Relation of Health to Racial Capacity: The Example of Mexico. *Geographical Review* 11: 243–264.

_____. 1924. *The Character of Races as Influenced by Physical Environment, Natural Selection and Historical Development.* New York: Charles Scribner & Sons.

_____. 1935. *Tomorrow's Children: The Goal of Eugenics.* New York: Wiley.

Huntington, E., and F. D. Cushing. 1924. *Principles of Human Geography.* New York: John Wiley and Sons.

Hurley, A. 1997. Fiasco at Wagner Electric: Environmental Justice and Urban Geography in St Louis. *Environmental History* 2(4): 460–481.

Ihlanfeldt, K. R. 1992. Intraurban wage gradients: evidence by race, gender, occupational class, and sector. *Journal of Urban Economics,* 32: 70–91.

Ingram, D. R. 1971. The Concept of Accessibility: A Search for an Operational Form. *Regional Studies* 5: 101–107.

Institute of Medicine, Committee on Environmental Justice: Research, Education, and Health Policy Needs. 1999. *Towards Environmental Justice.* Washington, DC: National Academy Press.

International Council of Shopping Centers (ICSC). 2000. Fact Sheet. www.icsc.org (accessed May 21, 2001).

James, F. J., and E. A. Tynan. 1986. Segregation and Discrimination of Hispanic Americans: An Exploratory Analysis. In J. M. Goering, ed., *Housing Desegregation and Federal Policy.* Chapel Hill: The University of North Carolina Press.

James, P. E. 1972. *All Possible Worlds.* Indianapolis: Odyssey Press.

Jencks, C. 1992. *Rethinking Social Policy: Race, Poverty and the Underclass.* Cambridge, MA: Harvard University Press.

Johnston-Anumonwo, I. 1992. The Influence of Household Type on Gender Differences in Work Trip Distance. *Professional Geographer* 44(2): 161–169.

_____. 1997a. Gender, Race and Determinants of Commuting: New York in 1990. *Urban Geography* 18: 192–212.

_____. 1997b. Race, Gender, and Constrained Work Trips in Buffalo, NY, 1990. *Professional Geographer* 49: 306–317.

Kain, J. F. 1968. Housing Segregation, Negro Employment and Metropolitan Decentralization. *Quarterly Journal of Economics* 82: 175–197.

Kales, S. N., G. N. Polyhronopoulos, M. Castro, R. H. Goldman, and D. Christiani. 1997. Injuries Caused by Hazardous Materials Accidents. *Annals of Emergency Medicine* 30: 598–603.

Kaplan, D. H., and S. R. Holloway. 1998. *Segregation in Cities.* Washington, DC: Association of American Geographers.

Kasarda, J. D. 1990. Structural Factors Affecting the Location and Timing of Urban Underclass Growth. *Urban Geography* 11: 234–264.

Kelley, M. A., J. D. Perloff, N. M. Morris, and L. Wangyue. 1993. Access to Primary Care Among Young African-American Children in Chicago. *Journal of Health and Social Policy* 5(2): 35–48.

Kempen, E. V. 1997. Poverty Pockets and Life Chances: On The Role of Place in Shaping Social Equality. *American Behavioral Scientist* 41(3): 430–449.

Kennedy, R. 2000. Racial Trends in the Administration of Criminal Justice. In N. J. Smelser, W. J. Wilson, and F. Mitchell, eds., *America Becoming: Racial Trends and Their Consequences.* Volume 1. Washington, DC: National Academy Press, 1–20.

Kevels, D. J. 1985. *In the Name of Eugenics. Genetics and the Uses of Human Heredity.* New York: Alfred A. Knopf.

Kington, R. S., and H. W. Nickens. 2000. Racial and Ethnic Differences in Health: Recent Trends, Current Patterns, Future Directions. In N. J. Smelser, W. J. Wilson, and F. Mitchell, eds., *America Becoming: Racial Trends and Their Consequences*. Volume 2. Washington, DC: National Academy Press, 253–310.

Knox, P., and S. Pinch. 2000. *Urban Social Geography*. Essex: Pearson Education Ltd.

Kobayashi, A., and L. Peake. 2000. Racism Out of Place: Thoughts on Whiteness and Antiracist Geography in the New Millenium. *Annals of the Association of American Geographers* 90(2): 392–403.

Kraft, M. E., and D. Scheberle. 1995. Environmental Justice and Allocation of Risk: The Case of Lead and Public Health. *Policy Studies Journal* 23(1): 113–122.

Krieg, E. J. 1995. A Socio-historical Interpretation of Toxic Waste Sites: The Case of Greater Boston. *American Journal of Economics and Sociology* 54(1): 1–13.

Lagunda, J. 1995. I Could Not Cope with Life. In Y. L. Espritu, ed., *Filipino American Lives*. Philadelphia: Temple University Press.

Leigh, W. A. 1989. Barriers to Fair Housing for Black Women. *Sex Roles* 21: 69–84.

Li, W. 1998. Anatomy of a New Ethnic Settlement: The Chinese Ethnoburb in Los Angeles. *Urban Studies* 35(3): 479–501.

Liu, F. 1997. Dynamics and Causation of Environmental Equity: Locally Unwanted Land Uses, and Neighborhood Changes. *Environmental Management* 21(5): 643–656.

Logan, J., and M. Schneider. 1984. Racial Segregation and Racial Change in American Suburbs: 1970–1980. *American Journal of Sociology* 89: 874–888.

Long, L., and D. DeAre. 1981. The Suburbanization of Blacks. *American Demographics* 3: 16–21, 44.

Lopez, D. E., E. Popkin, and E. Telles. 1996. Central Americans: At the Bottom, Struggling to Get Ahead. In R. Waldinger and M. Bozorgmehr, *Ethnic Los Angeles*. New York: Russell Sage Foundation, 279–304.

Ma, L. E., and J. H. Ma. 1982. *The Chinese of Oakland. Unsung Builders*. Oakland: Oakland Chinese History Center.

Madden, J. F. 1981. Why Women Work Closer to Home. *Urban Studies* 18: 181–194.

Marable, M. 2000. *How Capitalism Underdeveloped Black America* (updated edition). Cambridge, MA: South End Press.

Margai, F. L. 2001. Health Risks and Environmental Inequality: A Geographical Analysis of Accidental Releases of Hazardous Materials. *Professional Geographer* 53(3): 422–436.

Margai, F. L., S. G. Walter, J. W. Frazier, and R. Brink. 1997. Exploring the Potential Environmental Sources and Associations of Childhood Lead Poisoning. *Applied Geographic Studies* 1(4): 253–270.

Massey, D. S. 2000. Residential Segregation and Neighborhood Conditions in U.S. Metropolitan Areas. In N. J. Smelser, W. J. Wilson, and F. Mitchell, eds., *America Becoming: Racial Trends and Their Consequences*. Volume 1. Washington, DC: National Academy Press, 391–434.

Massey, D. S., and M. L. Eggers. 1990. The Ecology of Inequality: Minorities and the Ecology of Inequality: Minorities and the Concentration of Poverty. *American Journal of Sociology* 95(5): 1153–1188.

Massey, D. S., A. B. Gross, and K. Shibuya. 1994. Migrating Segregation and the Geographic Concentration of Poverty. *American Sociological Review* 59 (June): 425–445.

Massey, D. S., and B. P. Mullan. 1984. Process of Hispanic and Black Spatial Assimilation. *American Journal of Sociology* 89(4): 836–873.

Massey, D. S., and N. A. Denton. 1993. *American Apartheid: Segregation and the Making of the Underclass.* Cambridge, MA: Harvard University Press.

_____. 1987. The Effect of Residential Segregation on Black Social and Economic Well-Being. *Social Forces* 66(1): 29–56.

_____. 1988. Suburbanization and Segregation in U.S. Metropolitan Areas. *American Journal of Sociology* 94: 592–626.

McKee, P. 1999. *Producing American Races.* Durham, NC: Duke University Press.

McLafferty, S., and V. Preston. 1991. Gender, Race, and Computing Among Service Sector Workers. *Professional Geographer* 43: 1–15.

_____. 1996. Spatial Mismatch and Employment in a Decade of Restructuring. *Professional Geographer* 48: 420–431.

_____. 1997. Gender, race and determinants of commuting: New York in 1990. *Urban Geography* 18: 192–212.

McWilliams, C. 1943. The Zoot-Suit Riots (1943). In J. Boskin, 1976, *Urban Racial Violence in the Twentieth Century.* London: Glencoe Press, 61–64 (originally published in the *New Republic,* June 21, 1943, 818–820).

Miller, G. 2001, March 4. Experts Say Downturn Affects Minorities First. Associated Press.

Miller, H. J. 1999. Measuring Space-Time Accessibility Benefits Within Transportation and Computational Procedures. *Geographical Analysis* 31(1): 1–26.

Miller, L. 1964. Government's Responsibility for Racial Segregation. In R. Denton, ed., *Race and Property.* Berkeley: Berkeley Press.

Miller, S. C. 1969. *The Unwelcome Immigrant.* Berkeley: Berkeley Press.

Mitchell, J. T., D. S. K. Thomas, and S. L. Cutter. 1999. Dumping in Dixie Revisited: The Evolution of Environmental Injustices in South Carolina. *Social Science Quarterly* 80(2): 229–243.

Moffitt, R. A., and P. T. Gottschalk. 2001. Ethnic and Racial Differences in Welfare Receipt in the United States. In N. J. Smelser, W. J. Wilson, and F. Mitchell, eds., *America Becoming: Racial Trends and Their Consequences.* Volume 2. Washington, DC: National Academy Press, 152–173.

Mohai, P., and B. Bryant. 1992. Environmental Racism: Reviewing the Evidence. In B. Bryant and P. Mohai, eds. *Race and the Incidence of Environmental Hazards.* Boulder, CO: Westview Press, 163–176.

Muller, P. 1981. *Contemporary Suburban America.* Englewood Cliffs, NJ: Prentice Hall.

Murakami, E., and J. Young. 1999. Daily Travel by Persons with Low Income. In U.S. Department of Transportation, *Searching for Solutions: A Policy Discussion Series.* Washington DC: U.S. Department of Transportation, Federal Highway Administration, 65–84.

National Oceanic and Atmospheric Information (NOAA) and U.S. Environmental Protection Agency (USEPA). 1995. *User's Manual for Areal Locations of Hazardous Atmospheres.* Washington DC: National Safety Council.

Nayga, R. M., and N. Z. Weinberg. 1999. Supermarket Access in the Inner Cities. *Journal of Retailing and Consumer Services* 6: 141–145.

Neeno, M. K. 1996. *Ending the Stalemate: Moving Urban Housing and Development into the Mainstream of America's Future.* New York: University Press of America.

Neuman, E. 1994. A New Lease on Life Beyond the Inner City. *Insight on the News* 10(11): 6–10.

Oliver, M., and T. M. Shapiro. 2000. Wealth and Racial Stratification. In N. J. Smelser, W. J. Wilson, and F. Mitchell, eds., *America Becoming: Racial Trends and Their Consequences*. Volume 2. Washington, DC: National Academy Press, 222–251.

Omi, M. A. 2000. The Changing Meaning of Race in N. J. In N. J. Smelser, W. J. Wilson, and F. Mitchell, eds., *America Becoming: Racial Trends and Their Consequences*. Volume 1. Washington, DC: National Academy Press, 243–263.

Ong, P. 1997. Is Racism Permanent? In C. Hartman, ed., *Double Exposure: Poverty and Race in America*. New York: M. E. Sharpe, 28–29.

Oppenheimer, G. M. 2001. Paradigm Lost: Race, Ethnicity, and the Search for a New Population Taxonomy. *American Journal of Public Health* 91(7): 1049–1055.

Organization for Economic Cooperation and Development (OECD). 1997. Better Understanding of Our Cities: The Role of Urban Indicators. Paris, France: OECD Publications Service.

Orloff, L. E. 1997. Is Racism Permanent? In C. Hartman, ed., *Double Exposure: Poverty and Race in America*. New York: M. E. Sharpe, 24–28.

Ortiz, V. 1996. The Mexican Origin Population: Permanent Working Class or Emerging Middle Class? In R. Waldinger and M. Bozorgmehr, eds., *Ethnic Los Angeles*. New York: Russell Sage Foundation, 247–278.

Padilla, J. 1997. Is Racism Permanent? In C. Hartman, ed., *Double Exposure: Race and Poverty in America*. New York: M. E. Sharpe, 31–35.

Pastor, M., Jr. 2000. Geography and Opportunity. In N. J. Smelser, W. J. Wilson, and F. Mitchell, eds., *America Becoming: Racial Trends and Their Consequences*. Volume 1. Washington, DC: National Academy Press, 435–46.

Phillips, K. 1978, May. The Balkanization of America. *Harper's*: 37–47.

Phillips, L., and H. Gray. 1996. *Accidents Do Happen: Toxic Chemical Accidents Patterns in the United States*. Boston: National Environmental Law Center.

Pisarski, A. 1987. *Commuting in America*. Westport, CT: Eno Foundation.

Polluck, P. H., and E. M. Vittas. 1995. Who Bears the Burden of Environmental Pollution? Race, Ethnicity and Environmental Equity in Florida. *Social Science Quarterly* 76: 294–327.

Porter, M. 1995. The Competitive Advantage of the Inner City. *Harvard Business Review* 73: 55–71.

Public Interest Research Groups (PIRG). 1998. *Too Close to Home: A Report on Chemical Accidents Risks in the United States*. http://www.pirg.org/enviro/toxics/home98 (accessed March 10, 2001).

Pulido, L. 1996. Introduction: Environmental Racism. *Urban Geography* 17(5): 377–379.

Pulido, L. 2000. Rethinking Environmental Racism: White Privilege and Urban Development in Southern California. *Annals of the Association of American Geographers* 90(1): 12–40.

Pulido, L., S. Sidawi, and R. O. Vos. 1996. An Archaelogy of Environmental Racism in Los Angeles. *Urban Geography* 17(5): 419–439.

Reeve, H. (translator), F. Bowen (revisions), and P. Bradley, ed. A. de Tocqueville. 1835. *Democracy in America*. Volume 1. New York: Alfred A. Knopf (reprinted in J. Boskin, 1976).

Right-to-Know Network. 1998. accessed 1998. (www.rtk.net).

Riis, J. A. 1971. *How the Other Half Lives* (Reprint of 1901 edition). New York: Dover Publications.

Ringer, B. B., and E. R. Lawless. 1989. *Race-Ethnicity and Society.* New York: Routledge.

Rivera-Batiz, F. L. 1994. *Puerto Ricans in the United States: A Changing Reality.* Washington, DC: National Puerto Rican Coalition.

Rivkin, S. G. 1994. Residential Segregation and School Integration. *Sociology of Education* 67 (October): 279–292.

Rodney, R. 1982. *How Europe Underdeveloped Africa.* Washington, DC: Howard University Press.

Rogers, H. R. 1987. Black Americans and the Feminization of Poverty: The Intervening Effects of Unemployment. *Journal of Black Studies* 17: 402–417.

Rose, H. 1969a. The Origin and Pattern of Development of Urban Black Social Areas. *Journal of Geography* (September): 324–330.

_____. 1969b. *Social Processes in the City: Race and Urban Residential Choice.* Resource Paper No. 6. Washington, DC: Association of American Geographers, Commission on College Geography.

_____. 1971. *The Black Ghetto: A Spatial Behavioral Perspective.* Englewood Cliffs, NJ: Prentice Hall.

Rosenbaum, E. 1996. Racial/Ethnic Differences in Home Ownership and Housing Quality, 1991. *Social Problems* 43(4): 403–426.

Sanders, R. 1990. Integrating Race and Ethnicity into Geographic Gender Studies. *Professional Geographer* 42: 228–230.

Santiago, A. M., and G. Galster. 1995. Puerto Rican Segregation in the U.S.: Cause or Consequence of Economic Status? *Social Problems* 42(3): 361–389.

Sathisan, S. K., and N. Srinivasan. 1998. Evaluation of Accessibility of Urban Transportation Networks. *Transportation Research Record* 1617(19–1356): 78–83.

Schaefer, R. T. 1995. *Race and Ethnicity in the United States.* New York: Harper Collins.

Schneider, M., and T. Phelan. 1990. Blacks and Jobs: Never the Twain Shall Meet? *Urban Affairs Quarterly* 26: 299–312.

Scott, M., S. L. Cutter, C. Menzel, M. Ji, and D. Wagner. 1997. Spatial Accuracy of EPA's Environmental Databases and Their Use in Environmental Equity Analyses. *Applied Geographic Studies* 1(1): 45–61.

Semple, R. K., and A. G. Phillips. 1982. The Spatial Evolution of Corporate Headquarters Within an Urban System. *Urban Geography* 3: 258–279.

Semple, R. K., et al. 1985. Perspective on Corporate Headquarters Relocation in the United States. *Urban Geography* 6: 370–391.

Shenton, J. P., and G. Brown, eds. 1978. *Ethnic Groups in American Life.* New York: the *New York Times,* Arno Press.

Shipman, P. 1994. *The Evolution of Racism: Human Differences and the Use of and Abuse of Science.* New York: Simon & Schuster.

Shrestha, N. R. 1997. A Postmodern View or Denial of Historical Integrity? The Poverty of Yapa's View of Poverty. *Annals of the Association of American Geographers* 87(4): 709–716.

Smiley, T., ed. 2001. *How to Make Black America Better.* New York: Random House.

Smith, A. K. 1995, October 9. Does Coverage Depend on Color? With Homeowner's Insurance, It Might. *U.S. News and World Report,* 85.

Smith, J. P. 2000. Race and Ethnicity in the Labor Market: Trends over the Short and Long Term. In N. J. Smelser, W. J. Wilson, and F. Mitchell, eds., *America Becoming: Racial Trends and Their Consequences*. Volume 2. Washington, DC: National Academy Press, 52–97.

Smith, N. 1986. Gentrification, the Frontier, and the Restructuring of Urban Space. In S. Fainstein, and S. Campbell, *Readings in Urban Theory*. 1996. Malden, MA: Blackwell.

Soja, E. W. 2000. *Postmetropolis: Critical Studies of Cities and Regions*. Oxford: Blackwell.

Song, S. 1996. Some Tests of Alternative Accessibility Measures: A Population Density Approach. *Land Economics* 72(4): 474–482.

Squires, G. D., and W. Velez. 1996. Mortgage Lending and Race: Is Discrimination Still A Factor? *Environment and Planning* 28: 1199–1208.

Stanback, T. M. 1991. The New Suburbanization: Challenge to the Central City. Boulder, CO: Westview Press.

Stearns, L., and J. Logan. 1986. The Racial Restructuring of the Housing Market and Segregation in Suburban Areas. *Social Forces* 65: 28–42.

Steinberg, S. 1989. *The Ethnic Myth*. Boston: Beacon Press.

_____. 2001. *Turning Back: The Retreat from Racial Justice in American Thought and Policy*. Boston: Beacon Press.

Suffolk County Planning Department. 1999. Suffolk County, New York; An Overview. http://www.co.suffolk.ny.us/planning/overview.html#POPULATION (accessed July 12, 2000).

Talen, E. 2001. School, Community and Spatial Equity: An Empirical Investigation of Access to Elementary Schools in West Virginia. *Annals of the Association of American Geographers* 91(3): 465–486.

Tatum, B. D. 1999. *Why Are All the Black Kids Sitting Together in the Cafeteria?* New York: Basic Books.

Taylor, B. D., and P. M. Ong. 1995. Spatial Mismatch or Automobile Mismatch? An Examination of Race, Residence and Commuting in US Metropolitan Areas. *Urban Studies* 32: 1453–73.

Tettey-Fio, E. 1999. An Analysis of Mini-Market Site and Pricing in Areas of Minority Concentration. In F. A. Schoolmaster, ed., *Papers and Proceedings of the Applied Geography Conferences*. Volume 22. Charlotte: University of North Carolina at Charlotte, 27–33.

Thomas, G. E., ed. 1995. *Race and Ethnicity in America: Meeting the Challenge in the 21st Century*. Washington, DC: Taylor & Francis.

Thomas, S. B. 2001. The Color Line: Race Matters in the Elimination of Health Disparities. *American Journal of Public Health* 91(7): 1046–1048.

Tienda, M., and Li Ding-Tzann. 1987. Minority Concentration and Earning Inequality: Blacks, Hispanics, and Asians Compared. *American Journal of Sociology* 93(1): 141–165.

Tigges, L. M., I. Brown, and G. Green. 1998. Social Isolation of the Urban Poor: Race, Class, and Neighborhood Effect on Social Resources. *Sociological Quarterly* 39(1): 53–77.

Turner, S. C. 1997. Barriers to a Better Break: Employer Discrimination and Spatial Mismatch in Metropolitan Detroit. *Journal of Urban Affairs* 19: 123–141.

United Church of Christ (UCC). 1987. Toxic Wastes in the United States: A National Report on the Racial and Socio-economic Characteristics of Communities with Hazardous Waste Sites. New York: United Church of Christ, Commission for Racial Justice.

Urbanowicz, C. F. 1996. Urbanowicz on Darwin. www.csuchico.edu/curban/Darwin/ Darwin Sem -S95 (accessed June 12, 2001).

U.S. Census Bureau. 1990 Census of Population and Housing. Washington, DC.

_____. 1992. Census of Population and Housing: Public-Use Microdata Samples, Technical Documentation. Washington, DC.

_____. 1993a. 1990 Census of Population: Social and Economic Characteristics, Metropolitan Areas. 1990 CP–2–IB. Washington, DC.

_____. 1993b. 1990 Census of Housing: Detailed Housing Characteristics, Metropolitan Areas. 1990 CH–2–1B. Washington, DC.

_____. 1997. 1997 U.S. Population Estimates. www.census.gov (accessed July 10, 2000).

U.S. Department of Commerce. 1982. The Journey to Work in the United States: 1979. Current Population Reports P23, Special Studies No. 122. Washington, DC.

U.S. Department of Housing and Urban Development, Fair Housing and Equal Opportunity. 1996. Fair Housing Planning Guide. Volume 1. McLean, VA: Fair Housing Information Clearing House.

U.S. Department of Transportation, Federal Highway Administration. 1999. Searching for Solutions: A Policy Discussion Series (Proceedings from the Nationwide Personal Transportation Survey Symposium, October 1997). Washington, DC.

U.S. Environmental Protection Agency. 1992. Environmental Equity: Reducing Risk for All Communities. Volumes 1 and 2. Office of Policy, Planning and Evaluation. EPA230–R–92–008 and EPA230–R–92–008A. Washington, DC: Government Printing Office.

_____. 1995. Environmental Justice Strategy: Executive Order 12898. Office of Administration and Resources Management 3103. EPA/200–R–95–002. Washington, DC: Government Printing Office.

U.S. General Accounting Office (USGAO). 1983. Siting of Hazardous Waste Landfills and Their Correlation with Racial and Socio-economic Status of Surrounding Communities. Washington, DC: Government Printing Office.

U. S. News and World Report. 2002. The Danger of Strangers Within. March 11, p. 12.

USA Today. 1991, November 11. By the Numbers, Tracking Segregation in 219 Metro Areas. 3a.

Van Kempen, E. 1997. Poverty Pockets and Life Chances: On the Role of Place Shaping Social Inequality. American Behavioral Scientist 41(3): 430–449.

Vaughn, R. J., and M. E. Vogel. 1979. The Urban Impacts of Federal Policies: Volume 4, Population and Residential Location. Santa Monica: Rand Corporation.

Von Furstenberg, G. M., B. Harrison, and A. Horowitz, eds. 1974. Patterns of Racial Discrimination. New York: D. C. Health.

Waldinger, R. 1996. Still the Promised City? African Americans and New Immigrants in Post-Industrial New York. Cambridge, MA: Harvard University Press.

Waldinger, R., and M. Bozorgmehr, eds. 1996. Ethnic Los Angeles. New York: Russell Sage Foundation.

Walsh, E., R. Warland, and D. C. Smith. 1993. Backyards, NIMBYs, and Incinerator Sitings: Implications for Social Movement Theory. *Social Problems* 40(1): 25–38.

Wang, Fahui. 2000. Modeling Commuting Patterns in Chicago in a GIS Environment: A Job Accessibility Perspective. *Professional Geographer* 52(1): 120–133.

Ward, D. 1968. The Emergence of Central Immigrant Ghettoes in American Cities: 1840–1920. *Annals of the Association of American Geographers* 58(2): 343–359.

Weibull, J. W. 1980. On the Numerical Measurement of Accessibility. *Environment and Planning A* 12: 53–67.

Weir, M. 1997. "Commentaries." In C. Hartman, ed., *Double Exposure: Race and Poverty in America.* New York: M. E. Sharpe. pp. 223–25.

Weiss, K. B., and D. K. Wagener. 1990. Changing Patterns of Asthma Mortality: Identifying Target Populations at High Risk. *Journal of the American Medical Association* 264: 1683–1687.

West, C. 1993. *Race Matters.* Boston: Beacon Press.

Wheeler, J. O. 1985. Corporate Links with Financial Institutions: The Role of the Metropolitan Hierarchy. *Annals of the Association of American Geographers* 76(4): 262–274.

Williams, D. R. 2000. Racial Variations in Adult Health Staus: Patterns, Paradoxes, and Prospects. In N. J. Smelser, W. J. Wilson, and F. Mitchell, eds., *America Becoming: Racial Trends and Their Consequences.* Volume 2. Washington, DC: National Academy Press, 371–410.

Wilson, B. 2002. Critically Understanding Race-Connected Practices: A Reading of W. E. B. Du Bois and Richard Wright. *Professional Geographer* 54(1): 31–41.

Wilson, W. J. 1980. *The Declining Significance of Race: Blacks and Changing American Institutions.* 2nd ed. Chicago: University of Chicago Press.

_____. 1987. *The Truly Disadvantaged.* Chicago: Chicago University Press.

_____. 1996. *When Work Disappears. The World of the New Urban Poor.* New York: Vintage Books.

Wong, D. 1999. An Index of Chinese Residential Segregation. *Urban Geography* 20(7): 635–647.

Wong, D. W. S. 2000. Ethnic Integration and Spatial Segregation of the Chinese Population. *Asian Ethnicity* 1: 53–72.

Woods and Poole Economics. 2000. *2000 MSA Profile: Metropolitan Area Projections to 2025.* Washington, DC.

Wright, R. 1994, July 31. The Perversion of Darwinism. *New York Times,* 34. Review of Shipman, P. 1994. *The Evolution of Racism. Human Differences and the Use and Abuse of Science.* New York: Simon & Schuster.

Yandle, T., and D. Burton. 1996. Re-examining Environmental Justice: A Statistical Analysis of Historical Hazardous Waste Landfill Siting Patterns in Metropolitan Texas. *Social Science Quarterly* 77(3): 477–492.

Young, A. E. 1993. Banking on the Inner City. *Common Cause Magazine* 19(4): 35.

Young, I. M. 1990. *Justice and the Politics of Difference.* Princeton, NJ: Princeton University Press.

Young, R. M. 1998. Herbert Spencer and "Inevitable" Progress. www.shef.ac.uk (accessed June 21, 1999).

Zack, J. 1992. Banks Caught Red-Handed on Redlining. *Business and Society Review* 80 (Winter): 54–56.

Zax, J. F. 1990. Race and Commutes. *Journal of Urban Economics* 28: 336–348.

Zelinsky, W. 1992. *The Cultural Geography of the United States: A Revised Edition.* Englewood Cliffs, NJ: Prentice Hall.

Zhou, M. 2001. Contemporary Immigration and the Dynamics of Race and Ethnicity. In N. J. Smelser, W. J. Wilson, and F. Mitchell, eds., *America Becoming: Racial Trends and Their Consequences.* Volume 1. Washington, DC: National Academy Press, 200–241.

Index

293